CU00828243

The Oxfordshire Record Society

Volume 76

Methodism in Victorian Oxford

Methodism in Victorian Oxford

The Oxford Wesleyan Local Preachers' Book 1830–1902

———◆———

Edited by Martin Wellings

The Boydell Press
Oxfordshire Record Society
Volume 76

First published 2023

An Oxfordshire Record Society publication
Published by Boydell & Brewer Ltd
PO Box 9, Woodbridge, Suffolk IP12 3DF, UK
and Boydell & Brewer Inc.
668 Mt Hope Avenue, Rochester, NY 14620–2731, USA
website: www.boydellandbrewer.com

ISBN 978-0-902509-79-5

A CIP catalogue record for this book is available
from the British Library

The publisher has no responsibility for the continued existence or accuracy of
URLs for external or third-party internet websites referred to in this book, and
does not guarantee that any content on such websites is, or will remain, accurate
or appropriate

This publication is printed on acid-free paper

Printed and bound in Great Britain by TJ Books Limited, Padstow, Cornwall

For Fiona

Contents

—◈—

Illustrations

Figure

Maps

Foreword

Martin Wellings's *Methodism in Victorian Oxford* is a remarkable achievement. The extensive research required to identify so many relatively little-known individuals is set in the context of the Oxford Wesleyan Lay Preachers Book 1830–1902 and of wider Victorian Oxfordshire.

The original Lay Preachers Book is presented here from its manuscript form and made generally accessible for the first time. The volume captures the tensions in Wesleyan Methodism, between ministers and laity, central or local control, and what Wellings calls 'respectability or revivalism'.

The period of this volume was one of growth, from 700 members of Wesley's connexion in the county in 1791 to thousands by 1902. Buildings also increased to accommodate them.

Oxfordshire in religious terms was always dominated by the city of Oxford and this was the case in Methodism. Nevertheless, the rest of the county was not neglected, and frequent missions and chapel building occurred outside Oxford. Saving souls in villages was as important as in towns.

The records of the local preachers provide a window into a world we have lost. Sermons were still a significant attraction and effective preachers could move and motivate their audiences. Wesleyan preachers were trained, and assessed, their activities driven by the circuit preaching plans that identified which preacher would go to which church. These plans were at the institutional heart of the county's Methodism.

The preachers' meetings were the means by which this system was maintained. Their business tended to focus on problems to be solved, and so instances of neglect, misbehaviour, occasional 'buffooneries', and complaints predominate. But the care and dedication with which the preachers addressed these issues is testimony to their seriousness of purpose and the sense that they were doing God's business. The meetings demonstrate preachers' self-assessment and their concern with improvement. They gave of themselves, often walking sometimes long distances to the local services and varying congregations to which they were to preach.

This Oxfordshire Record Society volume 76 is an impressive contribution to the study of Victorian Oxfordshire, Methodism, and wider society. Wellings has brought his subject into the light through meticulous research and editing. His introduction provides an important assessment of the position of Victorian Methodism and will be a key source for scholars in the future.

The Society is delighted to have been able to publish two new volumes – 75 and 76 – during 2022–3. It is most grateful to the Greening Lamborn Trust for grants towards their publication costs.

Kate Tiller, Chair
Oxfordshire Record Society

Acknowledgements

This edition of the Oxford Wesleyan Local Preachers' minutes has been a work in progress for a long time and consequently many debts of gratitude have been accumulated as it has moved towards completion. Any and all errors, of course, remain entirely my own.

Thanks are due, first, to the Oxford Methodist Circuit and to the Trustees for Methodist Church Purposes for kind permission to transcribe and publish these records. The Circuit archives are in the care of the Oxfordshire History Centre, and I am deeply grateful to Mark Priddey and his colleagues at the Centre for their expert and cheerful assistance at every stage of the project. In particular, the catalogue of the archive, compiled and updated by Alison Smith, has been invaluable in guiding and facilitating my research.

Pursuing Local Preachers and the history of preaching has taken me to the Bodleian Library, the British Library and to the Methodist collections in the John Rylands University Library of Manchester, and I am glad to recognise the professional skills of the staff of each institution. The Wesley Historical Society Library and the resources of the Oxford Centre for Methodism and Church History at Oxford Brookes University have been especially helpful, and I am indebted to Dr Peter Forsaith and Tom Dobson for their support and encouragement.

I would like to thank Frances Lyons, Reference Librarian of the General Commission on Archives and History, The United Methodist Church, for supplying scans of Oxfordshire preaching plans of the 1820s from the Marriott collection at Drew University, and Rose Hill Methodist Church and Wesley Memorial Church, Oxford, for allowing me to photograph plans in their custody. I am glad to record my gratitude to Alison Butler and Liam Tiller, who enhanced and improved the image of the 1839 Oxford plan, to Graham Kirby for generous access to his collection of Oxford plans and directories from the early twentieth century, and to Peter Hemmings, who kindly provided photographs of Wantage Circuit plans from 1840 and 1847, showing a number of preachers who served in Oxford before the circuit reorganisation of 1837.

I have benefitted tremendously from conversations and correspondence with people working on local and family history in Oxford and Oxfordshire and with church members willing to share stories of Local Preachers mentioned in these minutes. I am particularly grateful to Donald and Judith Thompson, Edward and Margaret Minte, Richard and Vi Banbury, Alison Butler, Anthea Hogger, Robert

Sackett, John Lenton, Shirley Martin, Stephanie Jenkins, Malcolm Graham and Liz Woolley. John Banbury generously lent some cuttings about Gabriel George Banbury and an unpublished memoir of the doyen of Oxford Free Methodism.

I am very grateful to the editorial committee of the Oxfordshire Record Society for commissioning this project, in particular to Professor William Whyte, who suggested it, and to Dr Kate Tiller, who has helped me bring it to fruition. Through Dr Tiller I have also been able to draw on the cartographic skills of Giles Darkes, whose wonderful maps locate the Wesleyan preaching places in and around Oxford.

Finally, I want to thank Fiona Macdonald, who has lived with the Oxford Local Preachers for the whole of our married life, and to whom I gladly dedicate this book, with inexpressible gratitude and love.

Martin Wellings

Editorial Conventions

The Oxford Wesleyan Local Preachers' minutes are the work of many hands, particularly in the first four decades when the minute-taker was generally the junior minister stationed in the Circuit for at most three years. Contractions, abbreviations and idiosyncratic spelling and punctuation abound, but the general principle applied here has been to intervene only when it was deemed necessary to offer a note of clarification.

In places the text is difficult to read. Conjectural reconstructions are marked [*conj.*] and indecipherable words and phrases are indicated by [*indeciph.*], using square brackets and italic text.

Where a line or ditto marks are used to indicate repetition, the relevant text has been added, using square brackets and an explanatory endnote.

Square brackets have also been used to mark occasional corrections to dates of meetings.

Meetings typically followed a set sequence of business, and this is discussed in the Introduction (pages 47–61). The question and answer format of the original record has been retained.

Abbreviations

———◈———

DMBI	*A Dictionary of Methodism in Britain and Ireland*
HMCGB	*A History of the Methodist Church in Great Britain*
JOJ	*Jackson's Oxford Journal*
JRULM	John Rylands University Library of Manchester
MR	*Methodist Recorder and General Christian Chronicle*
OC	*Oxford Chronicle and Reading Gazette*
ODFCM	*Oxford and District Free Church Magazine*
ODNB	*Oxford Dictionary of National Biography*
OHC	Oxfordshire History Centre
OMCA	Oxford Methodist Circuit Archives
OMM	*Oxford Methodist Magazine*
OWMCM	*Oxford Wesleyan Methodist Circuit Magazine*
VCH	*Victoria County History*
WMM	*Wesleyan Methodist Magazine*

Introduction

In the introduction to his *Methodism: Empire of the Spirit* (2005) David Hempton retrieves the story of what he describes as 'a revealing encounter' from late-Victorian Oxford.[1] At a meeting chaired by Mark Pattison, Rector of Lincoln College, Hugh Price Hughes, Superintendent Minister of the Oxford Wesleyan Circuit from 1881–84, asked why Oxford possessed no adequate memorial to John Wesley, 'one of the greatest' sons of the University. Pattison queried the superlative, whereupon Hughes observed that Wesley was 'the founder of a Church which numbers twenty-five millions'. Pattison again interjected: "'No, no, Mr Hughes … twenty-five thousand you mean, not twenty-five millions.'" Hughes reached for his pocket-book for statistical evidence, and 'a correspondence ensued … upon Wesley's claims to greatness.'[2]

Hempton sees this encounter as a put-down, demonstrating Pattison's 'Oxonian chauvinism', but for Hughes' daughter and biographer it was an example of her father's willingness to assert Methodism's claim to recognition in circles where it had hitherto been disregarded. Hughes was the second minister to serve the newly built Wesley Memorial Church, opened in 1878; a building carefully designed to make a striking visual impact and to assert the place of Methodism in a city of dreaming spires.[3]

Central to the life and mission of Methodism, and expressive of its character and community, were the Local Preachers, lay volunteers who led the majority of worship services for the Wesleyans in this period. This volume presents the records of the quarterly Local Preachers' Meeting in the Oxford Wesleyan Circuit from 1830 until 1902, spanning the Victorian era in the city of Oxford, its suburbs and an extensive rural hinterland. Before turning to the text itself, this introduction sets the scene by offering a brief outline of the development of Wesleyan Methodism in the nineteenth century, first in Great Britain and then specifically in and around Oxford,

---

1   David Hempton, *Methodism: Empire of the Spirit* (New Haven and London: Yale UP, 2005), 1.
2   Dorothea Price Hughes, *The Life of Hugh Price Hughes* (London: Hodder and Stoughton, 1904), 161–2.
3   Martin Wellings, 'The building of Wesley Memorial Church, Oxford', in *Building the Church* (*The Chapels Society Journal*, volume 2) (2016), 21–35. For 'that sweet City with her dreaming spires', see Matthew Arnold, *Thyrsis* (1865), 1.19.

and by explaining the significance and place of preaching and Local Preachers in contemporary Methodism.

Wesleyan Methodism in the Nineteenth Century

Wesleyan Methodism was the largest and most cohesive of the new religious movements brought to birth by the eighteenth-century Evangelical Revival.[4] It owed its origins and its name to two clergy brothers, John Wesley (1703–91) and his younger sibling Charles (1707–88).[5] Raised in a Lincolnshire rectory in the best traditions of High Church piety, the Wesleys studied at Oxford University in the 1720s, and were instrumental in the formation of a student group whose disciplined and sometimes anxious spirituality attracted a variety of mocking nicknames: 'Bible Moths', 'Supererogation Men', 'Holy Club', and, from 1733, 'Methodists'.[6] In 1735 the brothers left England for the new colony of Georgia, intending to nurture a pristine Christian community on the virgin soil of the New World.[7] This proved to be an unsuccessful, uncomfortable and short-lived experience, but it introduced them to Moravian and Pietist groups, and thus to several of the streams already feeding a pan-European and transatlantic current of spiritual renewal.[8] In a Moravian meeting in London in the spring of 1738 John Wesley experienced an evangelical conversion, moving from a conviction of sin and failure to a sense of grace and assurance; Charles Wesley had reached a similar assurance several days earlier.[9] The Wesleys joined the network of evangelical societies in London, and in 1739 they began open-air preaching, at the invitation of George Whitefield (1714–70), a member of the Oxford 'Holy Club' who was already gaining a reputation as a popular orator.[10]

Mid-eighteenth-century evangelicalism was a rich mosaic of influences, bringing Puritanism and Pietism, High Church spirituality and Old Dissent, impulses from

---

4   There is a vast bibliography on the Revival. For accessible accounts, see Mark A. Noll, *The Rise of Evangelicalism* (Leicester: Apollos, 2004) and D. W. Bebbington, *Evangelicalism in Modern Britain. A History from the 1730s to the 1980s* (London: Unwin Hyman, 1989), 20–74.

5   Standard biographies of the Wesley brothers are Henry D. Rack, *Reasonable Enthusiast. John Wesley and the Rise of Methodism* (London: Epworth Press, 1989) and Gary Best, *Charles Wesley. A Biography* (Peterborough: Epworth Press, 2006).

6   Rack, *Reasonable Enthusiast*, 91–2.

7   The fullest account and analysis may be found in Geordan Hammond, *John Wesley in America. Restoring Primitive Christianity* (Oxford: OUP, 2014).

8   For the wider European contexts of the revival, see W. R. Ward, *The Protestant Evangelical Awakening* (Cambridge: CUP, 1992) and idem., 'Power and piety: the origins of religious revival in the early eighteenth century', in Andrew Chandler (ed.), *Evangelicalism, Piety and Politics. The Selected Writings of W. R. Ward* (Farnham: Ashgate, 2014), 73–91.

9   Noll, *Rise of Evangelicalism*, 87–9.

10   Richard P. Heitzenrater, *Wesley and the People Called Methodists* (Nashville: Abingdon Press, 2013 [second edition]), 108–9.

Central Europe and the Atlantic seaboard, and traditions from Wales, England and Scotland into creative and sometimes fractious combinations. Across this diversity, evangelicals shared a commitment to individual transformation through a response to the gospel, recovering the Reformation emphasis on justification by grace through faith, and linking this doctrinal affirmation to personal experience: evangelical religion was 'experimental', not simply cerebral, and evangelicals held that faith was authenticated in both feelings and practice.[11] If preaching was the most visible method of communication, evangelicals also sought to disseminate their message through publications, informal gatherings and personal conversation. Drawing on the legacy of seventeenth-century religious societies and on the close fellowship of the Pietists and the Moravians, small groups were central to the structure of the revival, offering safe spaces for testimony and support, mutual accountability and discipline, and the development of talents for leadership and public speaking.[12]

Tensions over doctrine and practice soon emerged in the nascent evangelical movement. Most evangelicals inclined to a Calvinist theology, emphasising human helplessness and divine grace, but the Wesleys championed an evangelical Arminianism, affirming the universal offer of the gospel.[13] This led to a break with Whitefield and the Welsh evangelical leader Howell Harris, and meant that relations between the Wesleys' Methodism and those evangelicals in the Church of England and the Dissenting denominations who adhered to Calvinism continued to be uneasy into the next century. At the same time, the Wesleys' insistence on the value of a structured and disciplined spirituality – the benefits of public worship, prayer and the sacraments as 'means of grace' even for those not yet awakened and converted – provoked a separation from the Moravians.[14] While contemporaries used 'Methodist' as a sneering soubriquet for all supporters of the revival, Calvinist and Arminian, the qualifier 'Wesleyan' needs to be added to those who allied themselves with the Wesley brothers.

By the early 1740s, therefore, the Wesleys had established their own strand of the revival. Over the next half-century, through tireless itinerant preaching and the absorption of networks founded by other evangelists, the Wesleys built up a 'connexion' of societies across the country. By 1791 there were 72,000 members in John Wesley's Connexion in Great Britain.[15] Members were required to attend a

---

11   Noll, *Rise of Evangelicalism*, 93. Compare 'Salvation by Faith', in John Wesley, *Sermons on Several Occasions* (London: Epworth Press, 1944), 3 (§I.4).

12   Heitzenrater, *Wesley and the People Called Methodists*, 114–16.

13   See Herbert Boyd McGonigle, *Sufficient Saving Grace. John Wesley's Evangelical Arminianism* (Carlisle: Paternoster, 2001).

14   Heitzenrater, *Wesley and the People Called Methodists*, 117–20; Rack, *Reasonable Enthusiast*, 198–207.

15   *Minutes of the Methodist Conferences* (London: Thomas Cordeux, 1812), 1, 243–4. The total of 72, 476 included 13,700 in Ireland.

weekly fellowship meeting, a 'class', as well as the society's Sunday worship service.[16] Societies were grouped into 'circuits' – there were 115 circuits in 1791[17] – each supervised by a small team of itinerant stipendiary preachers, supported by voluntary 'local' preachers. The itinerants were sent ('stationed') to their respective circuits each summer, initially by Wesley himself, and later by Wesley in consultation with the Conference, a gathering of preachers that met annually from 1744. Some Methodist societies built or acquired chapels; disputes with independent-minded trustees soon taught Wesley to insist that property should be held on a Model Deed, vesting it in the Connexion and ensuring that it was reserved for the use of preachers appointed by the Conference. In 1784 Wesley enrolled a Deed of Declaration in Chancery, bequeathing control of the Connexion and its property after his death to the Conference, thus giving institutional continuity to the movement.[18] This institutional evolution took place while the Wesleyan Connexion remained a voluntary organisation within the Church of England, and the Wesley brothers retained their lifelong standing as clergymen of the Established Church.

Over the next century the Wesleyan movement achieved phenomenal growth. In 1851, at the time of the Religious Census, the membership figure for England and Wales alone had increased to 358,000; the Wesleyans' claim of 1,544,528 attendances on Census Sunday supports the estimate of three to five adherents for every individual who had accepted the discipline of membership.[19] In 1791 there were three hundred Travelling Preachers; sixty years later there were just over a thousand Wesleyan ministers.[20] The four hundred preaching houses of 1791 had grown to 6579 places of worship, and there were 446 circuits under the authority of the Wesleyan Conference in Great Britain.[21] Half a century later, in 1901, the Wesleyans recorded a membership of 454,982 in 8508 churches, grouped in 790 circuits, served by 2202 ministers and more than 18,000 Local Preachers.[22] As well as the sheer weight of numbers, the Wesleyans had also achieved an impressive geographical spread across the country, with especially strong representation in

---

16   John Lawson, 'The People Called Methodists 2: "Our Discipline"', in Rupert Davies and Gordon Rupp (eds), *A History of the Methodist Church in Great Britain*, 1 (London: Epworth Press, 1965), 183–209.

17   *Minutes of Conferences*, 1, 236–9, including 28 in Ireland

18   Rack, *Reasonable Enthusiast*, 502–5.

19   Hempton, *Methodism: Empire of the Spirit*, 1–2. The 1851 Census recorded attendances, not attendees, and the relationship between those categories has been interrogated by historians. A figure of 924,000 Wesleyan attendees has been calculated from the attendances by Michael R. Watts: *The Dissenters*, 2, *The Expansion of Evangelical Nonconformity* (Oxford: Clarendon Press, 1995), 22–9, with table at 28.

20   The Wesleys' itinerant or travelling preachers evolved into Wesleyan Methodist ministers in the early nineteenth century, but ministers might still be referred to as 'itinerants' or 'travelling preachers'.

21   *Minutes of Conference* 1850, 398 (circuits) and 421 (members).

22   *Minutes of Conference* 1901, 538.

manufacturing and industrial areas.[23] The majority of Wesleyans were working class, but as the century wore on, the proportion of middle-class members increased, and the denomination celebrated its involvement in municipal government and in Parliament, with lists of 'Methodist Mayors' in the Wesleyan newspapers.[24]

Many attempts have been made to map the ebb and flow of Wesleyan membership against political, economic and social developments, and to study regional and sub-regional variations.[25] Recent work on Victorian revivals by David Bebbington has drawn attention to the interplay between context, spontaneity and planning,[26] and these elements contribute to an understanding of Methodist growth in this period. Socio-economic and political circumstances could be conducive to the creation of a receptive audience, so that, for instance, awareness of mortality during cholera outbreaks might predispose people to respond to the Christian message. Methodism's vibrant and informal spirituality, expressed in songs and in extemporary prayer and preaching, had an appeal. There was an expectation too that individual Methodists would share their faith, and the structure of small groups supplied a training ground for testimony and public speaking. In his acerbic *Portraiture of Methodism* (1807) the disgruntled ex-Methodist Joseph Nightingale described how prayer leaders might introduce Methodism to a new area through conversation, creating an opening for a prayer meeting and then for preaching and the formation of a class.[27] Rather than requiring heavy investment in the provision of a church building, a parsonage, a school and an endowment to support a resident clergyman, Wesleyan church growth in the first decades of the nineteenth century relied on lay volunteers and rented premises, supported by the circuit's Travelling and Local Preachers, and it was the Local Preachers who were often instrumental in the early stages of this light-touch expansion. From the 1850s spontaneous local initiative was supplemented by a connexionally directed Home Mission programme, with specially designated ministers and paid lay agents spearheading Wesleyan outreach.[28] This new strategy, described by David Bebbington as a 'revolution', preceded the 'Forward Movement' of the 1880s and the appointment of stipendiary

23   Henry D. Rack, 'Wesleyan Methodism 1849–1902', in Rupert Davies, A. Raymond George and Gordon Rupp (eds), *A History of the Methodist Church in Great Britain*, 3 (London: Epworth Press, 1983), 122–6.
24   Clive D. Field, 'The social structure of English Methodism: eighteenth–twentieth centuries', *British Journal of Sociology*, 28 (1977), 199–225; for an example of the celebration of municipal influence, 'Methodism and the Municipalities' and 'Methodism and the Lord Mayor's Show', *MR*, 14 November 1907, 5, 9.
25   See the bibliography in Hempton, *Methodism: Empire of the Spirit*, 262–5.
26   David Bebbington, *Victorian Religious Revivals. Culture and Piety in Local and Global Contexts* (Oxford: OUP, 2012), 83–106.
27   Joseph Nightingale, *A Portraiture of Methodism* (London: Longman, Hurst, Rees, and Orme, 1807), 270–1.
28   David W. Bebbington, 'The Mid-Victorian Revolution in Wesleyan Methodist Home Mission', *Journal of Ecclesiastical History* 70.1 (January 2019), 77–97.

or salaried Connexional Evangelists, like the Oxford Wesleyan Josiah Nix.[29] Although Wesleyan rhetoric continued to insist that every minister was a 'Home Missionary' and every preacher an evangelist, there was a tendency towards the professionalisation of outreach and the institutionalisation of revivals.

Growth mattered for the Wesleyans. They celebrated it, reported and recorded it, and, as the encounter between Hugh Price Hughes and Mark Pattison demonstrated, they appealed to it as evidence of God's approval of their theology and polity. Expansion, however, also brought challenges and problems, as Methodism at all levels became larger and more complicated in its structures and mechanisms.

At national level, John Wesley's first Conference in 1744 comprised just ten people. The 1784 Deed of Declaration specified a membership of one hundred named Travelling Preachers, the so-called 'Legal Hundred', but Wesley recommended that a wider fellowship should be involved in decision-making. By the nineteenth century the Conference gathered several hundred Wesleyan ministers, who met for two to three weeks each summer to determine questions of doctrine, polity and policy for the Connexion. Subject only to the constraints of the Deed of Declaration, the Conference had absolute authority over all aspects of Connexional life. It was, in Jabez Bunting's phrase, 'the living Wesley',[30] empowered to admit, ordain, station, discipline and exclude ministers, interpret doctrine, raise funds from the circuits and initiate new organisations. John Bowmer likened the Conference to the chapter-meeting of a religious order,[31] and its devotional framework, its tone of piety and its inquiries into ministerial character evoked the intimate and sometimes uncomfortable fellowship of the local class-meeting, but the sheer size of the assembly offered scope for grandstanding oratory, political manoeuvring, personal rivalries and elements of group-think. The Conference, moreover, was an exclusively ministerial body. Pressure for lay representation was resisted in the 1790s, 1820s, 1830s and 1840s, and was not finally conceded until 1878; the first lay woman was not admitted to the Conference until 1894. Lay involvement in decision-making came through committees of review, meeting before the Conference to examine the work of Connexional departments, and through the provision made in 1835 for circuit Quarterly Meetings to send memorials to the Conference on matters of concern. Given that the Conference was not obliged to accept these memorials, options for disgruntled lay Wesleyans were limited to pamphleteering, public meetings or resignation.

John Wesley's Methodism had a very slender administrative structure: its most substantial element was the Book Room, Wesley's publishing enterprise, which

29   For Josiah Nix (1847–1924), see below, and also 'Death of Mr Josiah Nix', *MR*, 3 April 1924, 4, and 'Reminiscences of Josiah Nix', *MR*, 10 April 1924, 7.
30   John Bowmer, *Pastor and People. A Study of Church and Ministry in Methodism from the death of John Wesley (1791) to the death of Jabez Bunting (1858)* (London: Epworth Press, 1975), 52.
31   Bowmer, *Pastor and People*, 58.

was a vital source of funds for the movement.[32] As the Connexion grew, so the supporting structures increased in size and scope. The Book Room expanded its catalogue, adding to the monthly *Magazine* and standard works of Methodist theology a range of hymnals, tracts, biographies, periodicals and other titles. Wesley does not seem to have been particularly interested in foreign missions, but after his death, Thomas Coke (1747–1814) championed missionary enterprise.[33] A concern lest Wesleyans be inveigled into supporting the work of the pan-evangelical London Missionary Society, thus diverting funds away from the Connexion, led to the creation of the Wesleyan Methodist Missionary Society in 1818,[34] and this became a very substantial institution, supervising mission stations in every continent and managing a large budget. At a time when the officers of the Conference, the annually elected President and Secretary, did this work in tandem with circuit appointments, the WMMS had a permanent secretariat of four ministers and a London base. Local fundraising for missions mobilised support and consolidated commitment, while the annual missionary anniversaries, with guest preachers and tea-meetings, were highlights of the Methodist year.

In 1834 the Conference accepted a proposal to create a Theological Institution for the training of ministers. This added another element to the Connexional system, as colleges were opened, first at Hoxton, and then at Richmond and Didsbury, with tutors seconded and funds raised to support the work. It also marked a change of approach, from an apprenticeship model of training to a seminary style of minis-terial education.[35] As will be seen, a development welcomed by some was regarded by others with deep suspicion as a betrayal of 'Methodism as it was'. The Institution, however, survived and thrived, adding further outposts at Headingley (1868) and Handsworth (1881). Meanwhile, the Wesleyans embarked on a major programme of school building from the early 1840s, adding teacher-training colleges at Westminster (1851) and Southlands (1872). Kingswood, Wesley's boarding school for the sons of his itinerant preachers, was joined by other Methodist proprietary schools, including The Leys School, Cambridge (1875), designed to cater for affluent Wesleyan families with Oxbridge aspirations for their sons.[36]

In the circuits and societies too, expansion brought both opportunities and challenges. The opportunities included growing resources, scope for a plethora of

32   Clive Murray Norris, *The Financing of John Wesley's Methodism c. 1740–1800* (Oxford: OUP, 2017), 177–90.

33   John Vickers, *Thomas Coke. Apostle of Methodism* (London: Epworth Press, 1969).

34   On tensions between the LMS and the Wesleyans, see Roger H. Martin, *Evangelicals United: Ecumenical Stirrings in Pre-Victorian Britain, 1795–1830* (Metuchen, N. J. and London: Scarecrow, 1983), 64–8.

35   Tim Macquiban, 'Practical Piety or Lettered Learning', *PWHS* 50.3 (October 1995), 83–107.

36   Martin Wellings, '"In perfect harmony with the spirit of the age": The Oxford University Wesley Guild, 1883–1914', in Morwenna Ludlow, Charlotte Methuen and Andrew Spicer (eds), *Churches and Education (Studies in Church History* 55) (Cambridge: CUP, 2019), 480–1.

activities, from tract societies to choirs to Sunday schools, and funds for new and larger buildings, as cottage-meetings and rented rooms were replaced by 'neat' and 'commodious' chapels and then by neo-Gothic edifices.[37] The presence of the well-to-do and the upwardly mobile both prompted and enabled the drive for more comfortable and elegant buildings: chapel trustees looked to pew rents to raise funds, and so sought to match the tastes and expectations of 'respectable' members of the congregation. More preaching places meant smaller circuits, as the eighteenth-century model of a few places scattered over a wide area, served by itinerants working a peripatetic six-week round gave way to a circuit based on a substantial urban centre with a fringe of villages, and the ministers based in the 'circuit town'. The countervailing challenge was often financial, as over-enthusiastic local leaders embarked on ambitious building schemes, and ran into debt, or as shortage of funds meant that there were struggles in meeting the costs of ministry.

Many of these issues were foreshadowed in John Wesley's lifetime, as the Connexion grew in size from a tight-knit community amenable to Wesley's personal knowledge and guidance to a larger body, more diverse, more assertive, and in Clive Norris' phrase, 'almost ungovernable'.[38] A new generation of leaders after 1791, epitomised by Jabez Bunting (1779–1858), managed the challenges of success not only by strengthening and developing the institutions of Wesleyanism, but also by insisting on the absolute authority of the Conference, replacing Wesley's personal prestige and charisma with a theory of ministerial control. Unsurprisingly, this provoked strenuous opposition.

Wesleyan Methodism's numerical growth and institutional development was matched by a growing denominational consciousness, expressed in an evolving relationship to the Church of England on the one hand and to historic Dissent on the other.

The question of the Wesleyans' relationship to the Church of England was a recurrent issue during the lifetimes of the Wesley brothers, and it became sharper after their deaths.[39] Both brothers consistently emphasised their loyalty to the Church, disclaimed any intention of separation, and expressed what Jeremy Gregory has described as 'at times surprisingly bitter and prejudiced' attitudes towards Dissent.[40] Wesleyans were strongly discouraged from holding services in 'Church

---

37   The monthly *Wesleyan Methodist Magazine* carried many reports of chapel openings, and 'commodious' was the favourite adjective through the 1830s.
38   Clive Murray Norris, '"Here is the voice of the people": Authority and Conflict in Eighteenth-Century Methodism', *Wesley and Methodist Studies* 11.1 (2019), 21.
39   See Martin Wellings, 'Wesleyan Methodism and Nonconformity', in David Bebbington and David Ceri Jones (eds), *Evangelicalism and Dissent in Modern England and Wales* (Abingdon and New York: Routledge, 2021).
40   Jeremy Gregory, '"In the Church I will live and die": John Wesley, the Church of England and Methodism', in William Gibson and Robert G. Ingram (eds), *Religious Identities in Britain, 1660–1832* (Aldershot: Ashgate, 2005), 175.

Hours' and Wesleyan worship was portrayed as a supplement, not an alternative to regular attendance at the parish church.

Charles Wesley was more consistent in holding the line against separation than his elder brother.[41] John Wesley, by ordaining Methodist preachers for service in America in 1784, breached the discipline of the Church of England, much to Charles' dismay, and by the 1790s pressure for the Wesleyans to clarify a separate identity had increased among both preachers and members. The 1795 Plan of Pacification resolved the tension within Methodism by allowing local Methodist societies to apply to the Conference for permission for the sacraments to be celebrated by the preachers, and the number so applying steadily increased over succeeding years. There was, however, no formal separation from the Church. Some Wesleyans continued to profess a dual loyalty, and to structure Sunday morning worship around the *Book of Common Prayer*, or John Wesley's abridgement of the Prayer Book, originally designed for Methodists in North America. At the Wesleyans' flagship chapel in City Road, London, the trustees ensured that Holy Communion was celebrated by a clergyman of the Church of England until the 1820s,[42] and Wesleyans continued to attend Anglican services in some areas as late as the 1860s.[43] Although some voices were very critical of the Established Church – Daniel Isaac in the 1810s and Joseph Rayner Stephens in the 1830s, for example[44] – the official stance of the Connexion was to stand aloof from Dissent, to support the principle of Establishment, and to assert the unique place of Wesleyan Methodism in 'our middle position between the religious parties of the land'.[45]

Two points need to be made about the Wesleyans' ecclesial identity in the years after 1791. The first is that, whatever the rhetoric, Wesleyan Methodism was in fact operating as a separate denomination within a generation of John Wesley's death. Wesleyans were holding Sunday services in direct competition with parish churches; they were appointing stipendiary preachers to exercise pastoral care of Methodist societies; they were sustaining and extending a network of religious communities and creating an institutional superstructure entirely outside the control of the parochial and diocesan system of the Church of England. It took several decades for the Wesleyans to adopt the style 'Reverend' for their Travelling Preachers, to call them 'ministers', and then to resume the practice of ordination, but the reality

41   Discussed in detail in Gareth Lloyd, *Charles Wesley and the Struggle for Methodist Identity* (Oxford: OUP, 2007).
42   George J. Stevenson, *City Road Chapel, London, and its Associations Historical, Biographical, and Memorial* (London: George J. Stevenson, 1872), 153.
43   Edward Royle, 'When did the Methodists stop attending their parish churches?', *Proceedings of the Wesley Historical Society* 56.6 (2008), 275–96.
44   Daniel Isaac, *Ecclesiastical Claims Investigated and the Liberty of the Pulpit Defended* (Edinburgh: C. Stewart, 1815); Michael S. Edwards, *Purge this Realm. A Life of Joseph Rayner Stephens* (London: Epworth Press, 1994), 9–17.
45   'The Annual Address of the Conference to the Methodist Societies', *Wesleyan Methodist Magazine* iv (fourth series), October 1848, 1131.

of separation existed from the 1790s.[46] When Jabez Bunting declined Anglican ordination in 1801, he was well aware that Methodism was already distinct from the Church in theology, liturgy, organisation and ethos.[47]

The second point is that in the first half of the nineteenth century a series of developments placed the Wesleyan 'middle position' under considerable strain. First, as denominational loyalties and institutions grew stronger and as pastoral reforms in the Church of England led a new generation of Anglican incumbents to insist on an exclusive commitment to the parish church, local Wesleyans came under pressure to choose between church and chapel.[48] Second, from the 1820s a renewed emphasis on Calvinist theology and Anglican Churchmanship drove a wedge between Wesleyans and Evangelicals in the Church of England, with Wesleyans noticing and complaining about hostile articles in the Evangelical press.[49] Third, the rise of the Oxford Movement from 1833 added both depth and volume to long-standing High Church criticisms of Methodism and also provoked Wesleyan fears that the Church of England was drifting towards Rome.[50] Several decades of polemic meant that by the last quarter of the century most Wesleyans felt further from the Church of England than their forebears, and a closer relationship was developing with evangelical Nonconformity. Wesleyans, who had looked askance at 'political Dissent' from the early 1800s through to the 1850s, now became active participants in the Free Church Council movement of the 1890s, and high-profile advocates of the 'Nonconformist Conscience'.[51] Moreover, with a muting of confessional Calvinism and a growing 'church consciousness' across all the Free Church denominations, Wesleyans increasingly shared a common chapel culture with Congregationalists, Baptists and other branches of the Methodist family.[52]

46   Margaret Batty, 'The contribution of local preachers to the life of the Wesleyan Methodist Church until 1932, and to the Methodist Church after 1932, in England', MA thesis, University of Leeds, 1969, 142, dates the change of style to 1818 and use of the word 'minister' to 1827; ordination by the imposition of hands was considered in 1822, and introduced in 1836: William Peirce, *The Ecclesiastical Principles and Polity of the Wesleyan Methodists* (London: Wesleyan Conference Office, 1873 (third edition)), 278–9.

47   Benjamin Gregory, *Side Lights on the Conflicts of Methodism during the Second Quarter of the Nineteenth Century* (London: Cassell and Co., 1898), 361.

48   Frances Knight, *The Nineteenth Century Church and English Society* (Cambridge: CUP, 1995), 24–36, 71.

49   See, for example, 'The Christian Observer and the Methodists', *WMM* xii (third series), January 1833, 32–43 and February 1833, 106–12; 'Intolerance of Evangelical Clergymen', *WMM*, March 1833, 186–91.

50   Mats Selén, *The Oxford Movement and Wesleyan Methodism in England* (Lund: Lund University Press, 1992).

51   For the role of Hugh Price Hughes in this development, see Christopher Oldstone-Moore, *Hugh Price Hughes. Founder of a new Methodism, Conscience of a new Nonconformity* (Cardiff: University of Wales Press, 1999).

52   For evocations of chapel culture, see Clyde Binfield, *So Down to Prayers. Studies in English Nonconformity 1780–1920* (London: J.M. Dent and Sons, 1977) and Charles D.

The growth and evolution of Wesleyan Methodism in the nineteenth century took place against a backdrop of tensions and difficulties, some of which resulted in secessions or expulsions from the movement. Although only one of these had serious repercussions in Oxford, it is worth summarising them briefly before making some more general points about the fault-lines running through Methodism in this period.[53]

Shortly after John Wesley's death the debate about the shape of Methodism provoked radical proposals from one of the younger preachers, Alexander Kilham (1762–98). Kilham's advocacy of greater democracy in Methodism, linked to his alleged sympathy for French Republicanism, led to his expulsion in 1796 and to the formation of the Methodist New Connexion.

A decade later, stirrings of revival in forms disapproved of by the Conference stimulated the creation of the Primitive Methodists (1808) and the Bible Christians (1815).

In 1826 the decision by the trustees of the newly built Brunswick chapel in Leeds to install an organ divided opinion in the circuit. The majority of class leaders and Local Preachers opposed the decision, but the Conference overruled them, and a thousand members seceded and formed the Leeds Protestant Methodists.

Opposition to the Theological Institution in 1834 coalesced around a senior preacher, Dr Samuel Warren. What may have been thwarted ambition on Warren's part joined with political and social grievances and personality conflicts in Liverpool, Manchester and Rochdale to give birth to the Wesleyan Methodist Association in 1835.[54] The Protestant Methodists joined with the Association in the following year.

From 1839 the Conference was troubled by anonymous satirical publications, attacking the 'metropolitan hierarchy' of Methodism. Between 1844 and 1849 a series of *Fly Sheets from the Private Correspondent* appeared, accusing Bunting and his allies of corruption and tyranny. The Conference of 1849 sought to determine the authorship of the *Fly Sheets* by questioning those suspected – James Everett (1784–1872), Samuel Dunn (1797–1882) and William Griffith (1806–83). Everett refused to attend the Conference; Dunn and Griffith declined to give the undertakings required; and all three were expelled. This was a catalyst for an explosion of protest in which ambitions for reform, long-standing grievances and local antagonisms merged. Supporters of the 'Three Expelled' organised mass meetings, petitioned for their reinstatement, and withheld contributions to Methodist funds.

Cashdollar, *A Spiritual Home. Life in British and American Reformed Congregations, 1830–1915* (University Park, PA: Penn State UP, 2000). A contemporary picture may be found in W. Haslam Mills, *Grey Pastures* (London: Chatto and Windus, 1924).

53   For this section, see John T. Wilkinson, 'The Rise of Other Methodist Traditions', in Rupert Davies, A. Raymond George and Gordon Rupp (eds), *A History of the Methodist Church in Great Britain*, 2 (London: Epworth Press, 1978), 276–329.

54   See D.A. Gowland, *Methodist Secessions. The Origins of Free Methodism in Three Lancashire Towns* (Manchester: Chetham Society, 1979).

Superintendents responded with expulsions, and rival Reform societies were set up. Until 1856 the Reformers continued to petition the Conference; in 1857 most of the Reformers joined with the Association to form the United Methodist Free Churches, while the remainder constituted the Wesleyan Reform Union. It has been estimated that the controversy cost Wesleyan Methodism 100,000 members.

Behind the controversies which erupted between 1796 and 1857 a number of common elements may be detected, and three may be mentioned here. The first, a recurring issue from the 1790s at least until the 1870s, involved the balance between ministerial authority and the rights of the laity. A call for lay representation in the Conference was first voiced by Alexander Kilham in the 1790s,[55] and it was repeated in the 1820s, 1830s, 1840s and 1850s. Although a small number of the itinerants sympathised with the call, most rallied behind the claim that the ministry was a 'collective pastorate' with unique authority, and that this must not be diluted by admitting lay people into the Conference. Advocates of change were either expelled, like Kilham in 1796, or withdrew from the Connexion, like George Steward in 1853.[56] Lay involvement in decision-making came through 'mixed' committees of ministers and lay members, appointed by the Conference to share in the management of Connexional funds, and, from 1861, through committees of review, including representatives nominated by the District Meetings, which gathered before the Conference to examine the work of Connexional departments. By the early 1870s the manifest inefficiency of the committees had rallied influential support for lay representation, and a scheme for a two-session assembly – first, a session open to all ministers and dealing with pastoral matters, and then a session composed of equal numbers of elected lay and ordained representatives handling the Connexion's temporal affairs – was approved in 1876 and implemented in 1878. This did not entirely settle the issue: debates about the relationship between the two sessions continued through the 1890s and echoes of nineteenth-century arguments reverberated in the negotiations for Methodist Union in the 1920s, but much of the antagonism of the earlier period was avoided.[57]

Linked to the question of ministerial authority and the rights of the laity, secondly, was the issue of local autonomy and central control. In one way John Wesley's Methodism empowered and gave agency to lay people, giving them roles and responsibilities as class leaders, stewards, trustees and Local Preachers. Methodism was a voluntary organisation, entirely dependent on the work, money and goodwill of its members, and Wesley tempered his instinctive autocracy with an alertness to local sensibilities. As the movement grew, however, and as Wesleyan leaders

---

55   Bowmer, *Pastor and People*, 46–50.
56   *Minutes of Conference* xii (1855), 191, and see George Steward, *The Principles of Church Government and their Application to Wesleyan Methodism* (London: Hamilton, Adams, and Co., 1853).
57   Martin Wellings, '"Making haste slowly": The Campaign for Lay Representation in the Wesleyan Conference, 1871–78', *PWHS* 53.2 (May 2001), 25–37.

sought to navigate the choppy waters of political and social unrest, the emphasis on 'walking according to rule' increased. The most notorious example of central intervention came in the Leeds organ controversy of 1826, when the Conference overruled local opinion. From the 1820s through to the 1850s argument raged as to whether Leaders' Meetings, Quarterly Meetings and Local Preachers' Meetings should control their own membership and elect their own officers, or whether these powers resided *ex officio* with the ministers. Since class leaders and Local Preachers were rooted in local communities, while ministers stayed in an appointment for at most three years, it was easy for the ministerial/lay debate to become elided with a local/central tension. Mid-century conflicts led the Conference to underline the constitutional partnership, under which ministers nominated officers and meetings approved or vetoed the appointments. Local resistance to central direction, however, did not disappear, even if it was expressed in quiet non-compliance, rather than noisy protest.

The third issue vexing the Connexion in the nineteenth century was the tension between respectability and revivalism. This should not be stated as a simple binary opposition: all Methodists were in favour of revival, although some were deeply sceptical of revivalism, and some of the most affluent and respectable Wesleyans lent their weight and their financial support to revival movements. Freelance revivalists, however, could upset local societies and disrupt Connexional discipline, and they could bring Wesleyanism as a whole into disrepute. They could also be exploited as a stalking-horse for criticism of the leadership – for being spiritually lukewarm or ineffective, too concerned with polite culture or social status, or unfaithful to authentic Methodism. This may well help to explain the unenthusiastic reception given by the Conference to the American preachers Lorenzo 'Crazy' Dow in 1805–07 and James Caughey in 1841–47. Dow's advocacy of North American-style camp meetings helped to stimulate the development of Primitive Methodism, while Caughey's protracted mission in the early 1840s played into the campaign against Bunting and his friends which resulted in the Reform crisis of 1849.[58] Part of the problem may have been in determining whether authentic revival as a phenomenon should be spontaneous or could be worked up, and whether it should grow naturally and unpredictably from local church life or come with a guest preacher and extensive advertising. By the 1870s, in the wake of Moody and Sankey, revivals were meticulously planned and carefully controlled, so that Hugh Price Hughes could claim that the result of a 'revival mission' was pre-determined by the efficiency of the preparations.[59]

As Wesleyan Methodism sought to cope with the challenges of success, therefore, a series of tensions emerged. The call for lay representation was repeated. The claim

---

58   Gregory, *Side Lights*, 390, 403. I owe this reference to Dr James E. Pedlar.
59   On Moody and Sankey, see John Kent, *Holding the Fort. Studies in Victorian Revivalism* (London: Epworth Press, 1978), 132–235; Hugh Price Hughes, 'Revival Missions', *Christian Miscellany and Family Visitor*, March 1881, 123.

that the ministry was a 'collective pastorate' with unique authority was rebutted, and the power of the Conference centrally and of ministers locally was called into question. The direction of development; the management of revivalism; the creation of institutions; the quest for respectability – all were criticised. There were national flashpoints: the expulsion of Alexander Kilham and the formation of the New Connexion; the banning of camp meetings and the subsequent development of Primitive Methodism; the Leeds organ controversy; the Warrenite secession; the *Fly Sheets* and the Reform agitation of 1849. Beneath the surface, however, local issues and personality clashes meshed with a continuing national debate about the identity and direction of Wesleyanism.

Two broad narratives ran through Wesleyan Methodism in the nineteenth century, presenting quite different interpretations of the life of the Connexion. The first, the official and the dominant narrative, celebrated success, pointing to the numerical growth of Methodism in Great Britain and the Empire, calculating the value of Wesleyan real estate, and taking a not-so-quiet pride in the increasing presence of Wesleyans in the professions, in municipal life, in the universities and in Parliament. This narrative recognised that Methodism had changed and developed since the days of the Wesleys, but it affirmed that in theology and polity – 'our doctrines' and 'our discipline' – the leaders of the Connexion had been faithful to the inheritance bequeathed by the founders, principally John Wesley himself. The 'old Connexion', they maintained, represented authentic Methodism, wisely and appropriately adapted to changing circumstances.

The second narrative saw things quite differently. Its varied advocates – Alexander Kilham and the founders of the New Connexion in the 1790s, Primitive Methodists and Bible Christians in the 1810s, the Leeds Protestant Methodists of the 1820s, the Associationists of the 1830s and the Wesleyan Reformers of the late 1840s – held that 'Methodism as it is' had departed from 'Methodism as it was'. Opinions differed as to when, how and why this declension had occurred, and how much effort should be expended in trying to put things right. The Primitive Methodists and the Bible Christians, whose revivalism did not keep in step with the model of Wesleyanism being crafted in the 1810s, accepted expulsion and struck out on their own, building new movements by pioneer evangelism. Kilham's New Connexion, the Leeds Protestant Methodists of the 1820s, the founders of the Wesleyan Methodist Association in the 1830s and the Reformers of 1849, on the other hand, fought back against the Wesleyan leadership, contested the narrative of faithfulness, and appealed to the wider membership, the courts, the press, and public opinion for support. Although the warfare was at its most fierce in the first half of the century, the bitterness lived on, surfacing in biographies of the protagonists into the 1870s and 1880s.[60]

---

60 See, for example, Richard Chew, *James Everett. A Biography* (London: Hodder and Stoughton, 1875), v–vi, 293, 378–9, and the critical references in the *Wesleyan Methodist*

In the heat of debate, particularly a debate inflamed by religious rhetoric and a Manichaean division between the children of light and the agents of darkness, there was little attempt on either side to understand the mindset and motivation of the other. For the Reformers, Bunting and his friends were 'the Clique' dominating the Conference for reasons of personal aggrandisement; for many ministers and leading lay members of the Connexion, the Associationists and the Reformers were 'agitators', disloyal, self-seeking and spiteful. The Reformers could not or would not appreciate the task of consolidation and reform which transformed Wesley's rather rickety Connexion into the largest Protestant Free Church in England by 1851; the Conference loyalists could not or would not admit the errors of judgment and the systemic weaknesses which made tens of thousands of Wesleyans sympathetic to the cause of the 'Three Expelled'.[61]

Growth in numbers and in structures, in institutional complexity and social aspirations; issues of denominational identity; conflicts over power, personalities and reform: all marked the history of Wesleyan Methodism in the nineteenth century. Attention must now be given to the way these themes played out in Oxford Methodism in this period.

Methodism in Oxford, 1830–1902

In 1791 there was a single Oxfordshire Wesleyan Circuit, with 700 members, served by three Travelling Preachers. Joseph Entwisle, stationed there as a fledgling itinerant in 1787–88, recalled that the Circuit covered parts of four counties and that there were only four chapels: at Oxford, Wallingford, High Wycombe and Witney; most of the Wesleyan societies met and worshipped in private houses. The junior preachers' accommodation was rudimentary, consisting of a rented garret room in New Inn Hall Lane, but they spent most of their time riding round the vast Circuit, fulfilling a regular six-week schedule of preaching appointments and visits.[62]

Over the next forty years new circuits were formed,[63] centred on Newbury (1795), Witney (1803), Whitchurch/Aylesbury (1810),[64] Chipping Norton (1813) and High Wycombe (1815). The earliest extant preaching plan, for May–July 1823,

---

Magazine to Chew's *William Griffith: Memorials and Letters* and Joseph Kirsop's *Historic Sketches of Free Methodism*: WMM, November 1885, 878–80.

61   This internal Methodist battle echoed the rhetoric and methods of evangelical campaigns on moral and political issues: see D.W. Bebbington, *The Nonconformist Conscience. Chapel and Politics 1870–1914* (London: George Allen and Unwin, 1982), 14–17.

62   *Minutes of Conference* 1791, 243; Joseph Entwisle, *Memoir of the Rev. Joseph Entwisle, fifty-four years a Wesleyan Minister* (Bristol: N. Lomas, 1848), 29–42.

63   Details in Joseph Hall, *Hall's Circuits and Ministers* (London: Wesleyan Methodist Book Room, 1897), with an alphabetical list of the circuits.

64   Whitchurch was the head of the circuit from 1810 until 1822: *Hall's Circuits and Ministers*, 12.

shows twenty-three preaching places, including six chapels.[65] Eight of the places and two of the chapels went into the newly formed Watlington Circuit in the following year,[66] and Samuel Warren's *Chronicles of Wesleyan Methodism*, published in 1827, recorded four chapels and 315 members in the Oxford Circuit.[67] At this date the Circuit extended north to Wootton, Woodstock and Tackley, east to Garsington, west to Eynsham and Hanborough, and south to Upton and Blewbury. Ten years later the places south of the Thames were transferred to the Wantage Circuit, leaving Oxford with fifteen societies, and thereafter the geography of the Circuit remained stable for the rest of the century.

Before the 1820s the surviving records of the Oxford Circuit are sparse, and are limited to deeds and conveyances relating to the chapels, occasional references in manuscript minutes of the District Meeting, and a single account book.[68] From 1825 the records also include the Schedule Books, compiled each quarter by the Superintendent and tabulating membership changes in each class and society. These membership and financial records, together with the Local Preachers' Book, make it possible to reconstruct the history of the Circuit in much more detail. In addition, two manuscript histories survive, one compiled in the 1890s by James Nix, and the other written up in the 1930s by his son Frank.[69]

To give an account of the fluctuating fortunes of Methodism in each place in the Oxford Circuit over three-quarters of a century is beyond the scope of this introduction, and there is much more work to be done on the specific history of the different societies. Local examples, however, may be used to illustrate a broader narrative of the Circuit's development between 1830 and 1902, against which the records in the Local Preachers' Book may be read.

From the mid-1820s through to the mid-1840s the Oxford Wesleyans seem to have experienced a time of steady if unspectacular growth. Despite the loss of a third of its societies to Wantage in 1837, the Circuit's membership increased from the 315 noted by Warren in 1827 to a peak of 690 in 1843.[70] New preaching places were licensed, including Beckley, Iffley, Marston, Hampton Poyle and Sandford;[71]

65   Plan of the Oxford Circuit, from the Marriott Collection, Drew University, Madison, N.J. Ref. D2003-038. I am very grateful to Frances Lyons, Reference Librarian of the General Commission on Archives and History, The United Methodist Church, for supplying a scan of this document.

66   Hall, *Hall's Circuits and Ministers*, 233.

67   Samuel Warren, *Chronicles of Wesleyan Methodism* (London: John Stephens, 1827), 2, 164. (Both parts are bound in one volume).

68   Oxfordshire History Centre, Oxford Methodist Circuit archive [hereafter OMCA], NM5/A/F1/1, Oxford Circuit Stewards' Account Book, 1815–24.

69   OHC, OMCA, NM5/A/MS1/1 [Nix 1] and NM5/A/MS1/2 [Nix 2]. Parts of each history were published in, respectively, the *Oxford Free Church Magazine* and the *Oxford Methodist Magazine*.

70   OHC, OMCA, NM5/A/A2/3, Circuit Schedule Book 1839–44, Midsummer 1843.

71   OHC, OMCA, NM5/A/A4/1, Local Preachers' Minute Book 1830–66, 17 Sept 1830; 4 March 1831; 2 July 1833; 3 April 1834; 2 July 1834.

chapels were opened at Woodstock, Combe, Headington Quarry and Iffley.[72] In 1829 fifteen places were listed in the Circuit Stewards' Account Book for contributions to the Circuit's budget. Six months later this had increased to twenty-seven, before falling to seventeen in the autumn of 1830.[73] These early records demonstrate the fluidity and flexibility of the Wesleyan system in this period. The Local Preachers' Book and the preaching plan mark the places where the Wesleyans were sending preachers, including ones where preaching might be tried for a quarter or two, and then dropped, like Kidlington and Wolvercote, sometimes because it was difficult to secure a suitable site or venue.[74] The Account Book lists the places where the Wesleyan presence was deemed solid enough to expect a contribution towards the costs of ministry, assessed according to membership. Even where preaching was successfully established and sustained over several years, building a chapel might take a long time.[75] Corbett Cooke, Superintendent in 1837–39, left a note for his successor recording 'a great Increase at Bladon' with 'eighty persons now meeting in class', and prospects for 'great good' at Woodstock and 'several other places' too.[76] The membership at Bladon almost doubled in the latter part of 1839, and although there was a gentle reduction over the next two years, Cooke's hopes for a chapel in the village were realised in 1843.[77] Through the 1840s Bladon, with a membership between 61 and 80, was second only in strength to the city centre society. The New Inn Hall Street cause, with more than 200 members and thriving Sunday and day schools, inevitably supplied a lot of the Circuit's revenue and many of its Local Preachers; it also enjoyed almost exclusively ministerial appointments for its Sunday services.

In 1826 the first Primitive Methodist preachers appeared in Oxford, and they received a hostile reception from the local population. Further attempts in 1835 and 1838 led to the establishment of a Primitive Methodist society in St Ebbe's, and this became the head of a circuit in 1845.[78] This seems to have scarcely impinged on the consciousness of the Wesleyans, except when Primitive Methodist Local

72   OHC, OMCA, Nix 2, loose page, gives dates for Woodstock (1824) and Combe (1835); cutting from the *Oxford Methodist Magazine*, April 1935, dates Iffley (Rose Hill) chapel to 1835. Nix 1 dates the first chapel at Headington Quarry to 1831; Lady De Villiers, 'Headington', in Mary D. Lobel (ed.), *Victoria County History of Oxford*, v (Oxford: OUP, 1957), 167, says 1830.

73   OHC, OMCA, NM5/A/F1/3, Circuit Stewards' Account Book, 1829–69, entries for 1829 and for March, June and October 1830.

74   OHC, OMCA, NM5/A/A4/1, Local Preachers' Minute Book 1830–66, 17 September 1830 and 27 March 1839

75   As will be seen later, in the last quarter of the century the Wesleyans were much quicker to build chapels.

76   OHC, OMCA, Circuit Schedule Book 1839-44, Midsummer 1839.

77   Janet Cooper, 'Bladon', in Alan Crossley (ed.), *Victoria County History of Oxford*, xii (Oxford: OUP, 1990), 34.

78   John Petty, *The History of the Primitive Methodist Connexion* (London: R. Davies, 1864), 448–9.

Preachers applied to join the Old Connexion.[79] Meanwhile, the only local reference to the Connexional troubles of the 1830s was a warm endorsement given to the national leadership by John Pike, doyen of the Oxford Wesleyan lay elite, who added his name to a letter denouncing the 'destructive designs' of Warren's Grand Central Association.[80]

Two decades of apparent harmony came to an end in the late 1840s, as the Oxford Circuit was caught up in the controversy over Wesleyan Reform. Here, as elsewhere in the country, local issues became entangled with the rhetoric around the *Fly Sheets* and controversy over the authority of the Conference and the ministers.

In summer 1849, as the Wesleyan Conference was voting to expel James Everett, Samuel Dunn and William Griffith from the ministry, the Oxford Circuit was preparing to say farewell to its Superintendent, John Wesley Button, who had completed a three-year appointment in the city. Tensions had, however, been building between Button and his junior colleague, William Hopewell, and some long-established local leaders. The presenting cause of the conflict involved Josiah Crapper, a schoolmaster, a member of a leading Wesleyan family in the city, a class leader at New Inn Hall Street, and secretary of the Wesleyan Sunday School committee.[81] Crapper was a Local Preacher, and was also son-in-law of Maximilian Wilson, Superintendent of the Circuit from 1841–44. Josiah Crapper seems to have been active in seeking to develop Methodist work in Summertown, to the north of the city, and he was deputed by the Local Preachers' Meeting in 1847 to obtain a suitable room in the village for Methodist preaching.[82] In June 1849, however, 'a conversation took place' in the Local Preachers' Meeting 'in reference to Brother Crapper supplying [i.e. preaching at], and administering the Sacrament to, the Independent Church at Summertown'. According to the record, the meeting asked Crapper to desist; he refused; and his name was therefore removed from the preaching plan.[83]

The minutes of the June meeting, taken by Hopewell, give no hint of any further controversy. However, on 18 August the *Oxford Chronicle* reported that fifteen 'well-known and highly-respected' Local Preachers had protested against 'the illegal proceedings at the last local preachers' meeting, which was improperly influenced by those in power, having for its object the expulsion of our much-respected and talented townsman, Mr J.M. Crapper ...' The fifteen protestors, it was further

79   See, for example, the Local Preachers' minutes for 25 June 1845, referring to the arrival of Brother Cox from 'the Ranters'.
80   'Funds of the Methodist Connexion', *WMM* xiv (third series), January 1835, 64–70, with Pike's name at 70. Pike ran a business selling china and glassware, and had been instrumental in the building of the New Inn Hall Street chapel in 1818. For a brief report of his death, see *WMM*, March 1845, 293–4.
81   James Nix gave an account of the local controversy in OHC, OMCA, Nix 1, ff 29–31.
82   OHC, OMCA, NM5/A/A4/1, Local Preachers' Minute Book 1830–66, March and September 1847.
83   OHC, OMCA, NM5/A/A4/1, Local Preachers' Minute Book 1830–66, 20 June 1849.

reported, had also been dropped from the plan.[84] The following week 'A Looker-on' contributed to the *Chronicle* an account of Button's final service, swiftly moving from praise of his 'grasp of intellect and powers of mind beyond the ordinary class of preachers' to criticism of his 'spirit of domination' and his 'misrepresentation and tyrannical dealing'.[85] Over succeeding weeks conflicting accounts of the case emerged. Two of the New Inn Hall Street trustees wrote to support Button, while William Bartlett, another senior Local Preacher, claimed that Crapper's willingness to preach for the Independents had been discussed the previous December, and approved by the Preachers' Meeting. Button, however, according to Bartlett, had refused to give Crapper any appointments and had brought disciplinary charges in June without any warning.[86]

It may be seen how the Crapper case could be read in parallel with the expulsion of Everett, Dunn and Griffith, as an example of an overbearing minister defying proper process and natural justice in pursuit of a personal vendetta. Clearly some of the mostly anonymous correspondents in the *Chronicle* strove to make exactly that connection. At this stage in the dispute, however, Button's action was still being defended by people who later joined the Reformers, including William Leggatt and G.G. Banbury.[87] It may be suggested that it was only as the national Reform campaign developed and gathered pace, and as Conference loyalists hit back with vituperation and expulsions, that disaffection in Oxford increased. Calm and moderate Superintendents could sometimes defuse Reform sympathies; unfortunately, Button's successor in Oxford, Joseph Earnshaw, was unwell, and responsibility devolved to his neighbour from Witney, Charles Westlake, who took a hard line, enforcing discipline and only re-admitting those preachers who expressed contrition.

Over the next two years the situation deteriorated. A steady stream of news and comment favourable to the Reformers and hostile to the Conference reached Oxford through reports in the *Chronicle* and through the weekly pro-Reform paper the *Wesleyan Times*. A public meeting was held in late October 1849 to express sympathy with the 'Three Expelled';[88] Oxford sent delegates to a Reform meeting in London in March 1850;[89] and in July 1850 Dunn and Griffith addressed a crowded gathering in the Adullam Chapel, Oxford's largest Dissenting place of worship.[90] When Hopewell quarrelled with the New Inn Hall Street Sunday School and Westlake made an unpopular nomination of a Circuit Steward, these actions were seen as further

84   'City and County Intelligence', *OC*, 18 August 1849.
85   'Wesleyans', *OC*, 25 August 1849.
86   Edward Thurland and W. Wiseman to editor, *OC*, 1 September 1849; William Bartlett to editor, *OC*, 8 September 1849.
87   'City and County Intelligence', *OC*, 1 September 1849.
88   'Meeting to Sympathise with the Expelled Wesleyan Ministers', *OC*, 27 October 1849.
89   'Conference Despotism', *OC*, 23 March 1850; compare 'The Oxford Delegates', *Watchman and Wesleyan Advertiser*, 27 March 1850, 102, for a very critical description of the Oxford Reformers, with a reply by James Goold in the *OC*, 4 May 1850.
90   'The Revs S. Dunn and W. Griffith at Oxford', *OC*, 13 July 1850.

examples of ministerial highhandedness.[91] The ministers' main problem, of course, was that they were unavoidably associated with the policy of the Conference, which was to refuse to negotiate with the Reformers. Those who withheld contributions to Connexional funds, like Leggatt , or who preached for the Reformers, like Fred Clements, were subject to discipline; others, like G.G. Banbury, opted to resign.[92] The Reformers gradually established their own alternative 'Wesleyan' societies, and began to publish their own preaching plan.[93] In 1857 the Reformers in the Oxford Circuit decided to join the United Methodist Free Churches, and this lonely UMFC outpost was sustained until Methodist Union in 1932.[94]

The protracted controversy over Wesleyan Reform cost the Oxford Circuit dear. Membership fell from 558 in September 1849 to 397 in September 1851, reaching a low point of 338 in December 1852. Annotations in the Schedule Books record local classes as 'doubtful' and report a succession of class leaders as 'Gone to the Agitators'.[95] Rival Reform societies were set up in Oxford, Woodstock and Combe, draining support from the Wesleyan cause, while the societies at Kidlington, Kirtlington and Iffley dwindled to extinction in the early 1850s. A dozen Local Preachers resigned or were expelled, and they formed the backbone of the Reformers' preaching plan. When Benjamin Gregory was appointed to the Oxford Circuit in 1857, his son recorded that 'he found Methodism in a truly pitiable condition', with congregations small, and 'finances strained to the verge of bankruptcy'.[96] Allowing for a biographer's exaggeration, in order to emphasise the transformation achieved in a matter of months, the 1850s were a difficult decade for the Circuit, and the damage caused by the Reform dissensions was long lasting.

Through the 1860s there was a gradual recovery in membership and confidence. Although the Circuit continued to rely on an annual grant from the Wesleyan Contingent Fund to cover its costs, membership grew and stabilised, and a new chapel was built at Headington Quarry in 1860.[97] More importantly, a concerted effort was made to clear the accumulating debt on the New Inn Hall Street chapel,

91   James Nix saw Westlake's refusal to withdraw his nomination as the reason why concil-iation failed: Nix 1, 31. The Quarterly Meeting minutes for this period have not survived. For Hopewell's conflict with the Sunday School, see OHC, OMCA NM5/25/A14/1, Oxford Wesleyan Sunday and Day Schools Committee minute book, 1842–73, 1 October 1849.
92   OHC, OMCA, NM5/A/A4/1, Local Preachers' Minute Book 1830–66, 18 December 1850 [Leggatt]; 25 June 1851 [Clements and Banbury].
93   See 'W.D.' [= William Downing], 'United Methodist Free Church', in the Oxford Free Church Magazine, June 1897, 45–6. Downing was the UMFC minister in Oxford from 1897–1906.
94   Oxford was in the London District of the UMFC, with Cheltenham as its nearest neigh-bouring circuit; most of the local Reformers joined the Wesleyan Reform Union, rather than the UMFC.
95   OHC, OMCA, NM5/A/A2/4, Circuit Schedule Book 1845-56, March 1851.
96   [J.R. Gregory], Benjamin Gregory, DD. Autobiographical Reflections, edited, with Memorials of his Later Life, by his Eldest Son (London: Hodder and Stoughton, 1903), 407.
97   De Villiers, 'Headington', 167.

thus freeing the Oxford trustees to assist the Circuit with its financial difficulties, and also opening up possibilities for the expansion of Wesleyan work in the city. During this period the population of Oxford steadily increased, with significant suburban development to the north, south and east of the city.[98] At the same time, legislation in the 1850s had opened undergraduate degrees at the University to non-Anglicans, and by the later 1860s there was growing pressure to abolish the remaining tests which excluded Nonconformists from higher degrees and fellowships. Upwardly mobile Wesleyan families were already sending their sons to Oxford, and there was an awareness that this was set to increase.

Between the arrival of Richard Bell as Superintendent in 1869 and the departure of Hugh Price Hughes in 1884, the position of Wesleyan Methodism in and around Oxford was transformed. Bell developed an ambitious scheme for a new city centre chapel, designed to cater for the growing urban population and to equip Methodism to reach the University. He also proposed the creation of a new circuit, centred on Woodstock, to enable a more effective concentration of ministerial efforts both in the city and in the rural hinterland.[99]

Over the next decade and a half Bell's scheme underwent considerable alterations,[100] but the eventual outcome resembled in broad outline, if not in precise detail, his vision for new buildings, more staff and 'aggressive action'. In 1878 the Wesley Memorial Chapel was opened on the New Inn Hall Street site, giving the Wesleyans an imposing Gothic building, complete with tower and spire, close to the city centre. Suburban outposts were established in Jericho, Botley and East Oxford. By the end of 1876 there was a designated weekly Class meeting, led by the Superintendent, for the small group of Wesleyan undergraduates at the University.[101] Although the plan to divide the Circuit was not taken forward, in 1874 an application was made for a third minister, supported by a Connexional Home Missions grant, to work in the villages around Woodstock, and, although this was a time of agricultural depression and rural depopulation, growth and development took place in all the villages over the next dozen years, and a new chapel opened in Bladon in 1877.[102] In March 1881 the Circuit welcomed a visiting evangelist, Robinson Watson, to lead an innovative fourteen-day mission, supported by extensive advertising, and significant membership growth followed.[103]

98   Malcolm Graham, 'The suburbs of Victorian Oxford: growth in a pre-industrial city', PhD thesis, University of Leicester, 1985, 10–14.
99   Richard Bell, 'Methodism in the University Towns', *MR*, 2 December 1870, 656. This was in line with latest Wesleyan thinking on rural mission: Bebbington, 'Wesleyan Methodist Home Mission', 94–5.
100 See Wellings, 'The building of Wesley Memorial Church', for an account of the evolving schemes.
101 OHC, OMCA, NM5/A/A2/6, Circuit Schedule Book 1869–78, December 1876.
102 OHC, OMCA, NM5/A/A3/1, Quarterly Meeting minute book 1861–88, minutes, 25 March 1874; Janet Cooper, 'Bladon', 34.
103 'Revival Intelligence', *MR*, 18 March 1881, 164; 'Mr Robinson Watson's Services', *OC*, 12 March 1881, 5.

The initiatives begun in the 1870s were taken up and developed during the ministry of Hugh Price Hughes (1881–84).[104] Hughes' claim to have 'revived' Oxford Methodism failed to give due credit to the work of his predecessors, but he undeniably consolidated and extended the achievements of the previous decade. Watson's converts were organised into mission bands to promote evangelism and enhance the impact of the Local Preachers; conventions were held to enthuse class leaders, society stewards and Sunday school teachers; small gatherings of wealthy individuals were convened to elicit financial backing for Hughes's projects;[105] and work among students grew with the creation of the Wesley Guild in 1883.[106] At his first Quarterly Meeting Hughes 'mentioned that he purposed holding special Evangelistic Services in every Chapel throughout the Circuit at the commencement of the ensuing year'.[107] A special meeting of Local Preachers in May 1882 planned open-air services on successive Sundays in the summer months, assigning a team of preachers to each. A year later, in preparation for the summer 1883 campaign, arrangements were made to print 10,000 hymn sheets for these services.[108] In the city, the New Inn Hall Street congregation marched through the city centre to an open-air service in a field near Magdalen College. Hughes led an Eight-Day Mission in the city, preceded by house-to-house canvassing, and this method was then extended to the villages.[109]

Within the city, new chapels were built in New Hinksey (1882), William Street (1883) and Walton Street (1883), while Hughes sought to extend Methodist work in the villages as well as in the city. The special Local Preachers' meeting in May 1882 drew up a list of seven villages where 'open-air work should be commenced'. A new list was presented in April 1884, with groups of preachers appointed for the summer months and a note that 'Mr Railton should render service with a cornet'.[110] In 1898 Hughes described the 'flying visits' by his 'Gospel chariots', recalling that '[a]s the result … several additional chapels have been erected since I left the Circuit'.[111]

---

104 For this section, see Martin Wellings, 'Hugh Price Hughes and "The Revival of Oxford Methodism"', *Methodist History*, 58.3 (April 2020), 152–64.

105 Hugh Price Hughes, 'The Revival of Oxford Methodism', in 'H.K.' [Nehemiah Curnock], *Hugh Price Hughes: Leader of the Forward Movement* (London: Charles H. Kelly, 1903), 17–18; OHC, OMCA, NM5/A/A3/1, Quarterly Meeting minute book 1861–88, minutes, 28 September 1881; Nix 1; J.E. Oxley, *A History of Wesley Memorial Church, Oxford 1818–1968* (Oxford: The Oxonian Press, 1968), 80–1.

106 Wellings, 'In perfect harmony with the spirit of the age'.

107 OHC, OMCA, NM5/A/A3/1, Quarterly Meeting minute book 1861–88, minutes, 28 September 1881.

108 OHC, OMCA, NM5/A/A4/2, Local Preachers' Minute Book 1867–1902, 10 May 1882 and 9 April 1883.

109 Hughes, 'Revival of Oxford Methodism', 19.

110 OHC, OMCA, NM5/A/A4/2, Local Preachers' Minute Book 1867–1902, 10 May 1882 and 16 April 1884.

111 Hughes, 'Revival of Oxford Methodism', 20.

Hughes left a new society and chapel at Eynsham, and a new society at Beckley, and re-established a Wesleyan presence at Charlton.

Between 1869 and 1884 the Wesleyan membership in the Oxford Circuit more than doubled, from 449 to 943.[112] The total exceeded 500 in the early 1870s, and then fluctuated between 470 and 510 for the next decade. The period of spectacular growth began in 1881, with an increase in the first quarter from 503 to 537, and then 566, 614, and 641, reaching 694 in March 1882. The biggest increase was reported in June 1882, when Hughes recorded a membership of 897, including 225 new members, a net increase of 203 in the quarter and 331 in the year. Although the largest numerical increase was at New Inn Hall Street, every society in the Circuit, except the tiny cause at Charlton-on-Otmoor, received at least one new member, and several of the village societies doubled their membership.[113] Growth, therefore, was neither an exclusively urban nor suburban phenomenon. The increases of 1881–84, moreover, reversed a decade of gradual decline in many of the villages.[114]

Hughes' ministry in Oxford became the stuff of Wesleyan legend, and due allowance needs to be made both for hagiography and for Hughes' own genius for self-promotion. In the early 1880s, however, the Oxford Circuit was significantly strengthened, and the confidence and momentum generated continued into the twentieth century. With small fluctuations, the membership figures held up well, although recruitment of new members sometimes struggled to keep pace with removals and resignations, so that in 1885–6, for example, 133 new members were received, and twenty-six moved into the circuit, but seventy-one left the area, seventy-four ceased to be members and eleven died, leaving a net increase of just three.[115] Hughes' strategic decision to pay attention to the villages as well as the city bore fruit in circuit initiatives to fund new chapels at Islip, Beckley, Combe, Wootton and New Headington in the 1880s and 1890s;[116] meanwhile, the modest mission room in William Street was replaced in 1904 by a commanding new chapel on the Cowley Road.[117] The corps of Local Preachers continued to grow; open-air services were held in the city and in the villages in the summer months; and special missions

112   Figures in this paragraph and the next calculated from the Schedule Books.
113   Headington Quarry increased from 44 to 84, Wootton from 20 to 47, Coombe from 25 to 43, Horspath from 4 to 11.
114   A majority of the villages had fewer members in 1880 than 1869. Although this coincided with the onset of late-nineteenth century agricultural depression and consequent depopulation, Wesleyan records do not ascribe this to the transfer or migration of members.
115   OHC, OMCA, NM5/A/A3/1, Quarterly Meeting minute book 1861–88, minutes, 31 March 1886.
116   Minutes, 30 December 1885 (Islip and Beckley), 30 March 1887 (Wootton and New Headington); the Combe chapel was replaced by a new building in 1893.
117   John Boylan, *Cowley Road Methodist Church Centre Oxford. Centenary 1904–2004* (Oxford: Cowley Road Methodist Church Centre, 2004). The architect, Stephen Salter, FRIBA, belonged to a prominent Oxford Wesleyan family.

were organised.[118] By the end of the century there was an active Nonconformist Council (later Free Church Council) in the city, with close ties to the city council as well as the business community; Wesleyans were well represented in every sphere of Oxford's commercial, philanthropic and political life; and the Wesley Guild bore witness to a Wesleyan presence in the University: two of the Guild's stalwarts, F.E. Corley and E.E. Genner, were Senior Members of the University and Local Preachers.[119] Wesleyan Methodism had come a long way since the early nineteenth century, when acquiring a city centre site for a chapel required subterfuge, and the proctors visited Wesleyan services to ensure that no undergraduates were present.[120]

Although the texts under consideration here are minutes of business meetings, the principal concern of the participants was the ministry of preaching. It is, therefore, appropriate to offer an outline of the place of preaching in nineteenth-century Wesleyan Methodism and to note the assumptions and expectations which underpinned it.

Preaching in Wesleyan Methodism

The years between the Glorious Revolution in 1688 and the death of Queen Victoria in 1901 have been described as 'a "golden age" of sermon culture in Britain'.[121] This judgment, emerging from the developing discipline of sermon studies, can be supported on a number of grounds. First, note may be taken of the sheer quantity of sermons preached in this period. William Gibson has estimated the total for the years 1689–1901 at around a quarter of a billion;[122] it may be suggested that the distribution of this aggregate figure should be weighted towards the Victorian era, overlapping with the Oxford Local Preachers' minutes considered here, both because of the expansion of places of worship in this period and because nineteenth-century reformers, like Bishop Samuel Wilberforce, insisted that the parochial clergy should preach at least once, and preferably twice, each Sunday.[123] Secondly, as a commentator in the *Monthly Review* observed in 1827, sermons comprised one of the most widely published forms of literature, rivalled only by novels: these categories comprised 'the two most remarkable departments of modern literature

---

118   For example, OHC, OMCA, NM5/A/A3/1, Quarterly Meeting minute book 1861–88, minutes, 25 March 1885.
119   For Ferrand Edward Corley (1877–1937) and Ernest Ely Genner (1877–1930), see *DMBI*, accessed 7 November 2019.
120   Oxley, *Wesley Memorial Church*, 9–11.
121   William Gibson, 'The British Sermon 1689–1901: Quantities, Performance, and Culture', in Keith A. Francis and William Gibson (eds), *The Oxford Handbook of the British Sermon 1689–1901* (Oxford: OUP, 2012), 5.
122   Gibson, 'British Sermon 1689–1901', 7.
123   Ronald K. Pugh, 'The episcopate of Samuel Wilberforce, Bishop of Oxford, 1845–69, and of Winchester, 1869–73, with special reference to the administration of the diocese of Oxford', DPhil thesis, University of Oxford, 1957, 169.

for extent'.[124] Thirdly, as the emphasis on preaching and the burgeoning market for published sermons indicate, there was an apparently insatiable public appetite for hearing and reading sermons. Fourthly, all denominations were concerned to improve the quality of preaching, whether through initial ministerial training, inspection and exhortation, modelling best practice, or the production of guides to homiletics. Finally, the vitality and success of a congregation was seen to be inextricably connected to the effectiveness of the preaching ministry. Popular preachers drew and retained congregations, and this was demonstrated by such varied orators as John Henry Newman at St Mary's, Oxford, in the 1830s, R.W. Dale at Carrs Lane, Birmingham, from 1859 to 1895 and Alexander Maclaren at Union Chapel, Manchester, from 1858 to 1910.[125] Charles Haddon Spurgeon, most celebrated of all the Victorian pulpit giants, created and sustained a congregation in excess of 5000 at the Metropolitan Tabernacle in South London between 1861 and 1892.[126] The rigid three-year itinerancy written into Wesley's Deed of Declaration made the long tenures of Anglican, Congregationalist and Baptist incumbents impossible for the Wesleyans until the rule was modified in the 1890s, so the association of one preacher with one congregation was not a feature of Victorian Wesleyanism. The Wesleyans had their star preachers, however, and they were in demand for chapel openings, anniversaries, and missionary meetings: all events needing a large congregation and a substantial collection. The opening of the New Inn Hall Street chapel in Oxford in 1818, for example, was marked by sermons from Adam Clarke, Richard Watson and Jabez Bunting; Joseph Benson came on the following Sunday.[127] In 1877 Benjamin Gregory and W.M. Punshon came for the stone-laying of the new building, while the opening of the Wesley Memorial Chapel a year later was followed by a month of visits by special preachers for Sunday and midweek services.[128] The appeal of special sermons may be judged by an incident recorded in the Local Preachers' minutes for March 1838: two of the Oxford preachers missed their Sunday appointments because they opted to stay in the city to attend the anniversary sermons instead.

If preaching was important for all varieties of Christians during the nineteenth century, it held a special place for the heirs of the Evangelical Revival, including the Wesleyan Methodists. Evangelicals of all persuasions were committed to delivering the gospel message, and there were many methods of doing this, from conversation

---

124 'Modern Sermons', *Monthly Review*, March 1827, 225.
125 For Dale, a Congregationalist, see A.W.W. Dale, *The Life of R.W. Dale of Birmingham* (London: Hodder and Stoughton, 1898); for the Baptist Maclaren, J.Y.H. Briggs, 'McLaren (Maclaren), Alexander', in Timothy Larsen (ed.), *Biographical Dictionary of Evangelicals* (Leicester: IVP, 2003), 397–9.
126 J. Armstrong, 'Spurgeon, Charles Haddon', in Larsen, *Biographical Dictionary of Evangelicals*, 624–7.
127 Oxley, *Wesley Memorial Church*, 11.
128 Oxley, *Wesley Memorial Church*, 27–8.

and correspondence to tracts and books, but preaching was the pre-eminent mode of communication. The example was set by George Whitefield and the Wesley brothers from the beginning of the Revival in the 1730s, and it is significant that when the Wesleyans celebrated their centenary, they chose to do so in 1839, not 1838, marking the anniversary not of John Wesley's 'warmed heart' in Aldersgate Street, but of the beginning of 'field preaching' a year later.[129] Over thirty-five years Whitefield preached an estimated 18,000 sermons, while John Wesley travelled perhaps a quarter of a million miles and preached 40,000 times in an itinerant ministry spanning half a century.[130] For the early evangelicals, the preacher was, in William Cowper's phrase, 'the legate of the skies', and preaching was

> 'the most important and effectual guard,
> Support and ornament of virtue's cause.'[131]

This high view of preaching was sustained throughout the nineteenth century. A contributor to the *Wesleyan Methodist Magazine* in January 1831, reflecting on the evolution of Methodism from a religious society ancillary to the Church of England into a fully fledged church, found it necessary to remind readers that there was more to public worship than going 'to preaching' and hearing sermons, but this advice may have fallen on deaf ears.[132] Reviewing 'The Modern British Pulpit' in June 1854, a writer in the Wesleyans' *London Quarterly Review* affirmed: 'The Pulpit ... cannot be too highly estimated. Nothing can equal it in importance, nothing compare with it in beneficial results.'[133] Thirty years later, Charles Garrett, giving the Ex-President's Charge to newly ordained Wesleyan ministers, reminded them that 'you are called especially to be *preachers*'.[134] Preaching was a 'sacred institution', urged James Harrison Rigg, while for William Arthur, it was 'the most powerful engine for promoting the religious and social welfare of the nation.'[135] In the early and middle years of the nineteenth century the *Wesleyan Methodist Magazine* carried sermons and scriptural expositions in most of its monthly issues, and although this diminished in later decades, full sermons were still occasionally published, while reviews of printed sermons became even more frequent as the market expanded. In addition, memoirs and obituaries in the *Magazine* bore witness to the power of

---

129 Thomas Jackson, *The Centenary of Wesleyan Methodism* (London: John Mason, 1839), 67–9.

130 James Downey, *The Eighteenth-Century Pulpit* (Oxford: Clarendon, 1969), 156, 210.

131 William Cowper, *The Task* (1785), Book Two.

132 E.T., 'On profiting from hearing sermons', *WMM*, January 1831, 25.

133 'The Modern British Pulpit', *LQR*, June 1854, 349. This article quotes Cowper, but without attribution, suggesting that the poem was considered well known to a Wesleyan readership.

134 'Faithful Stewardship', in Charles Garrett, *Loving Counsels. Sermons and Addresses* (London: T. Woolmer, 1887), 9. (Italics in original).

135 J.H. Rigg, 'The Pulpit: Professor Butler's Sermons', *LQR*, January 1857, 461; William Arthur [?], 'Home Heathenism', *LQR*, October 1855, 181.

preaching to bring people to saving faith. Most, like Mrs Judith Ally Leverett, of Aylesbury, the Revd Thomas Cooper, and Mrs Susanna Sykes came to faith through the impact of the spoken word;[136] but others, like John Gould, of Barnstaple, and Samuel Beaven, of Devizes, were awakened through reading the published sermons of Whitefield and Wesley.[137]

Wesleyan preaching in this period may be characterised by three elements, at least in aspiration. First, it was intentionally plain in style. When John Wesley wrote in the preface to the first volume of his *Sermons on Several Occasions* (1746) that 'I design plain truth for plain people',[138] he both took a stand within the homiletic mainstream of eighteenth-century preaching and also set a benchmark for Methodist preachers of future generations.

Clarity of language, simplicity of structure and an avoidance of jargon and ostentatious learning had been championed in the British pulpit since the middle of the seventeenth century, in the precept and practice of John Wilkins, Gilbert Burnet and John Tillotson.[139] Whitefield and the Wesley brothers took up this 'plain' style and married it to an unapologetically evangelical theology. For John Wesley, clarity was crucial: contemporaries confirmed that his style was 'neat, simple, and perspicuous' and a lady who heard him preach in 1790 exclaimed in surprise: 'Why, the poorest person in the chapel might have understood him!'[140]

Wesley's four volumes of *Sermons on Several Occasions* were published as official statements of Methodist doctrine, but they also served as homiletic models for Methodist preachers: the *Sermons* were required reading for Local Preachers as well as candidates for the ministry, and progress towards accreditation meant passing an oral examination on their contents. It is not surprising, therefore, that Wesley's emphasis on plainness recurs throughout the nineteenth century, in advice given to preachers, in reviews of works on homiletics, and in the qualities praised in obituaries and memoirs. Writing 'On the Office of a Local Preacher' in the *Wesleyan Methodist Magazine* in May 1832, 'Gamma' advised a neat and perspicuous plan of sermonizing.[141] The *London Quarterly* in June 1854 praised the Wesleys for 'a simple and pointed style of address', and complained that the modern pulpit tended towards 'miserable poverty of thought, arrayed in language either vapid or

---

136 'Recent Deaths', *WMM*, December 1834, 956; 'Memoir of the Late Rev. Thomas Cooper', *WMM*, January 1835, 2; 'Memoir of Mrs John Sykes, of Leeds', *WMM*, November 1836, 814.
137 'Memoir of Mr John Gould, of Barnstaple', *WMM*, March 1824, 145; 'Memoir of Mr Samuel Beaven', *WMM*, May 1824, 289.
138 'Preface', in Albert C. Outler (ed.), *Sermons* (*Works of John Wesley*, vols 1–4; Nashville: Abingdon, 1984–87), 1: 104.
139 Rolf P. Lessenich, *Elements of Public Oratory in Eighteenth Century England (1660–1800)* (Cologne: Böhlau, 1972).
140 John Whitehead, *The Life of the Rev. John Wesley, MA* (London: Couchman, 1796), 2:466; 'Anecdote of Mr Wesley', *WMM*, January 1825, 25.
141 'On the Office of Local Preachers', *WMM*, May 1832, 333.

bombastic.'[142] Thirty years later, in an article on 'Our Local Preachers: Preparation for the Pulpit', William Willmer Pocock, a Wesleyan Local Preacher, recommended use of 'the plainest, simplest, most unmistakeable language'.[143] Among numerous examples in the obituaries, John Bagnall, a Local Preacher in Carmarthen, was praised for his 'lucid, pointed and practical' discourses', while William Harrison, of Addingham, was remembered for 'his plain and affectionate sermons'.[144]

Wesleyan preaching, secondly, was intended to be evangelical in emphasis. Adam Clarke, whose *Letter to a Methodist Preacher on his Entrance into the Work of the Ministry* (1800) was one of the first formal works of Wesleyan homiletics, urged a young colleague, Samuel Woolmer: 'Preach a present, free and full salvation, wherever you go, whether they hear, or whether they will forbear. Preach Jesus; preach his atonement; preach his dying love. This will do more in awakening sinners than all the fire in hell.'[145] The same note was sounded in the Revd Robert Johnson's dying message to the Local Preachers of the Hull Circuit, recorded in his memoir in the *Magazine*: 'Tell them to preach Christ: nothing else will do. Christ for us, Christ with us, Christ in us; Christ all and in all. Tell them to preach Scriptural Christianity. All philosophical and metaphysical disquisitions are chaff.'[146]

The evangelical emphasis comprised two elements. One, as already indicated in the words of Clarke and Johnson, was doctrinal. Wesleyans were expected to proclaim an evangelical gospel, centring on the love of God for all (the Wesleys' evangelical Arminianism), the atonement, the need and possibility of new birth, and the call to holiness of heart and life. Sermons which failed to sound this evangelical note were criticised, so that, for example, a volume of *Parochial Sermons* by John Armstrong, the High Church Bishop of Grahamstown, was described by the *London Quarterly* as practical and cultivated, but 'sadly defective' because lacking 'proper evangelical colouring'.[147] Likewise, Charles Kingsley's *Sermons for the Times* (1855) were earnest, plain and colloquial – all qualities likely to commend them to a Wesleyan readership – but 'seriously erroneous and mischievous' in doctrine.[148]

The other element of the evangelical emphasis was earnestness. Wesleyan preachers were expected to speak from the heart, with energy and conviction. Rigg, writing in 1857, defined a sermon as 'in substance a divine message, but in form an earnest human speech'.[149] Praising the transformation of Scottish preaching through the example of Thomas Chalmers, the *London Quarterly* contrasted Chalmers'

---

142 'The Modern British Pulpit', *LQR*, June 1854, 362, 367.
143 W.W. Pocock, 'Our Local Preachers: Preparation for the Pulpit', *WMM*, February 1885, 95.
144 'Recent Deaths', *WMM*, July 1832, 537; 'Recent Deaths', *WMM*, January 1835, 79.
145 'Memoir of the Rev. Samuel Woolmer', *WMM*, May 1830, 296.
146 'Memoir of the Rev. Robert Johnson', *WMM*, April 1830, 225.
147 'Brief Literary Notices', *LQR*, January 1855, 557–8.
148 'Brief Literary Notices', *LQR*, January 1856, 559–60.
149 'The Pulpit', *LQR*, January 1857, 465.

'warm and masculine theology' with the 'vapid morality' of the Moderates in the Kirk, whose preaching was 'more like a stagnant pool than the river of life'. In the opinion of the same writer, the early Methodist preachers were 'possessed ... of masculine intellects, of warm hearts, and a simple and pointed style of address.' In the next generation, Robert Newton was celebrated for his 'evangelical simplicity and power'.[150] Earnestness, then, was a combination of personal sincerity and immediate religious experience, conviction of the importance of the message and of persuading hearers to respond, energy in delivery, and a sense of dependence on God for inspiration and guidance. For many Wesleyan commentators, earnestness could co-exist with deficiencies in education and infelicities of style, so that John Greeves, in his biography of the Bedfordshire Local Preacher William Cumberland, admitted that Cumberland's style was 'very homely, and sometimes degenerated into coarseness, or ludicrousness; but his simplicity and sincerity ... and a manner exceedingly earnest, affectionate, and winning; rendered him not only acceptable, but even popular, wherever he went'.[151] Earnestness would always trump formal eloquence: reviewing a volume of sermons by the Hon. and Revd A.T. Lyttelton in March 1894, the *Methodist Recorder* observed that the sermons were 'thoughtful and even able ... but too smooth and polished to pierce, perhaps to reach, the conscience of the ordinary hearer or reader'. The volume, said the reviewer, was 'eminently characteristic of an Anglican clergyman'.[152] By contrast, a few years earlier a writer described 'A Sunday Evening at Scarborough' in the *Magazine*, with a preacher whose energy and pathos held a crowded congregation, comprising 'all sorts and conditions of men' in 'rapt attention' for an hour.[153]

Plain in style; evangelical in emphasis; Wesleyan preaching, thirdly, was expected to be extempore in delivery. In the Pastoral Session of the Wesleyan Conference in 1894 the Revd Joseph Posnett complained that some theological college students were reading their sermons, and pronounced this 'a most bitter calamity' and 'a Methodist abomination'.[154] Representatives of the colleges hastened to repudiate the practice, but Posnett had touched on a recurring issue in the nineteenth century literature: whether sermons could (or should) be written and read, written and memorised, or delivered extempore.

Wesleyan commentators acknowledged that there were some famous, popular and evangelical preachers who read their sermons from manuscript. Thomas Chalmers was cited as an example, although in a context which indicated

150 'The Modern British Pulpit', LQR, June 1854, 355, 362–3.
151 John Greeves, *Memorials of William Cumberland, of Bedford* (London: J. Mason, 1834), 37.
152 'Readable Books and Articles', MR, 22 March 1894, 190. The book was Lyttelton's *College and University Sermons* (1894).
153 'A Sunday Evening at Scarborough', WMM, October 1888, 765–8.
154 'Reading of Sermons', MR, 2 August 1894, 573.

disapproval of the practice.[155] George Maunder, Superintendent in Oxford from 1876, was, remembered James Nix, 'a slave to the manuscript', but nonetheless 'his sermons were full of go and delivered with pathetic energy'.[156] The Wesleyan consensus, however, was that a manuscript came between preacher and congregation, preventing eye-contact and inhibiting an ability to adapt creatively to the response of the hearers and to the mood of the moment. For William Arthur, writing in 1855, reading in the pulpit was 'an evil', partly because 'few men read well, because few read naturally', and partly because reading tended to 'destroy all eloquence, by freezing the noble currents of emotion'.[157] Rigg agreed, arguing that a congregation needs 'the vivid play of living speech'.[158]

The practice of learning sermons and delivering them from memory (memoriter) was also generally disapproved. Reflecting in 1901 on a lifetime of preaching, Rigg admitted that he had adopted the memoriter style as a young Local Preacher in the early 1840s but had soon abandoned it as 'a burden and bondage'.[159] Wesleyan writers agreed that memorisation wasted time, over-taxed the memory, and resulted in sermons which might be perfectly prepared, but lacking in warmth.

The ideal for the Wesleyan commentators was a sermon premeditated in preparation but delivered extempore. Anticipating objections, they emphasised that extempore preaching did not mean preaching 'without the least previous study': this was 'gross ignorance and vanity'.[160] Preachers should read widely and think deeply, allow a subject to mature in their minds, organise the sermon into appropriate divisions, and then leave the mind open to 'the natural laws of suggestion and free speech'.[161] Rigg acknowledged that this required practice, and that it could be a temptation to those with 'a facility of superficial declamation'.[162] It could result in even the most experienced preachers losing the thread of their discourse. Overall, however, it produced the most fluent, natural and effective preaching, responding to the occasion. A topic 'closely premeditated, hardly written at all' allowed a preacher like Robert Newton to take the same basic structure and adapt it to a particular congregation, in effect producing a new sermon each time.[163]

Wesleyan confidence in plain, earnest, evangelical, extempore preaching was largely sustained through the Victorian era, but concerns about the waning effectiveness of the pulpit appeared from time to time. Sometimes a high-profile intervention by a leading preacher or public intellectual sparked debate, as when the

155 'On Preaching', LQR, July 1867, 388–9.
156 OHC, OMCA, Nix, 1, 39.
157 'Home Heathenism', LQR, October 1855, 184.
158 'On Preaching', LQR, July 1867, 387.
159 J.H. Rigg, Scenes and Studies in the Ministry of our Lord (London: Kelly, 1901), v–vi.
160 'An Essay on Extemporary Preaching', Methodist Magazine, August 1815, 577.
161 'On Preaching', LQR, July 1867, 403.
162 'Extempore Preaching', LQR, January 1872, 457.
163 'On Preaching', LQR, July 1867, 380.

Congregationalist J. Baldwin Brown published an article in *The Nineteenth Century* asking, 'Is the pulpit losing its power?' or when J.P. Mahaffy produced *The Decay of Modern Preaching* in 1882. At other times the newspapers or the heavyweight quarterlies reflected on the place of preaching in contemporary society. For the religious press, the state of the pulpit was always topical. Setting aside the jeremiads about sermons that were too short, too long, too intellectual or too shallow, there were occasions when serious consideration was given to the ability of preachers and preaching to reach those outside the ranks of regular worshippers, a concern discussed in a symposium in the *Wesleyan Methodist Magazine* in 1887. By this time, the language of 'efficiency' was being used for the training and support of preachers, and one manifestation of this development was the burgeoning of handbooks, Bible commentaries and journals intended to resource preachers – a trend treated to a scathing review by J.H. Rigg in the *London Quarterly* in July 1884.[164]

Rigg's 1884 article on 'Aids to Preaching' considered the sermon skeletons and expository serials not only from the standpoint of professional preachers but also from the perspective of Local Preachers. Rigg recognised a reality overlooked by much of the literature on the nineteenth-century pulpit: that the majority of Sunday services in the Methodist denominations were conducted by Local Preachers, and not by ministers.[165] With that in mind, attention may now be turned to the particular place of Local Preachers in Wesleyan polity and church life.

Local Preachers in Wesleyan Methodism

Preaching was fundamental to the development and expansion of the Wesleys' Methodism. The questions of who should preach, however, and how they should be selected, trained and authorised, and then how preaching should be organised, took decades to determine. The first Methodist preachers were the Wesley brothers and a small group of like-minded clergy friends. Very soon, however, lay members of the Methodist societies began to preach, and John Wesley assigned them to travel the far-flung 'rounds' or 'circuits' of his connexion. As John Lenton has shown, in the eighteenth century the Wesleyans had a band of 'travelling preachers', full-time itinerants, funded by the movement and available for deployment at John Wesley's discretion, a body of 'local preachers', who were self-supporting and tied by employment and family commitments to a particular area, and 'semi-itinerants', who had more constraints than the travelling preachers but more flexibility than the local preachers.[166] It was quite possible for individuals to move between these categories:

---

164   'Aids to Preaching', *LQR*, July 1884.
165   In 1883, seven out of eight Wesleyan preachers were lay rather than ordained: Kenneth D. Brown, *A Social History of the Nonconformist Ministry in England and Wales 1800–1930* (Oxford: Clarendon Press, 1988), 143.
166   John Lenton, *John Wesley's Preachers. A Social and Statistical Analysis of the British and Irish Preachers Who Entered the Methodist Itinerancy before 1791* (Milton Keynes: Paternoster,

for itinerants to 'locate', often when the rigours of annual redeployment became too onerous, or when health or family circumstances changed, or for 'local' preachers to sense a call to the itinerancy. John Bagnall, for example, whose death was noted in the *Magazine* in July 1832, was a Travelling Preacher for three years before settling in Carmarthen and becoming a Local Preacher there for the remainder of his life;[167] on the other hand, all travelling preachers began as Local Preachers. As indicated by the nomenclature, the difference was about availability for deployment ('stationing', in the Wesleyan terminology), and not about a distinction between lay and ordained, because the only ordained preachers were those already in Anglican orders, like John Fletcher, or those few 'set apart' by Wesley from 1784 onwards, first for work in America, and later for Scotland and England. Wesleyan Local Preachers, then, were not distinctively 'lay' preachers, but rather preachers whose work was focussed in a particular area. For John Wesley, as Margaret Batty has demonstrated, all his preachers formed one body, and the 'local' preachers were simply those members of that body not currently available for stationing.[168]

By the 1780s, as the Methodist movement grew, there is evidence to suggest that John Wesley's personal knowledge and control of the preachers was coming under strain. Wesley was concerned about what he saw as the pretensions or independence of Local Preachers and about the ambitions of the itinerants.[169] These tensions were not resolved, and the adjustments that took place after Wesley's death saw a much clearer official distinction emerge between the Travelling Preachers and the Local Preachers. Only the Travelling Preachers were admitted to the Conference, the Connexion's governing body. Only the Travelling Preachers were subject to the discipline of stationing, and eligible for a stipend and allowances. The Wesleyan leadership developed an understanding of authority vested in a 'collective pastorate', embodied in the Conference, and differentiated from the lay membership of the Connexion. One visible indication of this change was the alteration in the labelling of the portraits of Travelling Preachers in the *Magazine*, as the title 'Preacher of the Gospel' was replaced by the ministerial style 'Rev'.[170] The introduction of seminary-style training in 1834 and the resumption of ordination by the laying on of hands in 1836 confirmed the evolution of Wesley's Travelling Preachers into a trained, ordained, stipendiary ministry.

The development of the Wesleyan collective pastorate, with its theological under-pinning and institutional expression, was by no means painless. During the 1790s, for instance, Alexander Kilham urged that Local Preachers should be selected by

---

2009), 293, 315.

167 'Recent Deaths', *WMM*, July 1832, 537.

168 Margaret Batty, 'Origins: The Age of Wesley', in Geoffrey Milburn and Margaret Batty (eds), *Workaday Preachers. The Story of Methodist Local Preaching* (London: Methodist Publishing House, 1995), 21.

169 Batty, 'Origins', 29–30.

170 Batty, 'Contribution of Local Preachers', 142, dates the introduction of 'Rev' to 1818 and the official use of 'minister' to 1827.

'the people', and not just by the itinerants and that local Leaders' Meetings should be involved in the process of accreditation. Meanwhile Conference regulations provoked resentment by ordering Local Preachers to attend their classes and keep their appointments, insisting that only ministers should conduct baptisms and celebrate Holy Communion, and rebuking Local Preachers who sought to register under the Toleration Act to avoid conscription.[171] When William Hatton, a veteran Yorkshire Local Preacher, published his *Brief Account of the Rise and Progress of the Local Preachers* in 1817, he expressed the hope that a greater understanding of the work of Local Preachers would increase the esteem in which they were held, and that a new generation of Travelling Preachers would not 'attempt to lord it over their local brethren'.[172] Hatton's description of the value of Local Preachers, 'personal, pecuniary and religious',[173] to Methodism suggested that Local Preachers were feeling at best under-appreciated and at worst demeaned by the pretensions of the itinerants. A decade after the publication of Hatton's *Brief Account* it was Local Preachers who took the lead in the controversy that divided the Wesleyan cause in Leeds, as local opinion resisted the Conference's ruling on the installation of an organ in the Brunswick chapel.

A significant development in this period was the addition of quarterly Circuit Local Preachers' Meetings to the Wesleyan polity in 1796. The record of the decision was typically laconic:

> Respecting the admission of persons to be local preachers, Let the Superintendent regularly meet the local preachers once a quarter, and let none be admitted but those that are proposed and approved at that meeting; and if in any Circuit this be not practicable, let them be proposed and approved at the quarterly meeting.[174]

Whether this was a concession by the Conference to the influence of Local Preachers, or an attempt to deflect calls for greater participation in decision-making, or a move to ensure that Local Preachers were kept firmly within their circuits and subject to ministerial oversight, the mechanism of the quarterly meeting proved crucial to the corporate life and identity of the Local Preachers over the next century, and beyond.[175] The evolution of the Local Preachers' Meeting will be considered below, but the 1796 regulation about 'the admission of persons to be local preachers' prompts an examination first of the process by which a person might become a Wesleyan Local Preacher.

The structure and ethos of Wesleyanism encouraged testimony and evangelism. Members of the society were expected to speak of their religious experience in the weekly class meeting, and Wesleyans were active in evangelism, whether in

171 Batty, 'Contribution', 69–72, 82, 91, 134–5.
172 William Hatton, *A Brief Account of the Rise and Progress of the Local Preachers, and of Local Preaching, among the Methodists* (Leeds: E. Baines, n.d. [1817]), 4, 58.
173 Hatton, *Brief Account*, 38.
174 *Minutes of Conferences*, 1, 349 [1796].
175 Batty, 'Contribution of Local Preachers', 81–5.

conversation or through more organised endeavours, like the prayer meetings described by Joseph Nightingale.[176] Those whose fluency in the class or prayer meeting suggested an aptitude for preaching might be nominated to 'exhort'. Strictly speaking, exhorters were supposed to limit themselves to sharing a message of personal testimony, and were not permitted to 'take a text', or preach a sermon from a biblical verse. Whether this distinction was carefully observed in practice is doubtful. Permission to exhort was conveyed by a written note from the Superintendent, on the authority of the Local Preachers' Meeting, and the quarterly meeting kept the progress of the exhorters under regular review. Meanwhile, the exhorters were listed on the quarterly plan of preaching appointments in the circuit, sometimes by name, but more often by initials only.[177]

From exhorting, an aspiring Local Preacher would move to a period 'on trial', during which they would continue to conduct services, but with the added responsibility of preaching, 'taking a text' from the Bible as the basis for a sermon. Each quarterly meeting would hear reports on progress from whichever Local Preachers might have heard the preacher 'on trial'; if necessary, experienced preachers might be deputed by the meeting to bring a report to the next gathering. When judged ready, the preacher on trial would be required to face an oral examination in the Local Preachers' Meeting, exploring their Christian experience, their call to preach, and their knowledge of and fidelity to Wesleyan doctrine, as set out in John Wesley's *Sermons* and his *Explanatory Notes upon the New Testament*. The successful candidate would then become a fully accredited Local Preacher, listed on the quarterly preaching plan.

The process of admission changed very little in the course of the nineteenth century. Officially designated prayer leaders seemed to have faded away by the middle of the century, but Oxford Wesleyan plans continued to print separate lists of exhorters and preachers on trial, and those testing a call to preach continued to be monitored quarter by quarter, and then appear for oral examination before accreditation. Two developments, however, may be mentioned.

First, there was a gradual move to greater regulation and consistency across the Connexion. When William Peirce compiled his *Ecclesiastical Principles and Polity of the Wesleyan Methodists* in 1854, he observed apropos the Local Preachers' Meeting that 'There are but few positive laws relating to this useful class of officers. Common usage, not written law, determines, for the most part, all connected with the admission and government of this numerous and respectable body.' Peirce noted that there was no set term to the period a trainee Local Preacher might serve 'on trial': it was six months in most circuits, but 'the usage is not uniform'.[178] The 1868

176 Nightingale, *Portraiture of Methodism*, 270–1.
177 See, for example, the Oxford Plan of 1823, with separate lists of exhorters and prayer leaders, all indicated by initials.
178 William Peirce, *Ecclesiastical Principles and Polity of the Wesleyan Methodists* (London: Hamilton, Adams and Co., 1854), 312–13.

edition of the *Principles and Polity* picked up a change: 'since 1852 a probation of twelve months has become general.'[179] The reforms of 1894, considered below, codified this, requiring a minimum of twelve months' probation.[180]

The other instance of consistency concerned the vexed question of whether a Local Preacher fully accredited in one circuit had the right to transfer to another circuit without further examination. Discussions and correspondence in preparation for the report to the Conference of 1894 revealed that there was some variation in practice on this, and that some circuits had refused to accept transferred preachers unless they were willing to undergo a trial service.[181] The Conference ruled that 'Every duly accredited Local Preacher is entitled to be placed, without renewed Trial or Examination, upon the Plan of any Circuit to which he may remove; provided he present his Note of Removal and current Circuit Plan.'[182] The *Methodist Recorder* hailed this decision as an affirmation of the Connexional status of Local Preachers; Price Hughes observed that listing a Local Preacher on the plan did not oblige a reluctant Superintendent to give them any appointments.[183]

The second development which unfolded in the course of the century concerned the training of preachers. The early model of training was fundamentally an apprenticeship, where an inexperienced preacher accompanied a fully accredited colleague, learning by observation and practice. Sometimes a more drastic approach was taken, and a preacher with a note from the Superintendent was simply sent to 'take a few appointments in the country places', in the presence of a senior preacher, as a test of ability.[184] From the first decades of the century, however, preachers were also encouraged to read and to study. Hatton recommended at least consulting a Commentary, suggesting Burkitt as the most useful.[185] 'Gamma', writing in the *Magazine* in 1832, thought that Local Preachers should have 'a comprehensive grasp of mind in regard to the Gospel scheme of salvation', that they should be familiar with the works of Wesley and Fletcher, and that they should have access to a good Commentary.[186] Far more elaborate proposals were brought forward, for example by William Robinson, in his *Essay on Lay Ministry* (1832). Robinson recommended Local Preachers to build up a library, including Richard Watson's

179   Peirce, *Principles and Polity* (1868 edition), 352.
180   *Minutes of Conference*, 1894, 459.
181   'The Local Preachers. Proceedings of the Special Committee', *MR*, 1 February 1894, 68.
182   *Minutes of Conference*, 1894, 458–9.
183   'Local Preachers', *MR*, 1 February 1894, 72; 'Proceedings of the Special Committee', *MR*, 1 February 1894, 68.
184   Peirce, *Principles and Polity*, 318.
185   Hatton, *Brief Account*, 67. For William Burkitt (1650–1703) and his *Expository Notes, with Practical Observations, on the New Testament* (1700), see 'Burkitt, William' in *ODNB*.
186   'On the Office of Local Preachers', *WMM*, April 1832, 335.

Theological Dictionary and his *Institutes*,[187] Horn's *Introduction*,[188] Paley's *Works*,[189] and Wesley's *Sermons* and *Notes*. At some points in his treatise Robinson came close to acknowledging that many Local Preachers lacked the time, the resources and the educational background to master all these weighty tomes, but he continued to urge that much could be accomplished by '*moderate* industry'.[190]

By the last quarter of the century Wesleyan commentators were more aware of, or more explicit in recognising, the range of backgrounds and educational opportunities among the Local Preachers. They were also more concerned about the need to raise the standard of preaching if the Church was to appeal to an increasingly literate and educated population. The *Methodist Recorder* might fulminate that 'School Board education is destroying much of the colour and music and vigorous vitality of the old English rural type', and protest that 'we do not want … the local preacher to be cut to pattern or moulded in a shape',[191] but others argued that entertaining idiosyncrasy in the pulpit risked losing the rising generation. Proposals were therefore brought forward in 1894 for Connexional examinations to supplement the local supervision of training. Caution prevailed, however, and although reading lists were issued and a Union for Biblical and Homiletical Study established, participation in any of these ventures remained optional until the 1930s.[192]

If the process of accreditation remained much the same through the nineteenth century, so did the place of Local Preachers in the Wesleyan polity. There was some incremental adjustment to the Connexional constitution, so that in 1852, for example, Local Preachers of three years' standing were made *ex officio* members of the Circuit Quarterly Meeting. The admission of lay representatives into the Conference in 1878 brought a significant number of Local Preachers into the Wesleyans' governing body. Connexional and district Local Preachers' committees were set up in 1885.[193] The biggest change, however, happened in 1894, when almost a century of disparate regulations about Local Preachers were codified and a standard agenda for the meetings was laid down. The agenda, printed in the *Minutes of Conference* in the form of thirteen questions, covered the traditional topics of character and competence, recruitment, resignations, training, and changes to times

187   Richard Watson, *A Biblical and Theological Dictionary* (London: John Mason, 1837) and *Theological Institutes* (London: John Mason, 1823–9).

188   Presumably Thomas Hartwell Horne's *A Compendious Introduction to the Study of the Bible* (London: Thomas Cadell, 1827)

189   William Paley, *Works* (Edinburgh, 1829).

190   William Robinson, *An Essay on Lay Ministry; particularly on that of Wesleyan Local Preachers* (London: Mason, 1832), 39, 179.

191   'Editorial Notes', *MR*, 24 May 1894, 339.

192   Martin Wellings and Andrew Wood, 'Facets of Formation: Theology through Training', in Clive Marsh, Brian Beck, Angela Shier-Jones and Helen Wareing (eds), *Unmasking Methodist Theology* (London: Continuum, 2004), 75–6.

193   Batty, 'Contribution of Local Preachers', 213, 255.

and places of worship. It brought uniformity and provided explanatory comments and justification for the inquiries made.[194]

Just over a year later, C.O. Eldridge, a Wesleyan minister with a long-standing interest in Local Preachers, published *Local Preachers and Village Methodism* (1895).[195] Eldridge took the view that the future of Methodism, especially in the small towns and villages, depended on 'a trained local ministry', and that the Church had not really tackled the challenges of training, organisation and effectiveness posed by the changing social, religious and educational circumstances of the late nineteenth century.[196] He held that the reforms of 1894 were helpful, but insufficient; they failed to address, for example, the 'utterly uninteresting and profitless' Preachers' Meetings, or to grasp the nettle of training. For Eldridge, the Conference had focussed on status, while the real problem was indifference among the preachers.[197] Attendance at the Preachers' Meeting, and the way the meeting was used, were for him indicators of the motivation of the preachers and the vitality of the circuit. It will be seen below how these factors played out in the Oxford Wesleyan Circuit between the 1830s and the turn of the century.

Deployment: The Preaching Plan

Reference has already been made to the quarterly plan or the preaching plan, and this was a vital element in the organisation of any Wesleyan circuit.[198] The plan was a grid, formed by listing preaching places down the left-hand side of a sheet of paper and listing dates across the top of the sheet. The boxes in the grid were then filled by placing in each box the name of the preacher assigned to conduct worship in that place on that day. The earliest plans were handwritten, dating back to the 1770s; by the end of the eighteenth century, plans were printed. Early plans only included the names and appointments of the Local Preachers; one for the Hinckley Circuit from 1807 marked the spaces with an asterisk and the explanation that these gaps would be filled by 'An Itinerant';[199] but within a decade or so of this the Travelling Preachers as well as the Local Preachers were fully included. The Preachers were listed by name, seniority and category: first the Travelling Preachers; then the fully accredited Local Preachers; then the Preachers 'on trial'; then the Exhorters; then the Prayer Leaders. Perhaps to save space, everyone was assigned a number, and

194   *Minutes of Conference*, 1894, 456–62.
195   Eldridge's other books included *The Lay Preachers' Handbook* (1894).
196   C.O. Eldridge, *Local Preachers and Village Methodism* (Rochdale: Joyful News Book Depot, 1895), 12.
197   Eldridge, *Local Preachers and Village Methodism*, 126–7, 134.
198   For this section, see E. Alan Rose, 'Local Preachers and the Preaching Plan', in Milburn and Batty, *Workaday Preachers*, 143–63. For an example, see the Oxford Wesleyan Preachers' Plan for January to April 1839 reproduced in this volume.
199   I am grateful to the Revd Canon Helen D. Cameron for drawing this plan to my attention, and to the Revd Dr Tim Woolley for supplying a scan.

numbers rather than names were printed in the grid. Later in the century surnames were used in the grid, but an order of seniority was retained in the list. This was not solely about longevity in service: promotion to the head of the list was a matter of decision and a mark of respect,[200] while a lapse in behaviour could result in demotion or removal altogether for one or more quarters. Since the plan was a public document, this indication of public disgrace carried some weight. Preachers who returned to a circuit after an absence, or who resumed preaching after a period of retirement, were anxious to be restored to their former place on the plan, and not to start again at the foot of the list. To achieve accreditation was to 'come onto full plan'; to 'give up one's plan' was to resign as a Local Preacher.

Three observations may be drawn from the extant plans.[201] One is that almost all the Sunday morning and evening services in the New Inn Hall Street chapel were conducted by the ministers: Local Preachers were only appointed for Sunday afternoon services, perhaps the service connected to the Sunday School. Whether this was the ministers' choice, or partly a reflection of pressure from the pew-holders and trustees, is difficult to determine. At the end of the century, with a larger ministerial staff, more chapels and a greater range of Local Preachers, the pattern was not dissimilar: only a few of the Local Preachers were given appointments in the city chapels.

A second observation is that Local Preachers were deployed across the Circuit according to availability and not according to location. Local Preachers were not planned with greater frequency in their home places and were not used as *de facto* local pastors.

The third observation is that Local Preachers carried a heavy load of appointments. Some preached on eleven or twelve Sundays in the quarter, with significant journeys to their appointments. The saving grace, perhaps, was that they were not planned more than once in the same place, so allowing for the possibility of preparing one sermon and using it many times.

The Oxford Local Preachers' Book

As already noted, the Wesleyan Conference instituted quarterly Local Preachers' meetings in 1796. The first entries in the Oxford Local Preacher's Minute Book, for March and June 1830, indicate that there was at least one previous volume of

---

200 Thus in April 1835, the Oxford preachers resolved that Joseph Ostler should take the first place in the list on the plan.

201 Plans for the Oxford Wesleyan Circuit survive for May–July 1823 (Drew University), November 1834–February 1835 (Rose Hill Methodist Church), January–April 1839 (Wesley Memorial Methodist Church), May–October 1866 (JRULM), October–December 1876 (JRULM), July–September 1878 (Wesley Memorial Methodist Church), October 1886 – January 1887 (JRULM) and July–October 1888 (JRULM). From July 1890 an almost complete set is held by the Oxfordshire History Centre.

minutes, now lost.[202] Two stout books, the first seven by nine inches, with unruled pages and the second six by eight inches, with ruled pages, labelled respectively 'From 1830 to Dec. 26th 1866 Oxford Local Preachers' Book' and 'Minute Book of Local Preachers' Meetings, Oxford, Mar. 27, 1867 to Dec. 22, 1902' are now the oldest extant records of Oxford's Wesleyan Local Preachers' meetings, maintaining a sequence broken only four times in seventy-two years: the missing entries are December 1831; June, September and December 1841; December 1852; and September 1880. Until September 1870 the minutes were taken by one of the Circuit's ministers,[203] usually the junior of the two stationed in Oxford; from September 1870 the meeting elected one of its number as secretary.[204] Since the maximum term of a minister's appointment was three years and many of the junior ministers served for only one or two years, for the first forty years of this collection the minute-taker changed frequently, with corresponding variety in the style, length and legibility of the minutes. In the second period, five longer-serving secretaries kept the record, also with varying style, length and legibility.

Nearly every entry begins with a date, usually recording the day and month of the meeting.[205] The Conference specified that the Superintendent should meet with the Local Preachers once a quarter and the normal rhythm was for the meetings to be held in September, December, March and June, occasionally straying into early October, January, April and July. In 1830–31 Friday was a popular day for the meeting, but from the 1840s onwards Wednesday becomes the favoured day, perhaps because shopkeepers and self-employed artisans felt able to allow themselves a half-day's break in the middle of the week; Wednesday was also market day in Oxford, and most of the country carriers travelled to the city only on Wednesdays and Saturdays.[206] The time of meeting is only mentioned once: on Wednesday 28 September 1870 the preachers met at two o'clock. By this time, it had become customary for the Local Preachers' Meeting and the Circuit Quarterly Meeting to take place on the same day, with the preachers meeting in the early afternoon, the stewards later and the Quarterly Meeting last. This was convenient for all concerned:

202   March and 18 June 1830, referring to a minute of the meeting of 18 December 1829.
203   With the single exception of 4 April 1840, when Benjamin Watkins took the minutes in the absence of the Rev. Thomas Thompson.
204   The secretaries were Hugh Railton (1870–73), William Roberts (1874–80), Tom Skinner (1880–90), James Hastings (1890–93) and Henry Liddell (from 1894).
205   A small number of meetings are undated, or the year is omitted; a few are dated by season, for instance 'Lady Day' or 'Midsummer' or 'Christmas'; in a few cases the date is placed at the end of the minutes.
206   Janet Cooper, 'Markets and fairs', in Alan Crossley (ed.), *Victoria County History of Oxford*, iv (Oxford: OUP, 1979), 305. An official early closing day is not listed in Oxford directories until the early 1900s, when Thursday was the designated day: *Kelly's Directory of Berkshire, Bucks and Oxon, 1907* (London, 1907), 280. See also Alan Crossley, Chris Day and Janet Cooper, *Shopping in Oxford* (Oxford Preservation Trust Occasional Papers No. 4) (Oxford: Oxford Preservation Trust, 1983), 31.

from 1854 onwards, Local Preachers of three years' standing were automatically members of the Quarterly Meeting, and many Local Preachers also served as class leaders or society stewards.[207] This pattern endured until the 1890s, when the Local Preachers' Meeting was moved, first from the beginning to the end of the sequence, with a starting time of six o'clock, and then to a different day altogether. A later time may have suited those whose employment made it difficult for them to attend mid-afternoon meetings, but the Local Preachers resolved in December 1900 that the traditional pattern of meeting on the same day as the Quarterly Meeting should be restored, perhaps to encourage attendance.[208]

Very few of the minutes specify a venue for the meeting. Where a venue is mentioned, it is almost invariably 'Oxford', with a few references to 'Oxford vestry', 'chapel vestry' or (the most explicit) 'chapel vestry, New Inn Hall Lane'.[209] The only other venues mentioned are Woodstock (once, in June 1883) and Bladon (five times, from June 1870 to July 1901, always in the summer).

After date and venue, the minutes record attendance. The Superintendent, as chair of the meeting, is named first, followed by other ministers, and then the Local Preachers. Nomenclature varies: 'Mr' for the ministers and 'Brother' for the Local Preachers in 1830, with 'Rev.' appearing for the first time in January 1833, but not used with any apparent consistency thereafter. Whatever the differences in terminology and title, the separation between the ministers and Local Preachers is punctiliously observed, by both ministerial and lay secretaries, reflecting the practice of listing the names of the Travelling and Local Preachers separately on the preaching plan.

In most of the minutes, the ministers listed are those exercising pastoral responsibility in the Oxford Circuit. There are, however, a few additional names: John Langston, a supernumerary who was sent to Oxford as a result of disciplinary troubles in the Watlington Circuit in 1842–43; Charles Westlake, acting Superintendent in 1849–50; George Savery, who retired to Oxford in 1881; and Elijah Sumner, an Oxford Local Preacher who became a Wesleyan missionary, and spent a year's furlough from the West Indies in the city in 1891. Most intriguing of all is James Wilson (1814–1902). Wilson was a minister of the Methodist New Connexion, who retired to Oxfordshire in 1875, eventually settling in Islip, where

207 Peirce, *Principles and Polity*, 354–6. The reforms of 1894 extended this to all fully accredited Local Preachers: *Minutes of Conference* 1894, 459. The local application in Oxford is indicated by the correlation of dates in these minutes with the Quarterly Meeting records: OHC, OMCA, NM5/A/A3/1, Circuit Quarterly Meeting minute book, 1861–88. For some of the period the two meetings shared the same secretary.
208 Resolution of 10 December 1900. Judging by extant plans and directories, the resolution was not heeded, and Local Preachers' Meetings continued to be held on different days from the Quarterly Meeting.
209 January 1834.

he died in 1902.[210] He appears on the Oxford preaching plan from the late 1880s and was society steward at Islip in the 1890s. Although he never attended the Local Preachers' Meeting, the minutes of 24 March 1902 record a warm tribute to him and send condolences to his family. This active involvement with Oxford Wesleyanism may explain why Wilson's obituary in the Methodist New Connexion *Minutes of Conference* took care to assert that 'to the last he lost none of his enthusiastic preference for his own Denomination.'[211]

Some of the minutes make a distinction between the fully accredited Local Preachers and those exploring a call to preach, as preachers 'on trial' or as exhorters.[212] Most, however, put all the 'local brethren' into a single list.

The attendance list prompts one further observation and two questions. The observation is that all the preachers recorded in these minute books are men. Although several women are mentioned in the text – Mrs Brockless, of Islip, commemorated by the Local Preachers in 1890,[213] Mrs Gardiner, who provided a preaching room in The Crescent through the 1880s,[214] and Mrs Smith, of Woodstock, who brought a complaint against Joseph Foster in 1861[215] – the minutes do not reflect the vital role of women as members, supporters and leaders in the Wesleyan movement in the nineteenth century.[216] The reason for this omission is that, although John Wesley recognised that women as well as men might be called to preach, by the early nineteenth century the Wesleyans were restricting women's preaching to women's meetings and Sunday schools.[217] There were exceptions and there were also examples of women defying or subverting the ban,[218] but there is no evidence in the Oxford minutes of women serving as Local Preachers in this period. The first woman officially recognised as a Local Preacher in Oxford was

---

210   Wilson's only son, John Cook Wilson (1849–1915), was a fellow of Oriel College from 1874 and Wykeham Professor of Logic from 1889.

211   Methodist New Connexion *Minutes of Conference* 1902, 8–10.

212   For example, 19 March 1830, where the four preachers on trial are listed separately, after the fully accredited preachers.

213   September 1890.

214   September 1880 and 30 December 1889. The Gardiners were not Wesleyans, and their Room had previously been hired by the Free Church of England for Sunday services.

215   December 1861.

216   See the pioneering study by Linda Wilson, *Constrained by Zeal. Female Spirituality amongst Nonconformists 1825–1875* (Carlisle: Paternoster, 2000). One of the Wesleyan women in the sample studied here is Matilda Pike (1808–69), of Oxford: 47–8, citing her advice to a young preacher, and 272.

217   E. Dorothy Graham, 'Women Local Preachers', in Milburn and Batty, *Workaday Preachers*, 165–90, esp. 168–73.

218   See John H. Lenton, '"Labouring for the Lord": Women Preachers in Wesleyan Methodism, 1802–1932: A Revisionist View', in Richard Sykes (ed.), *Beyond the Boundaries: Preaching in the Wesleyan Tradition* (Oxford: Applied Theology Press, 1988) and John Lenton, Clive Murray Norris and Linda A. Ryan (eds), *Women, Preachers, Methodists* (Oxford: Oxford Centre for Methodism and Church History, 2020).

Irene Whelpton, daughter of one of the Circuit ministers, who was received as a Local Preacher on trial in March 1914, four years before the Wesleyan Conference resolved that women were eligible to become fully accredited Local Preachers.[219] The second, Jessie Eltham, who arrived in Oxford from Banbury in 1919, already fully accredited, was the niece by marriage of two long-serving Oxford Local Preachers, Samuel Watson and James Hastings.[220]

The first question prompted by the list concerns the proportion of the Circuit's preachers who attended the quarterly meetings. The minutes do not include apologies for absence, and it was only in 1961 that the Conference added attendance at the meeting to the formal duties of a Local Preacher.[221] Comparing the full list of Local Preachers on the plan with the names recorded in the minute books suggests that most preachers attended some meetings, but very few attended all. Attendance was highest in the 1830s, with just two or three absentees among twenty or twenty-five preachers in 1834–35 and 1838–39. By the 1860s, when the Circuit claimed around thirty preachers, attendance at many meetings had fallen to half the total body and this continued through to the end of the century, as the total climbed to sixty in 1888 and fifty-one in 1900. In February 1902 an attendance of twenty-nine was achieved, but this was a special meeting, with tea provided by James Nix and an address on 'Bible Study for Local Preachers' by E.E. Genner.

There is no easily discernible pattern of attendance. With most meetings taking place in Oxford, it is not surprising that William Bloomfield (1808–?), of Tackley, and John Barratt (1802–82), of Wootton, both farm labourers, seldom attended the meetings, although Jonathan Skidmore (1829–1901), who lived in Tackley and worked on the railway, was often present. Joseph Adams (1818–1903), of Bladon, a prosperous baker and farmer, did attend regularly until well into his sixties; his older contemporary John Danbury (1811–99), a Bladon stonemason, did not attend for the last thirty years of his long life. Some of the Oxford-based artisans like the tailor David Price Clifford (1838–1902) and the joiner Tom Dawson (1863–1946) attended most meetings; conversely, Walter Slaughter (1853–1909), who ran a successful grocer's business in St Clement's, attended a mere ten meetings in eighteen years.

The second question prompted by the list is more difficult to answer: who were the Local Preachers? What sort of people became Wesleyan Local Preachers in Victorian Oxford? Were there significant changes over time, and are they reflected in these minutes?

---

219   OHC, OMCA, NM5/A/A4/3, Local Preachers' Quarterly Minute Book 1903–30, minutes for 19 March 1914; John S. Simon, *A Summary of Methodist Law and Discipline* (London: Methodist Publishing House, fifth edition, 1923), 169.

220   For Jessie Eltham, see OHC, OMCA, NM5/A/A4/3, Local Preachers' Quarterly Minute Book 1903–30, minutes for 18 December 1919.

221   'Regulations Regarding Local Preachers', in Standing Orders: Amendments', *Minutes of Conference* 1961, 71. Compare the supporting report in *Agenda of Conference* 1961, 473. I am very grateful to Susan Howdle for this reference.

Taking change over time first, in absolute terms, the number of Local Preachers on the Oxford plan increased substantially in the years covered by these minutes, from twenty-four in 1834–35 to sixty-two in 1902. There were fewer local Wesleyan societies in 1902 (twenty-five places on the plan in 1834; nineteen in 1902), but the membership had increased from 620 to 771.[222] Evidently the proportion of Local Preachers to members and Local Preachers to societies had grown considerably. This comparison across seventy-five years, however, conceals both the decline in membership in the years after the Reform crisis and then the increase in the 1870s and 1880s, when, as noted above, membership soared from 500 to nearly 900. Between thirty and forty new Local Preachers were accredited during those decades of exceptional growth, and it may be suggested that this created an expectation of new vocations which continued to fuel recruitment into the twentieth century.

Turning to the names behind the statistics, in the course of editing and annotating the minutes many of the individuals whose names appear in the records have been identified, partly from internal evidence in the text, partly from other Oxford Methodist sources, partly from local newspapers and trade directories, partly from the transcribed or digitised Methodist and parochial registers published by the Oxfordshire Family History Society, and partly from the decennial census returns available online. Triangulating these sources has made it possible to establish dates and places of birth and death for many of the preachers, and to identify their trade or profession. Some 430 names appear in the minutes and around 310 have been definitely or plausibly identified; of those still to be traced, many appear only fleetingly, as potential preachers who did not pursue the calling or as fully accredited preachers arriving in Oxford from elsewhere but then swiftly moving on. Further investigation will be needed to increase the number of individuals whose outline biographies can be established with greater certainty, but a sampling of data from the 1830s, 1860s and 1890s allows some comparisons to be made and some tentative conclusions to be drawn.

Looking first at birthplaces, in the 1830s, three-quarters of the preachers (twenty-seven out of thirty-seven) were born in Oxford, the Circuit's wider hinterland or the county of Oxfordshire. Arrivals from further afield were mostly from neighbouring counties, like George King from Quainton (Bucks) and Joseph Nutt from Long Compton (Warwickshire); Thomas Jones, who moved from Yorkshire in 1837 to take up the tenancy of a farm in Islip, was unusual in this period. It should be noted that although only three of the preachers were born in Oxford itself, many more had moved into the city from the neighbouring villages and market towns by the time their names were listed on the preaching plan.[223]

---

222 Figures taken from extant plans; membership from OHC, OMCA, NM5/A/A2/1, Circuit Schedule Book 1825–36, (Members in Society in the Oxford Circuit, September 1835); Minutes of Conference 1902, 542

223 The earliest extant preaching plans list preachers simply by surname, without indicating a place of residence; by the 1850s a place is added; later in the century fuller names and postal

A similar pattern may be observed thirty years later. Of forty-eight preachers identified in the minutes of the 1860s, seven were born in Oxford, twenty-three within the Circuit, a further eight in the county, and just eight further afield, with Berkshire, Bedfordshire and Wiltshire accounting for four of them. The preacher furthest from his birthplace was Hugh Railton, born in Barnard Castle. Again, the city had drawn people from the rural hinterland – William Embury from Bloxham, George Keene from Witney, William Merry from Hanborough, Thomas Howard from Thame.

By the 1890s a considerable change had taken place. Eighteen of the ninety-seven preachers were born in the city itself, twenty-one in the wider Circuit and fourteen in the county. Almost half of the cohort, however – forty-one of the ninety-seven – were born elsewhere, from Swimbridge (Devon) to Sevenoaks (Kent) and Bere Regis (Dorset) to Gateshead, by way of Oundle, Ontario and Ootacamund (South India). As well as reflecting a much larger sample, the greater diversity of backgrounds in the late nineteenth century also bore witness to the rapid growth of Oxford's population in this period and to the impact of the admission of Wesleyans to the University.[224] It should be noted that travel was not one way: if Alfred Harris, born in South India, could come to Oxford to study, Frank Embury, born in Oxford, could leave his native city to work on construction projects in the Orange Free State and then serve as Superintendent of the Industrial School at Karur, Trichinopoly.[225] A web of imperial contacts, commercial, educational, administrative and ecclesiastical, touched the lives of the Oxford preachers, especially towards the end of the century.

Moving from origins to occupations, each sample reveals a wide range of jobs and professions. In the 1830s thirty-seven preachers are engaged in twenty different occupations, mostly reflecting the crafts and trades of the city's shopkeepers and skilled artisans. The most numerous of these are bootmakers (five), stonemasons (five) and tailors (three); in addition, there are three farmers, a shepherd, a farm labourer, and five schoolmasters. In the 1860s among twenty-two occupations, masons and bootmakers are still numerous (four each), exceeded only by bakers (five) and farm labourers (eight). The range has expanded to reflect the evolving economic life of the city, with two printers, two railway workers, two confectioners and a hairdresser. Another increase has taken place by the 1890s, with ninety-seven preachers engaged in forty-three different occupations. Traditional crafts are still represented – carpenter and joiner (four), mason, builder, bricklayer, plumber – with

---

addresses are given, particularly for preachers in the city.

224 The preachers born in Oundle, Ontario and Ootacamund, A.E. Taylor, Perry Dobson and Alfred Herschell Harris respectively, were all undergraduates.

225 Embury's departure and return are noted in the minutes for June 1892 and September 1894; for a brief biography, see the entry for the Embury family on the website of St Sepulchre's cemetery, Oxford: http://www.stsepulchres.org.uk/burials/embury_william.html, accessed 23 March 2022.

the addition of gas fitter – as are the retail trades – tailor (five), draper, grocer (six), bootmaker, baker, ironmonger and stationer. The presence of several draper's assistants testifies to the growth of larger shops, with lodgings for unmarried workers on site.[226] White-collar occupations include four clerks, two Inland Revenue officers, two schoolmasters, an auctioneer, a solicitor and a classical copyist,[227] as well as three salaried lay employees of the circuit and a full-time temperance advocate.[228] John Henry Salter, the boat builder, and Frederick Edens, coal merchant, represent Oxford's entrepreneurs. The records also show an astronomer,[229] a monumental mason, a photographer and a dentist. Last, but not least, thirteen students are listed in the minutes, forming the largest single occupational category in this period.

A simple list of occupations does not indicate levels of prosperity and the same descriptor may conceal as much as it reveals. Horace Ashdown and Walter Slaughter were both grocers in the 1880s, but Ashdown went bankrupt in 1889–90, while Slaughter built and sustained a successful business which enabled him to donate significant sums to the extension of Wesleyan work in East Oxford.[230] John Freeman and John Henry Roff were both clerks in the 1890s, but Freeman's employment as a clerk was short-term, and he soon entered the Wesleyan ministry, while Roff ended his career selling insurance for the Prudential. In an earlier generation James Nix and Thomas Howard were also clerks: Nix rose to be Chief Clerk at the Oxford Post Office and Howard was chief clerk and then a partner in the building firm of Symm and Co.; both men left very substantial estates.[231] The Local Preachers' Meeting brought together men of substantial means, like Henry Leake, who could afford to build a new chapel at Rose Hill, donate it to the Wesleyan Connexion, and then, after a disastrous collapse in membership during the Reform controversy, buy it back from the Wesleyans and give it to the Free Methodists,[232] and William Wheeler, of Hampton Poyle, described in the census as 'Wesleyan Local Preacher and Agricultural Labourer'.[233] At the end of the century, the Salter brothers, councillors and later aldermen and Mayors of Oxford, served alongside Jonathan Skidmore, of Tackley, who worked on the Great Western Railway until retirement

---

226 On preaching plans of the late 1880s and early 1890s several preachers give their address as 13 Queen Street, the premises of Charles Badcock and Co., drapers.

227 J.M. King.

228 J.R. Weatherill, District Superintendent for the United Kingdom Alliance.

229 Walter Wickham, FRAS.

230 Boylan, *Cowley Road Methodist Church Centre*, 1–6; 'Editorial Notes', *OWMCM* January 1908, 2, records Slaughter's donation of £400 towards reducing the debt on the Wesley Hall premises.

231 According to the probate records, Nix left £7924 in 1909 and Howard £10,800 a year earlier. J.H. Roff's estate in 1932 amounted to £574.

232 G.G. Banbury, 'Oxford Circuit', *UMFC Magazine*, May 1863, 328, and W.J.S. Bayliss, 'How Rose Hill Chapel Began', *OMM*, April 1935, 36–7. Leake is one of the few Local Preachers styled 'Esq' in the Wesleyan records.

233 Thus the 1871 Census. Wheeler began preaching in 1836, three years after Henry Leake.

and died at Sunset Cottage, the home on St Clement's provided by Walter Slaughter for 'poor aged Christians'.[234]

A sample of the minutes also sheds light on the age profile of the Local Preachers and on the age when Wesleyans were likely to experience a call to preach. In each of the sample decades there are a number of very senior preachers – Joseph Ostler (born 1771) and Thomas Meek (born 1775) in the 1830s; Meek and George Brown (born 1781) in the 1860s; and John Danbury and Edward Reed (born 1811), James Hitchman (born 1812), Charles Harper (born 1813) and Joseph Adams (born 1818) in the 1890s. In each decade, however, most of the preachers are aged between 20 and 40, and in each decade the majority of those who begin preaching do so before the age of 26. There are some exceptions: the tailor Joseph Bailey began at 47 in 1832, and Isaac Leworthy was 56 when he was added to the Oxford preaching plan in 1894, but these are rare cases, and it is possible that Leworthy was already a preacher when he came to Oxford in the early 1890s.[235] Some preachers begin in their teens, most in their early twenties, while habits of life and faith are forming and, at least in the earlier part of the century, while the physical demands of walking long distances to preaching appointments could perhaps more easily be met.

Judging by the names recorded in the minutes, therefore, the Oxford Local Preachers present a cross-section of the city and county's middling sort: some professional and businessmen, many tradesmen, many skilled artisans, and some labourers. Many were born locally or had migrated into the city from Oxford's rural hinterland, but by the end of the century origins had become much more diverse. Most of the preachers were young or in early middle-age, but the cohort included a number of very senior men as well. The significant change from the 1880s is the arrival of a group of undergraduates, many from Wesleyan schools and from ministerial or more affluent families. For some, preaching was the beginning of a lifetime of Christian service, in ordained or lay ministry.[236] For others, it may have been a phase in development from inherited or adolescent faith to a different outlook.[237]

Tracing identity also makes it possible to explore family connections and continuities. In the close-knit world of Wesleyan Methodism and Nonconformity, it is

---

234 For the Salters, see Simon Wenham, *Pleasure Boating on the Thames. A History of Salter Bros 1858–Present Day* (Stroud: The History Press, 2014), esp. 188–93 and 197–9; for Jonathan Skidmore, J.N. [James Nix], 'The Late Mr Jonathan Skidmore', *ODFCM*, September 1901, 45–6.

235 Leworthy was in his native Swimbridge, Devon, in 1891 and 1901; his daughter Margaret Ann taught at the East Oxford British School until 1899: 'Oxford School Board', *JOJ*, 11 March 1899, 4.

236 From the 1890s, F.W. Lewis and W.F. Lofthouse entered the Wesleyan ministry, while F.S. Goudge and H.A. Lester took Anglican orders. E.E. Genner and F.E. Corley were not ordained, but were dedicated lay Methodists.

237 For instance, T.C. Piggott, who came on trial in 1885 and who later experienced a crisis of faith: T.C. Piggott and Thomas Durley, *Life and Letters of Henry James Piggott of Rome* (London: Epworth Press, 1921), 286.

not surprising that chapel families intermarried. Thus, for example, Joseph Ostler (1771–1849) was the father-in-law of T.G. Smith (1808–92), and Benjamin Watkins (1816–44) married Sarah Bailey, whose father and brother were Local Preachers.[238] James and Josiah Nix had two brothers-in-law who were also Local Preachers,[239] and at least three nephews who explored the calling.[240] The most prolific dynasty of preachers, however, was the Danbury family at Bladon. Over four generations, the family of John and Selena Danbury provided seven Local Preachers[241] and there were another six in a wider cousinhood of Sumners and Grimmetts.[242]

After recording the date and place of assembling and noting the attendance, the minutes turn to the business of the meeting. Both agenda and minutes were shaped by the question-and-answer format adopted by John Wesley at the first Methodist Conference in 1744, a model retained by the Conference and by other Wesleyan meetings well into the twentieth century.

The first question remained essentially the same throughout the seventy-two years of the minutes: 'Are there any objections to any of the Brethren touching their moral character – soundness in the faith – attention to discipline – and ability for their work?' Writing in October 1833 Alfred Barrett made it explicit that: 'They were examined one by one', indicating that the names of the Local Preachers were read out, and opportunity given for any objections to be voiced. Whether this practice was sustained as the number of preachers increased from twenty-one in the early 1830s to more than fifty in 1902 cannot be determined from the minutes, but the question: 'Any objections?' remained at the top of the agenda for the entire period.

Barrett recorded 'None' in answer to the question about objections. Many of the minutes, however, do report problems. The most frequent objection is that a preacher has 'disappointed' or 'neglected' a congregation by failing to fulfil an appointment. The Wesleyan system depended on its volunteer Local Preachers arriving to lead worship, as directed by the preaching plan, and preachers who were unable to keep an appointment were expected to arrange an accredited substitute, a requirement printed on the plan throughout the period.[243] Many of the minutes,

---

238 Benjamin Watkins entered the Wesleyan ministry in 1840, married Sarah Bailey in November 1842, and they sailed for the Gold Coast. Within eighteen months both had died: *Minutes of Conference* 1844, 18.

239 Joseph Colegrove and Frederick Edens.

240 William Colegrove, Joseph Colegrove (junior) and Henry Elijah Sumner. James Nix's son, Philp Wamsley Nix, was also a Local Preacher.

241 John Danbury (1811–99), John Wesley Danbury (1849–77), Harry Danbury (1859–85), Harry William Danbury (1879–1958), Charles Gladstone Danbury (1885–1953), Henry Albert Smith (1878–1971) and Edward James Smith (1873–1948).

242 Joseph Danbury (1845–1929), John Grimmett (1835–1917), Gabriel Woodward (1856–1937), Joseph Nappin (1863–1935), Elijah Henry Sumner (1842–1916) and Henry Elijah Sumner (1877–1963).

243 The extant plan for 1834–35 includes this reminder: 'It is particularly requested that each Preacher will conscientiously attend to his own appointment, or in case of indisposition &c

however, note at least one instance of 'disappointment', and some record multiple omissions. Sometimes the preacher concerned was present to explain, apologise or rebut the accusation; sometimes the secretary was directed to write for an explanation or to require the offender to attend the next meeting to give an account of what had happened.

The minutes seldom give a cause for missed appointments. In September 1875 the usually reliable James Nix admitted overlooking an appointment at Horspath, because he was away from Oxford at the time. Far more culpable were George Scarsbrook and Daniel Young, who missed their appointments at Oxford and Wheatley in spring 1838 because they wished to attend the anniversary sermons in the city centre chapel. The impact on a congregation is captured in the minutes of 24 September 1890, which record that 'Bro Vallis on Aug 17 failed to send a supply to Cranham St but a note arrived on Sunday morning that he would be unable to attend.' The secretary added: 'The Superintendent promised to point out to him the inconvenience of such a course.' The stewards and congregation at the Cranham Street Mission, faced with an empty pulpit and a note of apology, might have used a more forthright term.

Even when preachers arranged substitutes or 'supplies' to cover appointments, problems could still arise. Sometimes the substitute proved unreliable and failed to arrive. Moreover, as noted in 1834, the Wesleyans insisted that the substitute should be an accredited Local Preacher, and complaints recur through the minutes of unaccredited or unauthorised people being drafted in to fill gaps in the plan. The earliest example appears in March 1831, at Abingdon, and the last in March 1894, at Cranham Street. On the latter occasion, Enoch Salt, the Superintendent, 'exhorted the brethren to strict attention to prescribed duties and strongly urged them in cases of necessity to supply only comprehensively accredited substitutes'.

Many reasons may be inferred for occasionally missing appointments: ill-health, inclement weather, forgetfulness. There are examples, however, of preachers who defaulted frequently and of places which were often 'neglected'. The former may have been indicative of temporary disgruntlement, as when William Leggatt missed a series of appointments at Combe in 1838–40, or of a waning commitment to preaching or to Wesleyanism, as with William Cheney, who between 1831 and 1837 resigned twice, was restored twice, and was then dropped from the plan, having missed numerous appointments across the Circuit. When particular places suffered frequent 'neglect', like Beckley and Cuddesdon in the 1880s and 1890s, it may be suspected that preachers felt disinclined to travel to very small congregations in distant locations: both causes began in the 1880s, as part of the legacy of Hugh Price Hughes' 'spirit of daring adventure', but Beckley required regular efforts by the preachers to 'revive the work', while an article in the *Methodist Recorder* in 1913 admitted that often the Cuddesdon congregation consisted of just 'faithful Mrs Shirley'.[244]

get it supplied by one whose name is on the plan, or who has a note from the Superintendent.'
244 *OMM*, September 1936, and 'Faithful Mrs Shirley', *MR*, 9 January 1913, 15–16.

A second recurring source of objection in the minutes is neglect of the class meeting. All Wesleyan Methodists were required to belong to a class and to attend its weekly meeting. At intervals through the nineteenth century the place of the class in the Wesleyan system was debated, but although challenged and eventually modified, the structure was retained.[245] In March 1889, as investigation by a Conference committee was reaching its conclusion, 'The rule of the Connexion requiring every Local Preacher to meet in Class was brought prominently before the meeting & it was unanimously agreed that a circular letter (drawn up by the Superintendent & the Secretary) be sent to every Local Preacher giving the Rule in full and desiring that he inform the next meeting in whose class he met.' This inquiry revealed that two of the preachers, James Hastings and Joseph Shirley, were not currently members of a class; neither was keen to join one, although by December Shirley was expressing his 'strong sympathy' with class meetings and 'said he intended joining a class during the qr', whereupon the topic seems to have been dropped.

Some Wesleyans evidently found the discipline of the class irksome or failed to establish a rapport with a particular class leader or group. From the very beginning of the minutes, non-attendance at the class appears, with brothers Pearson and Cheney reprimanded in September 1830 for neglecting to meet. In the next decade James Lindars' persistent failure to attend a class eventually led to his removal from the plan, and a similar fate befell Edwin Kent in 1872, but only after nearly twenty years of procrastination and numerous second chances.

Several other lapses in 'moral character' are scattered through the minutes. Allegations of drunkenness were brought against brother Osborn of Charlton in 1857 and Joseph Belcher in 1885. William Symons was reprimanded for playing unsuitable games in 1865 and Daniel Young for 'trifling' in 1840. Young also offended Wesleyan Sabbatarianism, by taking picture-frames to one of his appointments. Similar scruples about working on the Sabbath led to charges against the Woodstock glover Thomas Meek in 1831, resulting in his absence from the plan for more than twenty years.[246] Young's 'trifling' extended to taking a young woman to his Sunday appointments; similar behaviour may be inferred in the case of John Danbury, expelled for 'gross immorality' in September 1836, a month after his marriage and two months before the birth of his eldest son. Meek and Danbury were eventually reinstated, and their obituaries made no reference to youthful indiscretions.[247]

245 Henry Rack, 'Wesleyan Methodism 1849–1902', in *HMCGB*, 3, 158–62.
246 For an example of a strict interpretation of the Sabbath, see the critical comments in the review of Horatio Smith's *Festivals, Games and Amusements*, *WMM*, August 1831, 556–8. The Wesleyan Conference supported Sir Andrew Agnew's bill for the better observance of the Lord's Day in 1833 and 1836, and a series of five 'Letters on the Sabbath' were published in the *WMM* in 1833: *WMM*, February to June 1833 and September 1833, 638–9. For Agnew's campaign, see Ian Bradley, *The Call to Seriousness* (London: Jonathan Cape, 1976), 104–5.
247 For Meek, see *JOJ*, 13 April 1872, 8, recording that he had been a Local Preacher for 'more than half a century'; for Danbury, see *JOJ*, 12 August 1899, 10, recording sixty-six years' service as a Local Preacher.

If Young, Danbury and Meek faced strict discipline, other preachers were treated with considerable leniency. John Harris of Tackley admitted in 1866 that he had struck his wife, 'under circumstances of great provocation', and was suspended for one quarter. Thirty years later the Oxford schoolmaster Arthur Leyland killed a woman in a hit-and-run cycling accident and again was suspended for a single quarter.[248] Falling into debt loomed large in the Wesleyan catalogue of moral delinquency, but neither Horace Ashdown, whose grocer's shop failed in 1889, nor Frederick Edens, who ran into problems in the coal business in 1897, was treated harshly: indeed, the preachers clubbed together to raise a subscription to help Ashdown over his difficulties.[249] John Wesley Hussey, already expelled by March 1830 but whose fate lingers as a warning in the first entry in the minute book, was probably also a victim of financial misfortune, but he attempted to clear his debts by embezzling money from his employer, was caught, and narrowly escaped transportation.[250] Another preacher who served a prison sentence was Walter Gilder, convicted of indecent exposure in the University Parks in August 1884. The minutes refer in very guarded terms to Gilder's 'case', but the local press reported 'considerable interest' because of his position as a Local Preacher. Two fellow preachers, James Nix and Robert Buckell, were prepared to pledge £50 each to enable Gilder to appeal against conviction by the city magistrates, but to no avail. Gilder was quietly dropped from the plan and left Oxford shortly afterwards.[251]

On two occasions Local Preachers' responses to wider events raised questions of discipline. One was the controversy over Wesleyan Reform, discussed above, which began locally with the expulsion of Josiah Crapper in the summer of 1849 and continued at least until 1851,[252] with further expulsions, resignations and one case of a preacher gate-crashing a meeting from which he had been excluded.[253] Twenty years later a political controversy came before the Local Preachers' Meeting, when in September 1872 Albert Henman tried to persuade the meeting to censure Christopher Holloway for his involvement in the National Agricultural Labourers' Union. The preachers refused to entertain the charge, and it was Henman who resigned.[254]

248 'An Oxford Schoolmaster charged with manslaughter', JOJ, 14 December 1895, 8.
249 JOJ, 11 January 1890, 5; OHC, OMCR, NM5/A/A4/3, Local Preachers' Quarterly minute book, 1903–30, minute for 26 September 1907, on the whereabouts of the fund raised to help Ashdown.
250 John Wesley Hussey was committed for trial for embezzlement in February 1830: JOJ, 6 February 1830, 3. He was employed by John Pike, Oxford's leading lay Wesleyan.
251 'Indecent Conduct in the University Parks', OC, 16 August 1884, 5, 'Latest News', Oxford Times, 16 August 1884, 8, and 'The Alleged Indecent Conduct in the University Parks', JOJ, 23 August 1884, 8.
252 There are some indications of continuing reverberations until 1853, with Joseph Adams withdrawing briefly from the plan 'from a scruple of conscience'.
253 Benjamin Scott, in March 1851.
254 For Holloway's activities in the NALU, see Pamela L.R. Horn, 'Christopher Holloway: an Oxfordshire Trade Union Leader', Oxoniensia 33 (1968), 125–36 and Mark Curthoys,

There are comparatively few references in the minutes to questions of competence or doctrinal orthodoxy. Threaded through the meetings of the 1840s are frequent expostulations about Billy Birmingham, whose style of preaching ('labored eccentricities') and fondness for freelance revivalism exasperated his colleagues. Daniel Young's competence was questioned in autumn 1838 and experienced preachers were deputed to report on his sermons. Jonathan Skidmore was advised to pay more attention to pulpit preparation and Thomas Irons was told to make his sermons shorter. Apart from John Marcham, whose grasp of 'Wesleyan orthodoxy' was questioned in September 1844 and Percy Armstrong, who was accused of 'preaching unmethodistic doctrine' in 1887, the only theological controversy in the minutes arose in 1846 when William Ray began to advocate Swedenborgianism. Ray soon departed, was leading a Swedenborgian congregation in St Clement's by 1851, and eventually became a minister of the New Jerusalem Church.[255]

After resolving matters of character and discipline, the minutes consider recruitment, training and accreditation. The structure of the minutes mirrors the questions asked at the Conference about Wesleyan Travelling Preachers, beginning with those at the end of their training, and sometimes even using the language of reception into full connexion for Local Preachers about to go 'on full plan'.[256] It may be more helpful to begin the journey from recruitment to accreditation at the start rather than the end and to consider how the process of becoming a Local Preacher was initiated.

Across the period covered by the Oxford minutes there was some fluidity in categories of Wesleyan lay leadership in worship. The 1823 Oxford plan lists four groups: preachers, preachers on trial, exhorters and prayer leaders.[257] Prayer leaders are mentioned only once in the Oxford minutes, in December 1845. Their role, according to Joseph Nightingale, was to bring people to the Methodist meetings;[258] in some places there was a separate prayer leaders' plan, and it may be seen that leading in prayer and evangelism might well prepare someone to consider a call to preach.[259] Later in the century a similar role was fulfilled by Mission Bands, first formed in Oxford in 1882 and revived in the 1890s, with the brief 'to secure by

---

'Oxfordshire's Tolpuddle? The Case of the Ascott Martyrs', *Oxoniensia* 86 (2021), 159–78, at 167–8. His position as a Local Preacher was noted by a critical correspondent in *JOJ*, 14 September 1872, 5.

255 Kate Tiller, *Church and Chapel in Oxfordshire 1851*, (Oxford: Oxfordshire Record Society, 1987), 76.

256 To be received into full connexion (with the Conference) has been standard Methodist terminology for Travelling Preachers (ministers/presbyters) since the Wesleys, but now sounds unusual when applied to Local Preachers. It is used in the minutes in the 1830s, but not thereafter.

257 Madison, N.J, Drew University, Ref. D2003-038, Marriott Collection, Oxford Plan, 1823.

258 Nightingale, *Portraiture of Methodism*, 270–1.

259 See, for example, Albert Jewell, 'The "Grand Life" of a nineteenth-century Cornish Methodist', *PWHS* 63.4 (2022), 164–5.

invitation as large a congregation as possible, and to assist the appointed preacher in any way that he may request.'[260] As organised in the 1890s, Mission Bands included some accredited Local Preachers among their members, but also functioned as a testing-ground for potential preachers.

Prayer leaders and Mission Bands worked in groups; the exhorter had sole responsibility for a service, and in the 1830s to be an exhorter was to be on the first rung of the ladder to accreditation as a Local Preacher. The question in the minutes: 'Are any proposed as exhorters?' marks the beginning of the process of testing and formation, leading on to 'Are any received on Trial?' and then to accreditation: 'Are any to be received into full connexion as Local Preachers?' Later in the century the category of exhorter seems to have evolved from a transitional role to a permanent one, and the question 'Any one to be an exhorter?' is separated from the question 'Any one to receive a note?', with the latter being the first stage on the road to accreditation. Perhaps it was recognised that there was a continuing role for those who might never succeed in passing the tests for accreditation and some remained exhorters for a long time. Conversely the difference in status could be keenly felt: when it was suggested in December 1893 that Moses Smith should be moved to the exhorters' list after repeated postponement of his final examination, he chose instead to resign from the plan.

The question 'Who receive a note?' invites a terse response, and the minutes generally record 'none' or simply list names, without saying much about the candidate or the originator of the suggestion. Sometimes a proposer is mentioned, so that in March 1901 David Price Clifford proposed that Brother Mortimer of Forest Hill be given a note, and the meeting concurred. Why Clifford made the suggestion and whether Mortimer knew that he intended to do so cannot be determined. Even this level of detail is unusual: more often the record states simply that a name has been discussed and the Superintendent asked to have a conversation with the person suggested. When no more is heard of the name, it may be concluded either that the Superintendent thought them unsuitable or that they declined the invitation.

Trainee Local Preachers began by working with more experienced preachers; thus, when John Danbury was received as an exhorter in September 1835, he was assigned to accompany Joseph Ostler, William Leggatt and William Bartlett to some of their appointments. Before accreditation preachers had to demonstrate their competence by conducting a service in the presence of the Superintendent and confirm their sincerity and understanding of Wesleyan doctrine by passing an oral examination at the Local Preachers' Meeting. The examination, testing conversion, current Christian experience and theological knowledge, drew on John Wesley's *Sermons* and his *Notes on the New Testament*. The minutes explain the process, recording, for example, in September 1844:

---

260 OHC, OMCA, NM5/A/A1/1, Circuit plans and directories, plan for January to April 1897.

The Brethren Barrett & Danbury have completed the prescribed period of probation but not having been heard by the Superintendent the necessary preliminary to their reception according to rule – it is agreed that Bro. Barrett shall preach before Mr Fisher on Sunday afternoon Novr 3rd at Wootton and Bro. Danbury on Sunday afternoon Nov. 17th in the Morning Chapel – and it is further agreed that the appointments of the Brethren in the early part of next Plan shall be so arranged as to give them an opportunity as frequently as possible, of hearing Messrs Barrett & Danbury, so that the Meeting may be in possession of full information respecting their fitness for our work.

Evidently the examination was a significant challenge to many preachers, because it was often postponed: in December 1840, for instance, Brothers Wheeler, Smith and Lindars were eligible for examination, but had not read the *Notes* and *Sermons*, so remained on trial for a further quarter; in March 1841 Smith and Wheeler passed the examination, but Lindars did not appear at the meeting.

As well as training new preachers from within the existing Oxford membership, Local Preachers were also recruited by transfer from other Wesleyan circuits and from other denominations. The minutes note the arrival of fully accredited preachers and preachers on trial from elsewhere in the Connexion. In the 1830s and 1840s most are from neighbouring circuits: Brackley, Banbury, Wantage, Watlington, Witney and Swindon, although Henry Barford came from London, James Goold from Midsomer Norton and Thomas Jones from York. Thereafter, although preachers continue to arrive from Oxfordshire, Buckinghamshire and Berkshire, there are also arrivals from Camborne and Maidstone,[261] Guernsey and Bedale,[262] and even from Ceylon and New Zealand,[263] reflecting both the expansion of Oxford's population from the 1850s and the new opportunities for Wesleyans created by the gradual repeal of the university tests in 1854 and 1871.

New arrivals were supposed to bring credentials – either a letter of commendation from the Superintendent of their previous circuit, or a preaching plan showing their status. When Brother Osborn arrived in June 1853, he came without the appropriate documents, so Robert Day, the Oxford Superintendent, was asked to make inquiries. William Gibson, who arrived from Thame in 1876, was approved for inclusion on the plan, 'as soon as his credentials are received'. Albert Henman, on the other hand, 'having brought his credentials' from Bedford was 'cordially received' in March 1863. In March 1872 it was resolved that 'In future, Local Preachers coming to reside in the Oxford Circuit have no appointments until they have been heard and pass a satisfactory Examination.' Connexionally this was a contentious issue. It was raised during the discussions of revised regulations for Local Preachers in 1894 and the Conference ruled against it.[264]

---

261 Hugh Allen and Henry Lester.
262 William Hankin and John Fryer.
263 John Blazé and William Torr.
264 See, for example, 'The status and training of Local Preachers', *MR*, 22 February 1894, 126 and 'The Local Preachers. Proceedings of the Special Committee', *MR*, 1 February 1894, 68.

Transfers from other Wesleyan circuits were common in this period, but the minutes also record occasional arrivals from other denominations – usually other branches of the Methodist movement. Most were Primitive Methodists, sometimes designated 'Ranters' in the minutes. Brother Cox arrived in 1845 but was dropped two years later 'on account of reiterated neglect of his appointments'. Charles Elford transferred to the Wesleyans in 1848 and John Allen and Charles Harper followed suit in 1854. Harper remained a Wesleyan Local Preacher until 1897. William Dingle, a very senior preacher with the Primitive Methodists, transferred in 1870, and David Price Clifford joined the Wesleyans in 1885.

The three Bible Christians who are noted as arrivals in the minutes, H.W. Horwill, W.G. Torr and O.K. Hobbs, were all students. The Wesleyans did, however, gain a few preachers from the local Free Methodists, most notably Robert Buckell, who switched denominations in 1882. Buckell became Mayor of Oxford in 1885, but resigned from the plan three years later, much to the Wesleyans' chagrin.

Gains, then, were balanced by losses. The minutes ask: 'Any one left the Circuit? Any one resigned? Any one died?' Preachers were lost to the Free Methodists, especially during the Reform controversy. There was also a steady outflow of preachers from Oxford to other circuits, including migration to North America and Africa. Some Oxford Local Preachers entered the Wesleyan ministry; some were ordained in other denominations, particularly Congregationalism.[265] Some resigned through ill-health or other commitments: Henry Brown found that he could no longer walk long distances to his appointments; John Towle's business took him away from home frequently; Thomas Smith was fully occupied as Sunday School Superintendent. In some cases, the Meeting was reluctant to accept a resignation, so that John King attempted to resign several times through the 1890s, due to ill-health, but was persuaded to stay on the plan. This might indicate an evolving understanding of what it meant to be a Local Preacher, from a more functional view in the 1830s to a lifelong calling by the 1890s, reflected in the retention of ageing or infirm preachers on the list. Other preachers resigned when their services were criticised[266] or when their persistent neglect of appointments attracted adverse comment – the Vallis brothers were particularly prone to resignation through the 1890s and beyond.[267]

Deaths are recorded, sometimes with obituary tributes. Joseph Bailey, senior, who died in February 1854, received a typical Wesleyan obituary, comparable to the innumerable reports of 'recent deaths' in the *Wesleyan Methodist Magazine*:

> Bro Bailey had been removed from his labours by the hand of death during the last Quarter. He was called away very suddenly, but was prepared for his solemn

---

265 Including Henry Sumner and William Freeman. Henry Leake and Josiah Crapper also leant towards Congregationalism.
266 Thus Brother Harris in March 1872.
267 Thomas Vallis resigned at least three times and Albert George Vallis once.

change. He for many years maintained the purity, consistency, and uprightness of the christian without reproach. Under various trying dispensations of providence, he was sustained by the grace of God. As a local preacher, he was very acceptable and useful – his sermons shewed him to be a man of reading – reflection and much prayer. He walked with God, and was not, for God took him.

Very different is the much longer obituary of Jonathan Skidmore, written for the *Oxford and District Free Church Magazine* in 1901 and pasted into the minute book. Although equally edifying in tone, it offers far more information about its subject's life, background and activities.[268]

As well as preachers, the minutes also concern themselves with places, asking 'Are any alterations to be made in regard to the places on the plan?' This question could be developed in several directions.

First, the Local Preachers' Meeting took the lead in setting times of worship. There were some well-established patterns, particularly the seasonal alteration of midweek evening service times in the villages. This was so familiar that the minutes sometimes record versions of 'the usual winter alterations' or 'Winter hours in country places', with an earlier start reflecting the shorter working day in the winter. Other changes were much more eclectic, with experimentation between morning, afternoon and evening services on Sundays, and minor variations of time. In some cases, the aim was to allow a preacher to take an afternoon appointment in one place and an evening appointment in another, or for preachers going to adjacent villages to travel together: hence the arrangements agreed in March 1836 for the pattern of afternoon and evening services at Drayton, Harwell and Steventon. In other cases, the reason seems to have been to see which times would be most effective in gathering a congregation and sometimes this involved frequent changes: between 1882 and 1893, for example, the service at Eynsham was switched between morning and afternoon seven times. The larger and more stable places rarely changed, and if they did, it was at their own request, so that, for example, Sunday afternoon services were discontinued at New Inn Hall Street in 1860. The minutes do show evidence of consultation: the proposal to settle on morning and evening services at Bladon in 1863 was to be implemented 'if agreeable to the friends', while some of the changes at Eynsham were delayed, pending discussion between the Rev. Henry Jefford and the local members.

The second alteration with regard to places was the approval of new venues for Wesleyan preaching, in response to the question: 'Are there any new Places to be taken on the Plan?' This question receives an affirmative answer seventy-three times in the minutes, with a further thirty-eight occasions when a new place is suggested

268 For changing styles and conventions in obituaries and deathbed narratives, see Mary Riso, *The Narrative of the Good Death* (Farnham: Ashgate, 2015) and David W. Bebbington, 'The deathbed piety of Evangelical Nonconformists in the nineteenth century', in David W. Bebbington, *The Evangelical Quadrilateral* (Waco: Baylor University Press, 2021), 1, 209–33.

but not immediately followed up. More than a quarter of the meetings, therefore, note a new outlet for preaching. In most cases the record simply mentions a place, but sometimes reasons are given. Thus, in June 1830 the meeting agreed to provide preaching in the Oxford parish of St Thomas's, without saying more, but also set out in some detail its reasons for exploring a new work in Summertown, combining need and opportunity:

Qu. 7 What is the opinion of this Meeting concerning Somer-Town?

Ans We think it highly desirable that we should have a place open for preaching in that populous neighbourhood and as several persons formerly members of our Society are resident there, but on account of no class meeting in that neighbourhood its vicinity have neglected that means, & also a chapel unoccupied standing in the centre of the town, we earnestly request Mr Stamp to take those measures he may deem necessary to introduce Methodist preaching.

Sixty years later, in June 1890, a suggestion that Methodist preaching be introduced in Sunnymede, on the northern outskirts of Summertown, came in response to a request from local residents, some presumably Methodist members or adherents.

If Summertown in the early 1830s represents the meeting identifying an opportunity, New Headington in the 1880s shows the preachers giving formal recognition to work already in progress. The Wesleyans tried to sustain a cause in New Headington between 1842 and 1846 and again in 1862–65, but neither effort proved successful. From the mid-1880s, however, meetings for worship were held in Thomas Vallis's house in New High Street and by the time the Local Preachers agreed in March 1885 'to place New Headington on the Plan for a Sunday evening appointm[en]t', the service had been going 'for some time'; in November 1888 the foundation stones were laid for a new chapel.[269]

Reading the Local Preachers' minutes in conjunction with the Quarterly Meeting minutes shows an evolution in Wesleyan mission strategy from the 1830s through to the 1890s. The 1830s and 1840s represent a continuation of the entrepreneurial evangelism of Wesleyanism in the first decades of the nineteenth century, when open-air preaching, cottage meetings and revivals were features of a growing, dynamic and often spontaneous movement. Private homes were licensed for worship, new places appeared briefly on the preaching plan and then disappeared, and it was possible for Local Preachers like the extrovert Billy Birmingham to attempt to export the revivalism of Headington Quarry to other villages. Nineteen new ventures were tried in the 1830s and fifteen in the 1840s.[270] Thereafter the Reform controversy drained resources and sapped confidence, so only seven new

269 Michael S. Edwards, The *Lime Walk Story. A Fortieth Anniversary Souvenir History, 1885–1972* (Witney: The Witney Press, 1972), 5.
270 Some of these were repeated attempts to establish a footing in the same places.

ventures were attempted in the 1850s and five in the 1860s. Although the number fell to three in the 1870s, this masked the consolidation of the Circuit's membership and finances and the development of a strategy to reach Oxford's growing suburbs with purpose-built chapels and salaried lay evangelists, complementing the efforts of the Local Preachers.[271] This laid the foundations for significant growth in the early 1880s, supplying the personnel, money and confidence for another period of expansion, both in the suburbs and in the villages, with twenty-five new places attempted or considered.

The evangelism promoted by Hugh Price Hughes in the 1880s made extensive use of open-air preaching, deploying Local Preachers and mission bands to take Methodism to the villages. Special meetings were held to organise these services until June 1888, when it was agreed that the open-air services would be incorporated into the regular plan. In these years, the Circuit's strategy also included planting chapels in new places, a marked contrast to the earlier years of the century, when many established Wesleyan societies did not possess their own premises. The minutes show the consequences, in answering the question which complements the inquiry about new places: 'Any place to be given up?' In many cases no explanation is given, but sometimes the stated reason is the loss of a rented room, as, for example, at Kidlington in 1830 and 1867, or lack of success in finding suitable accommodation, as at Marston in 1861 and 1867. When the cause failed through loss of members to the Reformers, as at Kirtlington in 1864 or Iffley (Rose Hill), no reference to this appears in the Local Preachers' minutes.

The minutes reveal that some places were tried repeatedly, but without success. There were numerous attempts to establish a Wesleyan presence in Marston, Wolvercote and Summertown, and several in Botley and Wheatley. The minutes do not record any discussion of why these efforts failed, or why perseverance elsewhere succeeded, nor do they comment on the presence of other Christian groups in those places, except for an Evangelical Union at Botley in 1871. When noting the 'claims' or 'needs' of villages in the 1880s, no indication is given that the presence of a parish church might suffice for the spiritual care of the community, but the Quarterly Meeting minutes of the same period show that the Wesleyans believed that these villages were in desperate need of a Nonconformist place of worship, offering a wholesome alternative to the Established Church.[272] This outlook, a marked contrast to the attitude of the earlier period and reflecting a much more negative appraisal of

---

271 The first bespoke 'school chapel' or 'mission school' opened in Cranham Street, Jericho, in 1871, with George Ford, a Wesleyan home missionary (and Local Preacher) assigned to develop the work there: 'Wesleyan Missionary School', *OC*, 25 November 1871, 5. Ford was based nearby, living at 9 Cardigan Street. For the wider application of this policy, see Bebbington, 'Wesleyan Methodist Home Mission'.
272 See, for example, the decision to build a chapel in Garsington: OHC, OMCA, NM5/A/ A3/1, Quarterly Meeting minute book 1861–88, minutes for 25 March 1885.

the Church of England,[273] was shared by the Oxford Nonconformist Council, later the Oxford and District Free Church Council, and helps to explain Wesleyan persistence in trying to sustain a presence in places like Dorchester and Cuddesdon.[274]

It has already been seen that struggling causes could be a reason for Local Preachers neglecting their appointments: a long walk on Sunday to preach to 'faithful Mrs Shirley' at Cuddesdon tested the commitment of many preachers. More positively, the minutes show Local Preachers volunteering to take a special interest in some of the weaker places. In September 1865, for example, Hugh Railton, Charles Hunt and James Nix were given responsibility for the work at Marston, while in March 1901 R.W. Baker offered to conduct eleven out of the quarter's thirteen services at Beckley. In March 1894 brothers Nix, Clifford and Wickham were deputed to visit Islip, 'to confer with the brethren there on the best method of improving the state of the Society and of conducting the Sunday school'. Where a village society had no class leader, Local Preachers were asked to conduct a class meeting in conjunction with their Sunday appointments; in 1896 this was formalised when Clifford, Solloway and Field were appointed to meet the classes at New Hinksey, Islip and Cuddesdon respectively.[275] These were temporary arrangements; the most persistent and successful endeavour was William Richings' commitment to Horspath, which began in 1892, when he volunteered to go each week to 'revive the work' and continued until his death in 1910, the year a new chapel was opened in the village. The meeting agreed in June 1896 that Richings' daughter could also travel to Horspath in the preachers' conveyance to assist her father.

Hints may be gleaned from the Local Preachers' minutes about the health or otherwise – usually otherwise – of Wesleyan work in different places, but there is very little explicit discussion of the strength or weakness of the societies. Need may be inferred from regular changes in service times, reducing from two services each Sunday to one, decisions to assign particular preachers to give continuity, or special efforts to revive the work. The appointment of a committee generally indicates problems, as at Islip in 1894 or Eynsham in 1899, but details remain elusive. Conversely, the new and thriving suburban chapel in East Oxford (William Street, opened in 1883) receives very few references, while its grander equivalent in North Oxford (Walton Street, also 1883) is not mentioned at all, although Walton

273   Compare the analysis of the interplay between mid-century village evangelism, ritualism and the re-orientation of Wesleyanism towards the Free Churches in Bebbington, 'Wesleyan Methodist Home Mission', 95–6.

274   For the attitude of the Free Church Council, see James Nix, 'Our Village Free Churches', *ODFCM*, March 1897, 17–19.

275   A reminder to preachers appointed for Beckley, Forest Hill, Islip, Eynsham, Garsington, Cuddesdon, Woodstock and Wootton to meet the classes on Sunday appears on the plan from July 1896: OHC, OMCA, NM5/A/A1/1, Circuit plans and directories, plan for July to October 1896.

Street's success may be the unexpressed reason for the gradual decline of the nearby Cranham Street Mission and its quest in 1886 for a different pattern of Sunday worship to attract a new congregation.

Although not specifically about places, mention may be made here of another topic which recurs in the minutes: the practical challenge of getting preachers to their appointments. Distances were formidable: G.G. Banbury recalled Joseph Ostler walking from Abingdon to Woodstock, then to Chipping Norton, and finally returning home, having covered some fifty miles and preached three times in a single day.[276] Half a century later, Alfred Gregory reported walking from Oxford to Bladon, then to Combe, and getting lost on the return journey, requiring a lengthy detour and a trip of some twenty miles.[277] With these distances in mind, a committee was appointed in September 1837 'to procure suitable conveyance for the Preachers when appointed to the Country places.' Changes in times of services and of preaching places inevitably affected the route taken by the conveyance and the minutes record the varying arrangements. For half a century the minutes suggest that there was a single large vehicle, travelling in the direction of Woodstock, Wootton and Tackley, with occasional diversions to Islip and Charlton. In autumn 1887, however, it was decided that it would be cheaper and more practical to use two smaller pony traps, one travelling to Woodstock, Wootton and Tackley and the other to Bladon, Combe and Eynsham. These vehicles left the Martyrs' Memorial in the morning; another vehicle set off in the afternoon for Garsington, Horspath and Cuddesdon.

A series of problems beset the preachers' transport. One was securing adequate vehicles: Arthur Pearson was asked in June 1891 to secure a stronger horse and a larger trap for the Garsington route, but in November and December 1891 he failed to find any vehicle at all on three occasions. Another challenge was paying the hire charges. A subscription system was set up in 1850, with a hopeful resolution: 'That the friends at the country places be affectionately requested to contribute as much as they can towards this object.' By the late 1860s a Horse Hire Fund was in operation, with a treasurer and committee. A decade later George Maunder, Superintendent from 1876–78, handed over the profits from the sale of the preaching plan to bail out the Fund, and designated collections were instigated on specific Sundays.[278] In 1881 the Horse Hire Fund was renamed the Circuit Mission Fund, but the financial problems continued. In addition, the Local Preachers' Meeting had occasion to urge country societies to take good care of a hired or borrowed horse. In 1847 a message was sent to the friends at Charlton-on-Otmoor 'requesting them to pay more attention to their Horse, especially in reference to provinder', and pointing

276 Manuscript memoir of Gabriel George Banbury, by John Brownjohn (1912), 28.
277 Letter of 1871, in Benjamin Gregory, *Consecrated Culture: Memorials of Benjamin Alfred Gregory* (London: T. Woolmer, 1885), 97.
278 First marked on the plan in July-September 1878, with a collection at Tackley on 4 August.

out that 'Mr Boffin, the lender, complains and threatens to refuse to lend unless the horse be properly fed.' In similar vein, the friends at Tackley and Wootton were reminded in 1885 'that they might reasonably be expected to bear the Expense of stabling the Horse for the appointed preacher'. Just one reproachful reference appears in the minutes to a preacher failing to arrive on time at the rendezvous for the departure of the conveyance, but the reminder to be PUNCTUAL was printed on the plan in block capitals.[279] The minutes do not discuss the challenge of driving the conveyance, but the Bladon jubilee number of the *Oxford Wesleyan Methodist Circuit Magazine* contained several stories of preachers' hair-raising journeys and narrow escapes.[280]

In most quarters, confirming attendance, inquiring into character, reviewing arrivals and departures and agreeing on times and places of preaching fills the minutes. In December 1887, however, the Superintendent, John Martin, 'stated that if the routine business of the Meeting could be got through more expeditiously a discussion upon some Theological or other subject might profitably be taken up at the close', Through the century several such attempts were made to foster theological discussion or to offer papers on biblical studies or the craft of preaching. Thus, in December 1870, 'Two papers were read ... on subjects relating to the work of preaching'. Bro. J. King spoke on 'Our Work' and Bro. Stiles on the 'Conditions of a Sinner's Acceptance with God'. In 1893 Enoch Salt suggested that a paper on 'the best method of conducting the ordinary preaching service' would be helpful; Walter Wickham volunteered to prepare one, but there is no evidence that it was ever presented. In 1894 D.P. Clifford offered to give a paper on a Gospel text and in December 1895 Alfred Archer 'introduced a discussion on the best means of increasing the Local Preachers' efficiency in the villages', a topical subject.[281] In February 1902 a special meeting convened to hear E.E. Genner, classical scholar and Fellow of Magdalen, speak on 'Bible Study for Local Preachers'. Moving beyond the meeting itself, plans were laid in 1837 to create a Local Preachers' Library, a subject which was raised again in 1888–89, while in 1894 'Bro Wickham placed before the meeting the advisability of forming a Home Reading Union in connection with the Allan Library' – the collection donated to the Wesleyan Connexion in 1884, for the

---

279 OHC, OMCA, NM5/A/A1/1, Circuit plans and directories, plans for the 1890s. The reference in the minutes is to William Richings, in June 1885.

280 John H. Ritson, 'My first Sunday at Bladon' and [Anon.], 'The Road to Bladon: Some Adventures Recalled', in *OWMCM*, June 1927, 43–4 and 47–8.

281 In 1894–95 the Joyful News Book Depot, Rochdale, published *Homely Counsels for Village Preachers*, by Joseph Bush, a Past President of the Wesleyan Conference, and C.O. Eldridge's *Local Preachers and Village Methodism*. These books were part of a wider conversation about the position of Methodism in rural areas and wider debate about changing patterns of rural life: see, for example, G.F. Millin, *Life in Our Villages* (London: Cassell and Co., 1891) and Enoch Salt, 'Parish Councils and Village Methodism', *WMM*, October 1894, 692–4.

use of ministers.[282] A theological society was mooted in 1882 and a monthly meeting for mutual improvement in 1890. In the same year plans were laid for a Local Preachers' Convention and this duly took place in 1891. It may be noted that many of these schemes for study, discussion and development took place as the number of Local Preachers in the Oxford Circuit was increasing, as access to education was improving, and as the training, resourcing and effectiveness of Local Preachers were being debated in the Conference and the Wesleyan press.[283] Amidst all of these worthy endeavours at self-improvement, there are also examples of compassionate concern for those struggling with ill-health or bereavement, good wishes for those recently married and one occasion when James Nix provided tea for the preachers, albeit perhaps as an incentive to ensure a large attendance for Genner's paper on Bible study. In lighter vein, in June 1891 James Chapman suggested 'that the Local Preachers with their friends should have a picnic during the summer'. Typically, a committee was appointed to investigate; no definitive record of the event survives, but it may be hoped that this rare opportunity for Oxford's hard-working Local Preachers to set business aside and relax did in fact take place.

It is impossible to overestimate the importance of Local Preachers to the maintenance and extension of Wesleyan Methodism in the nineteenth century. The records presented here, although often terse, afford insights into the selection, training and deployment of the preachers and the ebb and flow of Wesleyanism in the city and the countryside. They also enable an exploration of the rhythms of Methodist life and spirituality and shed light on personalities and controversies. At a time when Methodism was growing in strength, influence and confidence, they have a significant contribution to make in understanding a movement whose place in nineteenth-century Oxford and Oxfordshire has often been overshadowed or overlooked.[284]

282 See 'Allan Library', in *DMBI*, and Clive Field, 'The Allan Library: A Victorian Methodist Odyssey', *Bulletin of the John Rylands Library* 89.2 (2013), 69–105.
283 As well as the discussions leading up to the Conference of 1894, see, for example, William Unsworth, 'The training and employment of Local Preachers', *WMM*, June 1893, 440–4.
284 By comparison with the extensive historiography of the Oxford Movement and the diocesan reforms of Bishop Samuel Wilberforce, Methodism and Protestant Nonconformity in Oxfordshire have received little attention, although this has been remedied in recent volumes of the *Victoria County History of Oxford* and in the pioneering research of Kate Tiller: see, for instance, *Church and Chapel in Oxfordshire in 1851* and '"The desert begins to blossom": Oxfordshire and Primitive Methodism, 1824–1860', *Oxoniensia* 71 (2006), 85–109.

Figure 1. Wesleyan Methodist Preaching Plan for the Oxford Circuit, January to April 1839. Photograph: Alison Butler.

Map 1.   Preaching places in the Oxford Wesleyan Circuit
(County). Giles Darkes © Oxfordshire Record Society.

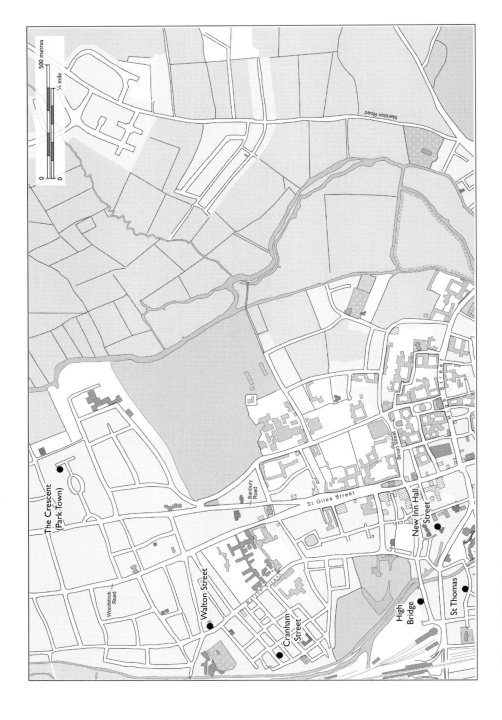

500 metres

¼ mile

Marston Road

The Crescent
(Park-Town)

Woodstock
Road

Banbury
Road

St Giles Street

Walton Street

Cranham
Street

Broad Street

New Inn Hall
Street

High
Bridge

St Thomas

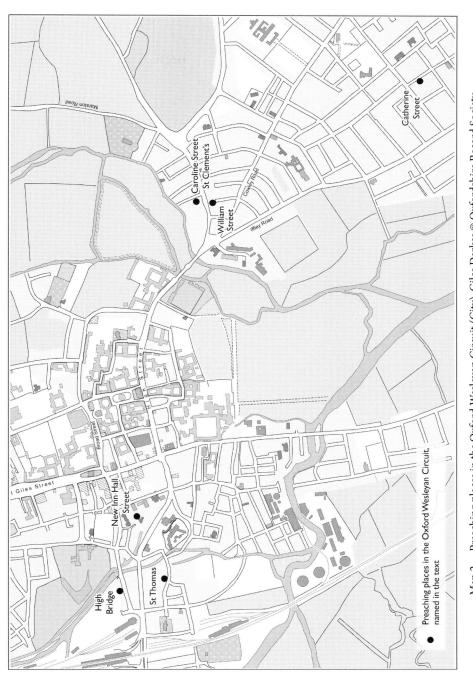

Map 2. Preaching places in the Oxford Wesleyan Circuit (City). Giles Darkes © Oxfordshire Record Society.

From 1830

to

Dec. 26th 1866

Oxford

Local Preachers'

Book

19 March 1830

Oxford,[1] 19th March, 1830

Minutes of the Oxford Circuit Local preachers' meeting.

Present[2]

Mess. Stamp[3] & Loutit[4] and Brors Ostler,[5] Jackson,[6] Bartlett,[7] Brown[8] & Legget.[9]

------- Cheney,[10] Ward,[11] Smith,[12] & Crapper.[13]

I. Are there any objections to any of the Brethn touching their moral character – soundness in the faith – attention to discipline – and ability for their work?

A. None – except

1. Br. Greenhill[14] having disappointed[15] Woodstock[16] on the 7th of Feb. & Murcot[17] on the 31st of Jan. last, a note be written to him, specially requesting his attendance at the next Local Preachers' Meeting to account for this neglect of discipline.

1   The principal chapel in the Oxford Wesleyan Circuit was in New Inn Hall Street and opened in 1818.

2   Loutit begins by listing the two ministers, then the fully accredited Local Preachers, and then, on a separate line, those testing a call to preach as exhorters or preachers on trial.

3   John Sundius Stamp (1799–1849), Superintendent of the Oxford Wesleyan Circuit, 1829–31. For his subsequent career and departure from the Wesleyan ministry, see Alison W. Kirk, Simon R. Valentine and W. Leary, 'Stamp family' in the online edition of the *DMBI* and *Wesleyan Times*, 1 August 1849, 491 and 495.

4   James Loutit (1801–85), junior minister in the Oxford Circuit, 1829–30: *Minutes of Conference* 1885, 22–3.

5   Joseph Ostler (c.1771–1849), mason or bricklayer, of Oxford.

6   Henry Jackson was a member at New Inn Hall Street in the 1829 class lists: OHC, OMCA, NM5/A/A2/1, Oxford Circuit Book, 1825–36.

7   William Bartlett (1799–1875), master carpenter, of Oxford.

8   George Brown (c.1771–1860), saddler, of Oxford.

9   William Leggatt (1801–87), ironmonger, of Woodstock.

10   William Cheney (c. 1806–?), schoolmaster, of Oxford.

11   Perhaps Charles Ward (1800–?), a member at New Inn Hall Street in 1827 and Bartlett's brother-in-law.

12   John Smith (1803–98), last and bootmaker, of Oxford.

13   Josiah Munday Crapper (1810–92), schoolmaster, of Oxford.

14   Joseph Greenhill (1796–1861), brickmaker, of Headington Quarry. Greenhill witnessed an application for the registration of a house for worship in 1824 and his dwelling was licensed for worship in 1826: OHC, Oxford Diocesan Archives, DIOC/1/D/2, certificates for religious worship, c. 645 (1823–34).

15   i.e., failed to keep his appointment to preach.

16   The Woodstock Wesleyan chapel opened in 1824.

17   The Wesleyans did not succeed in establishing a presence in Murcott, but the Primitive Methodists opened a chapel there in 1843: Kate Tiller (ed.), *Church and Chapel in Oxfordshire 1851* (Oxford: Oxfordshire Record Society, 1987), 70.

2. That the names of J. Hussey[1] and B. Warren,[2] be left of the plan.

3. That Mr. Leonard[3] is removed.[4]

II. Are there any of the Brethren in debt?

A. None, except one, who is exerting himself to discharge it.[5]

III. Are there any to be received into full connexion,[6] as local preachers?

A. Brs Cheney & Saunders,[7] whose period of trial is now completed, but whose reception is postponed, from their not having, as yet, been able to comply with the 4th Res. of Quest. 7th in the Minutes of last meeting.[8]

IV. Are there any to be received on trial?

A. 1. Thos Bent [*conj.*] of the Newport Pagnell Circuit who comes duly recommended.[9]

2. Josiah Crapper.

V. Are there any miscellaneous Resolutions?

A. 1. Complaints having been made, with respect to the disappointment of places by the local preachers, it was unanimously agreed – that should any Br. in future be charged with this, he shall be called solemnly, in presence of the meeting, to account for the neglect, & if unable to justify himself, shall be admonished, put back on trial, or suspended as to the superintendt may appear fit.

2. That from the painful circumstances which have recently occurred in the cases of Hussey and Warren, as well as from regard to our private & public character, we unanimously agree that the 2nd quest. in these minutes,[10] shall be put, once a quarter, to every local preacher, local preacher on trial, & exhorter on this plan.[11]

1   Probably John Wesley Hussey (1796–1867), committed for trial at the Oxford City Sessions in February 1830 for embezzlement from his employer. The employer, John Pike, was a prominent Oxford Methodist. Hussey pleaded guilty at trial, was sentenced to seven years' transportation, but was pardoned after serving three years' imprisonment at the Millbank Penitentiary. See *JOJ*, 6 Feb 1830, 3, and 24 April 1830, 3.

2   Benjamin Warren (1767–1837) was listed as leader of the Abingdon Class in June 1829: OHC, OMCA, NM5/A/A2/1, Oxford Circuit Book, 1825–36. If the 'painful circumstances' which led to his removal from the plan involved debt, Warren nonetheless died as a prosperous currier and leather seller in Stony Stratford seven years later.

3   Perhaps Benjamin Leonard, who appears in the minutes in 1838.

4   i.e., has left the Oxford Circuit.

5   Marginal annotation: 'Church'.

6   The origins of Wesleyanism in groups and individuals working 'in connexion with' John Wesley were reflected in the enduring description of the Wesleyan denomination as a Connexion (retaining the eighteenth-century spelling). The terminology of trial, probation and reception into full connexion (with the annual Conference) was used for the itinerant or Travelling Preachers; here Loutit uses it for Local Preachers as well.

7   Probably James Saunders.

8   Not extant, but probably requiring a candidate for admission as a Local Preacher to have read John Wesley's *Sermons* and *Notes on the New Testament*.

9   A Local Preacher moving from one place to another was expected to bring a letter of commendation from his previous circuit and a copy of the preaching plan on which he was listed as a preacher in good standing.

10   i.e., whether any preacher was in debt.

11   Indicating the descending order of seniority, from fully accredited Local Preachers to preachers on trial to those testing a call as exhorters.

In name of the Meeting,
J. Loutite, Sec[y].[1]

18 June 1830

Oxford, June 18th, 1830.
Minutes of the Oxford Circuit Local Preachers Meeting.
Present Mr. Stamp and Messrs Bartlett, Brown, Meek,[2] Leggatt, Ostler, Greenhill, Lane, Jackson and
Messrs Saunders, Cheney, Goodman[3] J Crapper Bent and Smith.
Qu I Are there any objections to any of the Bretheren touching their moral character soundness in the faith attention to discipline and ability for the Work?
Ans. None, except
Bro Martin[4] of Blewberry having disappointed Southmoor[5] on the 6th of June a note shall be written to him specially requesting his attendance at the next Local preachers Meeting to account for this neglect of discipline.
Qu 2. Are there any to be received in full connection?
Ansr. 1 Bro Geo. Scaresbrook[6] from the Brackley Circuit on condition of producing a Note of Recommendation from the Superintendant of that place.
2. Bro. W. Cheney who completed his period of probation three months ago, but is continued on trial having neglected to comply with the Requisition of the Local preachers Meeting held 18 Dec 1829 Quest VII. Sect. 4.
3. Bro. J. Saunders also who has not fully complied with the Regulation and requests three months longer period.
Qu. 3. Are there any to be received on trial?
Ansr Daniel Lousley of Blewberry.[7]
Qu 4. Are there any to be received as exhorters?
None.
Qu 5. Are any alterations to be made in regard to the places on the plan?
Ansr The alterations made in reference to the time of preaching at Woodstock at the Meeting 18th Dec 1829 not having been attended with the anticipated results, the hours of service are now to be half past two in the afternoon and six o'clock in the evening.
Qu. 6 Are any additional places to be taken on the plan?
Ans. The Parish of St Thomas in the city of Oxford.

1   Until 1870 the junior minister in the Circuit acted as secretary of the Local Preachers' Meeting. Many of the minutes were signed by the secretary, as record-keeper, rather than by the Superintendent, as chair of the meeting.
2   Thomas Meek (c.1775–1872), glover, of Woodstock.
3   Although named as William Goodman in December 1830, a more likely identification is James Goodman (1794–?1854), wheelwright, of Abingdon.
4   Probably James Martin (1795–1878), basket maker, of Blewbury.
5   There was a Wesleyan chapel at Southmoor by 1823: Drew University, Madison, NJ, Marriott Collection, D2003-038, Oxford Plan, 1823.
6   George Scarsbrook (1805-81), baker.
7   Daniel Lousley (1793–1853), farmer, of Blewbury.

Qu. 7 What is the opinion of this Meeting concerning Somer-Town?
Ans We think it highly desirable that we should have a place open for preaching in that populous neighbourhood and as several persons formerly members of our Society are resident there, but on account of no class meeting in that neighbourhood its vicinity have neglected that means, & also a chapel unoccupied standing in the centre of the town, we earnestly request Mr Stamp to take those measures he may deem necessary to introduce Methodist preaching.[1]
Qu. 8 What is the opinion of the meeting respecting Kidlington?
Ans. We agree to try it another Quarter.
In behalf of the Meeting, Jno. S. Stamp.

17 September 1830
Minutes of the Oxford Circuit Local Preachers Meeting held 17th Sept 1830.
Present Messrs Stamp, Bartlett, Brown, Leggatt, Ostler, Martin, Lane, Jackson, Scarsbrook, Goodman, Crapper, Church,[2] Smith and Saunders.
Qu. 1 Are there any objections to any of the Brethren touching their moral character, soundness in the faith attention to discipline and ability for the work?
Ansr 1 Bro. Pearson[3] having neglected to supply Yarnton[4] on the 8th of August and Steventon on the 22nd of same month shall be requested to attend the next meeting and account for the same and also for neglecting for nearly three months meeting in Class.[5]
2. Bro. Cheney for neglecting Woodstock on Aug. 1 and Murcot and Charlton on the 22nd and neglecting Blewberry[6] and his Class shall also be specially summoned to attend the ensuing meeting to account for this negligence.
Qu. 2 Who have died this Quarter?
Ansr James Mawbey.
Qu. 3 Who are to be recieved in full connection this Quarter?
Ansr 1 James Saunders who is still eligible but the same obstacle continues as mentioned 3 months ago.
2. William Cheney and Willm Harper who are eligible but absent.[7]
Qu. 4 Are any to be recieved on trial?
Ansr Thomas Church.
Qu. 5 Are any to be proposed as exhorters?

1   Summertown first developed in the 1820s and had a population in excess of 500 by 1832. A Baptist chapel was built in Middle Way in 1824 but was disused by 1830: Alan Crossley (ed.), *VCH*, 4, *The City of Oxford* (Oxford: OUP, 1979), 196, 418.
2   Thomas Church (1795–1854), tailor, of Oxford.
3   George Pearson (1792–1874), mason, of Oxford.
4   Dropped from the preaching plan in March 1831.
5   Weekly attendance at the class meeting, a gathering for testimony and mutual accountability, was a requirement of Methodist discipline.
6   One of the larger country societies, with a chapel opened in 1826: Kate Tiller (ed.), *Berkshire Religious Census 1851* (Reading: Berkshire Record Society, 2010), 10.
7   Completion of the period of training required an oral examination at the LP Meeting.

Ansr None.
Qu. 6 Are any alterations to be made on the ensuing plan?
Ans 1 The morning preaching at Harwell to be given up.[1]
2 Kidlington on account of the death of Mr Jos Hale[2] and the sale of the property to be relinquished.
3 Jericho preaching to be on Thursday in lieu of Tuesday.
4 Preaching at Steventon [*conj.*] only in the evening.
Qu. 7 Are any new places to be taken on the Plan?
Ansr 1 <u>Kirtlington</u> where Mr Wakefield has provided a place for preaching.[3] The service to take place in the evening at 6 o'clock.
2. <u>Beckley</u> where preaching shall commence at 5 o'clock in the Evening.
Signed for & in behalf of the Meeting Jno S. Stamp.

17 December 1830

Minutes of the Oxford Local preachers Meeting held Decr 17 1830
Present Messrs Stamp & Hickman,[4] Brown, Ostler, Greenhill, Scarsbrook, Cheney, Goodman, Crapper, Smith.
Quest. 1 Are there any objections to any of the Brethren? None. N.B. Bro: Bent neglected Blewberry on Nov. 21 and Marcham and Steventon in the evening.[5]
Qu: 2 Who are to be received in full connection.
Ansr William Goodman.
Qu: N.B. Bro. Sa[u]nders, Cheney and Harpur are eligible and on account of absence their reception is postponed.
Qu: 3 Are any to be received as exhorters?
Ans. None. John Mobley[6] may receive a note from the Superintendant authorizing him to engage occasionally as an exhorter.
Qu: 4 Are there any alterations to be made on the ensuing plan?
Ans. The times of preaching at Steventon to be ½ p 2 and 5 p.m.
Pro. Sec. Jno S. Stamp.

1   Leaving Harwell with an evening service only.
2   Perhaps Joseph Hall (1791–1830), coal merchant, corn factor, and baker, whose property, including six houses in Kidlington, was advertised for sale by auction in July 1830: *JOJ*, 31 July 1830, 2. Hall was a Leader in the Kidlington Wesleyan Society in June 1826: OHC, OMCA, NM5/A/A2/1, Oxford Circuit Book, 1825–36.
3   John Wakefield, grocer, of Kirtlington, registered a tenement in Kirtlington as a place for religious worship on 15 September 1830: OHC, Oxford Diocesan Archives, DIOC/1/D/2, certificates for religious worship, c. 645 (1823–34), f.165.
4   Henry Hickman (1802–46), junior minister in the Oxford Circuit, 1830-31: *Minutes of Conference* 1846, 302–3.
5   Steventon and Marcham had afternoon and evening services and the appointed preacher was supposed to lead both; presumably Bent preached in the afternoon and then went home, missing the evening service.
6   John Mobley (1813–59), butcher, of Oxford.

4 March 1831

Minutes of a Meeting of the Local Preachers of the Oxford Circuit March 4: 1831
Present Messrs Stamp, Bartlett, Brown, Leggatt, Ostler, Greenhill, Lane, Jackson,
Scarsbrook, Cheney, Crapper, Harper, Smith, Church, Bent, Mobley.

Quest. I Are there any objections to any of the brethren?

Ansr 1 This meeting manifests disapprobation of Bro. Martin employing to fill the
pulpit at Abingdon a Brother who is considered ineligible and who has never been
appointed there by the Superintendant.[1]

2. This meeting also calls upon Bro. Pearson to shew reason why he neglected
Beckley Jany 23 1831. Bro. Bent neglecting Yarnton Feb. 13th and Bro. Church for
neglecting Southmoor Feby 20 and Jericho Feby 24 1831.

Quest. II Do any Brethren retire from the plan?

Ansr Thomas Widdows who has appeared on the plan under the signature of W[2]
removing from the Circuit.

Quest. III Who are eligible to be received into full connection?

Ansr Brethn Saunders, Cheney, Harper, Crapper and Bent.

Quest. IV Are any now to be received?

Ansr William Cheney and Josiah Crapper. NB The absence of the other Brethren
precludes their reception this evening.

Quest. V Are any to be received on trial?

Ansr None.

Quest. VI Who are to be received as exhorters?

Ansr John Mobley.

Quest. VII What alterations are to take place on the plan?

Ansr 1 Preaching at Kirtlington to take place at ½ p 2 in the afternoon and at 6
o'clock in the evening.

    2 Yarnton for the present to be left off the plan.

Quest. VIII What place is to be taken on the plan?

Ansr Iffley. The Service to commence at 6 o'clock in the evening.

Signed in behalf of the Meeting Jno S. Stamp Chairman.

10 June 1831

Minutes of a Meeting of the Local preachers of the Oxford Circuit held 10th June
1831

Present Messrs Stamp, Bartlett, Ostler, Meek, Brown, Jackson, Scarsbrook, Cheney,
Mobley.

Qu I Are there any objections to any of the Brethren?

---

1   Control of the preaching appointments was jealously guarded by the Superintendent.

2   Until the second half of the nineteenth century preachers were identified on the grid
of services on the quarterly preaching plan by numbers or letters, rather than their full
names, presumably to save space. A key was printed on the plan. Preachers in training were
sometimes indicated in that list by initials only.

Ansr The Meeting complained of Br. Pearson neglecting several places whither he was appointed ~~had~~ and not even seeking a supply from the preachers who are on the plan.[1]

Qu II Do any Brethren retire from the plan?

Ansr 1 Bro. Saunders having tendered his resignation. The Meeting accepts it.
   2 Bro. Lane and Bro. Bant on account of having left the circuit.

Quest. III Who are eligible to be received into full connection?

Ansr William Harper and Daniel Lousley.

Qu IV Are any now to be received?

Ansr No. ~~Boththe~~ Both the Brethren just named are absent.

Qu V What alteration takes place on the plan?

Ansr The preaching at Woodstock to be at 11 in the Morning and at 6 in the Evening.

Jno. S. Stamp Chairman.

16 September 1831

Minutes of a Meeting of the Local preachers of the Oxford Circuit, held at Oxford 16th September 1831

Present Messrs Stamp, Bartlett, Brown, Leggatt, Ostler, Pearson, Jackson, Scarsbrook, Cheney, Crapper, Harper, Smith and Mobley.

Quest I Are there any objections to any of the Brethren?

Ansr This Meeting having heard with regret of certain transactions which occurred in the house of Bro. Thos Meek on Sunday Aug 21 ult. in which the sanctity of the Sabbath was grossly violated Unanimously resolve that Bro. Meek shall be requested to meet the Local Brethren, to account for and explain these proceedings and that the preachers[2] ~~who~~ shall be specially summoned to attend for this purpose in the Vestry of the Wesleyan Chapel Oxford on Friday the 30th day of September 1831 at 6 o'clock in the Evening.

Quest II Who are eligible in respect to the continuance on the plan to be received as accredited preachers?

Ansr Willm Harper, Daniel Lousley and Thos Church.

Quest III Who are now to be received?

Ansr None. NB (1) Bro. Harper is continued on trial solely on account of not having complied with the resolution of a Meeting of the Local Brethren 18th Decr 1829. See Quest VII Art 4. (2) Dan: Lousley and Thos Church are absent.

Quest IV Who are now to be received on trial?

Ansr John Smith and John Mobley.

Quest V Are any to be received as exhorters?

Ansr None.

Quest VI What alterations are to take place on the plan?

---

1   A preacher unable to fulfil an appointment was expected to find an accredited substitute to 'supply' in his place.

2   'that the preachers' inserted in the margin.

Ansr 1 The Preaching at Bladon[1] during the winter to begin at ½ past 5 in the Evening.[2]
　　2 The Preaching at Kirtlington.
　　3 The Preaching at Jericho.
Quest VII What places are to be removed from the plan?
Ansr Jericho and St Thomas.
Quest VIII Are any fresh places to be tried.
Ansr None at present.
Signed Jno. S. Stamp Chairman.

30 September 1831

Sept 30th 1831
Present Messrs Stamp, Tarr,[3] Bartlett, Ostler, Brown, Leggatt, Cheney, Crapper, Mobley, Harper, Greenhill, Church.
A letter was received from Mr Meek in which he declared that the violation of the Sabbath already alluded to, was contrary to his wishes and commands and committing his cause into the hands of the brethren. They resolve
1st That this Meeting, considering the standing of Bro. Meek in the Socy[4] exceedingly regrets that he should so far disregard the authority vested in him as the head of a family, as to suffer the Sabbath to be violated by his children in the making of mourning on that day.[5]
2 That this Meeting would especially recognize the principle that the Head of a family is answerable to the Church & to God for transactions which occur under his roof & that it is his especial duty to prevent all such proceedings as would be prejudicial to the character and interest of Religious Society.
* 3rd & 4th See the other side.[6]
* That acting on this principle, this Meeting feels it to be their duty to admonish and reprove Bro. Meek, for this violation which they consider might have been prevented, and, apprehensive lest his employment as Local Preacher might have conduced to this neglect of family discipline, resolve that until the next Quarterly

---

1　In 1823 Bladon was linked with Hanborough for Sunday services. Wesleyan support steadily grew through the 1830s and the first chapel was opened in 1843: Tiller, *Church and Chapel in Oxfordshire*, 12.
2　First reference to a recurring theme: service times in the villages were adjusted for winter and summer evenings.
3　William Tarr (1802–74), junior minister in the Oxford Circuit, 1831–32. Tarr resigned from the ministry in 1858: *Minutes of Conference* 1858, 26, but continued to describe himself in census returns as a 'retired Wesleyan minister'.
4　i.e., the Wesleyan Methodist Society.
5　Meek was a glover; presumably members of his household were working on Sunday to fulfil a commission for mourning attire.
6　Notes of the meeting were completed at the foot of the facing page, beneath the minutes of 16 March 1832.

Meeting he have no appointment on the plan, in order that he may fully attend to the spiritual affairs and controuling of his family.

16 March 1832

March 16th 1832[1]
Revd Messrs Stamp and Tarr. Also Messrs Bartlett, Leggatt, Ostler, Greenhill, Scarsbrook, Cheney, Crapper, Smith, Mobley, Birmingham.[2]
Q 1st Are there any objections to any of[3] the bretheren. Bro. Jackson answerable for having omitted to attend his appointments at Woodstock & Forest Hill.
Q 2 Are any of the bretheren eligible to be received in full
Ans Bro. Harper, Lousley, Church.
Qu 3 Are any to be received as exhorters?
Ansr Bro. Birmingham.
Mr Stamp is requested to converse with Brethn Sandars and Brown[4] on the subject of local preaching.

15 June 1832

June 15th 1832
Present Messrs Stamp, Bartlett, Brown, Leggatt, Ostler, Greenhill, Scarsbrook, Cheney, Jos Crapper, Church, Smith, Mobley, Birmingham.
Qu. 1 Are there any objections to the Preachers?
Ans. Bro. Martin neglected Harwell – also Bro. Jackson Apl 29th he wilfully[5]
Qu 2 What is the opinion of the Meeting respecting Bro. Meek?
This meeting regrets that the evil complained of still exists in full form. And they cannot consistently with the principles laid down in the resolutions of Sept 30 1831 remove the restriction then laid upon him.
2 That this resolution be communicated to Mr Meek.
Qu 3 Are any to be received in full connection
Bro Harper and Bro Lousley eligible but are not present consequently not rec'd at present. Bro. Church present not but has not read Mr Wesley's Notes on the NT.[6]
Qu 4 That Who remain as exhorters?
Ansr Bro. Birmingham.
Qu. 5 Who are proposed as exhorters?
Henry Brown.
James Hitchman.[7]

1   There are no minutes for a meeting in December 1831.
2   William Birmingham (1809–75), shoemaker, of Headington.
3   'any of' inserted above the main text.
4   Henry Brown (see below, 15 June 1832).
5   Acknowledging that some of the missed appointments were unintended.
6   John Wesley's *Explanatory Notes Upon the New Testament* (1755), part of the doctrinal standards of the Wesleyan Connexion.
7   James Hitchman (1811–96), tailor, of Oxford.

Qu. 6 Are any persons to receive notes from the Supt?
Ansr James Wait.[1]
Qu 7 Is there there any alteration in any of the places?
Ansr None.
Qu 8 Are any fresh places to be taken on to the plan?
Ansr Nuneham & Clifton are proposed, but it is considered that sufficient attention could not at present be paid to them.
Signed Jno. S. Stamp Chairman.

14 September 1832

Sept 14th 1832
Present Messr Adams,[2] Barrett,[3] Bartlett, Brown, Leggatt, Ostler, Greenhill, Scarsbrook, Goodman, Cheney, Crapper, Church, Smith, Mobley, Birmingham, Hitchman, Brown & Harper.
Qu. 1 Are there any objections to any of the Bretheren?
Ansr Bro. Whitmell is answerable for having neglected his appointment & taking away his congregation 12th Augt.[4]
Qu. 2 What is the judgement of the Meeting with reference to Bro. Meek's case?
Ansr A The cause of complaint not being entirely removed the bretheren are of opinion that his name may stand upon the plan during the ensuing Quarter, but without any appointments. Yet that a hope shall be held out to him of a restoration to office in case of an improvement in his domestic management.
Qu. 3 Do any retire from the plan?
Ansr Bro. Jackson, he having left the Society.[5]
Qu. 4 Are any to be received in full connection?

1   James Wait(e) died in September 1835, and is possibly the James Wheat, of Headington Quarry, buried at St Andrew's, Headington, on 15 September 1835. James Wait was listed as a member at Headington Quarry in 1832, and a member on trial in 1829: OHC, OMCA, NM5/A/A2/1, Oxford Circuit Book, 1825–36.
2   John H. Adams (1788–1846), Superintendent of the Oxford Circuit, 1832–35: *Minutes of Conference* 1847, 453.
3   Alfred Barrett (1808–76), junior minister in the Oxford Circuit, 1832–33: *Minutes of Conference* 1877, 14–17.
4   Thomas Whitmell, of Bletchingdon, an excise officer. His daughter Rhoda was baptised at New Inn Hall Street in January 1832. In Mary D. Lobel (ed.), *VCH*, 6, *Ploughley Hundred* (London: OUP, 1959), 70, it is noted that there were two Methodist places of worship in Bletchingdon in the early 1830s, so one may have been the congregation Whitmell 'took away' from the Wesleyans. Whitmell registered his own dwelling for religious worship in April 1830: OHC, Oxford Diocesan Archives, DIOC/1/D/2, certificates for religious worship, c. 645 (1823–34), f.155. Although the LP Minutes make no reference to reinstatement, Whitmell was listed on the Wesleyan preaching plan for November 1834–February 1835 as a Local Preacher in good standing.
5   i.e., resigned his membership of the Wesleyan Connexion.

eligible Bro. Harper; but wishes on account of his present state of health still to remain on trial.

also Bro. Lousley, but not present.

    J. Church, but has not read Mr Wesley's Notes.[1]

    J. Smith ~~do~~ the same

    J. Mobley the same.

therefore none are at present received.

Qu. 5th Do any remain as exhorters?

Ansr Bro. Birmingham.

Qu. 6th Are any proposed as exhorters?

Ansr None. Three young men at Abingdon & one at Harwell may be employed at the discretion of the Supt.

Qu. 7th Are any proposed as eligible to receive a note from the Superintendant?

Ansr The following persons are proposed.

Messrs Wait,[2] Towle,[3] Prentice[4] & Bailey.[5]

Qu. 8 Shall there be any alteration with reference to any of the places

Ansr Southmoor shall be supplied only in the afternoon during the next Quarter.

Qu. 9 Are any new places proposed?

Ansr None at present.

Sept 14th 1832 Alfred Barrett Secy.

2 January 1833

Jany 2nd 1833

Present Revd[6] Messrs Adams & Barrett, also Messrs Ostler, Bartlett, Brown, Leggatt, Martin, Greenhill, Pearson, Goodman, Cheney, Crapper, Smith, Birmingham, Hitchman, Brooks,[7] Simpson[8] & H. Brown.

Qu. 1 Are there any objections to the Preachers?

Ansr Bro. Church neglected Kirtlington.

Bro. Mobley also neglected several appointments and apparently without reason – this meeting therefore deems him answerable.

Qu. 2d What is the judgement of the Meeting with refe to Bro. Meeks case?

---

1   See note 1 for the previous meeting.

2   James Waite (d. 1835).

3   John Towle (1796–1885), tailor and later paper maker, of Oxford. As Mayor of Oxford 1856–57, Towle identified as a Wesleyan, and was buried in the New Inn Hall Street chapel graveyard.

4   John Prentice (1802–63), whitesmith, of Oxford.

5   Joseph Bailey (1785–1854), tailor, of Oxford.

6   First use of 'Revd' for the Wesleyan ministers.

7   Possibly Aaron Brooks, listed as a member at Abingdon in 1832: OHC, OMCA, NM5/A/A2/1, Oxford Circuit Book, 1825–36.

8   William Simpson (1811–bef. 61), shoemaker, of Abingdon.

Moved by Bro. Cheney and seconded by Bro. Bartlett that Bro. Meek be received into full employment again upon the plan.

Qu. 3d Are any received into full connexion?

Ansr None. Messr Church, Lousley & Mobley are eligible but not present.

Qu. 4th Are any received on Trial?

Ansr Bro. Birmingham with a recommendation that he shall use every endeavour to improve himself.

Also Bro. Brown & Bro. Hitchman.

Qu. 5th Are any proposed to come on the plan as exhorters?

Ansr Brethn Simpson and Brooks of Abingdon. also Bro. Saunders and Br. Towle. Also Bro. Wait as a candidate and Sumner if approved.

Qu. 6th Are any proposed to go out occasionally by permission of a note from the Superintendent?

Ansr Bro. King.[1]

Qu. 7th Shall any alteration be made with reference to any of the places?

Ansr Hincksey shall be taken off the plan for the present?

Qu. 8th Are any new places proposed?

Ansr Cothill to be annexed to Marcham 2 o'clock the former & 5 the latter.[2] Also Clifton at 5 p.m.

1833 Jany 2nd Chapel Vestry.[3] Alfred Barrett Secy.

3 April 1833

April 3rd 1833

Present Revd Messrs Adams & Barrett, also Messrs Bartlett, Brown, Leggatt, Ostler, Scarsbrook, Cheney, Smith, Hitchman, Simpson, Mobley, Sumner, Waite and Birmingham.

Qu. 1st Are there any objections to any of the Preachers?

Bro. Church omitted Headn Quarry without any substantial reason and is therefore answerable. Bro. Henry Brown neglected Wooton and another place, in consequence of which & of his stated inability to walk long journeys Bro. Bartlett moved & Bro. Ostler seconded that the question of his further continuance as a Local Preacher be referred to the discretion of Mr Adams.

N.B. Mr Adams subsequently intimated that it would be advisable to withdraw Bro. Henry Brown's name for the present.

Moved also that Bro. J. Towle's name be discontinued on the plan at present, his temporal occupation requiring him to be much from home.

Questn 2 Are there any bretheren to be received in full connexion? Ansr None.

3rd Are any bretheren to be received on Trial? Ansr None.

---

1   George King (1809–58), cordwainer, of Oxford.

2   So that the preacher appointed for Marcham at 5 p.m. could preach at the neighbouring hamlet of Cothill at 2 p.m.

3   Probably the vestry of the New Inn Hall Street chapel: see the entry for 1 January 1834.

4th Shall any young men be received on the plan as exhorters?

Bro. Wait and Sumner are eligible but they have not been heard – their reception therefore for the present deferred.

Bro. Henry Leake[1] of Iffley & Bro. Robins[2] of Abingdon shall be admitted as candidates by initial letter.[3]

5th Are any alterations to be made in any of the places?

The time of preaching at Harwell shall now be 6 o'clock. And at Bladon 6 o'clock. And at Beckley 6 o'clock.[4]

6th Are any new places to be taken in?

Ansr We will endeavour if possible to obtain footing in Kidlington.

2 July 1833

Oxford July 2nd 1833

Present Revd Messrs Adams & Barrett also Messrs Ostler, Bartlett, Cheney, Leggatt, Martin, Brown, Hitchman, Scarsbrook, Greenhill, Smith, Birmingham, Robins, Simpson, Sumner, Harper & Crapper.

Quest 1st Are there any objections to any of the bretheren?

Ansr Bro. Pearson om[itte]d Clifton 2d June & as far as we know without reason.

Bro. Henry Brown shall be discontinued from the plan henceforward – his name has been on ~~the~~ for the last quarter at his own request.

Bro. Meek having left the society is now no longer of course a local Preacher.

Questn 2 Are any bretheren to be received into full connexion?

Ansr None.

Questn 3 Are any bretheren to be received on Trial?

Ansr One. Bro. Simpson of Shippon his reception moved by Mr Barrett & seconded by Mr Ostler.

Questn 4 Are any to be received on the plan as exhorters?

Ansr Bro. Sumner of Forest Hill.

   Bro Waite, Headington Quarry.

Bro. Leake wishes at present to remain as he is, having only his initial letter upon the plan.

Questn 5th Shall any be received as Candidates?

---

1   Henry Leake (1809–86), gentleman, of Iffley.

2   Shadrach Rob[b]ins (1812–72), cordwainer, of Abingdon. Robins was a member of the Abingdon society in 1832 and had moved into the city by 1841: OHC, OMCA, NM5/A/A2/1, Oxford Circuit Book, 1825–36 and 1841 Census.

3   i.e., to appear in the list of preachers on the plan indicated by a letter only, rather than full name.

4   It was customary to make evening services later in the summer months. Given the Wesleyans' commitment to Sabbatarianism, demonstrated in the Meek case, this was presumably not a reflection of a longer working day, but of enabling preachers and congregations to take advantage of lighter evenings to travel to the services.

Ansr Bro. King who meets in Mr Evans' class.[1]
Questn 6th Are any alterations to be made in any place upon the plan?
Clifton for the present shall be discontinued.
Quest. 7th Shall any new places be taken upon the plan?
Ansr Kidlington at 6 ½ in the evening and Marston at 6 in the evening.
Alfred Barrett Sec[y].

2 October 1833

Oct 2nd 1833 Chapel Vestry
Present the Revd Messrs Adams and Barrett, also Messrs Ostler, Goodman, Cheney,
Leake, King, Smith, Waite, Simpson, Scarsbrook, Greenhill, Bartlett.
Qu 1st Are there any objections made to any of the bretheren?
Ansr None. They were examined one by one.[2]
Qu. 2nd Who are to be received into full connexion as local preachers?
Ansr Bro. Church, he having fulfilled the various conditional requirements.
Questn 3 Are any bretheren to be received on Trial?
Ansr None to be received on trial.
Questn 4th Are any bretheren to be received as exhorters?
Ansr Henry Leake of Iffley
    George King Oxford
Questn 5th Are any to be received as Candidates?
Ansr James Roberts provided his circumstances as an apprentice will allow of it.
Questn Shall any alteration be made with respect to places or times of services?
Ansr The evening service at Steventon shall now commence at 5 ½ o'clock.
    That at Beckley at 5 o'clock.
    Preaching at <u>Kidlington</u>, <u>Cothill</u> and <u>Marston</u> shall be discontinued until more
eligible places can be found.
Signed on behalf of the Meeting

Alfred Barrett Sec[y].

1 January 1834

~~Dec 31st~~ Jan 1st 1834
Present Revd Messrs Adams and Barrett also Messrs Brown, Leggatt, Greenhill,
Bartlett, Goodman, Crapper, Smith, Waite, Birmingham, Scarsbrook, King, Mobley,
Hitchman, Sumner, Simpson, Robins, Cheney, Ostler, Church
Questn 1st Are there any objections to any of the bretheren?

---

1   Daniel Evans (c. 1769–1846), who was leading two classes in Oxford by 1826: OHC,
OMCA, NM5/A/A2/1, Oxford Circuit Book, 1825–36. Evans was the builder of the New Inn
Hall Street chapel: Brian Law, *Building Oxford's Heritage* (Stadhampton: Prelude Promotion,
1998), 29–41.
2   This inquiry into character paralleled the practice for Wesleyan ministers at the District
Meeting and the Conference.

Bro Bartlett neglected Headn Quarry but for a justifiable cause.

Bro Cheney answerable for neglecting Marcham.

Bro Mobley censurable for several neglects, insomuch that the Meeting deemed it doubtful whether or not[1] it was proper to continue his name upon the plan. On further consideration however it was determined to continue to Bro Mobley his privileges for another quarter by way of probation.

Bro Sumner neglected Bletchington, apparently without reason, therefore answerable.

Quest 3d Are any to be received on Trial?

Ansr Bro Waite & Bro Sumner

    Bro Bailey if approvd of by Mr Adams.

Questn 4th Are any to be received as exhorters?

Ansr Bro. Robins of Abingdon.

Questn 5th Are any to be received as candidates? None.

Questn 6th Is any alteration suggested in reference to places.

    Service shall be held at Drayton in the afternoon.

Resolved also that in case any brother shall neglect his appointment without assigning a justifiable reason, shall have his name put down one in the order in which it stands upon the plan.[2]

Chapel Vestry 1834 Jany 1st

New Inn Hall lane Alfred Barrett Secy.

3 April 1834

Apl 3rd 1834

Present Messrs Adams and Barrett Also Messrs Ostler, Greenhill, Church, Martin, Cheney, Smith, Waite, Hitchman, King, Sumner, Crapper, Leake, Simpson, Goodman, Scarsbrook, Leggatt, Bartlett & Brown.

Questn 1st Are there any objections to any of the bretheren?

Ansr None.

Questn 2nd Are any bretheren to be received into full connexion?

Ansr Bro Hitchman is eligible but requested to wait another quarter & in the mean time preach before a senior local preacher in order that the meeting may be made acquainted with the opinion of that brother as to Bro Hitchman's qualifications.

Questn 3rd Are any to be received on Trial?

Ansr Bro Leake & Bro King.

Questn 4th Are any to be received as exhorters?

Ansr Bro Roberts.

Questn 5th Are any to be received on the plan as candidates?

---

1   'or not' inserted.

2   Local Preachers were listed on the preaching plan in order of seniority. Demotion in the list was a very public humiliation.

Ansr Bro Prentiss & Bro Perry[1]

Questn Shall any alteration be made in reference to places?

Ansr Kirtlington shall commence 5 ½ eveng ser[vice].

Hampton Poyle shall be taken on trial service at 9 in the morning.

Alfred Barrett Secy.

2 July 1834

July 2nd 1834

Present Messrs Adams and Barrett

Also Messrs Ostler, Brown, Leggatt, Scarsbrook, Church, Simpson, Sumner, Crapper, Smith, Hitchman, Greenhill, Cheney, Leake, Roberts, King, Birmingham & Prentiss.

Questn 1st Are there any objections to any of the bretheren?

Ansr None.

Questn 2 Are any to be received into full connexion as Local Preachers?

Ansr None.

Questn 4th Are any to be rec'd as exhorters?

Ansr Bro Prentice.

Questn 5 Are any to be rec'd as Candidates?

Ansr None.

Questn 6 Shall there be any alteration in any of the places?

Tubney shall be annexed to Southmoor & service shall commence at 10 ½ in the morning.[2]

Alfred Barrett Secy

July 2nd 1834

Chapel Vestry New Inn Hall lane.

----

1 October 1834

Present Rev. Mr Adams in the chair, Peterson,[3] Ostler, Leggatt, Goodman, Crapper, Leake, Wait, Prentice, Cheney, Sumner, Simpson, Roberts, Church, King, Scarsbrook, Bartlett, Birmingham.

Ques 1 Are there any objections to any of the brethren?

1   Identified in January 1835 as 'of Harwell'. William Perry was a member at Harwell in 1832: OHC, OMCA, NM5/A/A2/1, Oxford Circuit Book, 1825–36.

2   The service at Southmoor, two and a half miles from Tubney, was at 2.30 p.m.

3   William Peterson (1810–99), junior minister in the Oxford Circuit, 1834–36; left the Wesleyan ministry in 1846 and was ordained in the Church of England: *Minutes of Conference* 1846, 315; *Leeds Mercury*, 8 August 1846, 8.

Ans. Bro. Cheney has not attended all his appointments. After considerable discussion, Bro. C. was advised to resign his place among us, unless he would promise to fulfil all his appointments. Accordingly he gave up his plan.[1]
Ques. 2 Are any to be received into full connexion as Local Preachers?
Ans. Brethn Hitchman & Simpson have fulfilled the conditions of admission but decline being received before the brethren whose names on the Local list stand above theirs.[2]
Ques. 3 Are any to be received on trial?
Ans. Brethn Roberts & Prentice.
Ques. 4 Are any to be received as Exhorters?
Ans Bro. Ray.[3]
Ques. 5 Are any alterations to be made in the places?
Ans. During the next plan let the service at Kidlington commence at 5 p.m. & at Bladon at 5 ½ p.m.
Ques. 6 Is there any place to be received?
Ans. Sandford shall have preaching during the next Plan – to commence at 5 p.m.
Oct 1/34 W. Peterson.
Chapel Vestry
New Inn Hall Lane

1 January 1835
Present Rev. J.H. Adams Chairman W. Peterson Bartlett Brown Leggatt Ostler Scarsbrook Crapper Church Louseley Smith Birmingham, Hitchman, Simpson, Sumner, Waite, Leake, King, Prentice, Ray.
Ques. 1 Are there any objections to any of the brethren?
Ans None.
Ques. 2 Are any to be received into full connexion as Local Preachers?
Ans Breth. Louseley, Birmingham, Hitchman, Simpson, Sumner & Waite were examined & it was resolved that the Breth. Louseley, Hitchman, Simpson, Sumner be received & that the Breth. Birmingham & Waite be continued on trial.
Ques. 3 Are any to be received on trial?
Ans. Breth. Roberts & Prentice.
Ques. 4 Are any to be received as Exhorters?
Ans. Bro. Perry of Harwell.
Ques. 5 Are any alterations to be made in any of the places?

---

1   i.e., resigned as a Local Preacher. A preacher transferring to another circuit would be expected to produce a preaching plan as evidence of being an accredited Local Preacher, so to 'give up the plan' meant to resign.
2   On the extant preaching plan for November 1834 to February 1835 Lousley, Smith and Birmingham were senior to Hitchman and Simpson in the list of preachers on trial.
3   William Ray (1814–84), schoolmaster, of Rose Hill.

Ans. Let the Evening service during the next plan commence at 5 o'clock at Steventon & at 5 ½ at Bletchington.

Note:- At this Meeting a letter from Mr Cheney was read requesting to be employed on the next plan as a Local Preacher & also intimating his ability to fulfil all his appointments. After mature ~~debil~~ deliberation it was resolved that his request be complied with & that his name be the last on the list of the Local Preachers in full connexion.

Chapel Vestry Jan 1/35 W. Peterson.

1 April 1835

Chapel Vestry April 1/35

Present Mr Adams in the chair~~man~~ also the Brethren Peterson, Brown, Leggatt, Ostler, Martin, Greenhill, Church, Scarsbrook, Crapper, Goodman, King, Hitchman, Simpson, Smith, Perry, Birmingham, Waite, Leake, ~~King~~, Ray, Prentice.

1. Are there any objections to any of the brethren?
Ans. None.

Ques. 2 Are there any to be received into full connexion as Local Preachers?
Ans. Brethn Leake & King were examined & received. After some conversation about Brethn Birmingham & Waite it was resolved that they be continued on trial ~~another~~ for the present.

Qu. 3 Are any to be received on trial?
Ans. Bro. Ray.

Qu. 4 [Are any to be received][1] as Exhorters?
Ans. Mr Embling, who is to have but few appointments at present because of the delicacy of his health.[2]

Qu. 5 Are there any <u>new</u> places to be put on the plan?
Ans. Horsepath, to have preaching at 6 p.m.

Qu. 6 What alterations are to be made in the time of preaching?
Ans. On the next plan let the evening service begin at 5 ½ at Kirtlington and Sandford.

NB. At this meeting it was stated that Mr Cheney sent in his Plan a few days before his first appointment on it became due. It was also stated that he now regretted having done so; & it was suggested that he be employed on the next plan, but this the meeting rejected. It was also moved & supported by Brethn Leggatt & Crapper & adopted unanimously that Bro. Ostler on account of his seniority as a preacher should on the next Plan be No. 1.[3]

Chapel Vestry
April 1/35

W. Peterson.

---

1 Indicated in original by a line.
2 Embling does not appear on the 1839 plan.
3 Ostler stands at number 4 on the 1834–35 plan, after Bartlett, Brown and Leggatt.

1 July 1835

Minutes of a Local Preachers' Meeting for the Oxford Circuit Chapel Vestry July 1/35

Present Messrs Adams, Peterson, Ostler, Bartlett, Crapper.

Qu. 1 Are there any objections to any of the brethren? Ans. None.

Quest. 2 Are there any to be received into full connexion as Local Preachers?

Ans. Bro. Birmingham and Bro. Wait to be placed next to Bro. Sumner.

Ques. 3 Are there any to be received on trial?

Ans. Bro. Perry.

Ques. 4 [Are there any][1] to be received from other circuits?

Ans. Bro. Tidmas [*conj.*] of Bletchington, who comes accredited from the Brackley Circuit.[2]

Ques. 5 What alterations are to be made ~~during~~ on the next plan?

Let Coombe have two services every Sunday, to commence at 2 & 5.[3] Let the evening service at Kirtlington also begin at 5 & that at Bletchington at 5 ½.

William Peterson.

30 September 1835

Minutes of a Local Preachers' Meeting of the Oxford Circuit held in the Chapel Vestry Sep 30/35. Rev. S. Hope[4] in the chair.

Present

Ques. 1 Are there any objections to any of the brethren? Ans. None.

Ques. 2 Who has died since the last meeting?

Ans. Bro. Wait who died in peace.

Ques. 3 Who is to be received on trial? Bro. Harper who has returned from America.

Ques. 4 Who are to be received as Exhorters?

Ans. Bro. Danbury,[5] who shall accompany Brethn Ostler, Leggatt & Bartlett to some of their appointments, & Bro. Harris who shall go with Brethn Ostler & Crapper & Bartlett.[6]

Ques. 5 What alterations are to be made in the times of the services?

---

1   Indicated in original by a line.

2   Perhaps Richard Tidmas, baker, of Bletchingdon. In 1833 he married at Ambrosden and was then living at Arncot, a preaching place on the Brackley Wesleyan Circuit.

3   Membership at Combe fluctuated considerably in the 1820s and early 1830s and over the winter of 1834–35 Combe had services on Sunday afternoons, alternating with the neighbouring hamlet of East End. However a chapel was opened in the village in 1835, perhaps indicating greater stability and justifying the increase in provision: OHC, OMCA, NM5/A/A2/1, Oxford Circuit Book, 1825–36 and Tiller, *Church and Chapel in Oxfordshire*, 65.

4   Samuel Hope (1784–1847), Superintendent of the Oxford Circuit, 1835–37: *Minutes of Conference* 1848, 6–7.

5   John Danbury (1811–99), stonemason, of Bladon.

6   '& Bartlett' added in pencil.

Ans. Let the services at Coombe commence at 2 & 5 – Bladon at 2 & 5 ½ - Kirtlington at 2 & 5 – Iffley 2 ½ & 6 – Horsepath at 5.
Chapel Vestry,
New Inn Hall Lane William Peterson.

30 December 1835

Minutes of a Local Preachers' Meeting for the Oxford Circuit held Dec 30/35.
Rev. S. Hope in the chair.
Present W. Peterson, Ostler, Bartlett, Leggatt, Scarsbrook, Goodman, Crapper, Hitchman, Simpson, Birmingham, Leake, Prentice, Ray & Harper.
Question 1 Are there any objections to any of the brethren? Ans. None.
Ques. 2 Are there any to be received on trial? Ans. Bro. Perry of Harwell.
NB. Bro. Harper declined having his name continued on the Plan as his is not health is not sufficiently vigorous to sustain the fatigues of a Local Preachers work.
3. Who is to be received into full connexion as Local Preachers? Ans. Bro. Prentice has been the usual time on trial but he declines being examined at present, not having read the requisite works.
4. Who are to receive notes? Bro. Bolton to go with Bro. Ostler & Bro. Henry Huggins[1] of Blewbury to go with Bro. Martin. Harris and Danbury as before.
5. What Alterations shall be made on the next Plan in respect of the places?
Ans. Let Littleworth be given up. Let Wootton be inserted on the plan, for one service, alternately 10 ½ & 2.
Mem. It is very desirable the brethren be so planned that they be not obliged to come home alone e.g. Let Oxford Preachers be planned the same day at Marcham and S. Moor.[2]
Chapel Vestry William Peterson.

30 March 1836

Minutes of a Local Preachers' Meeting of the Oxford Circuit held March 30 1836
Rev. Samuel Hope in the chair.
Present Will. Peterson Ostler, Bartlett, Leggatt, Martin, Scaresbrook, Goodman, Crapper, Hitchman, Simpson, Birmingham, Leake, King, Prentice, Ray, Perry.
Question 1 Are there any objections to any of the brethren? Ans. None.
Question 2 Who are to be fully received as Local Preachers?
Ans. Brethn Prentice & Ray. Also Bro. Meek to have his name succeed the last of the Preachers residing in the Oxford Circuit.
Ques. 3 Who are to be fully received on Trial?
Ans. Bro. Danbury of Bladon. Also Brethn Bolton & Osborne but without having their names on the plan – each of them to be occasionally planned with a preacher.
Ques. 4 Who are to have notes? Ans. Bro. Huggins to go with Bro. Martin.

---

1   Henry Seth Huggins (1812–1901), blacksmith, of Blewbury.
2   Marcham and Southmoor each had an afternoon service at 2.30 p.m., allowing preachers returning to Oxford to meet on the way back.

Ques. 5 What alterations are to be made in the Times and Places?
Ans. Let the Evening service begin at Steventon at 5 ½ & let Drayton & Steventon & Steventon & Harwell be planned together & also Wootton Berks & Marcham when convenient.[1]
Chapel Vestry William Peterson

29 June 1836

June 29/36
Chapel Vestry
Present Rev. S. Hope, W. Peterson, Ostler, Bartlett, Leggatt, Greenhill, Scarsbrook, Goodman, Crapper, Simpson, Hitchman, Birmingham, Leake, Prentice, Ray, Perry, Danbury.
Question 1 Are there any objections to any of the brethren? Ans. None.
Ques. 2 Do any of the brethren retire from the work?
Ans. Bro. King voluntarily retires from the work & from society.
Ques. 3 Are any to be received on trial?
Ans. Bro. Bolton & Bro. Osborne.
Ques. 4 [Are any][2] to receive Notes?
Ans. James Osborne of Charlton[3] on condition of his meeting in class – to be planned at Kirtlington, Bletchington, Forest Hill & Wheatley.[4] Also Daniel Young[5] Junr & William Wheeler of Hampton Poyle.[6] Harry Huggins note to [be] removed.
Ques. 5 What alterations are to be made on the next Plan in reference to the Places?
Horsepath to be at 6. Shippon to be planned seperately. Wheatley to have preaching at 5 ½. William Peterson.

28 September 1836

Minutes of Local Preachers' Meeting Septr 28 1836
Present Rev. S. Hope – Bird,[7] Ostler, Bartlett, Leggatt, Martin, Scarsbrook, Goodman, Crapper, Church, Hitchman, Simpson, Birmingham, Meek, Prentice, Ray, Perry, Harris, Bolton, Osborne, Robins.
Ques. No. 1 Are there any objections to any of the Local Preachers?

---

1   Drayton had afternoon services, Harwell evening services, and Steventon both afternoon and evening services on the 1834–35 Plan.
2   Indicated in original by a line.
3   In the 1841 Census two James Osborns are listed at Charlton; both were farmers.
4   All relatively close to Charlton-on-Otmoor.
5   Possibly Daniel Young (1816–45), cabinet maker, of Oxford. See below, September 1840.
6   William Wheeler (1806–83), agricultural labourer, of Hampton Poyle.
7   William Bird, junior minister in the Oxford Circuit, 1836–37. Two William Birds are listed in the *Minutes of Conference* 1836, with William junior stationed in Oxford. In 1837 the younger William retired from the ministry 'for want of health': *Minutes of Conference* 1837, 141. The announcement of his death in the *Wesleyan Methodist Magazine* attributed his demise to a cold caught in Oxford in the severe winter of 1836–37: 'Recent Deaths', *WMM*, November 1837, 877.

Ans 1 Bro. Tidmas neglected Coombe on Sep. 25th.

2 Bro. Danbury having fallen into gross immorality is unanimously expelled.[1]

Ques. 2 Who is to be received on the plan.

Ans. Not any.

Ques. 3 Who is to be continued on trial by note. Ans. Bro. Osborne, Young, Wheeler, Huggins.

Ques. 4 Any to be received on Trial?

Ans 1 Bro Banbury[2] from Witney.

2 Bro Barratt Bro Stone[3]

Ques. 5 Any alteration to be made in the places?

Ans Coome to have preaching at 5 ½ o'clock.

W. Bird.

29 December 1836

Local Preacher's Minutes Dec. 29/36

Present Rev. S. Hope – Bird Ostler Brown Meek Allen Ray Robins Osborne Banbury Bolton Greenhill Leggatt Birmingham Young

Ques. 1 Are there any objections to any of the preachers?

Ans. That Bro Osborne be requested to meet in class.

Ques. 2 Any of the Brethren to be fully received on the Plan?

Ans None.

Ques. 3 Are any to be received on Trial?

Ans: Bro Barratt Bro Young

Ques. 4 Are any to be continued by Note?

Ans Bro Wheeler Bro Huggins

Ques. 5 Are any to receive notes?

Ans Bro Nutt[4] Bro Golding[5]

Ques. 6 Is there any alteration to be made in the Places?

Ans 1 Give up preaching at Wooton[6]

2 Put Marcham & Tubney together.

3. Resolved that there be preaching at Southmoor in the evening.

1   John Danbury married Selena Sumner at Bicester in August 1836 and their eldest son Ziba was born in November 1836, suggesting that the 'gross immorality' involved a pre-marital pregnancy.

2   Gabriel George Banbury (1815–1911), tailor, of Woodstock.

3   John Stone (1805–87), carrier, of Kingston Bagpuize. Stone appears on the Wantage Circuit plans for 1840 and 1847.

4   Joseph Nutt (1800–69), mason, of Iffley [conj.]. His daughter Mary Ann was baptised at New Inn Hall Street in May 1838 and he was a trustee of the Rose Hill chapel.

5   William Golding (or Goulding) (1805–95), gardener, of Steventon. Goulding appears on the 1840 and 1847 Wantage plans. For a biography, see Elizabeth Stuart-Langford, 'A Dweller among his own People', MR Winter Number 1901, 96–100. I am very grateful to Dr Peter Forsaith for supplying a copy of this article.

6   Wootton (Berkshire), rather than Wootton by Woodstock.

4. That there be preaching at Bletchington in the Evening.
5. That Littleworth & Wheatley be connected.
Willm Bird.

29 March 1837

Local Preachers' Meeting Mar 29/37
Present Bros Ostler, Leggatt, Goodgame, Ray, Simpson, Church, Tidmans, Young, Robins, Banbury, Harris, Hitchman, Smith, Birmingham, Barratt – Rev. S. Hope – Bird.
Ques. 1 Are there any objections to any of the preachers? Ans. None.
Ques. 2 Any to be received on Trial.
Ans. Bro. Wheeler.
(N.B. Bro. Huggins remain as before).
Ques. 3 Any to receive Notes of permission.
Ans. Zeph Grace.[1]
Ques. 4 Any person to be admitted in full
Ans. Bro. Cheyney.
Ques. 5 Any alteration in places.
1. That Harwell have preaching in the Evening at 6 ½ o'clock.
2. That Agburn W. [West Hagbourne [conj.]] have service at 9 ½ and Drayton at 2 ½ o'clock
3. That Wooton preaching be at 5 ½ o'clock.
4 That Littleworth have preaching at 3 ½ o'clock.
5 That Islip have preaching at 2 ½ o'clock and Ham. Poyle at 6 o'clock.
Oxon. March 29/37 Willm Bird.

28 June 1837

Local Preachers' Meeting 28 June 1837
Present
Saml Hope Chairman

Ostler	Leggatt	Greenhill
Bartlett	Martin	Simpson
Birmingham	Meek	Prentice
Ray	Perry	Harris
D. Young	Huggins	Allen
Scarisbrook	Crapper	Stone

Ques. 1 Are there any objections to any of the Brethren?
Ans To Bro Church for having neglected Wootton on the 21st May and Steventon on the 11th June. He is also objected to for not having regularly met in Class during the Quarter

---

1   Zephaniah Grace (1813–1901), shepherd, of Blewbury.

To Bro Cheney for having neglected Horsepath on the 25 June.

Ques. 2 Are there any Preachers to be received upon the Plan?

Ans None

Ques. 3 Are there any to be received on Trial?

Ans None

Ques. 4 Are there any to receive notes?

Ans Bro H. Huggins and Bro Grace to continue with a Note another Quarter.

 Br. W Goulding Steventon on Note

 Br. Etchells[1] Abingdon on Do

 Br W. Mitford[2] Oxford on Do

 Br W. Bateman Headn Quarry Do.

 Br. J Davies[3] Cowley

 Br. Ben^n Watkins[4] Oxford

Ques. 5 Any alterations in the Plan?

Ans Drayton at 2 o'clock instead of ½ past 2

 Sandford to be taken off the Plan

 Littleworth at 3 instead of ½ p 3

Ques. 6 Are there any new Places to be taken on the Plan?

Ans Murcott at 2 o'clock in connexion with Charlton.

 Saml Hope Chairman.

27 September 1837

Local Preachers' Meeting Sept 27th 1837

Present – Rev. C. Cooke[5] – Jos^h Heaton[6] – Bro^s Ostler – Brown – Leggatt – Greenhill – Crapper – Church – Hitchman – Birmingham – Tidmus – Prentice – Ray – Robbins – Harris – Young – Wheeler

Ques 1 Are there any objections to any of the Brethren?

---

1 James Etchells was Superintendent of the Chipping Norton Circuit, 1836–38, and his son, also James, married there in 1839. It is possible that this reference is to the younger James Etchells (1815–54).

2 William Mitford, or Midford (1807–68), whitesmith, of Oxford.

3 James Davis (1811–56), labourer, and then tea dealer, of Cowley [*conj.*].

4 Benjamin Watkins (1816–44), schoolmaster, of Oxford. Watkins entered the Wesleyan ministry, was sent to West Africa, and died a year after arriving in the Gold Coast: *Minutes of Conference* 1844, 18. Watkins' nomination as a candidate, signed by Thomas Rogers, was recorded in the Oxford District Meeting minutes for May 1840: JRULM, MARC, D223.3, Oxford District Meeting 1832–42.

5 Corbett Cooke (1787–1866), Superintendent of the Oxford Circuit, 1837–39. In addition to the obituary in *Minutes of Conference* 1866, 451–2, see also the brief account of Cooke's ministry in Oxford in [M.A. Cooke,] *The Upright Man; A Memorial Volume of the Rev. Corbett Cooke, Wesleyan Minister* (London: Conference Office and Guernsey: E. Le Lievre, 1868), 51–4.

6 Joseph Heaton (1813–92), junior minister in the Oxford Circuit, 1837–38: *Minutes of Conference* 1892, 32–3.

Bro[r] Cheney objected to for neglecting his appointments. Resolved that his name be left off the plan.

Ques 2 What Preachers on Trial are to be received on the regular Local Preachers Plan?

Brothers Robins and Harris.

Ques 3 Are any proposed for exhorters? None.

Ques. 4 Are there any alterations to be made in the arrangements of the places on the plan or in the times of preaching?

Woodstock shall commence in the morning at 10 ½ o'clock.

Ques. 5 Are any new Places to be taken upon the Plan?

St Clement's Chapel 2 ½ and 6 o'clock

Garsington 9 ½

Resolution – that a Committee consisting of Rev. C Cooke – Bros Ostler - Prentice and Bolton, be appointed to procure suitable conveyance for the Preachers when appointed to the Country places.

Joseph Heaton.

27 December 1837

Local Preachers' Meeting Dec 27 1837

Present Rev. C. Cooke – Josh Heaton – Bros Bartlett – Brown – Greenhill – Crapper – Leake – Robins – Harris – Bolton – Young – Davis – Watkins

Ques 1 Are there any objections to any of the Brethren? None.

[Ques] 2 What Brethren on Trial are to be received ~~on the~~ as regular Local Preachers. NB Br. Thomas Jones from the York Circuit to be received on Trial.[1]

[Ques] 3 What Exhorters are to be received on Trial?

Bros Mitford – Davis – Watkins

4 Are any proposed to be received on Trial? None.

5 Are there any alterations to be made in the arrangement of the Places on the plan or in the time of preaching?

Preaching at Islip 2 ½ and 5

    at Hampton 6 & Garsington 5 ½

Resolved that the following Persons be appointed as a Committee to solicit subscriptions for the purchase of books for ~~the~~ a Local Preachers' Library – The Travelling Preachers – Bros Ostler, Leake, Bolton, Bartlett, Crapper.

Jos[h] Heaton.

28 March 1838

Local Preachers' Meeting ~~Ð~~March 28th 1838

Present – Rev. C. Cooke – J. Heaton – Bros Ostler, Brown, Leggatt, Crapper, Hitchman, Birmingham, Leake, Robins, Harris, Banbury, Young, Jones, Davis, Watkins, Bateman, Mitford.

---

1   Thomas Jones (1816–? before 1891), farming at Islip by 1851.

Ques 1 Are there any objections to any of the Brethren – as to their moral and Religious character – their Belief of our Doctrines - Their attention to Discipline – Their ability for our work?

The Brethren regret that Oxford and Wheatley have been neglected by Bros Scarsbrook and Young staying from their appointments to hear Anniversary sermons[1] and hope that this will, for the future, be avoided.

2. What Brethren on Trial are to be received on the regular Local Preachers' Plan? None.

Quest 3 What Exhorters are to be received on Trial? None.

4 Are any Brethren to be proposed as Exhorters?

Br Thomas Smith to have a note on trial – also Br. Benj[n] Leonard (Coombe)[2] – also Rich[d] Hadland – (Horsepath).[3]

5 Are there any alterations to be made in the arrangement of the places on the plan or in the times of Preaching?

Kirtlington 5 ½

6 Where can we have Open Air Preaching?

St Clements at 2 o'clock

Jericho 9 once a fortnight

Stanton St Johns 2 ½ do - with Forest Hill

Kidlington to be joined with Hampton

Headington 9 ½ ~~Barton~~ Beckley

Wheatley 6

Jos[h] Heaton.

27 June 1838

Local Preachers' Meeting June 27th 1838

Present Rev. C. Cooke – J. Heaton – Ostler – Bartlett – Greenhill – Scarsbrook – Ray – Birmingham – Smith – Robins – Crapper – Watkins – Harris – Davis – Bateman – Bolton

Quest. 1 Are there any objections to any of the Brethren?

Br. Leggatt having neglected his appointment at Coombe Mr Cooke is requested to see him concerning it, and if he will not promise to take his appointments for the future, it is resolved that his name be left off the plan.

It is resolved that on account of the peculiar circumstances of Br. Barrett, his name be left off the plan.[4]

---

1   Chapel and Sunday School anniversary sermons, and the annual sermons for the Missionary Society, were significant events, drawing large congregations to hear invited celebrity preachers.

2   Benjamin Leonard (1813–80), schoolmaster.

3   Richard Hadland (1817–?).

4   Barratt does not appear on the 1839 plan. No further information is offered to explain the 'peculiar circumstances'.

Brother Young's competency for the work being questioned, it is resolved that Brs Ostler, Greenhill, Scarsbrook be appointed to hear him preach and to give their report next Quarterly Meeting.

Ques. 2 What Brethren on Trial are to be admitted on the regular Local Preachers' Plan? None.

Ques. 3 What Exhorters are to be received on Trial? None.

Ques. 4 Are any proposed to be admitted as Exhorters?

Br Hadland to have his note renewed but must preach <u>only</u> where Mr Cooke shall appoint.[1]

Ques. 5 What changes are to be made in the times of preaching and what new places are to be put on the plan?

Bletchington to be joined to Hampton.

That Br Birmingham be requested to engage a house at Wheatley for preaching.

Jos. Heaton.

26 September 1838

Local Preachers Meeting ~~June~~ Sept[r] 26th 1838

Present Rev[d] C. Cooke – Nightingale[2] – Ostler – Brown – Scarsbrook – Hitchman – Ray – Harris – Bateman – Watkins – Birmingham – Davis – Church – Prentice – Robins – Jones – Crapper

Ques. Are there any objections to any of the Brethren with reference to moral character, ability to preach, attention to discipline.

Enquiry to be made into the reason why Bro[r] Leggatt did not go to Coombe last Sabbath.

Bror Young's incompetency still being questioned, Bro. Nightingale is to have some conversation with him and Bros Crapper, Scarsbrook and Bartlett hear him preach.

The Brethren who have been on trial a year or longer be enjoined to read Mr Wesley's Sermons & Notes and be prepared for examination the next Local Preachers Meeting.

Bror Fathers[3] at Islip have a note on trial from Mr Cooke.

St Clements preaching at ½ 2.

Coombe 5 o'clock.

Kirtlington two & five

Wheatley 5 o'clock.

---

1   Suggesting that Hadland was accepting invitations to preach beyond the appointments assigned by the Superintendent.

2   Thomas Nightingale (1814–90), junior minister in the Oxford Circuit, 1838–39: *Minutes of Conference* 1890, 19–20.

3   Richard Fathers (1810–after 1873), stonemason.

26 December 1838

Local Preachers' Meeting Dec 26th 1838

Bros Cooke, Nightingale, Ostler, Brown, Greenhill, Leggatt, Ray, Crapper, Smith, Prentice, Watkins, Bolton, Young, Hitchman, Harris, Banbury, Birmingham, Bateman, Scarsbrooke, Leake, Bartlett.

Are there any obj[ns] to any of the Brethren?

Mr Cooke with Bros Ostler, Brown and Bartlett go to Woodstock on Friday Dec 28th to inquire into Bro. Meek's case.

Bro[r] Young preach on Monday 31st Dec 1838 at 6 o'clock.[1]

Bro[r] Bateman be received on trial.

Bro[r] Osborne [conj.] be received on the plan.

Are there any persons to be proposed as Local Preachers or on trial.

Bro[r] Lewis be received as an exhorter.

Bros Smith[2] & Banbury be received on the full plan.

Bro. Young be continued on trial another quarter, & several of the brethren be required to hear him.

Iffley ½ past ten.

Lower Wolvercott be received on the plan – to have preaching on Sunday Evening.[3]

27 March 1839

Local Preachers' Meeting March 27th

Present Messrs Cooke, Nightingale, Ostler, Bartlett, Brown, Scarsbrook, Church, Hitchman, Birmingham, Leake, Ray, Robins, Harris, Banbury, Jones, Davis, Watkins, Lewis.

Are there in any objns to any of ye Brethren in reference to moral & religious character, their punctuality in attending their appointments, doctrine – discipline – orthodoxy

That Bro[r] Young be censured for neglecting his appointments & continue on trial another quarter. *

That it is the opinion of this meeting that Bro[r] Bateman's name be ~~suspen~~ dropped from ye plan on account of want of health.

That ye Report of the Committee appointed to meet at Woodstock be received.

* Bro Young stated that it was thro' indisposition that he neglected Bladon.

That the case of Bros Meek & Leggat be referred to Mr Cooke.

Any proposed on trial.

Bro. Danbury have a note on trial –

Littleworth & Forest Hill be put together

Lower Woolvercott be put off the plan

Preaching at Bletchington at ½ 2 o'clock on Sunday.

---

1   Presumably a trial service, before experienced preachers, to test his competence.

2   This is John Smith, listed at 18 on the Jan–April 1839 plan, one place above G.G. Banbury.

3   Lower Wolvercote is listed on the Jan–April 1839 plan, with a service at 6 p.m. The next meeting resolved to discontinue this experiment.

? June 1839

Midsummer Local Preachers Meetg
Present Messrs Cooke Nightingale Smith Crapper Bartlett Hitchman Greenhill
Scaresbrook Young Harris Jones Ray Robins Lewis Banbury Leggatt Davis Watkins
Birmingham Church
1. Any objections to any of the Brethren on the usual points.
I. Res. that Mr Cooke see Bror Prentice before he makes the next plan and ask him
if he will take his appointments & if not, his name be dropped from the plan.
2. Are there any now to be received on the plan
II Res. that Bror Young be received on the Plan.
III Res. That Bror Leggatt be again received on the Plan, & according to the Rule
his name be put at the bottom of the Plan.[1]
IV Res. That Bro[r] Lewis be received on trial.
V Resn That Bro[r] Lindars[2] be received as an exhorter.
Any alterations in the places
Rs. VI Littlemore and Cowley have outdoor preaching alternately on Sunday
afternoon at 4 o'clock.
Rs VII Out door preaching at Old Woodstock every other Sunday aftern.
Res. IX That Brother Davis and Bro[r] Watkins be received on the plan.
X Meeting at St Clements on 14th July.[3]

9 October 1839

Minutes of Local Preachers Meeting Octr 9 [*conj.*] 1839
Present Revd Thomas Rogers[4] Chairman. T. Thompson,[5] Ostler, Brown, Smith,
Crapper, Hitchman, Scarisbrooke, Harris, Jones, Ray, Robins, Lewis, Watkins,
Birmingham, Leake & Prentice.
Question 1 Are there any objections to any of the Brethren?
1) Enquiry was made if Res 1 of the last Meeting had been complied with in
reference to Bro Prentice when it was found that domestic affliction was the cause
of the neglect complained of. Bro Prentice then stated that he thought it his duty
owing to the presence of severe domestic affliction to resign his office as a local
preacher, which resignation was accepted.
2) Resolved that the Brethren Bolton & Wheeler, having been on trial more than
the ordinary term, but not having submitted to an examination, be written to,
requesting them to attend the next local preachers meeting for that purpose.

1   Loss of seniority, in consequence of failure to fulfil appointments.
2   James Lindars (1811–?), saddler and harness maker, of Oxford [*conj.*].
3   No explanation was given of the purpose of this meeting or of its outcome.
4   Thomas Rogers (1778–1864), Superintendent of the Oxford Circuit, 1839–41: *Minutes of Conference* 1864, 18–19.
5   Thomas Thompson (1810–91), junior minister in the Oxford Circuit, 1839–41: *Minutes of Conference* 1891, 55.

3) Resolved that Bro Jones be requested to read Mr Wesley's Sermons[1] & prepare for his examination before the next local preachers Meeting.

Question 2 Are there any to be proposed to come on the plan this q[uarte]r?

1) Resolved that Bro Ths Smith do come on the plan as an Exhorter & that Mr Rogers be requested to see him on the subject.

2) That Bro Henry Smith[2] be received on trial on the plan.

Question 3 Are there any alterations to be made in any of the places?

1) Resolved that the preaching at St Clements be changed from 2 ½ to 10 ½.

T.T. Secretary.

6 January 1840

Minutes of Local Preachers Meeting Jany 6 1840.

Present Revd Thos Rogers, Chairman. Messrs Thompson, Brown, Harris, Robins, Jones, Leggat, Young, Smith, Banbury, Bolton, Leake, Scarisbrooke, Crapper, Birmingham, Church, Watkins, Hitchman & Lindars.

I Have any remarks to be made upon the minutes of the last meeting?

Res. I Mr Rogers having seen Bror Thomas Smith & reported – it was resolved that in consequence of his engagements as Superintendent of the Sunday School he do not come on the plan at present.

II Are there any objections to any of the brethren?

Res. II That Bro Wheeler be written to expressing the regret of the Meeting at his absence, & that he be required to attend the next local preachers meeting, & submit to his examination, on pain of his name being left off the plan.

III Are there any to propose to come on the plan.

IV Are there any alterations to take place at any of the places?

Res III 1) That St Clements be changed from morning to afternoon
    2) That Forest Hill have only one service.

V Are any now on trial to be fully received?

Res IV That Bro Bolton and Bro Jones be received in full Connexion.

VI Are any to be received on trial from exhorters?

Res V Bro Lindars. T.T. Secretary.

4 April 1840

Minutes of Local Preachers Meeting April 4th 1840

Present Revd Thomas Rogers Chairman & Messrs Ostler, Bartlett, Brown, Scaresbrook, Crapper, Church, Hitchman, Birmingham, Ray, Robbins, Harris, Smith, Banbury, Leggett, Young, Davis, Watkins, Jones, Wheeler, Lewis, Lindars, & Hadland.

---

1   John Wesley's *Sermons on Several Occasions* (1746–60), with his *Notes on the New Testament*, formed the doctrinal standards of Wesleyan Methodism, and were required reading for Local Preachers.

2   Henry Smith (1814–?), labourer, of Bladon. Smith was a Wesleyan village missionary by 1841 and later an Independent minister.

1. Are there any objections to any of the Bretheren?
Res. I That Brother Birmingham be requested to begin his services punctually at the appointed time.
2. Are there to [be] any alterations in any of the places?
Res. II That there be only one service at Hampton, that in the evening.
Ques. 3 Are there any to be received on the plan?
Res. III Brothers Thomas Smith as exhorter, also that Bro William Shepperd be allowed to exhort in company with Brothers Ostler, Bartlett, & Crapper. And Bro. Jno Barrett in company with Brothers Leggett & Banbury.[1]
B. Watkins in the absence of the Rev[d] T. Thompson, Secretary.

? June 1840

Minutes of Local Preachers Meeting June 1840
Present Rev[d] T. Rogers in the Chair, Leake, Ray, Brown, J. Smith. Lindors, Jones, Scarsbrook, Lewis, Hitchman & Harris.
Ques. 1 Are there any objections to any of the Brethren?
Decided to take Bro <u>Church</u>'s name off the plan; he not fulfilling his appointments. Mr Rogers to inform him of this decision. Mr Rogers to expostulate with Bro <u>Robins</u> for neglecting his appointments. Bro <u>Osborne</u>'s name to be continued on the plan, but without any appointments. If Bro Tho[s] Smith's name was on a previous plan (at Banbury), to be ~~received~~ placed in the next <u>on trial</u>.[2]

? September 1840

Local Preachers Meeting Sep[r] 1840
Present Rev T. Rogers in the Chair. Messrs Thompson, John Smith, B. Watkins, Harris, Ostler, Lindars, Bailey, Lewis, Scarsbrook, Hitchman, Young, Jones.
Ques. 1 Are there any objections to any of the Brethren?
Bro <u>Robins</u> censured for neglecting his appointments, but on the ground of a promise to amend, his name to be continued.
Bro <u>Osborne</u>'s name to be continued, but no appointment as before.
Bro <u>Young</u> charged with trifling, carrying picture frames to an appointment on Sunday, & taking a young woman with him to his appointments, etc etc: reprimanded by the Meeting, tendered his resignation which was accepted.[3]
Ques 2 Are there any alterations in any of the places?

1   Perhaps John Barrett (1802–82), of Wootton, admitted as an exhorter in September 1849. Living in Wootton, Barrett would be well placed to travel with Leggatt and Banbury, both based in Woodstock.
2   As well as checking Smith's credentials, this raised the question of whether a fully accredited Local Preacher from one circuit should be accepted in another without further examination. This issue was not finally resolved until 1894 and recurs at intervals in the Oxford minutes.
3   John Wesley warned his Travelling Preachers to 'converse sparingly and cautiously with women, particularly with young women': '"The Twelve Rules of a Helper", 1753', in *The Constitutional Practice and Discipline of the Methodist Church* (London: Methodist Publishing

The preaching at Horspath at 2 ½ instead of 6 o'clock in future.

Ques 3 Any brethren on trial to be ~~received~~ fully received on the plan. None.

Ques 4 Any Exhorters to be received on trial? The two now on the plan, Hadland & Smith. Bro Bailey's name to be again placed on the plan.

Oc 5 1840[1]

T.T.

? December 1840

Minutes of Local Preachers Meeting Dec[r] 1840

Present Rev[d] T. Rogers Chairman. Messrs T. Thompson, Greenhill, Ray, Jones, Smith, Wheeler, Lindars, Hadland, T. Smith, H. Smith, Lewis, Banbury, Scarsbrooke, Ostler, T.G. Smith,[2] Robins, Davis, & Bailey, & Bartlet.

Ques 1 Are there any objections to any of the preachers?

Bro Leggat having neglected Coombe, Wooton & Kirtlington; resolved that he be admonished.

Ques 2. Are there any to be fully received?

Bro[s] Wheeler, H. Smith, & Lindars having been on trial the accustomed time but not having read the Notes & Sermons[3] resolved that they remain on trial another quarter; & that during that time they be required to read them.

Ques 3. Are any proposed to come on trial.

Killingworth [conj.] Hedges[4] is to have a note from the Superintendent, & to be heard by some of the local preachers. Mr Rogers to see Bro Prentice before next meeting respecting his coming on the plan again.

Ques 4. Are there any alterations in any of the places?

Horspath to be altered from 2 ½ to 6 o'clock.

Ques 5. Are there any new places to be taken on the plan?

Waterheaton.

Dec. 28 1840

T.T.

? March 1841

Minutes of Local Preachers Meeting March 1841

Present The Rev[d] Tho. Rogers in the Chair, Messrs Thompson, Ostler, Bartlet, John Smith, Watkins, Hitchman, Jones, Wheeler, Ray, H. Smith, Lewis, Harris, T.G. Smith, T. Smith, Scarsbrook.

House, 1988), 1, 77. In this and in mixing his secular employment with spiritual work, Young failed to demonstrate the moral seriousness expected of a Local Preacher.

1   It evidently took Thompson some time to write up the minutes.

2   Thomas George Smith (1809–92), bootmaker and leather cutter, of Oxford.

3   John Wesley's *Sermons on Several Occasions* and his *Explanatory Notes upon the New Testament*.

4   Killingworth Hedges (1811–58), glove cutter, of Wootton (Oxon.). Thompson struggled with the first name.

Ques. 1. Are there any objections to any of the Preachers?

1. That as Bro <u>Birmingham</u> is now residing beyond the limits of this Circuit, & has not taken his appointments recently; resolved: that he be written to by Mr Rogers informing him that on the <u>sole</u> <u>condition</u> of his taking some appointments his name be continued on the plan.

2. Mr <u>Leake</u> having sent in his resignation resolved: since it appears that Mr Leake is still willing to take some appointments at Iffley Mr Rogers be requested to see him & to inform him that <u>on</u> <u>condition</u> of his name remaining on the plan his request may be complied with.

3. Bro <u>Robins</u> having again neglected his appointments; resolved: that his name be <u>taken off the plan</u>.

4. Bro <u>Osborne</u> continuing in a very afflicted state, & there being no probability of his speedy recovery; resolved: that his name be taken off the plan.

Ques 2 Are there any bretheren to be fully received upon the plan?

Bro^s <u>Wheeler</u> & H. <u>Smith</u> having read the Notes & Sermons[1] & submitted to an examination; resolved unanimously that they be fully received on the plan. Bro <u>Lindars</u> not being present; resolved: that he be required to attend the next Local Preachers Meeting for examination. (This is understood to be conditional; depending on Bro Lindars more frequent attendance at Class.)

Ques 3. Are there any proposed to come on trial?

<u>John Clements</u> of Cha[r]lton,[2] as an Exhorter.

Ques 4. Are there any alterations in any of the places.

<u>Islip</u> from 5 ½ to 6 o'clock.

Ques 5. Are there any new places to be taken on the plan.

None.

T.T. Mar 29. 1841.

30 March 1842

Minutes of Local Preachers Meeting 30th March 1842[3]

Present The Revd M. Wilson[4] Chairman Messrs Willan,[5] Greenhill, Scarsbrook, Hitchman, Birmingham, Ray, Harris, Banbury, Leggatt, Davis, Jones, Sargent,[6] T.G. Smith, Bartlett, Brown, J. Smith, Wheeler.

---

1   John Wesley's *Sermons on Several Occasions* and his *Explanatory Notes upon the New Testament*.

2   John Clements (1818–43), shoemaker, of Charlton.

3   The next entry in the minute book after March 1841.

4   Maximilian Wilson (1777–1857), Superintendent of the Oxford Circuit, 1841–43: *Minutes of Conference* 1857, 405–6.

5   William Willan (1817–94), junior minister in the Oxford Circuit, 1842–43: *Minutes of Conference* 1894, 32–3, noting particularly the impact of his ministry in Oxford.

6   George Sargeant (1817–99), of Oxford. He entered the Wesleyan ministry in 1847: *Minutes of Conference* 1899, 36–7, and F. Rought Wilson, *Life of George Sargeant. Wesleyan Missionary and First President of the West Indian Conference* (London: Charles H. Kelly, 1901).

Ques. 1. Are there any objections to any of the Preachers?
That brother Scarsebrook be requested to speak kindly and affectionately to brother Lindars respecting his more faithfully attending his appointments.
Ques 2. Are there any brethren to be fully received upon the plan?
Ques 3. Are there any proposed to come on Trial?
Ques ~~3~~ 4. Are there any persons to be proposed to come on the plan?
Brother John Danbury of Bladon to be received as an Exhorter.[1]
That brother Prentice be put on the plan as a Local Preacher if he promise punctually to attend his appointments.
That brother Edwd Hilliard[2] of Woodstock be received on the Plan as an Exhorter.
That brother Thos Barrett[3] be received on the plan as an Exhorter.
Ques 4. Are there any alterations in any of the places?
That there be preaching at Woodstock every Sunday afternoon at half past 2 o'clock and during the Summer months, when the weather is favourable, to preach in the open air.
Ques 5. Are there any new places to be received on the plan?
Ans. Woolvercott.

29 June 1842

Minutes of Local Preachers Meeting 29th June 1842
Present The Revd M. Wilson Chairman, Willan Ostler, Bartlett, Scarsbrook, Greenhill, Thomas Smith, Ray, Banbury, Leggatt, Davis, Jones, Sargent, Bailey, T.G. Smith, Brown.
Ques 1 Are there any objections to any of the Preachers?
Ans. None.
Ques 2 Are there any brethren to be fully received on the Plan?
Ans. None.
Ques 3. Are there any persons ~~to be~~ proposed to come on the Plan?
Ans. That bro Hedges be conversed with respect [to] his coming on the Plan; that bro Cripps be heard by bro Smith as regards his ability to exhort.
Ques 4. Are there any alterations in any of the places?
Ans. That the preaching at Kirtlington shall be in the morning instead of afternoon. And at Hampton in the afternoon instead of the morning.
Ques 5. Are there any new places to be received on the Plan.
Ans. Summers Town, & Kidlington.

1   Resuming local preaching after expulsion in September 1836.
2   Edward Hilliard (1813–88), locksmith, of Woodstock. In official records, the surname often appears as Stilliard.
3   Possibly Thomas Barrett (1800–78), labourer, of Wootton, received as an exhorter in September 1849.

28 September 1842

Minutes of Local Preachers Meeting 28th Sepr 1842

Present The Revd M. Wilson Chairman Messrs Willan, Scarsbrook, Ostler, Hitchman, Ray, Harris, Smith, Leggatt, Davis, Jones, Bailey, Wheeler, Sargent, T.G. Smith, Sumner,[1] Church, Clements, Smart,[2] Danbury, Bartlett, Greenhill, Birmingham, Brown, T. Smith & Lindars.

Ques 1. Are there any objections to any of the Preachers?

Ans. That brother Jones be seriously admonished respecting his late attendance to his appointments.

Ques. 2 Are there any brethren to be fully received on the Plan?

Ans. Bro Ewers,[3] an accredited Local Preacher from the Watlington Circuit.

Bro Clements, who has been on Trial for four quarters, & undergone a satisfactory examination be received on condition of his reading Mr Wesley's Notes on the New Testament & Sermons according to Rule.

Ques. 3. Are there any persons to come on Trial as a Local Preachers?

Ans. Bro Rogers. Bro Barrett. Bro Danbury.

Ques 4. Are there any persons to be received on the Plan as Exhorters?

Ans. Bro Hilliard of Woodstock, Bro Bailey Junr of Oxford.[4]

Ques. 5. Are there any alterations in any of the places?

Ans. Service at Summers Town to be in the evening. Service at Hampton to be in the evening. Service at Horsepath at 5 in the evening.

Ques. 6. Are there any new places to be received on the plan?

Ans. Headington on a week night.

28 December 1842

Minutes of Local Preachers Meeting
28th December 1842

Present The Revd M. Wilson Chairman. Messrs Willan Langston[5] Ostler Bartlett Brown Greenhill Scarsbrook Hitchman Birmingham Ray Banbury Leggatt Jones Sargent T G Smith Smart Danbury Haynes & Bailey Junr.

Ques 1. Are there any objections to any of the Preachers?

---

1   There is no mention of a Sumner on the 1839 Plan, so this may be a different person from the exhorter of 1833–35.

2   Richard Smart (1817–87), brother-in-law of Richard Fathers, of Islip [*conj.*].

3   Jonathan Ewers (1816–93).

4   Joseph Bailey (1824–50), tailor, of Oxford.

5   John Langston (c. 1797–1891) was stationed in the Oxford Circuit as a supernumerary minister, 1842–44. This followed his removal from the Watlington Circuit, after disciplinary charges brought against him by the Circuit Stewards were upheld by the District Meeting. After refusing to withdraw from the ministry, Langston ceased to be recognised as a Wesleyan minister in 1849: *Minutes of Conference* 1849, 185. I am grateful to John Lenton and Shirley Martin for details of Langston's life and career.

That bro Lindars be seen by Bro Willan and Scarsbrook respecting his meeting in Class.[1]

Ques 2. Are there any brethren to be fully received on the Plan?

~~Ques. 3~~ That bro. Smart be received on the Plan, having undergone a satisfactory examination. Also Robins.

Ques 3. Are there any persons to come on Trial as Local Preachers?

That bro ~~Robins~~ Pulker[2] of Charlton be heard on Sunday Jan[y] 1st by bro Ostler with a view to his being received as an Exhorter.

That bro Cripps be received on the plan as an Exhorter.

29 March 1843

Minutes of Local Preachers Meeting 29th March 1843

Present The Revd M. Wilson Chairman Mess[rs] Willan Ostler Bartlett Brown Scarsbrook Hitchman Ray Smith Banbury Leggatt Davis Jones Bailey Wheeler Sargent Lindars Tho[s] Smith T.G. Smith Sumner Danbury Hilliard & Bailey.

Ques. 1. Are there any objections to any of the Preachers?

Ques. 2 Are there any brethren ~~places~~ to come on the Plan?

Ques 3 Are there any person to come on trial?

Ques 4 Are there any persons to be received on the plan as Exhorters?

Bro Woodward[3] of Woodstock to ~~recei~~ have a Note from the Super allowing him to Exhort.

Ques 5. Are there any alterations in any of the places?

Ques. 6. Are there any new places to be received on the Plan?

28 June 1843

Minutes of Local Preachers Meeting 28 June 1843

Present The Rev[d] Max. Wilson Chairman The Revd Mess[rs] Willan & Langston Mess[rs] Ostler Bartlett Brown Scarsbrook Smith Banbury Leggatt Davis Jones H Smith Sargent Sumner Ewers Smart Danbury Bailey Jun[r] & Robins.

Ques. 1. Are there any objections to any of the Preachers?

Answer To Bro Lindars for omitting class meeting. Decision. That his name be kept on the plan for 3 months but with no appointment; that bro Scarsbrook be directed to endeavour to prevail on him to attend his Class.

Ques 2 Are there any ~~new places~~ brethren to come on the plan?

Ques 3 Are there any persons to come on Trial?

~~That~~ bro[rs] Shilliard[4] and Bailley Jun[r].

Ques 4. Are there any persons to be received on the plan as Exhorters?

---

1   Neglect of the weekly class meeting, a core element of Wesleyan spiritual discipline.
2   Charles Pulker (c. 1811–?), tailor, of Charlton-on-Otmoor.
3   Abel Woodward (1808–70), labourer, of Woodstock [*conj.*]. Abel Woodward was brother-in-law of William Leggatt.
4   Presumably a slip for 'Hilliard'.

Bro Woodward to be rec[d] as an Exhorter. Also bro Adams. Bro Buckell[1] receive a Note from Mr Wilson allowing him to Exhort.
Ques 5. Are there any alterations in any of the places?
Horsepath at 6.
Ques 6 Are there any new places to be received on the plan?
Cassington 6 o'clock. Headington 2 ½ & 6.

27 September 1843

Minutes of a Local Preachers' Meeting held September 27th 1843
Present – Rev. Max. Wilson Chairman Rev. Mess[rs] Dunn[2] and Langston, Mess[rs] Ostler, Brown, Scarsbrook, Hitchman, Ray, Banbury, Davis, Jones, Bailey, Wheeler, H. Smith, Sargent, Lindars, T. Smith, T.G. Smith, Sumner, Ewers, Smart, Robins, Danbury and Bailey Jun[r].
Ques 1. Are there any objections to any of the Brethren?
Ans[r] To Bro Birmingham, who neglected his appointments at Woodstock & Headington, & on the day of one of those appointments went to Charlton where he remained till the following Thursday intruding himself upon the hospitality of the friends who were ill-able to afford it, to the detriment of his character as a Local Preacher. Res[d] that an official note be sent to him expressive of the sense & feeling of the Meeting on the subject.[3]
2. That Bro. Haynes, who has appeared on the Trial list during this Quarter be dropt for want of ability for the work.
3. That Bro. Pulker's resignation of his place on the Exhorters' List be accepted.
4. That the Exhorter, answering to the initial P & th No. 42 on the present plan, be heard on Sunday Oct 1st at Headington by Mess[rs] Sargent & Robins & that their report of his qualifications for the work be presented to before the printing of the next plan to the Superintendant who shall decide as to his being retained.
Ques 2. Are there any Brethren to come on the Plan?
Ans[r] Bro. T. Smith, who is come duly accredited from the Newcastle-under-lyme Circuit.
Ques. 3. Have any Brethren died during the last Quarter?
Ans[r] This Meeting records its deep sense of the loss which has been sustained by the death of Bro[r] Stevens this Quarter & of the Brethren Harris & Clements in the course of the previous Quarter – and further this Meeting regards the unblemished integrity of their career as Local Preachers & their satisfactory departure in the faith and hope of the Gospel, as rendering their names worthy of a permanent record.

J.P.D. Sep 27/43.

---

1   Robert Buckell (1810–58), plumber, of Oxford.
2   James P. Dunn (1818–76), junior minister in the Oxford Circuit, 1843–45: *Minutes of Conference* 1877, 23–4.
3   See below, March 1848, for a more detailed account of a similar incident. Birmingham seems to have been undertaking freelance preaching tours in the Oxfordshire villages.

27 December 1843
Minutes of a Local Preachers' Meeting held in Oxford Chapel Vestry Dec[r] 27th 1843
Present Rev. Mess[rs] Wilson & Dunn The Breth[n] Ostler, Bartlett, Hitchman,
Scarsbrook, Ray, Banbury, Leggatt, Davis, Bailey, Wheeler, T.G. Smith, Sumner,
Ewers, Smart, Robins, T. Smith 2[d], Rogers, Bailey Jun[r], Buckle, Adams,[1] Palmer.[2]
The Minutes of the last Meeting having been read-
Ques. 1. Are there any objections to any of the Brethren?
Ans[r] Bro Birmingham neglected the Morning Chapel and Horsepath.
    2. To Bro Lindars, who has not met in Class. Res[d] that his name be left off the
plan.
    3. That a Committee consisting of Messrs Wilson, Dunn, Leggatt & Banbury be
appointed to investigate the dispute of Bro Danbury with the Trustees of Bladon
Chapel.
Miscellaneous Res.
That Bro Marcham[3] of Islip & Bro. Fred. Clements[4] of Charlton be permitted to
exhort on the authority of a Note from the Superintendent.
That the times of preaching at St Clements be 3 & 6.
That the afternoon preaching at Coombe be altered from ½ past 2 to 2 o'clock.
                                                                          J.D. Secy.

27 March 1844
Minutes of a Local Preachers' Meeting held in Oxford Chapel Vestry Mar: 27th 1844
Present Revd Messrs Wilson & Dunn Messrs Leggatt, Bailey, Smith 1st, Hitchman,
Smith 2nd, Robins, Hy Smith, Scarsbrook, Bailey Jun[r], Smart, Jones, Ray, Davis,
T.G. Smith, Buckle, Adams, Cripps.
Ques: 1. Are there any objections to any of the Brethren on the ground of character,
ability or attention to discipline?
Ansr None, with the exception of a complaint against Bro Birmingham on account
of certain labored eccentricities amounting to buffooneries to which he has recourse
in the Pulpit to the annoyance instead of the profiting of his congregations.
Res[d] That Mr Dunn be requested to converse with him on the subject & that if he
alter not, some further resolution of the Meeting be taken.
Miscellaneous Resolutions
1 That the Brethren Woodward Buckle and Adams be in the ordinary course
removed from the Exhorters' to the Trial List.
2 That Bro Clements of Charlton have a name on the Exhorters' List.

1   Joseph Adams (1818–1903), baker, of Bladon.
2   Probably John Palmer (1801–68), farmer, of Murcott.
3   Either John Marcham (1818–89) or his brother William (1816–80), both agricultural
labourers, of Islip. The June 1844 minutes identify John Marcham. In March 1856 it is reported
that Marcham is emigrating to Canada, but this was William, who died in Canada in 1880.
4   Frederick Clements (1822–59), boot and shoemaker, of Charlton-on-Otmoor.

3. That the times of preaching at St Clements in future be ½ past 2 and 6 o'clock.

4. That the Evening service at Headington be henceforth dropt.

5. That the appointment of the Brethren at Forest Hill on the new Plan be for the afternoon as well as the Evening.

Signed on behalf of the Meeting

J.P. Dunn

Secretary.

26 June 1844

Minutes of a Local Preachers' Meeting held in the vestry at Oxford June 26th 1844. Present Revds M. Wilson & J.P. Dunn Messrs Ostler, Bartlett, Brown, Scarsbrook, Ray, Leggatt, Banbury, Jones, Bailey, T.G. Smith, T. Smith 2, Rogers, Bailey Junr, Buckle, Palmer & Coker.

Ques: 1. Are there any objections to any of the Brethren on the grounds of ability, character, or attention to discipline?

Ansr None.

Miscellaneous Resolutions

Resd That Bro. Danbury be heard in the Morning Chapel[1] sometime in the month of September next by Messrs Ostler, Bartlett, & Scarsbrook, preparatory to his being received on the full plan.

2. That Bro Bailey Jr be heard on the 28th of July by Brethren Brown, Scarsbrook & Bartlett.

3. That Bro Clements be received on trial.

4. That Bro John Marcham be heard or conversed with by Messrs Wilson, Bartlett, Brown & Smith.

5. That the times of preaching at Wootton be 2 and 5 p.m.

6. That Messrs J.P. Dunn, Sargent, Leggatt, Banbury, T. Smith 2nd, Scarsbrook and Jones form a Committee to supply Kidlington with open-air preaching.

N.B. Bro Bailey Junr was examined before this Meeting as to ~~his~~ the reality of his conversion, and his knowledge of our doctrines and his examination was satisfactory.

Signed on behalf of the Meeting J.P. Dunn

Secretary.

---

1   The Morning Chapel and Tract Room was situated on the south-west corner of the New Inn Hall Street premises, between the main chapel and the schoolroom. See the sketch 'Ground Plan' 'drawn from memory by F.W.N[ix]' in the unpublished history of 'Methodism in Oxford' by James and Frank Nix, reproduced in Martin Wellings, 'The building of Wesley Memorial Church, Oxford', *Building the Church* (*The Chapels Society Journal*, vol. 2, 2016), 29. The name may have been copied from Wesley's Chapel in City Road, London, where the smaller Morning Chapel complemented the principal auditorium.

25 September 1844

Minutes of a Local Preachers' Meeting held in the Vestry at Oxford Sept 25th 1844. Present – Rev[d] T.R. Fisher[1] the Chairman Also Rev[d] J.P. Dunn & Mess[rs] Ostler, Bartlett, Scarsbrook, Hitchman, Ray, Banbury, Leggatt, Davies, Jones, H. Smith, Sargent, T.G. Smith, Robins, Bailey J[r], Ewers and Tho[s] Smith, also Messrs Barrett, Danbury, Buckle & Adams.

Ques: 1. Are there any objections to any of the Brethren on the grounds of moral character attention to discipline &c.

Ans[r] The Meeting not being satisfied as to the Wesleyan Orthodoxy of John Marcham whose name stands on the Exhorters' List, the Superintendent is respectfully requested to converse with him on the subject.

Ques. 2 Are there any to be received into full connexion as Local Preachers?

Ans[r] The Brethren Barrett & Danbury have completed the prescribed period of probation but not having been heard by the Superintendent the necessary preliminary to their reception according to rule – it is agreed that Bro. Barrett shall preach before Mr Fisher on Sunday afternoon Novr 3rd at Wootton and Bro. Danbury on Sunday afternoon Nov. 17th in the Morning Chapel - and it is further agreed that the appointments of the Brethren in the early part of next Plan shall be so arranged as to give them an opportunity as frequently as possible, of hearing Messrs Barrett & Danbury, so that the Meeting may be in possession of full information respecting their fitness for our work.

Ques: 3. What alterations in the times of Preaching is it desirable to adopt?

Ansr St Clements afternoon Preaching to be at ½ p[t] 2.

Coombe – preaching on the Lord's Day at 2 & 5.

Headington to have Evening Preaching during the Winter Months.

Miscellaneous

1st It is judged expedient that there should be preaching at High Bridge[2] for the six Sabbaths next ensuing from 5 to 6 o'clock p.m. and the following Brethren have agreed to undertake this duty in the order here stated.

Oct. 6th Bro. Hitchman. Oct 13th Bro. Thos Smith.

Oct. 20th Bro. Bailey Jun[r]. Oct 27th Bro. T.G. Smith.

Nov[r] 3rd Bro. Scarsbrook & Nov. 10th Bro. Robins.

---

1   Thomas R. Fisher (1806–90), Superintendent of the Oxford Circuit, 1844–46. Following a breakdown in health, Fisher retired from the Wesleyan ministry in the late 1840s and subsequently emigrated to New Zealand: 'Rev. T.R. Fisher', *The Press* (Christchurch), 22 January 1890, 2. I am grateful to Shirley Martin for this reference.

2   Alternative name for Hythe Bridge: Christopher Hibbert (ed.), *The Encyclopaedia of Oxford* (London: Macmillan, 1988), 190. It is unclear why this was chosen as a site for open-air preaching: the LNWR and GWR stations were not built at the western end of Hythe Bridge Street until the 1850s. The bridge was, however, close to the densely packed housing of Fisher Row and St Thomas's.

2nd By a unanimous vote of the Meeting Bro. Bartlett has been elected Treasurer and Bro. Scarsbrook Secretary to the Local Pr. Cash Fund who are hereby authorized to collect Subscriptions for the purpose of paying off the debt incurred by Cart-Hire. N.B. Their report to be presented to the next Meeting.
Signed J.P. Dunn
Secretary.

27 December 1844

Minutes of a Local Preachers' Meeting held in the Vestry at Oxford
Decr 27th 1844.
Present Revds T.R. Fisher & J.P. Dunn. Messrs Ostler, Bartlett, Brown, Scarsbrook, Crapper, Jno Smith, Sargent, Jones, Wheeler, Ewers, Tho. Smith, Smart, Bailey, Bailey Junr, Buckle, Adams, Cripps, Danbury.
Ques: 1 Are there any objections to any of the Brethren on the ground of moral character, attention to discipline etc.
Ans^r. Bro. Robins has in several instances neglected his appointments. The Meeting wish their deep regret to be recorded that this Brother should have been in some degree of careless of his work during the past Quarter and they desire to have conveyed to Bro. Robins an expression of their earnest hope that he will in future pay that punctual attention to his appointments on the plan to which he has virtually pledged himself by placing himself in this respect at the disposal of the Superintendent & which therefore the Meeting has a right to expect.
Ques: 2 Do any Brethren retire from the plan?
Ans^r. Bro. Leake, whose resignation is accepted. On this case it wa is resolved unanimously that the Local Preachers of the Oxford Circuit having heard the announcement of Mr Leake's determination to discontinue his connexion with them, are desirous of expressing their thanks to him for the services he has rendered the Circuit during the 9 years he has been one of them & also their undiminished esteem for his private and public character. And while they cannot conceal their regret that Mr Leake finds himself under the necessity, on conscientious grounds, of retiring from their body, they at the same time join in the expression of earnest wishes for his prosperity & happiness in whatever sphere of Christian labor & usefulness he may feel himself called upon to move.
Moved by Rev J.P. Dunn seconded by Mr T. Smith and adopted unanimously.[1]
Ques: 3 Are any to be received on the full Plan?
Ans^r Bro. Danbury who has passed through his probation satisfactorily to the Meeting.

---

1   In February 1845 Leake was 'set apart to the Christian ministry' by the Congregationalists of Frilford: *Evangelical Magazine and Missionary Chronicle*, May 1845, 259. I am indebted to Shirley Martin for this reference. Although Leake did not continue in the Congregational ministry, he subsequently played a significant part in the Reform controversies which divided Oxford Methodism from 1849 onwards.

Ques: 4 Are there any new places to be put on the plan?

Ans. It is judged expedient that enquiry be made & if found desirable that it be attempted to raise a Cause at Garsington. Messrs Ray & Davies are mentioned as the most suitable persons to make the proposed enquiry.

Signed on behalf of the Meeting

Jas. P. Dunn Secretary.

26 March 1845

Minutes of a Local Preachers' Meeting held in the Vestry Oxford March 26th 1845 Present Rev^{ds} T.R. Fisher & J.P. Dunn. Messrs Ostler, Bartlett, Scarsbrook, Crapper, Hitchman, Ray, J. Smith, Banbury, Leggatt, Davis, Jones, Sargent, Ewers, Robins, T. Smith, Rogers, Bailey J^r, Danbury, Buckell, Adams, Clements, Cripps, Palmer. Wm Marcham and Goold.[1]

Ques. 1 Are there any objections to any of the Brethren on the grounds of moral character, attention to discipline etc?

Ans^r The Meeting having received information that the Brethren Birmingham & Smart do not make it a point to maintain an uninterrupted connexion with the Society by keeping their names on some Class Book & meeting as frequently as they can – notwithstanding that, from the character of their employment they may be under the necessity of removing frequently from place to place - it is resolved that a letter shall be written to them on behalf of the Meeting, reminding them of that imperative Rule of Methodism which requires that every Local Preacher shall be under all circumstances a Member of Society.[2]

Ques. 2 Are any Brethren to be received from other Circuits?

Ans: Bro: Goold from the Midsomer Norton Circuit who has come duly accredited.

Ques: 3 Are there any to be received on the full Plan?

Ans. Bro. Buckle & Bro. Jos: Adams, whose examination has been satisfactory & who have complied with all the conditions previously required of them in order to their reception.

Ques: 4. Are there any alterations in the places and times of preaching?

Ans^r The afternoon preaching to be at ¼ to 3. Water Eaton preaching at 6 o'clk only.

Ques 5 Are any additional places to be recommended to be put on the plan?

Ansr The minute of the last Meeting with regard to Garsington having been neglected to be acted upon, it is proposed that it be adopted as the a Minute of this Meeting with a view to an enquiry being made next quarter as to it whether it has been carried into effect.

Bro. Leggatt engages to make enquiry at Kidlington in order to ascertain the propriety or otherwise of our endeavouring to establish a Cause in that village.

---

1   James Goold (1818–92),

2   Concern that Local Preachers should attend a weekly class meeting recurs in the minutes. Smart was employed through the 1840s variously as a baker, gate-keeper and toll-collector; Birmingham was a shoe-maker.

Marston is also spoken of as a probable scene of Methodist exertion.
In behalf of the Meeting
J.P. Dunn.

25 June 1845

Minutes of a Local Preachers' Meeting held in the Vestry June 25th 1845
Present Revd T.R. Fisher & J.P. Dunn. Messrs Ostler, Bartlett, Scarsbrook, Crapper, Hitchman, Jno Smith, Banbury, Leggatt, Davies, Bailey, Sargent, T.G. Smith, Bailey Junr, Goold, Danbury, Buckle & Adams.
Ques: 1 Are there any objections to any of the Brethren on the ground of moral Character, attention to discipline etc?
Ansr Bro. Birmingham has neglected Headington Quarry at a time when he was released from the duties of his worldly Calling so as to be able to have fulfilled the appointment had he been so disposed.
The Meeting resolve that a letter be written to him requiring him forthwith to furnish the Superintendent with an explanation of such neglect & if that explanation do not prove satisfactory that his name be not inserted on the next plan.
2. Bro. Ray neglected St Clements on 13th May without any assigned reason – that such neglect in the judgment of the Meeting is very reprehensible.
3. Bro. Sargent neglected Headington – attempted an explanation, but a very unsatisfactory one to the Meeting.
Ques. 2 Is there any alteration to be made in the order of the Names as they stand on the plan?
Ansr. Resd That Bro. Bailey's No. henceforth be 6, or rather that his place be next to Bro. Brown's & that Bro. Leggatt stand next in order on future plans.
Ques: 3 Are there any individuals to be admitted on trial on the plan?
Ansr Bro. Cox (alias) formerly in connexion with the Ranters,[1] who shall be placed on the Trial List – heard by the Superintendent in the course of the Quarter and examined next Local Preachers Meeting.
NB Bro. Clements shall also be heard by the Superintendent in the course of the Qr and examined next Local Preachers' Meeting.
Miscellaneous
That Headington preaching henceforth be at ½ past 2 only & Bladon afternoon preaching at ¼ to 3.
That Marston be put on the next plan and that there be preaching there in Miss Dolley's house at 6 o'clock every Sabbath Evening.
That Somers' Town & Kidlington also be put on the plan if places of for preaching can be obtained.
Signed on behalf of the Meeting J.P. Dunn Secy.
NB The Brethren Goold, Sargent, Hitchman have engaged to preach in the open air 3 times each according to appt in the course of this summer.

1   Less than complimentary term for Primitive Methodists.

? September 1845

Minutes of the Local Preachers' Meeting held at Oxford September 1845
Present Rev. T.R. Fisher Henry M. Harvard.[1]
Any objections to any of the brethren? None.
Any alterations to be made in the order of the brethren on the plan? Agreed that Bro. Robins stand next to Bro. Ray.
Are there any brethren to be received on the plan as accredited Local Preachers? Bro. Woodward who was examined and received accordingly the brethren Clements and Cox not being present their case was postponed.
Any brethren to be received from other circuits? Bro. Greenhill who has just returned from Brackley and who it was agreed should stand opposite to no. 8 on the plan.
Is there any alteration recommended in the times of preaching at any of the places? Recommended that Cassington preaching be at 2 & 5 on the Sabbath.
Are there any new places to be proposed? Somertown proposed and agreed to. Wolvercott & Kidlington, but nothing definite settled. Sunday evening preaching was to be resumed at Headington.

? December 1845

Minutes of the Local Preachers' Meeting held at Oxford December 1846[2].
Present Rev. T.R. Fisher, Henry M. Harvard. Breth[n] Robins, Ewers, Ostler, Bartlett, Buckell, Sargent, Ray, Jones, Crapper, Hitchman, Bailey.
Are there any objections to any of the Brethren? None.
Are there any to be received fully on the plan? Brethn Clements and Cox whose case is postponed as they are not present.
Are any to be received on trial? W. Marcham.[3] Memorand. A note has been given to Bro. Jos. Castle[4] authorizing him to preach and the Brethr. Gascoigne[5] and Fathers are also authorized as exhorters.
What preachers have left the circuit? None.
Have any been recd from other circuits? None.
Are any alterations expedient as to the places of preaching on the plan – any places to be discontinued or added or any alterations in the time of preaching, at either of these? None.
Mem. It was agreed that two notes should be addressed as follows viz to the friends at Woodstock on the subject of arranging to meet the Local Brethr appointed from

---

1   Henry M. Harvard (1814–93), junior minister in the Oxford Circuit, 1845–47: *Minutes of Conference* 1894, 19.
2   Harvard dated the minutes 1846, but this was a slip.
3   Perhaps William Marcham, of Islip: see minutes for December 1843.
4   Joseph Castle (1826–72), carpenter and joiner, of Woodstock [*conj.*]. Castle was identified in March 1846 as 'of Woodstock', which suggests that he was the Joseph Castle who later prospered as a builder in Oxford and was Mayor in 1868–69.
5   William Gascoigne (1815–87), labourer, of Islip.

Oxford to preach to them on that Sunday on which the cart does not travel that way. Second to the Prayer Leaders of Oxford urging them to attend to their country appointments in connection with the Local Preachers such union of labour having been frequently most useful.[1]

Dec. 24th 1846[2] Henry M. Harvard.

25 March 1846

Minutes of the Local Preachers' Meeting held at Oxford

Present Rev. T.R. Fisher & Henry M. Harvard. Messrs Bartlett, Ostler, Leggatt, Bailey, Banbury, J. Smith, Goold, Crapper, Scarsbrook, Bailey jun, Hitchman, Sargent, Davis, Ewers, Jones, Adams, Buckell, Ray, T.G. Smith.

The case of the Brethr Cox and Clements was postponed until the next meeting.

Mr Jos. Castle of Woodstock was received as an exhorter.

Bro. Jno Smith tendered his resignation as a preacher among us which was reluctantly accepted.[3]

It was agreed that Headington no longer remain on the plan. St Thomas, Jericho and St Clements were selected as places during the ensuing quarter for Open air preaching. The Brethr Hitchman Sargent Ewers J Smith Goold kindly consented to afford this service.

Mem. The Brethr Greenhill & Smart has left the circuit their acceptable services were now therefore no longer available.

Bro. Embury[4] was accepted also as a preacher on trial recommended from the Banbury Circuit.

Lady Day[5] 1846 Henry M. Harvard.

? June 1846

At the Loc. Preachers' Meeting at Oxford Midsummer.

Present Rev. T. ~~R. Fisher~~ Williams[6] & Henry M. Harvard Scarsbrook Bailey Embury Bailey jun Goold Jones T.G. Smith Adams Hitchman J. Smith Sargent Bartlett Ostler Crapper Ray Woodward Davis Castle Ewers Cripps Buckell Leggatt Banbury

1   The only reference in the minutes suggesting the presence of prayer leaders in the Oxford Circuit, supporting the Local Preachers. Prayer leaders are listed by their initials on the 1823 plan: Drew University, Madison, NJ, Marriott Collection, D2003-038, Oxford Plan, 1823; but not on any of the extant plans after 1830.

2   Again, a slip by the secretary.

3   According to an obituary in the *ODFCM*, June 1898, 34, Smith retired from local preaching because he thought the Circuit was sufficiently supplied with preachers and no longer needed his services in this role.

4   William Embury (1825–68), printer.

5   March.

6   Fisher was unable to complete his appointment, due to ill-health, and the temporary vacancy was filled by John Williams (1809–63), a recently returned missionary: *Minutes of*

Are there any objections to any of the brethren? Ans. It was ~~agreed~~ resolved that Bro. Cox be communicated with on the subj of neglecting his appointments and also Bro. Clements of Charlton.

That the brethr Cox & Clements be communicated with on the subject of their not coming for examination preparatory to reception on the plan as accredited loc. preachers & requested to come next quarter. It was noted that Bro. Coker has left the circuit.

Some conversation having arisen upon some views of ye[1] doctrine of the Trinity said to be entertained by Bro. Ray he was requested to give his views on that subject to the next quarterly Meeting.[2]

Wootton afternoon preaching was recommended to be at 2 ½.

It was agreed that preaching should be at Kidlington twice on the Lord's day.

Midsummer 1846 Henry M. Harvard.

? September 1846

At the Local Pr. Meeting held Oxford September 1846 Present Rev. J.W. Button[3] & Henry M. Harvard and the brethren Leggatt Ostler Scarsbrook Banbury Brown Adams Crapper Robins Hitchman Sargent Smith etc.

The brethren were examined each one.

It was requested that the brethren Cox Clements & Marcham appear before the next Meeting for examination in order to full reception as local Preachers

The brethr. Embury & Hartley were examined and recd. fully as local preachers.

Bro. Castle was recd. on trial. Bro. Stokes[4] was recommended to have a note authorizing him to preach.

The case of Marston was to be left to Mr Button and Mr Thurland.[5]

Noke was to be put upon the plan for preaching at 6 o'clock.

In reference to the case of Bro. Ray it was resolved that the peculiar views to which reference were made as held by him are unsound that he be requested to refrain from putting these forth among our people either from the pulpit by conversation or by distributing tracts and that he be affectionately requested to use the translation of Scripture in lieu of that which he has been understood to use.[6]

Henry M. Harvard.

Conference 1863, 430–1. Williams' journey from Manchester to Oxford took place at the Connexion's expense: Minutes of Conference 1846, 441.

1   Inserted into the text.

2   As the minutes of the next two meetings make clear, Ray had begun to hold and expound the beliefs of the New Jerusalem Church or Swedenborgians.

3   John Wesley Button (1798–1879), Superintendent of the Oxford Circuit, 1846–49: Minutes of Conference 1879, 39–40.

4   William Stokes, received on trial in September 1847.

5   Edward Thurland (1794–1879), chemist and druggist, a prominent Oxford Wesleyan.

6   According to the ODCC, Swedenborg's teaching 'does not admit of brief summary': 'Swedenborg, Emmanuel', ODCC, 1327–8. However, the New Jerusalem Church affirmed a revised canon, excluding those parts of the Protestant Bible lacking 'the internal Sense' defined by Swedenborg: G.E. Bentley, Jr, 'A Swedenborgian Bible', Blake: An Illustrated Quarterly, 24.2 (Fall 1990), 63–4. Whether Ray was using a New Jerusalem text, or simply

? December 1846

At a meeting of the Loc. Preachers held at Oxford for the December quarter 1846. Present the Ministers with the Brethren Ostler Leggatt Smith Bailey Scarsbrook Robins Banbury Sargent Fathers Jones J Smith Bartlett etc etc

A conversation was again held upon the case of Bro. W. Ray who has engaged no more to meet the questions already referred to according to the tenor of the last entry upon this subject. It was desired that a note be addressed to him requiring a reply in writing to the following enquiries. 1. Whether he have joined the Swedenborgians in Oxford. 2. If he hold the doctrines of justification & the witness of the Spirit according to the Wesley[n] Methodist standards.[1]

The Brethren Clements & Marcham were examined & fully received on the understanding that they should be heard preach by the Superintendent Minister, & approved.

Bro. Stokes was received as an exhorter.

It was observed that the Preaching at Bladon on the Sabbath would be till again altered in the morning instead of afternoon the evening preaching as before.

Water Eaton it was observed would be discontinued.

                                                            Henry M. Harvard.

? March 1847

At a meeting of the Local Preachers held at Oxford for the ~~June~~ March quarter 1847. Present the ministers of the circuit & the brethren Sargent Scarsbrook Hitchman Ostler Bailey Crapper Buckell Smith Hartley Gould Robins Embury Banbury & Adams etc.

Bro. Ray's case was again considered when it was thought that it would be advisable that his name should disappear from the plan.[2]

Bro. Sumner[3] was rec. [*conj.*] as on trial from the Wantage circuit as being of nine months standing.

The brethren Reaks & Richards[4] were admitted on trial.

It was agreed also that the preaching at Wootton should be in the morning instead of the afternoon of the Sunday.

---

giving a Swedenborgian interpretation to the familiar 1611 translation of the Bible cannot be determined from the record.

1   The New Church challenged the traditional Protestant emphasis on justification by faith alone, although Swedenborg's insistence on works of charity bore some similarity with Wesley's teaching on holiness. Swedenborg's writings on angels and spirits struck a different note from the Wesleyan understanding that God's Spirit bears witness with the believer's spirit that a person is accepted by God. For Wesleyans, this witness of the Spirit was fundamental to the believer's sense of assurance.

2   By March 1851 Ray was leading a New Jerusalem Church in St Clement's, Oxford: Kate Tiller (ed.), *Church and Chapel in Oxfordshire 1851* (Oxford: Oxfordshire Record Society, 1987), 76. Ray went on to be a minister of the New Jerusalem Church.

3   Possibly Ziba Sumner (1814–72), schoolmaster, who moved between Oxford and East Hanney in the 1840s.

4   George Brian Richards (1828–1904), bookseller, of Oxford.

That the preaching at Coombe be also at 11 in the morning of Sunday in lieu of the afternoon.

And that the same alteration be made at Islip.

It was agreed also that preaching should be tried at Somertown on the Sunday at 2 ½ & 6 & that the following brethren be a committee to fix upon an eligible room for the purpose viz. Messrs Crapper Gould Ewers Sargent & Buckell.

Henry M. Harvard.

? June 1847

At a meeting of the Local Preachers held at Oxford for the June Quarter of 1847 Resolved that Bro. Thos Turner be received on the Plan, the term of his trial having ended.

N.B. In consequence of Mr Harvard having lost the minutes of this meeting nothing further is known of it.

Wm Hopewell.[1]

29 September 1847

At a Meeting of the Local Preachers held in Oxford Sepr 29th 1847

Present: Bro^s Button, Hopewell, Brown, Leggatt, Scarsbrook, Crapper, Hichman, Banbury, Davis, Jones, Sargent, Ewers, T. Smith, Bailey Junr, Goold, Danbury, Buckle, Adams, Embury, Turner, Church, Reaks, Richards & Cripps.

1st Ques. Is there any objection to any Br^o?

Ans^r Yes. And recommended that Br^o Cox be drop[p]ed from the Plan, on account of reiterated neglect of his appointments.

2nd Ques. Any to be received on trial?

Ans^r. Yes. Br^o Wm Stokes.

3rd Ques. Are any received as Exhorters?

Ans^r. Yes. Br^o James Bonnar.[2]

4th Ques. Are any received from other Circuits?

Ans^r. Yes. Br^o James Marcham, who has been 3 years a preacher in the Swindon circuit.

6th Resolved that a note be addressed, through Mr Bonnar of Charlton,[3] to the Friends who entertain the Local Preachers there; requesting them to pay more attention to their Horse, especially in reference to provinder, and represent that, Mr Boffin,[4] the lender, complains and threatens to refuse to lend unless the horse be properly fed.

---

1   William Hopewell (1816–54), junior minister in the Oxford Circuit, 1847–49: *Minutes of Conference* 1854, 372–3.

2   Probably James Bonner (1825–1904), of Charlton-on-Otmoor. The family had emigrated to the USA by 1850.

3   Either James Bonner or his father Thomas (1789–1851), farmer, of Charlton-on-Otmoor.

4   James Boffin (1816–1900), baker and confectioner, a prominent Oxford Wesleyan.

7. Resol. That the following Brethren constitute a deputation, and wait upon Mr Bolton of Forest Hill;[1] to represent to him the desirability of erecting a Chapel there[2] Viz., Bros Crapper, Scarsbrook, Bartlett and Goold.

8. That Bro Crapper try to obtain a suitable place to preach in at Summer-town; as the place, till now used, may be had no longer.

Wm Hopewell

22 December 1847

Minutes of a Local Preachers' Meeting held in Oxford Decr 22nd 1847

Present Bros J.W. Button, W. Hopewell, Ostler, Bartlett, Bailey Snr, Leggatt, Scarsbrook, Crapper, Hitchman, Banbury, Wheeler, Ewers, T. Smith, Bailey Junr, Goold, Buckell, Adams, Embury, Clements, Marcham, Turner, Cox, Richards, Cripps, Gascoign, Bonner.

1st Quesn Is there any objection etc? Ansr No.

2nd Quesn Are any received on Trial? Ansr Bros Palmer, Fathers & Gascoign shall be heard preach at Kidlington on the 11th of January by Bros Bartlett, Crapper, Leggatt & Banbury and if their report be favourable the above named bretheren shall be received on trial.

3rd Quesn Are any received as Exhorters? Ansr No.

4th Quesn Are any received on the full Plan?

Ansr Bro Cox after undergoing an examination was unanimously received as a Local Preacher.

5th Quesn Any fresh places? Ansr Hinksey.

Wm Hopewell

22 March 1848

Minutes of a Local Preachers' Meeting held in Oxford March the 22nd 1848

Present J.W. Button, W. Hopewell, Brown, Bailey Snr, Bailey Junr, Embury, Hartley, Buckell, Banbury, Smith, Scarsbrook, Leggatt, Goold, Adams, Jones, Bartlett, Gascoign, Fathers, Davies, Ewers, Turner and Crapper.

1st Question. Are there any objections to any of the Brethn?

Ansr The Meeting was informed that Bror Birmingham neglects his work and to do to the utmost in his power to maintain his mother and sister, who reside with him. And also that he goes to places both in and out of the circuit to hold meetings and stay with the friends unsoliceted, sometimes taking with him Bror Hunt[3] whose

---

1   William Bolton of Forest Hill was a subscriber to the *Wesleyan Methodist Magazine* in the early 1840s: OHC, OMCA, NM5/A/A2/3, Oxford Circuit Schedule Book, 1839-45. John Bolton (1796–1865), a trustee of the New Inn Hall Street chapel, farmed at Forest Hill.

2   Joseph Thornton, 'Recollections and reminiscences by an octogenarian Methodist', *OMM* (n.d., cutting in the Nix collection of material on Oxford Methodist history, f. 89), dates the first chapel in Forest Hill to 1860 and to the initiative of James Boffin (see note 3 above).

3   Charles Hunt (1829–1910), tailor, of Headington, became an exhorter in 1849.

staid and industrial habits the meeting considers are endangered by such conduct. The meeting having attentively considered what was said, deems such proceeding on the part of Br° Birmingham calculated to disgrace the profession of Christianity and the office of Local Preacher sustained by him, and feels obliged to take some active measures to prevent such conduct in future. The meeting therefore invites Br[r] B. to come to the next quarterly meeting and either disprove these statements or assure it that he will act differently in future, and inform him that if he, as on other occasions, neglect to attend or promise as required, that his name will certainly be removed from the Plan the next quarter. Also that the Secretary send a copy of this minute to him.[1]

2nd Ques[n] Are any received on trial?

Ans[r] Yes. Charles Elford,[2] (who comes from the Primitive Methodists) that he be put on trial for one quarter, and informed by the Rev[d] J.W. Button that if his examination at the end of that period be satisfactory he will on its expiration be placed on the full Plan.

3rd Ques[n] Are any received as Exhorters?

Ans[r] Yes. Frederick Church[3] of St Clement's.

Ques[n]. Are any fresh places to be put on the plan?

Ans[r] Yes. Wolvercott, Oxon.

William Hopewell

21 June 1848

Minutes of a Local Preachers' Meeting held in Oxford June 21st 1848

Present The Rev[ds] J.W. Button, Will[m] Hopewell Mess[rs] Ostler, Leggatt, Buckell, Bailey Junr, Turner, Banbury, Hartley, Bartlett, Goold, Scarsbrook, Adams, Palmer, Birmingham, Elford, Jones, Richards & T.G. Smith.

1st Ques[n] Are there any objections to any of the Brethren?

The minute of the last meeting, relating to Br° Birmingham being read, Br[r] Birmingham defended himself and asked forgiveness if he had committed an offence. Whereon it was moved by Br° Crapper and seconded by Br° Bartlett 'That, this Meeting having heard Br[r] Birmingham's explanation, apology and promises, for the future not to offend in the like manner, accept the same.'

2nd Ques[n] Are any received on the full Plan?

Ans[r] Br° Elford (moved by Br° Crapper & sec[d] by Br° Goold)

---

1   A much more positive appraisal of Birmingham as a preacher with 'a passion for saving souls' is given in the *OMM*, May 1936, 46. Joseph Thornton, 'Recollections and reminiscences by an octogenarian Methodist', *OMM* (n.d., cutting in Nix Collection) recalls Birmingham and Charles Hunt as visitors to Forest Hill in the 1850s.

2   Charles Elford (1823–84), grocer, of St Clement's. Elford is the most junior preacher on the extant 1847 plan for the Oxford Primitive Methodist Circuit, reproduced in Kate Tiller, '"The desert begins to blossom": Oxfordshire and Primitive Methodism, 1824–1860', *Oxoniensia*, 71 (2006), (Oxford: OAHS, 2007), between pages 102 and 103.

3   Frederick Church (1827–92), tailor, of St Clement's.

Also Br° Richards (moved by Br° Leggatt and sec[d] by Br° T.G. Smith).

3rd Are any received on trial?

Ans[r] Br° Thomas Meek of Woodstock[1] (moved by Br° Bartlett se[d] by Br° Crapper).

W. Hopewell Sec[y].

20 September 1848

Minutes of a Local Preachers' Meeting held in Oxford September 20th 1848

Present The Revds J.W. Button W. Hopewell Messrs Bartlett, Bailey, Crapper, Hitchman, Birmingham, Robins, Banbury, Davies, Jones, Ewers, Goold, Adams, Embury, Ellford, Richards, Buckell & Church Junr.

1st Ques[n] Are there any objections to any of the Brethren? Agreed that the Rev[d] J.W. Button and Mr Crapper be deputed to wait on T.G. Smith and tender him advice in reference to the discipline of his son.[2]

2nd Is there any alteration in the times of public service?

Agreed, that the Evening Service at Oxford be altered from 6 o'C to 6 ½ o'C provided the Oxford Leaders' Meeting approve of the change.

W. Hopewell.

20 December 1848

Minutes of a Local Preachers' Meeting held in Oxford December 20th 1848

Present The Rev[ds] J.W. Button, Wm Hopewell Messrs Ostler, Bartlett, Brown, Leggatt, Crapper, Banbury, Jones, Wheeler, Goold, Danbury, Adams, Buckell, Scarsbrook, Hitchman, Bailey Jn[r], Clements, Marcham, Cox, Elford, Richards, Church Jn[r], Gascoign, Fathers, Cripps and Bailey Sn[r].

1st Quest[n] Are there any objections to any of the Brethren?

Ans[r] 1st A charge being brought against the moral character of Bro[r] Palmer it was Resolved that, a Leader's Meeting[3] be held on the case at Charlton on Christmas Day, to be composed of Brors Clements, Wheeler and the Leaders of Islip.

2[d] Bro[r] Robins having tendered his resignation on account of change in his doctrinal views, it was accepted and Bro[r] Elford appointed to take his place at Rose Hill on Sunday 31st inst.

2[d] Quest[n] Are any received on trial?

Ans[r] Bro Church Jun[r].

Resolved that the Rev[d] J.W. Button examine Bro[rs] Gascoign and Fathers at Islip, and if satisfied with their views of Wesleyan doctrine and discipline that they be received on the plan.

W. Hopewell

---

1   Restored after an absence of a dozen years.

2   There were three sons: Joseph (b. 1833), Caleb (b. 1836) and Joshua (b. 1836), all living in the family home in 1851 and working in their father's boot-making business. Josiah Crapper was an experienced schoolmaster, so perhaps considered an appropriate counsellor on juvenile discipline.

3   Meeting of the Leaders of the classes in the local Wesleyan congregation.

21 March 1849

Minutes of a Local Preachers' Meeting held in Oxford March 21st 1849
Present The Revds J.W. Button Wm Hopewell & Messieurs Ostler, Bartlett, Leggatt, Scarsbrook, Crapper, Hitchman, Birmingham, Davies, Jones, Smith, Ewers, Bailey Junr, Goold, Buckell, Adms, Embury, Clements, Richards and Church Junr.
1st The Revd J.W. Button stated that, Bror Palmer's case had been investigated according to the first minute of the last meeting and the accusation found groundless as it was unsupported by evidence.
Resol 2nd That Brors Gascoign and Fathers be received on the full plan.
Resol 3rd That Bror Castle be again received on trial, and that he be examined at the next meeting in order to his coming on the full plan.
Resol 4th that Brors B. Scott,[1] and Tarrant[2] be received on trial, but so appointed for the present as not to interfere with their engagements in the Sunday School.[3]
Willm Hopewell

20 June 1849

Minutes of a Local Preachers' Meeting held in Oxford June 20th 1849
Present The Revds J.W. Button W. Hopewell Messieurs Bartlett, Brown, Leggatt, Scarsbrook, Crapper, Hickman, Birmingham, Banbury, Davis, Jones, Bailey Jnr, Goold, Danbury, Buckell, Adams, Embury, Clements, Cox, Richards, Fathers, Church Jnr, Castle, Scott and Tarrant.
Bror Palmer sent in his resignation, but on deliberation it was aggreed 'That – the Resignation be not accepted, but that Bror Palmer's name be retained on the plan as usual; and that but a few morning appointments be given him the next quarter with the view of enabling him more conveniently to attend to his temporal duties.'[4]
1st Quesn Are there any objections to any of the Brethren?
A conversation took place in reference to Bror Crapper supplying, and administering the Sacrament to, the Independent Church at Summertown. When it was moved, by Bror Banbury, and seconded by Bror Adams & Resold 1st That this meeting does not consider Bror Crapper's Present Position, in relation to Methodism, a proper one.'
Also, it was moved by Bror Banbury, seconded by Bror Adams, and carried unanimously That – 'This meeting respectfully requests Bror Crapper to discontinue his connection with the Independents at Summertown, and come among us as a Local Bror, or discontinue his connection as a Local Preacher.' Mr Crapper refusing to

---

1   Benjamin Valentine Scott (1829–96), hatter and hosier, of Oxford.
2   William Henry Tarrant (1820–97).
3   Scott was secretary of the Sunday School Committee and both Scott and Tarrant were teachers: see OHC, OMCA, NM5/25/A14/1, Minutes of the Oxford Wesleyan Sunday and Day School Committee, 1842–73, 29 January 1848.
4   Palmer was a farmer. It is unclear if there was any connection between the charge brought against his moral character in December 1848 and the demands of his temporal duties mentioned here.

give up the aforesaid connection - it was further moved by the Revd J.W. Button and seconded by Bro^r Jones That 'If, previous to the plan going to press, Bro^r Crapper promise to give up his connection with the Summertown Independent Church, his name shall be continued on the plan.' Carried unanimously.[1]

2nd Ques^n Are any received on the full plan?

Bro^r Castle was examined, as required by the 3rd Resolution of the previous meeting, and his examination being satisfactory, he was unanimously received on the full plan.

Willm Hopewell Sec^y

26 September 1849

Minutes of a Local Preachers' Meeting held in Oxford Sept 26 1849

Present Rev^s C. Westlake[2] & Wm Hopewell Messrs Jeffreys, Bailey, Leggatt, Birmingham, Banbury, Jones, Wheeler, Bailey Junr, Danbury, Adams, Marcham, Ja^s Marcham, Richards, Gascoign, Cripps.

1st Question Are there any objections to any of the Brethren on the grounds of ability, character, or attention to discipline?

Ans None!

2nd Ques. Are any received on the plan as Exhorters?

Ans. Yes. Bror^s Thos. Barrett,[3] Kent,[4] John Barrett,[5] Howard & C. Hunt.

Resolved

1 That Bro. Palmer be examined by Mr Hopewell and if satisfactory be received on the plan.

2 That Bro T.G. Smith be again received on the plan, his name being placed last.

3 That this meeting records, with submission to the Divine will, the decease of Mr Jos^h Ostler, who for the period of 54 years fulfilled the duties of a Local Preacher with fidelity and acceptance. He died aged 78. His end was peaceful and triumphant.[6]

1   This minute does not reflect the account of the dispute published in the *Oxford Chronicle* in the summer and autumn of 1849, or in subsequent narratives sympathetic to the Reformers: see 'Wesleyans', *OC*, 25 August 1849. Crapper's connection with the Summertown Congregational Church continued, and he signed the return for the 1851 Religious Census, using the designation 'Preacher of the Gospel', used to describe Wesleyan ministers in the *WMM* until the 1820s: Tiller, *Church and Chapel in Oxfordshire 1851*, 99.

2   Charles Westlake (1805–58), Superintendent of the Witney Circuit. Button's successor as Superintendent in Oxford, Joseph Earnshaw (1798–1859), suffered from protracted ill-health in 1849–50, so Westlake took the chair at the Local Preachers' and Quarterly Meetings, and Richard Bell was stationed to cover the pastoral work: *Minutes of Conference* 1850, 554, where Bell is the 'additional Young Man' for whom £20 was allocated. For Westlake, see *Minutes of Conference* 1859, 204, and for Earnshaw, *Minutes of Conference* 1860, 397–8.

3   Thomas Barrett (1800–78), agricultural labourer, of Wootton (Oxon.).

4   Edwin Philip Kent (1817–85), hairdresser, of St Ebbe's.

5   John Barrett (1802–82), slater and plasterer, of Wootton (Oxon.).

6   Ostler's death was reported in *OC*, 18 August 1849.

3rd Question. Is there any alteration in the time of public services

Ans. Yes. That Mr Hopewell consult the Trustees of St Clements, and if they agree, that there be only an afternoon service at St Clements Chapel on the Sabbath, during the next quarter.

On the order of the day being read, after a long conversation on the case of Bro Crapper and the Brethren who resigned their work last quarter; it was moved by Bro Banbury, and seconded by Bro Danbury, and carried unanimously 'That this meeting approves of the conduct of the Rev[d] Mr Button, in regarding the protests of the professedly aggrieved Brethren, as a resignation of their official position as Local Preachers.'[1]

Willm Hopewell.

26 December 1849

Minutes of a Local Preachers' Meeting held in Oxford Dec[r] 26th 1849

Present The Revd[s] C. Westlake, W. Hopewell, R. Bell[2] Messieurs Bailey, Leggatt, Birmingham, Jones, Banbury, Wheeler, Bailey Jn[r], Danbury, Adams, Woodward, Marcham, Ja[s] Marcham, Richards, Fathers, T.G. Smith, Cripps, John Barratt, Kent and Howard.[3]

Resol. 1st That Bror[s] Thos. Barratt and Kent be received on trial.

2nd That Bror[s] Nicholls and Hunt[4] be rec[d] as Exhorters.

3rd That the Sunday service at St Clements be altered from the afternoon to the evening and that the evening services at Coombe be at 2 o'C instead of 2 ½ and at Charlton at 5 ½ instead of 6 o'C.

4th That the services of the Witney preachers be continued.[5]

A note was read from Bro[r] J. Ewers requesting to be restored to the plan. When it was moved by Bro[r] Bell and seconded by Bro[r] Jones that Mr Westlake converse with Bro[r] Ewers and if satisfied with his views that Bro[r] Ewers be restored, his name being placed at the bottom of the plan.[6]

Willm Hopewell.

20 March 1850

Minutes of a Local Preachers' Meeting held in Oxford March 20th 1850

1   'Wesleyans', *OC*, 25 August 1849, claimed that fifteen Local Preachers had resigned in sympathy with Josiah Crapper.

2   Richard Bell (1820–74), sent to supply in the Oxford Circuit, 1849–50, and stationed as Superintendent, 1869–72: *Minutes of Conference* 1875, 562.

3   Thomas Howard (1825–1908), builder's clerk, of Oxford. Howard was later Chief Clerk, and then partner, to Joshua Symm, an influential Oxford Wesleyan: Bryan R. Law, *Building Oxford's Heritage*, 62, 70.

4   Charles Hunt: see above, March 1848.

5   Local Preachers from Westlake's Witney Circuit were brought in to cover appointments in the Oxford Circuit, following the resignation of a substantial number of Oxford preachers.

6   Ewers was one of the preachers who had withdrawn, in support of Josiah Crapper.

Present The Revd[s] Jos[h] Earnshaw, W. Hopewell, R. Bell, with Messrs Bailey, Leggatt, Banbury, Davis, Jones, Danbury, Adams, Marcham, Richards, T.G. Smith, Ewers, Kent, Howard, John Barratt, Hunt.

Resol 1st This Meeting has the painful duty to record the decease of another of its members, Mr Joseph Bailey, who for a period of seven years attended to the duties of Local Preacher in the Oxford Circuit with fidelity and acceptance. He died in great peace aged 26 years.[1]

Resol 2nd That Bror[s] Ewers and Jones [and] Cox be again admitted on the Plan their names to be placed at the bottom.[2]

Resol 3rd That Bro[r] Howard be received on trial.

Resol 4 That the services of the Witney Local Preachers be continued.[3]

Resol 5 That the service at Rose Hill commence at 10 ½ AM and at Charlton at 6 o'C Also that there be service at St Clements at 3 in the aftern.

Resol 6 That the services on Good Friday be as follows Bro[r] Marcham at Woodstock. Bailey at Rose Hill. Richards at Bladon. Leggatt at Coombe. Kent at Tackley. Howard at Islip. Jas Marcham at Kidlington.

W. Hopewell.

3 July 1850

Minutes of a Local Preachers' Meeting held in Oxford July 3rd 1850

Present The Revd[s] Jos[h] Earnshaw, W. Hopewell, R. Bell, and Messrs Leggatt, Birmingham, Banbury, Jones, Adams, Clements, Marcham, T.G. Smith, Ewers, Cox, Howard, Cripps and Hunt.

Resol 1st That Bro[r] Barford,[4] from the City Road Circuit,[5] be placed on the Plan, and that his No. be 25.

2nd On a statement being made that Bro[r] Brown expressed his willingness to submit to Methodist Discipline and abstain from agitation should he be again received on the Plan: it was moved by W. Hopewell and sec[d] by Mr Smith: That in consideration of his age and the spirit manifested by Bro[r] Brown he take the place on the Plan he had before his name was drop[p]ed.

3[rd] On a similar statement to the above being made in reference to Mr Scott, it was resolved that:- Messrs Earnshaw and Leggatt wait on him and if they are satisfied that he intends, if readmitted on the plan, to observe the discipline of Methodism and abstain from agitation, that he again be placed on the plan as an exhorter.

Willm Hopewell.

---

1   OC, 2 February 1850.

2   More of the preachers who had resigned in summer 1849.

3   Local Preachers from the Witney Circuit, used to fill gaps left by the resignations of 1849.

4   Henry Alfred Barford (1817–89), tailor's foreman.

5   The circuit based on Wesley's Chapel, in City Road, London.

25 September 1850

Minutes of a Local Preachers' Meeting held in Oxford September 25/50
Present The Revs R. Day[1] J.E. Cooke[2] and Messrs Bailey, Leggat, Brown, Birmingham, Banbury, Davies, Jones, Wheeler, Adams, Gascoigne, Barford, Kent, Scott, Cripps & Howard.
Question 1st Are there any objections to any of the Preachers? None.
N.B. Bro. Woodward is unable to attend to his appts. It was also recommended that Mr Cooke should see Bro Nichols & encourage him to attend to his appointments. A conversation having taken place relative to the best mode of defraying the expenses of the Circt conveyance and several of the bretheren, & other friends having intimated their willingness to continue Quarterly subs it was moved by Mr Jones & seconded by Mr Bailey and Resolved unanimously:
'That the friends at the country places be affectionately requested to contribute as much as they can towards this object.'
Signed John Elmer Cooke
Sec.

18 December 1850

Minutes of a Local Preachers' Meeting held at Oxford Dec 18th 1851[3]
Present Revs R. Day J.E. Cooke and the bretheren Bailey Leggatt x Brown Birmingham Banbury Jones Danbury Adams Woodward Clements Meek Fathers Cox Barford Barratt Kent Howard Scott Cripps Hunt etc.
Question 1st Are there any objections to any of the Preachers? Ansr None.
Resolved unanimously
That as brother Kent has now passed his examination in a satisfactory manner, that he be now received as a fully accredited L. Preacher.
N.B. x The presence of Mr Leggatt was protested against by the Superintendent, as Mr Leggatt's Ticket had been withheld[4] in consequence of the factious course he had persisted in pursuing. Mr Leggatt then demanded a Trial at a Leaders Meeting[5] which was granted him. The Meeting took place at Woodstock Dec 30/1851:[6] And the following charges were preferred against him by the Superintendent

1   Robert Day (1794–1864), Superintendent of the Oxford Circuit, 1850–53: *Minutes of Conference* 1864, 15. The obituary notes that 'He was extremely jealous for the observance of all parts of our discipline': in other words, he was not prepared to conciliate those who sympathised with the Reform movement.
2   John Elmer Cooke (1817–86), junior minister in the Oxford Circuit, 1850–52: *Minutes of Conference* 1886, 30.
3   Should be 1850.
4   Quarterly ticket of membership. Withholding the ticket indicated suspension or expulsion from the Wesleyan Society.
5   Meeting of the Class Leaders of the local Society.
6   Should be 1850.

I That you have factiously withheld Class money and Quarterage[1] from Dec/49 to Dec/50 & by your example induced all the members of your Class to do likewise.

II That you have attended two Wesleyan Reform Meetings, since <u>last</u> September, one at Oxford at which you were Chairman[2] and the other at Bladon in which you took part.

III That you have stated that the Wesleyan Conference is an anti-Christian Institution - your words are 'I think the Conference one of the worst forms of anti-Christ ~~in existence~~ & will do all I can to put it down.'

Mr Leggatt did not attend the meeting: the charges were supported by evidence, & the unanimous vote of the meeting pronounced him 'Guilty,' & on the 9th Jany he received formal notice of his expulsion.

J.E. Cooke.

26 March 1851

Minutes of a Local Preacher's Meeting held at Oxford March 26/1851

Present Revs R. Day, J.E. Cooke and the bretheren Brown Birmingham Banbury Jones Wheeler Adams Clements Marcham Meek Gascoign Fathers T.G. Smith Cox Barford Kent Cripps Nicholls & Hunt.

Ques 1 Are there any objections to any of the Preachers?

A conversation took place in reference to the conduct of some of the bretheren in having preached for the Agitators[3] in this Circuit and allowing one of the expelled local preachers to take an appointment – the bretheren <u>Adams</u> and <u>Barford</u> expressed their purpose to <u>act in an honourable manner </u>during their connection with us and the subject dropped.

N.B. The presence of Mr Scott was protested against but he obstinately <u>refused</u> to withdraw.[4]

---

1   Wesleyan members were expected to pay one penny each week at their Class Meeting and one shilling when the Quarterly tickets were issued by the minister. These contributions were the mainstays of Wesleyan finance, and withholding payment was an effective tactic adopted by the Reformers.

2   In the autumn of 1850, the supporters of Wesleyan Reform held public meetings in Oxford and elsewhere. Leggatt was a member of the Reform Committee for the Oxford Circuit, charged with arranging a meeting at Bladon in October 1850: OHC, OMCA, NM5/B/A2/1, Circuit Wesleyan Reform committee minute book, 1850–54, minutes for 17 October 1850. A year earlier Leggatt took the chair at a 'meeting to sympathise with the expelled Wesleyan ministers', reported in the OC, 27 October 1849, but this does not seem to have provoked censure at the time.

3   i.e., the supporters of the Reform movement.

4   Scott was a member of the Reform Committee in Oxford as early as October 1850: OHC, OMCA, NM5/B/A2/1, Circuit Wesleyan Reform committee minute book, 1850–54, committee appointed at a public meeting held on 15 October 1850. It may be inferred that he had withdrawn or been expelled from Wesleyan membership, but sought to make a protest by attending the Local Preachers' Meeting.

Bro. Woodward having sent a note containing his resignation that resignation was accepted.

John E. Cooke Secy.

25 June 1851

Minutes of a Local Preacher's Meeting held at Oxford June 25/1851

Present Revs R. Day, J.E. Cooke & the bretheren Meek, Davis, Jones, Kent, Adams & Hunt.

Ques 1 Are there any objections to any of the preachers?

Res. 1: That bro. Pearson's name be left of[f] the plan.

2. That this Meeting deeply regrets the course which brother Clements has pursued in allowing an unauthorised person to to not take his appointment, and that on the same day he preached for the Reformers but as bro Clements refuses to promise that he will not repeat the offence - if he continues so to do – this meeting considers he has forfeited his place among us.[1]

N.B. The bretheren Banbury, Ewers & Barford sent in their resignation during the Quarter.[2]

John E. Cooke sec.

25 September 1851

Minutes of a Local Preachers' Meeting held at Oxford Sep 25/1851

Present Revs Day, Cooke & the bretheren Bailey, Jones, Smith, Church, Hunt, Danbury, Kent & Meek.

Res. 1st That in the event of the bretheren Adams & Cox not being to take their regular work after they have been conversed with by the Ministers upon the subject, their names shall not be on the next plan.[3]

Res. II That Mr Smith of Woodstock (an old Local preacher from the Brackley Circuit) be placed on the plan, next to Mr Kent.

Res. III That Bro. Hunt be heard preach preach during the Quarter by one of the Ministers, preparatory to his being received on Trial.

(Signed) J.E. Cooke sec.

---

1   Clements was a member of the Reform Committee from October 1850 and a preacher on the Reformers' plan by 1856: OHC, OMCA, NM5/B/A2/1, Circuit Wesleyan Reform committee minute book, 1850–54, committee appointed at a public meeting held on 15 October 1850 and NM5/A/A1/2, copy circuit plan for the Wesleyan Circuit (in fact a Reformers' plan).

2   Banbury, Ewers, and Barford were among the preachers who formed the first Reformers' plan in April 1851: OHC, OMCA, NM5/B/A2/1, Circuit Wesleyan Reform committee minute book, 1850–54, Minutes of the Reform Committee, 2 April 1851.

3   James Cox, of Kirtlington, joined the Reformers; Joseph Adams, of Bladon, stayed with the Wesleyans.

24 December 1851

Minutes of a Local Preachers' Meeting held at Oxford December 24th 1851
Present Revs Day, Cooke & the bretheren Brown, Jones, Marcham, Kent, Gascoigne,
J. Barratt, Cripps and Davis and Howard . T.G. Smith.
Question 1st Are there any objections to any of the Preachers?
Ans[r] It is resolved that Bro[r] Nichols be left off the Plan.
Res. II Bro Howard, having passed his examination in a satisfactory manner, his
nomination to the full plan was unanimously received supported.
Res III That Bro Hunt, who has preached before and to the satisfaction of, the
superintendent, shall now be received on Trial.
Res IV That a conversation be had with Mr Phipps of New Hinksey[1] and that the
preacher appointed at Oxford in the afternoon be requested to preach at Mr Phipps
house in the evening [conj.].[2]
                    Signed John Elmer Cooke secy.

24 March 1852

Minutes of a Local Preachers Meeting held in the vestry Oxford March 24/52
Present Revs Day & Cooke & the bretheren Jones Kent Cripps & G.B. Richards.[3]
Quest 1st Is there any objection to any of the Preachers? Ans[r] None.
Quest II Are there any suitable persons to be recommended as Exhorters?
Ans[r] Bro. Pearson[4] (Woodstock) & Turtle [conj.] (Coombe).[5]
Quest III Any alterations to be proposed in the time for holding services?
Ansr Coombe evening service to commence at ½ past 5 o'clock.
                    J.E. Cooke Secy.

30 June 1852

Minutes of a Local Preachers Meeting held in the vestry Oxford June 30/52
Present Revs Day & J.E. Cooke and the bretheren Brown Jones Gascoign T.G. Smith
Kent Howard Cripps & Danbury.
Question 1 Are there any objections to any of the bretheren? Ans[r] None.
A Note was received from Bro. Bailey tendering his resignation. Resolved:-
That this Meeting deeply sympathises with Bro. Bailey in his growing infirmities,
but in consideration of his long and acceptable services, cannot bring themselves
to drop his name from the Plan, and to meet the case respectfully request the

---

1   'of New Hinksey' inserted into the text. Possibly Charles Phipps (1825–63), shoemaker,
of North Hinksey.
2   Text has been overwritten: probably 'evening' over 'afternoon'.
3   George Brian Richards (1828–1904).
4   Charles Pearson (1829–1903), hairdresser, of Woodstock.
5   Perhaps Edward Turtle (1834/5–1910), shoemaker, of Combe, accepted as an exhorter
in 1885, or an elder brother.

Superintendent to allow Mr Bailey to choose the places most convenient for himself to attend.

    (Signed) John Elmer Cooke. Sec.

29 September 1852

Minutes of a Local Preachers Meeting held in the vestry of Oxford Chapel September 29th /52

Present Revs Day and Scott,[1] with the Brethren Jones, Fathers, Marcham, Hunt, Kent, Davis.

Question I[st] Are there any objections to any of the Brethren?

It was stated that Bro Adams had not fulfilled his appointment at Hampton Poyle on the 8th of August and at Oxford on the 12th of Septr, and enquiries were directed to be made concerning the cause.

Question IInd Are any to be received on Trial?

Ans[r] Bro Hillis, if the enquiries to be made concerning him are satisfactory.

Question IIIrd Are any alterations to be made in the times of services?

Ans[r] Service shall be held at Kirtlington at half past two in the afternoon.

It was determined that at the next meeting the Brethren Barratt and Hunt should be examined in order that they may be received as fully accredited Local Preachers.

                            Uriah Scott Secy.

30 March 1853

Minutes of a Local Preachers Meeting held in the vestry of Oxford Chapel March 30th 1853[2]

Present Revds Day & Howard, with the Bretheren Smith, Howard, Hunt, Adams, Barratt, Fathers, Jones, Meek, Davis & Gascoign.

Question I[st] Are there any objections to any of the Bretheren?

The Chairman upon coming to Bro Adams' name stated that he had rec[d] a note from Mr Adams which amounted to a resignation of his place on the Plan and which was read to the Bretheren. After a lengthened and dispassionate discussion Bro Adams decided upon adhering to the decision expressed in his note and his name was therefore withdrawn from the Plan.

Question IInd Are any to be received on Trial?

---

1   Uriah Scott (1820–[?] 59), junior minister in the Oxford Circuit, 1852–53. Scott left the Oxford Circuit midway through the year, following an order by the Yeovil magistrates for him to pay maintenance for an illegitimate child, and he had left the Wesleyan ministry by the Conference of 1853: *Minutes of Conference* 1853, 191. I am grateful to Shirley Martin and John Lenton for information about the court case.

2   This is the next entry in the Minute Book. Between September 1852 and March 1853 is a blank page, perhaps left for a record of the December 1852 meeting. The Yeovil court case took place in November 1852, with an unsuccessful appeal in January 1853, so it is possible that the meeting was held in late December, but that Scott left Oxford without writing up the minutes.

<u>Arranged</u> that Bro Cripps and Jno Barratt be heard during the Quarter for the purpose of being received on Trial.

The Chairman reported that Bro Foster, an authorised Local Preacher, had removed from the Leighton Buzzard [Circuit] to this Circuit and his name was ordered to be placed on the Plan.[1] <u>Bro Thos Barratt</u> was examined in Theology and questioned as to his approval of Methodist Discipline and unanimously received fully on the Plan.

Question IIIrd Any alterations to be made in times of service? Ans. No.

H.C. Howard Secy.

29 June 1853

Minutes of a Local Preachers Meeting held at Oxford June 29th 1853

Present Revds R. Day and H.C. Howard,[2] with the Bretheren Jones, Meek, Smith, Birmingham, Palmer & Hunt.

The Minutes of the last Meeting were read and confirmed.

Question I Are there any objections to any of the Bretheren? Ans None.

Question IInd Are there any to be rec[d] on Trial?

The Chairman reported that he had heard Bro Cripps in pursuance of the resolution of the last Quarterly meeting and suggested that no alteration of his place on the plan should be now made in which the Meeting concurred. Also that Bro Barratt had failed to supply the appoint[t] given him for the purpose of being heard & that therefore he remained in the same position.

Question III Are there any for full reception?

Bro Osborn from the [ ] Circuit;[3] it being understood that as Bro Osborn had not presented his credentials from his last Circuit that the Chairman should make the customary enquiries.

Question 4th Any alterations in times of service. No.

Miscellaneous

Certain of the Bretheren having failed to supply their appointments the Meeting expressed itself strongly upon the subject, and decided a Record to be made of its serious disapproval of such conduct.

The Chairman expressed his regret that the Bretheren at Headington had but seldom attended their classes.

This being the last Quarterly Meeting at which the Chairman would be present in this Circuit it was <u>moved</u> by Bro Smith ~~and~~ seconded by Bro Jones and unanimously

---

1   Joseph Foster (1814–80), farmer, of Combe.

2   Henry Charles Howard (1833–1912), junior minister in the Oxford Circuit, 1853–54. Howard became supernumerary in 1858, retired 'for want of health' in 1860, and was ordained deacon and priest by the Bishop of London in 1862 and 1863 respectively: *Minutes of Conference* 1860, 412; *Crockford's Clerical Directory* (London: Horace Cox, 1865), 323. I am grateful to Shirley Martin for information on Howard's later career.

3   A gap was left for the insertion of the name of the circuit. This may be George Osborn (1816–91), farmer, of Charlton-on-Otmoor, because Mr Osborn is 'of Charlton' in the December 1857 minutes.

resolved, that the thanks of the Meeting be presented to him for the kind and efficient manner in which he has conducted the affairs of the Meeting and the Circuit at large during the past 3 years.

Signed in behalf of the Meeting

H.C. Howard Secy.

28 September 1853

Minutes of a Local Preachers Meeting held in Oxford Sept[r] 28 1853

Present Revs Thos Harris[1] & Henry C. Howard and the Bretheren Brown, Jones, Smith, Howard, Hunt, Kent, Danbury, Cripps.

The Min. of the last Meeting were read and confirmed.

Question I Are there any objections to either of the Bretheren? Ans. No.

The case of Bro Adams was then introduced & discussed. It appearing that he had declined his work upon the Plan from a scruple of conscience now removed and not from any disaffection to Methodist Law &c it was moved by Bro Jones & seconded by Rev. H.C. Howard that his name be placed on the Plan in its original place. Carried Unanimously.[2]

Question II Any to be received on Trial as Exhorters?

Bro William Bloomfield of Tackley.[3]

Question III Any for full reception?

Bro G.B. Richards late Wes. Missionary.[4]

Question IV Any alteration in times of service?

Wootton from 5 to ½ p 5 & all the Country places from 7 to ½ p 6 on w[ee]k [conj.] days.

H.C. Howard

Secy.

26 December 1853

Minutes of a Local Preachers Meeting held in Oxford Decr 26[th] 1853

Present Revs Thos Harris & Henry C. Howard with Bretheren Smith, Richards, Jones, Meek, Marcham, Davies, Hunt, Howard, Wheeler, Bloomfield, Brown, Birmingham, Gascoign and Cripps.

---

1   Thomas Harris (1791–1863), Superintendent of the Oxford Circuit, 1853–54: *Minutes of Conference* 1864, 9–10.

2   Adams was a member of the Reform Committee in the Oxford Circuit in October 1850 and had sympathy with the movement: OHC, OMCA, NM5/B/A2/1, Circuit Wesleyan Reform committee minute book, 1850–54, committee appointed at a public meeting held on 15 October 1850. It would seem that he eventually decided to remain with the Wesleyan Connexion, and that this choice was accepted by the Local Preachers' Meeting.

3   William Bloomfield (1808–? [after 1871]), labourer, of Tackley.

4   See note for March 1852 on George Brian Richards. In the Census returns of 1891 and 1901 Richards described himself as a 'Wesleyan minister', but his name does not appear in the *Minutes of Conference*. 'Missionary' here might mean salaried lay evangelist or 'home missionary'.

The Min. of last Meeting were read & confirmed.
Question I Any objection to either of the Bretheren? Ans. No.
Question II Any to be rec[d] on Trial? Bro. J. Barratt of Wootton.
Question III Any to be fully rec[d]? No.
Question IV Any alteration in times of Service.

    Tackley to 11. Kidlington 6. Kirtlington ½ p 5.
    Bladon 6. Islip 6. Hampton Poyle 6.
    Headington Quarry 6. Rose Hill 6.

It was also decided that the double appoints given on the present plan should be discontinued.
It is announced that Bro Charlton had removed from the Circuit. Bros Davies, Wheeler, Bloomfield & Fathers to supply his appts.

Henry C. Howard
Secretary.

29 March 1854

Minutes of the Local Preachers Meeting held March 29th 1854
Present Rev Tho Harris in the Chair with the Brethren Jones Brown Davis Adams Meek Richards Gascoign Fathers Howard Hunt Smith Turtle[1] & Bloomfield.
Question I Any objections &c. None except that a complaint was made against Bro Birmingham that when he has no appointments on the plan he very rarely attended any place of worship and was ~~idling~~ loitering at home while his brethren were preaching at the Headington Quarry Chapel.
Resolved that a letter be written to him.
Ques 2 Any to be received on trial? Answer Bro Harper.[2]
Ques 3 Any to be fully received? Ans No.
Ques 4 Any to be permitted to preach by a Note from the Superintendent – Ans Bro Railton[3] of Oxford and Bro Saml Faulkner of Tackley.[4]
Ques 5 Any alterations. None of any consequence.
Bro Bailey had been removed from his labours by the hand of death during the last Quarter. He was called away very suddenly, but was prepared for his solemn change. He for many years maintained the purity, consistency, and uprightness of the christian without reproach. Under various trying dispensations of providence, he was sustained by the grace of God. As a local preacher, he was very acceptable

---

1   Possibly Edward Turtle (1834/5–1910), shoemaker, of Combe, and later of Woodstock.
2   Charles Harper (1813–97), baker, of Oxford.
3   Hugh Railton (1831–1907). In 1851 Railton was an apprentice confectioner in Barnard Castle, but during the 1850s he settled in Oxford, and married, and became book-keeper to a confectioner, perhaps his fellow-Wesleyan James Boffin.
4   Samuel Faulkner (1810–78), agricultural labourer, of Tackley.

and useful - his sermons shewed him to be a man of reading – reflection and much prayer. He walked with God, and was not, for God took him.[1]

26 June 1854

Local Preachers Meeting held in Oxford June 26th 1854

Present Revds Thos Harris & H.C. Howard with the Bretheren Wheeler Osborn Howard Bloomfield Birmingham Fathers Palmer Jones Hunt and John Allen[2] (lately belonging to the Primitive Methodists).

Question 1st Any objection to any of the Bretheren?

It was resolved that the Chairman address a letter to Bro Kent admonishing him of his neglect of his class-meeting – and also of his refusing to meet in the Society at Woodstock.

Question 2nd Are there any to be received on Trial?

Bro Railton to be received as an Exhorter.

Bro Faulkner to continue preaching on Note.

Resolved that John Allen and Charles Harper who have honourably retired from the Primitive Methodists having been fully accredited Local Preachers in that Connexion, be rec[d] on Trial, but in consid[n] of their position in the above-ment[d] Body they should remain on Trial one Quarter only.[3]

Question III Any alterations in time & place? No.

Henry C. Howard.

27 September 1854

Minutes of the Local Preacher's Meeting held September 27th 1854

Present Revs Thos. A. Rayner[4] and H.J. Piggott[5] with the brethren Brown, Davis, Jones, Wheeler, Danbury, Adams, Richards, Gascoign, Howard, Hunt.

Quest[n] I Any objection against any of the Brethr.

Answ. None.

Quest[n] II Any to be received on trial?

---

1   Bailey's sudden death was reported in the *OC*, 4 February 1854. The final sentence adapts the biblical account of the death of the patriarch Enoch in Genesis 5:24.

2   Possibly John Allen (c.1814–68), shoemaker, of St Ebbe's.

3   Harper appears on the 1847 Primitive Methodist Oxford Circuit plan: Kate Tiller, "'The desert begins to blossom': Oxfordshire and Primitive Methodism, 1824–1860', *Oxoniensia*, 71 (2006), (Oxford: OAHS, 2007), between pages 102 and 103.

4   Thomas Alexander Rayner (1814–85), Superintendent of the Oxford Circuit, 1854–57: *Minutes of Conference 1885*, 33.

5   Henry James Piggott (1831–1917), junior minister in the Oxford Circuit, 1854–55: *Minutes of Conference* 1918, 121. From 1860 until his death Piggott worked to establish Wesleyan Methodism in Italy. For his early ministry, including very brief references to his year in Oxford, see T.C. Piggott and T. Durley, *Life and Letters of Henry James Piggott, BA, of Rome* (London: Epworth Press, 1921), 18–36.

Answ. Bro. Railton. Also that Bro. Faulkner, and Bro. Skidmore,[1] both of Tackley, receive notes from Superintendent to preach before one or two of the Brethr, who shall report to the Next Quarterly Meeting. Also that Bro. Bloomfield of Tackley be heard by one or two of the brethr, & be reported as above.

III Any to be fully received?

That Bros Allen and Harper being absent their reception as accredited Local Preachers according to the minutes of the last Meeting be postponed.

IV Any alteration in time in any of the Places?

The Week evening preaching at 6 ½ instead of 7.

Henry J. Piggott.

27 December 1854

Minutes of the Local Preacher's Meeting held December 27th 1854

Present Revs Thos A. Rayner & H.J. Piggott, with ~~Brothers~~ the brethren Brown, Birmingham, Jones, Danbury, Adams, Hunt, Osborn, Foster, Bloomfield, Howard & Blunt.

Quest[n] 1 Any objection against any of the brethren?

That a note be sent to Bro Kent, to express the surprise of the meeting that he has not attended Class during the Quarter, and to intimate that, as a Local Preacher, he will be expected to meet with the Woodstock Society.

Quest[n] 2 Any to be received on trial?

That the ~~note of~~ minute of the last Meeting respecting Bros Faulkner and Skidmore be repeated.

Quest 3 Any to be fully received?

The full reception of Bros Harper & Allen again deferred owing to ~~the~~ their absence from the Meeting.

Quest. 4 Any alteration in time in any of the Places.

That enquiry be made at Rose Hill whether the preaching on the Sabbath morning could be conveniently changed to afternoon.

Quest[n] 5 Any fresh places to be received on the Plan.

That Forrest Hill be regularly supplied.

Henry J. Piggott.

28 March 1855

Minutes of a Local Preacher's Meeting held March 28th 1855

Present Revs T.A. Rayner & H.J. Piggott, with the brethren, Birmingham, Wheeler, Jones, Danbury, Adams, Marcham, Richards, Gascoign, Fathers, Hunt, Osborn, Harper, Allen, Railton, Bloomfield.

1. Any objection against any of the Brethren?

Answ. That the note of the last Meeting respecting Bro Kent be repeated.

2. Any to be received as accredited Local Preachers?

---

1   Possibly Jonathan Skidmore, of Tackley: see below, March 1859.

Bros Harper & Allen, having both made satisfactory statements respecting their personal experience, their belief in Methodist doctrine, & attachment to Methodist discipline, were unanimously received as accredited Local Preachers.

Bro Railton to be examined at the next Quarterly Meeting preparatory to his full reception, & during the quarter to be heard by one of the Ministers.

3. Any to be received on trial?

Bro Bloomfield to have an appointment at the Morning Chapel[1] during the next Quarter & to be heard by one of the Ministers.

Bro Faulkner to be put on the plan as an Exhorter.

4. Any alteration in any of the places?

The evening Service at Coombe to commence at 5 ½ o'clock.

5. Any new places to be received on the plan?

Answ. Botley.

Henry J. Piggott.

27 June 1855

Minutes of a Local Preachers Meeting held June 27th 1855

Present Revs T.A. Rayner & H.J. Piggott with the brethren Meek, Birmingham, Jones, Richards, Danbury, Harper, Cripps, J. Barratt, Gascoign, Bloomfield, Palmer, Wheeler, Adams, Hunt, Railton, Allen, T.G. Smith, Brown & Howard.

1. Any objection to the moral & religious character of any of the brethren?

Moved by Bro Richards and seconded by Bro Smith that certain rumours being afloat injurious to the character of Bro Osborn, it is the opinion of this Meeting that, if possible, his case be settled by the investigation of the Ministers, and, this failing, to avoid all occasion of offence, Bro Osborn do not take his appointments as a Local Preacher, until some decision be arrived at according to our rules in such a case.[2] The resolution was put to the meeting and adopted unanimously.

2. Any objection in point of Discipline? None.

3. Any on trial to be received as accredited Local Preachers?

Bro. J. Barrett and Bro. Railton, after being both examined in presence of the Meeting, were unanimously received as accredited Local Preachers.

4. Any to be received on trial? None.

5. [Any to be received][3] as Exhorters? None.

6. No alteration in time at any of the places.

7. No new places to be received on the plan.

H.J. Piggott.

---

1   See above, June 1844. The Morning Chapel was a smaller chapel within the New Inn Hall Street premises.

2   No detail is given about the 'injurious' rumours, but see below December 1857, when Osborn was formally charged with drunkenness.

3   Indicated in original by a line.

26 September 1855

Minutes of a Local Preachers' Meeting held Septr 26th 1855
Present The Revs T.A. Rayner (in the Chair) & H.J. Piggott, with the brethren Brown, Jones, Wheeler, Danbury, Adams, Marcham, Smith, Kent, Howard, Hunt, Osborn, Blunt, Harper, Allen, Railton, Bloomfield, Cripps and Faulkner.
1. Are there any objections to the moral & religious character of any of the brethren? None. Broth Osborn's case was made the subject of a long conversation, himself being present, and as a result the following resolution was moved by Bro Brown and seconded by Bro Howard and passed unanimously.
That Bro Osborn's case having been investigated, it is the unanimous opinion of this Meeting, that the Charges brought against him have not been sustained, and that he is entitled to the confidence of his brethren.
2. Are there any objections against any of the brethren in matters of discipline? None.
3. Are there any brethren on trial now to be fully received? None.
4. Are there any to be received on trial?
Bro David Harris,[1] having come from the Guildford Circuit duly authenticated as a Local Preacher on trial, to be placed in a similar position on our own plan. Also to receive instructions to prepare for examination next Quarter.
5. Are there any to be received as Exhorters?
Bro John Harris of Tackley.[2]
Bro James Nix[3] Jun[r] to receive a note from the Superintendent to preach occasionally during the Quarter.
6. Any alteration at any of the places?
Coombe Sunday evening service to commence at 5 ½.
Botley do at 6.
7. Any new places to be received?
Enquiries to be made about Kennington.
Henry J. Piggott (Secy).

26 December 1855

Minutes of a Local Preachers Meeting held December 26th 1855
Present Revs T.A. Rayner and H.J. Piggott, with the brethren Birmingham, Jones, Danbury, Adams, Meek, Howard, Hunt, Harper, Allen, J. Barrett, Railton & Cripps.
1. Any objections to the moral or religious character of any of the Brethren? None.
2. Any objections against any of the brethren in matters of discipline? None.

---

1   David Harris (1831–1916), leather grounder. Although he came to Oxford from Guildford, Harris had previously lived in Charlbury and returned there later in the year: see the December 1855 minutes.
2   Possibly John Harris (1823–1905), carter, of Tackley.
3   James Nix (1835–1909), Post Office clerk, of Oxford.

N.B. Bro Blunt has removed during the Quarter to London, and Bro D. Harris of Woodstock to the Witney Circuit.
3. Any to be received as accredited Local Preachers?
   Bro Bloomfield of Tackley to be requested to prepare for Examination at the next Meeting.
4. Any to be received on trial? None.
5. Any [to be received][1] as Exhorters?
   Bro. Jas Nix Junior.
   Also Bro Jno Grimmett[2] of Bladon to receive one or two appointments during the next Quarter.
6. Any alteration in any of the Places?
   Rose Hill morning service to commence at 11 o'clock.
   Kidlington afternoon do do at 2 ½.
7. Any new places to be received on the Plan? None.
                              Henry J. Piggott.

26 March 1856

Minutes of a Local Preachers' Meeting held March 26th 1856
Present the Revs T.A. Rayner & H.J. Piggott with the brethren Brown, Birmingham, Jones, Adams, Marcham, Meek, Palmer, Smith, Howard, Hunt, Foster, Railton, Bloomfield, Cripps & Faulkner & Jas Nix.
1. Any objections to the moral or religious character of any of the brethren? None.
2. Any objections agst any of the brethren in matters of discipline? None.
3. Any on trial to be received as accredited Local Preachers?
Bro Wm Bloomfield of Tackley having passed thro the usual examination to the satisfaction of the brethren was unanimously received.
4. Any to be received on trial?
   Bro C. Cripps of Islip,[3] proposed by Bro Adams, seconded by Bro J. Smith.
   Bro Faulkner of Tackley, propd by Bro Palmer, seconded by Bro Jones.
   Bro J. Harris of Tackley, propd by Bro Adams, seconded by Bro Jones.
   Bro J. Nix of Oxford, propd by Bro Railton, seconded by Bro Jones.
   Bro Jno Grimmett of Bladon, propd by Bro Adams, seconded by Bro Foster.
5. Any to be received as Exhorters? None.
6. Any alteration in any of the places?
   See minutes of last Meeting.
7. Any new places to be received on the Plan?
   Horspath to be enquired about.

1   Indicated in original by a line.
2   John Grimmett (1835–1917), agricultural labourer, of Bladon.
3   Charles Cripps (1834–1910), agricultural labourer, of Islip.

N.B. 1. Bro Marcham of Islip,[1] being about to leave for Canada, a resolution was unanimously passed, expressive of the affection & esteem of ~~the~~ his brethren & of their earnest wishes & prayers for his future usefulness & happiness & it was requested that a note be given him from the Superintendent embodying the substance of this Resolution.

2. Bro Busby having acted in the Capacity of Local Preacher in the St Albans Circuit & having removed hither during the Quarter, received on ~~to~~ the Plan.

Henry J. Piggott.

25 June 1856

Minutes of Meeting held Wednesday June 25th 1856
Present Rev. T.A. Rayner, Rev. H.J. Piggott, with the Brethren Brown, Jones, Adams, Meek, Smith, Howard, Hunt, Allen, Railton.
1. Any objections against the moral or religious character of any of the brethren? Answ. None.
2. Any objections against any of the brethren in respect of matters of discipline? Many complaints having been received from several of the places ~~on account of the ground that~~ to the effect that appointments have been grievously neglected during the Quarter, a lengthy conversation took place on the subject, and the desire was earnestly expressed by the Meeting that brethren would for the future except in cases of necessity attend to <u>their own</u> appointments.
3. Any to be received as Accredited Local Preachers?
None.
4. Any to be received on trial?
None.
5. Any alteration in any of the Places?
Kirtlington to be retained nominally on the Plan without appointments.[2]
6. Any new place to be received on the Plan?
None.
N.B. Horspath to have a few open air appointments, without being formally placed on the Plan.
Mem 1 Bro Davis of Rose Hill, for many years a faithful and acceptable labourer in this Circuit, has died in the Lord.
2 Bro Busby has removed to the Romford Circuit.

Henry J. Piggott

---

1   William Marcham.
2   The Kirtlington membership fell steeply during the Reform crisis and the Reformers were holding Sunday services in the village in 1856: OHC, OMCA, NM5/A/A1/2, copy circuit plan for the Wesleyan Circuit (in fact a Reformers' plan), January–March 1856.

24 September 1856

Minutes of Meeting held Wednesday Septr 24th /56
Present Revs T.A. Rayner & S.H. Morton,[1] with the breth[n] Allen, Jones, Wheeler, Nix, Railton, Hunt, Meek, Birmingham, Adams & Howard.
1. Any objections against the moral & religious character of any of the brethren? Ans[r] None.
2. Any objections against any of the brethren in respect of matters of discipline?
Several brethren have employed unauthorised substitutes, but have pledged themselves for the future either to take their own appointments or to get accredited supplies.
3. Any to be received as accredited Local preachers?
None.
4. Any to be received on trial?
None.
5. Any alteration in any of the places?
Charlton ½ past 2 instead of 2.
Botley to be removed from the plan.
6. Any new places to be received on the plan?
None.

S.H. Morton.

22 December 1856

Minutes of Meeting held Monday Dec: 22nd 1856
Present Revs T.A. Rayner, S.H. Morton with the brethn Osborne, Meek, Foster, Adams, Railton, Wheeler, Smith, Allen, Nix, Hunt.
1. Any objections against the moral & religious character of any of the brethren?
None. (Bro: Smith cautioned by the Superintendent with respect to his non- and late attendance at public service.)
2. Any objections against any of the brethren in respect of matters of discipline?
None.
3. Any to be received as accredited Local preachers?
None.
Brethren Cripps, Faulkner, J. Harris and J. Nix to preach trial sermons during the quarter, & be examined next Local preachers meeting.
4. Any to be received on trial?
Joseph Colegrove.[2]
5. Any alterations in any of the places?

1   Samuel Henry Morton (1831–91), junior minister in the Oxford Circuit, 1856–58: *Minutes of Conference* 1892, 15–16.
2   Joseph Colegrove (1835–79), shoemaker, of Oxford. See Mary Bright Rix, *Life of Emma Mathews* (Oxford: Hall, 1960), 18–21. When received on trial Colegrove had just married Rosa Nix, younger sister of James Nix.

None.
6. Any new places to be received on the plan?
None.

S.H. Morton.

25 March 1857

Minutes of meeting held Wedy 25th March 1857

Present Revs T.A. Rayner S.J. Morton with the brethren Brown, Jones, Foster, Colegrove, Hunt, Adams, Nix, Wheeler, Palmer, Birmingham, Grimmett, Cripps, Harris & Faulkner.

1. Are there any objections against the moral & religious character of any of the brethren?
2. Any objections against any of the brethren in respect of matters of discipline?
None.
3. Any to be received as accredited Local Preachers?
Bro. Cripps to be placed on the Exhorters List
Bro. Faulkner do do do
Bro. Harris be received as an accredited Local Preacher.
Bro. Nix do do do
4. Any to be received on Trial?
Resolved that there be a list of Exhorters, with the understanding that the Meeting does not commit itself to receive them as Local Preachers.
Resolved that Henry Tombs,[1] W. Roberts,[2] Luke Day[3] be received as Exhorters.
5. Any alteration in any of the places?
None.
6. Any new place to be received on the plan?
None.

S.H. Morton

24 June 1857

Minutes of meeting – held June 24th 1857

Present: Rev^{ds} T.A. Rayner& S.H. Morton with the brethren Brown, Smith, Hunt, Kent, Nix, Colegrove, Harper, Bloomfield, Jones.

1. Are there any objections against the moral & religious character of any of the brethren?
None.
2. Any objections against any of the brethren in respect of matters of discipline?
None.
Bro. Allen has left the Society.

---

1   Perhaps Henry Tombs (1838–87), confectioner, of Oxford.
2   William Roberts (1836–?1915), clerk, of Oxford.
3   Possibly Luke Day (1838–?), cordwainer, of Oxford.

Bro. Railton has removed from the circuit.

3. Any to be received as accredited Local preachers?

Bro. Merry[1] from the Witney Circuit.

Bro. Grimmett exam^n deferred until Xmas.

4. Any to be received on trial?

None.

5. Any alteration in any of the places?

None.

6. Any new places to be received on the plan.

None.

S.H. Morton.

30 June 1857

Minutes of Meeting held Wed^y Sep 30th 1857

Present:- Rev^{ds} ~~T.A. Rayner~~ B. Gregory[2] & S.H. Morton – with the brethren Meek, Jones, Adams, Harper, Birmingham, Grimmett, Bloomfield, Wheeler, Hunt, Danbury, Howard, Colegrove, Nix, Smith, Brown.

1. Are there any objections against the moral & religious character of any of the brethren?

None.

2. Any objections against any of the brethren in respect of matters of discipline?

None.

3. Any to be received as accredited Local preachers?

Bro^r Grimmett examin^n next meeting.

Bro^{rs} Hunt, Birmingham & Howard & Superint^{dt} to hear him preach his Trial Sermon.

Bro^r Colegrove's exam^n next meeting.

Bro^{rs} Brown, Smith & Harper to hear Sermon.

4. Any to be rec^d on Trial or as Exhorters?

Bro^r Roberts on Trial.

Mark Winter[3] proposed as Exhorter by Bro^r Meek, seconded by Bro^r Danbury.

Green prop^d by Bro. Smith, sec^d by Bro. Brown as Exhorter.

5. Any alteration in any of the places?

Winter hours in country places.[4]

---

1   William Merry (1828–62), stonemason.

2   Benjamin Gregory (1820–1900), Superintendent of the Oxford Circuit, 1857–60. In addition to the official obituary in the *Minutes of Conference* 1901, 125–7, an account of Gregory's ministry in Oxford may also be found in J.R. Gregory (ed.), *Benjamin Gregory, DD. Autobiographical Recollections … with Memorials of his Later Life* (London: Hodder and Stoughton, 1903), 407–23.

3   Mark Winter (1834–1916), leather dresser, of Wootton (Oxon).

4   Sunday and midweek services began earlier in the winter months.

6. Any new places to be received on the plan?
None.

S.H. Morton.

28 December 1857

Minutes of Meeting held Wednesday December 28th 1857[1]
Present:- the Revds B. Gregory & S.H. Morton with the brethren Howard, Osborne, Colegrove, Nix, Colegrove,[2] Roberts, Jones, Hunt, Palmer, Bloomfield, Harris, Birmingham, Foster, Brown, Adams, Harper.
1. Are there any objections against the moral & <u>religious</u> character of any of the brethren?
A charge was brought against Mr Osborne of Charlton to the following effect:-
On the 15th December 1857 Mr Savage[3] - a member of the Society – saw Mr Osborne – ~~in~~ as he believes – in a state of intoxication <u>at 5 minutes</u> to eight o'clock in the evening. Mr Osborne in reply stated, that after a day's hard toil - (having that day removed furniture from Woodstock to Charlton) – he did, in a Public House, take two glasses of ale, - but was not <u>intoxicated</u>.
Proposed by Mr Adams:- seconded by Mr Palmer that the following Local preachers with the Ministers be appointed a Committee to investigate this charge
Messrs Howard, Jones, Hunt, Adams, Foster, Fathers.
2. Any objections against any of the brethren in respect of matters of discipline?
Complaints made that certain of the brethren have obtained unaccredited supplies.[4]
This practice strongly reprehended and the brethren charged by the Superintendent not to repeat it.
3. Any to be received as accredited Local preachers?
Bro[rs] Grimmett & Colegrove passed thro their examination & reports of Sermons were made by Superintendent. Both accepted as accredited Local preachers.
4. Any to be rec[d] on Trial or as Exhorters?
John Hedges[5] as Exhorter.
Tho[s] Trafford[6] do.
5. Any alteration in any of the places?
No.

---

1   The numeral in the date has been corrected and is hard to decipher, but 28 December 1857 was a Wednesday.
2   Joseph Colegrove is listed twice.
3   Perhaps Charles Savage (1822–90), mason, of Bladon, whose son Charles and daughter Amy were baptised at New Inn Hall Street in 1852 and 1855 respectively.
4   i.e., people other than accredited Local Preachers to take their appointments.
5   John Hedges (1834–1922), labourer, of Headington Quarry. On Hedges and Thomas Trafford, see 'Methodism in the Oxford Circuit', *OMM*, January 1934, 1, preserved in F.W. Nix's collection of material on Oxford Methodist history, OHC, OMCA, NM5/A/MS1/2.
6   Thomas Trafford (1833–1915), agricultural labourer, of Headington. Obituary in the *OWMCM*, January 1916, 1–2.

6. Any new places to be received on the plan?
No.

S.H. Morton.

24 March 1858

Minutes of Meeting held Wednesday March 24th 1858
Present: Rev[ds] B. Gregory & S.H. Morton with the brethren Smith, Jones, Roberts, Hedges, Colegrove, Hunt, Adams, Danbury, Bloomfield, Fathers, Harper, Palmer, Grimmett, Trafford, Foster, Birmingham, Kent, Nix, Howard.
1. Are there any objections against the moral & religious character of any of the brethren?
With deep regret the superintendent stated that, being convinced of Mr Osborne's immorality – he had felt it to be his duty to withhold Bro[r] O's Ticket – and that consequently his name would be dropped from the plan.
A serious statement affecting Mr Grimmett's character had been made in course of the quarter to the superintendent - wh: was substantially acknowledged by Mr G. The meeting determined that he sh[d] not supply his appointments during the remainder of the quarter & that he sh[d] be admonished by the Superint[dt].
2. Any objections against any of the brethren in respect of matters of disciples [discipline]?
None.
3. Any to be rec[d] as accredited Local Preachers?
None.
4. Any to be rec[d] on Trial or as Exhorters?
~~Henry Tombs to be recd on Trial.~~
Bro[r] Horton to be rec[d] on Trial
Bro[r] Bloomfield to be rec[d] as an Exhorter.[1]
5. Any alteration in any of the places?
Coombe – 6 instead of ½ past 5 – ½ 2 inst[d] of 2.
6. Any new places to be rec[d] on the plan?
Cassington
Barton

S.H. Morton.

23 June 1858

Minutes of Meeting held Wednesday June 23rd 1858
Present: Rev[ds] B. Gregory – S.H. Morton – with the brethren Jones, Adams, Nix, Hunt, Harper, Barratt, Winter, Horton, Meek.
1. Are there any objections against the moral or religious character of any of the brethren?

---

1   Job Bloomfield (1834–72), agricultural labourer, of Tackley, who moved up to being a preacher on trial in June 1859.

None.

2. Are there any objections against any of the brethren in respect of matters discipline?

None.

3. Any to be rec^d as accredited Local Preachers?

Brethren Roberts & Horton – who are to preach during the quarter – and be examined next Meeting.

4. Any to be rec^d on Trial or as Exhorters?

– Brother Clarke[1] – proposed by Mr Jones and seconded by Mr Adams – on Trial.

John Hedges - to be rec^d on Trial – proposed by Mr Jones & seconded by Mr Adams

Thos Trafford do proposed by Mr Jones seconded by Mr Nix.

5. Any alteration in any of the places?

Cassington at 5 o'clock. Not afternoon.

Barton at 5 do.

6. Any new places to be received on the plan?

Horsepath – open air.

S.H. Morton Secy.

22 September 1858

Minutes of a Local Preachers' Meeting held on Wednesday Sep 22nd, 1858.

Present Revs B. Gregory (Chairman & A.J. French,[2] together with Brethren Brown, Meek, Harris, Horton, Grimmett, Adams, Hedges, Jones, Howard, Foster.

1. Are there any objections against the moral or religious character of any of the Brethren?

Ans. None.

2. Are there any objections in matters of discipline?

Kidlington had been disappointed by Brother Grimmett, and Islip by Bro. Danbury.

3. Are there any to be rec^d as accredited Local Preachers?

Brethren Roberts & Horton, after examination held, were unanimously received.

4. Are there any to be received on trial?

None.

5. Is there any alteration in the places?

Bladon, to have afternoon preaching instead of morning.

Kirtlington, to be continued with help from Tackley.

Cassington & Horspath, discontinued for the present.

Alfred J. French,

Secretary.

---

1   Jonas Clarke (1810–87), confectioner, of Woodstock.

2   Alfred John French (1835–1921), junior minister in the Oxford Circuit, 1858–59: *Minutes of Conference* 1922, 110–11.

26 December 1858

Minutes of a Local Preachers' Meeting held on Monday Dec. 26th, 1858.

Present Revs B. Gregory, A.J. French, together with Brethren Adams, Jones, Howard, Merry, Roberts, Harris, Nix, Wheeler, Bloomfield.

1. Are there any objections against the moral or religious character of any of the Brethren?

Ans. None.

2. Are there any objections in matters of discipline?

Rosehill has been disappointed by Brethren Harper & Colegrove.

3. Are there any to be received as accredited Local Preachers?

None.

4. Are there any to be received on trial?

Bro. Langden, from the Cheltenham Circuit.

5. Is there any alteration in any of the places?

None.

6. Are there any new places to be commenced?

Old Woodstock, in the afternoon.

23 March 1859

Minutes of a Local Preachers' Meeting held March 23rd, 1859

Present Revs B. Gregory & A.J. French, with Brethren Jones, Danbury, Adams, Meek, Smith, Kent, Palmer, Foster, Barratt, Nix, Colegrove, Clarke, J. Bloomfield, Wheeler, Hunt, Hedges, Horton, Harper, Howard.

Qu. 1. Are there any objections against any of the Brethren?

Ans. 1 Several of the Brethren, having neglected their appointments, as Brethren Nix, Danbury and others, were requested to make conscience of attending their apptmts.

Ans. 2 Bro. Grimmett's name is removed from the plan for the ensuing Quarter, to be afterwards re-admitted should his future conduct justify such a step.

Qu. 2 Are any to be received as Exhorters?

Ans. 1. Bro. Skidmore of Tackley [1]) to have their initials placed on the plan

   2. Bro. Holloway of Wootton [2])

   3. Bro. Albert Bishop of Wootton [3])

---

1   Jonathan Skidmore (1829–1901), railway labourer. A tribute, 'The Late Mr Jonathan Skidmore', by J.N. [James Nix] was published in the *ODFCM*, September 1901, 45–6 and a copy is pasted into the Local Preachers' minute book (see below, September 1901).

2   Christopher Holloway (1828–95), agricultural labourer, of Wootton (Oxon.). Later active in agricultural trade unionism: see Pamela L.R. Horn, 'Christopher Holloway: an Oxfordshire Trade Union Leader', *Oxoniensia* 33 (1968), 125–36.

3   Albert Bishop (1841–1910), son of a gardener, of Wootton (Oxon.). Accepted for the Wesleyan ministry in 1864: *Minutes of Conference* 1910, 148–9. See also Benjamin Gregory's recollection of Bishop as a young preacher in *WMM*, May 1888, 381–3.

Qu. 3 Any alterations to be made in time or place?
Ans. Coombe in the evening at 6 instead of 5 ½ o'clock.

22 June 1859

Minutes of a Local Preachers' Meeting held June 22nd 1859.
Present:- Revs B. Gregory (in the chair) & A.J. French, and Brethren Adams, Jones, Danbury, Bloomfield, Trafford, Meek, Horton, Harper, Nix, Roberts & Clarke.
Qu. 1 Are there any objections against any of the Brethren?
Ans. None. Bro. Grimmett's name to be restored to its former position on the plan.
Qu. 2 Are any to be received on the full plan?
Ans. 1 Bro. John Hedges, who has left the circuit.
    2 Bro. Thomas Trafford, who remains on trial another quarter.
Qu. 3 Are any to be received on trial?
Ans. Bro. Job Bloomfield, of Tackley.
Qu. 4 Are any to be received as Exhorters?
Ans 1 Bro. Buckingham, of Woodstock.[1]
    2 Bro. Preston, of Oxford.[2]
Qu. 4 Are there any alterations in times or places?
Ans. None.

Alfred J. French.

21 September 1859

Minutes of a Local Preachers' Meeting held Sep. 21st, 1859.
Present Rev. B. Gregory & Brethren Foster, Harris, Meek, Hunt, Adams, Skidmore.
Qu. 1 Are there any objections against any of the Brethren?
Ans None.
Qu. 2 Are any to be received on the full plan?
Ans Bro. Hitchman.[3]
Qu. 3 Are any to be received on trial?
Ans Brethren Skidmore, Holloway & Bishop.
Qu. 4 Are there any to be received as Exhorters?
Ans. None.
Qu. 5 Are there any alterations in times or places?
Ans. The evening service at Coombe to commence at 6.

21 December 1859

Minutes of a Local Preachers' Meeting held Dec. 21st, 1859.

---

1   Charles Buckingham (1813–71), licensed victualler, of Old Woodstock.
2   Charles James Preston (1841–1904), of Oxford. Preston entered the Wesleyan ministry in 1861: *Minutes of Conference* 1905, 138. See also Benjamin Gregory's recollection in *WMM*, May 1888, 381–3.
3   James Hitchman (1812–96), tailor, of Oxford.

Present, Revs B. Gregory & A.J. French and Brethren Palmer, Colegrove, Hedges, Bloomfield, Fathers, Trafford, Harris, Merry, Wheeler, Skidmore, Roberts, Howard & Horton.

Qu. 1 Are there any objections against any of the Brethren?

Ans. Several disappointments have occurred during the Q^r.

Qu. 2 Are any to be received on the full plan?

Ans. Brethren John Hedges & Thomas Trafford.

Alfred J. French.

21 March 1860

Minutes of a Local Preachers' Meeting held March 21st 1860

Present Revs B. Gregory, Alfred J. French, with Brethren Meek, J. Barratt, Bloomfield, Fathers, Skidmore, Horton, Holloway, Buckingham, Bishop, Harper, Ecclestone, Preston, Hedges, Adams, Wheeler, Clarke, Howard.

Question 1 Are there any objections against any of the Brethren?

Ans No.

Question 2 Are any to be received on the full plan?

Ans No.

Question 3 Are any to be received an Exhorters?

Ans No.

Question 4 Are there any alterations in times or places?

Ans No.

Alfred J. French.

27 June 1860

Minutes of a Local Preacher's Meeting held at Oxford, June[1] 27th 1860.

Present Revs B. Gregory & A.J. French, with Brethren Smith, Adams, Jones, Hunt, Grimmett, Ecclestone, Buckingham, Bishop, Foster, Bloomfield, Trafford, Clarke, Holloway, Meek, Nix.

Question 1 Are there any objections against any of the Brethren?

Ans No.

Qu. 2 Are there any to be rec^d on the full plan?

Ans No. N.B. Brethren Skidmore, Holloway & Bishop will have been on trial 12 months next Quarter.

Qu. 3 Are there any to be rec^d as Exhorters?

Ans No.

Qu. 4 Are there any alterations in times or places?

Ans No.

Alfred J. French.

---

1   The month has been corrected by writing 'June' over 'July'.

26 September 1860

Minutes of Local Preachers Meeting held Sept. 26 1860

Present Rev^{ds} F.F. Woolley[1] & C.H. Floyd[2] with Messrs Smith, Jones, Nix, Railton, Hunt, Roberts, Preston, Adams, Cripps, Foster, Howard, Ecclestone, Palmer, Merry &c.

1. Is there any objection against any Brother?

None.

2. Are any to be rec^d on the full plan?

Brethren Skidmore, Holloway & Bishop request that their examination be postponed. Bro. Preston, & the forementioned brethren are to be Examined at the Dec Mtg, & preach in the interim before the Super.

3. Any to be rec^d on trial? None.

4. Any removals to or from the Circuit? None.

5. Any alterations in times or places?

The usual winter alterations.[3]

Chas. H. Floyd.

26 December 1860

Local Preacher's Meeting held at Oxford, Dec. 26th 1860

Present Rev^{ds} F.F. Woolley & Chas. H. Floyd, with Messrs Jones, Wheeler, Danbury, Adams, Meek, Fathers, Smith &c.

1. No objection against any brother.

N.B. some disappointments having occurred thro' changes, the Meeting expressed its desire that the Brethren wd, as far as possible, fulfil their own apptments.[4]

2. Brethren Skidmore, Holloway, Bishop, Preston, & Buckingham were examined, & received as fully accredited Local Preachers.

3. None to be rec^d on trial.

4. No removals to, or from the Circuit.

5. The Sunday Afternoon Service in Oxford to be discontinued.

The Sunday Evening Service at Kirtlington to be discontinued.

The propriety of putting Horspath & Marston on the Plan to be considered & reported on at the next Meeting.

C.H.F.

---

1   Frederick Farmer Woolley (1816–78), Superintendent of the Oxford Circuit, 1860–61: *Minutes of Conference* 1878, 43–4.

2   Charles Hulme Floyd (1836–1919), junior minister in the Oxford Circuit, 1860–61. Floyd returned as Superintendent, 1878–81: *Minutes of Conference* 1920, 113.

3   i.e., earlier starting times for services in the rural parts of the Circuit.

4   Confusion through changing appointments meant that some congregations received no preacher at all, and were thus 'disappointed'.

Bro. Brown, (the oldest Local Preacher on the Plan), having died during the quarter, Brethren Smith, Howard & Harper were requested to prepare a record concerning him.[1]

27 March 1861

Local Preachers Mtg held at Oxford, March 27th 1861
Present Rev[d] F.F. Woolley & Mess[rs] Foster, Adams, Meek, Cripps, Preston, Wheeler, Railton, Hunt, Nix & Jones.
1. Any objection against a Brother? None.
2. Any to be rec[d] on full plan? None.
3. Any [to be received on][2] trial? None.
4. Any removals? Bro. Horton to Reading.
5. Any alteration in hours of Service?
The usual ones only.
6. No opening for indoor service having presented itself at Horspath & Marston, the Brethren Eggleston, Nix, Howard & Hunt were deputed, as a Sub-Committee, to arrange for outdoor service during the summer months.
Chas. H. Floyd
'This Meeting records, with submission to the Divine Will, the removal by death of its Senior Member, Bro. Brown, who for upwards of 40 years discharged the duties of a Local Preacher with fidelity & acceptance. He died in peace at the venerable age of 79.' (copy)

26 June 1861

Local Preacher's Meeting held at Oxford, June 26 1861
Present Rev[ds] F.F. Woolley & Chas H. Floyd with Mess[rs] Jones, Adams, Nix, Railton, Foster, Ecclestone, Bloomfield, Cripps &c.
1. Any objection against a Brother? None.
2. Any to be rec[d] on full plan? None.
3. Any [to be received][3] on trial? None.
4. Any removing from, or coming into the Circuit? None.
5. Any fresh place to be put on the plan?
Headington: service to commence at 3 o'clock on the Sabbath Afternoon.
6. The Committee, chosen at the March Quarterly Meeting, were again requested to arrange for out-door Services, if practicable, at Marston, Horspath & Headington.
Chas. H. Floyd

25 September 1861

Minutes of the Local Preachers Meeting held at Oxford Sept 25th 1861

---

1   For a note of the death of George Brown, see *OC*, 5 January 1861, 5.
2   Indicated in original by a line.
3   Indicated in original by a line.

Present Rev. W.R. Rogers[1] & P.B. Wamsley[2] Messrs Adams, Hitchman, Jones, Smith, Howard, Nix, Roberts, Grimmett, Ecclestone, Colegrove, Danbury, Fathers, Kent, Hunt, Harris, Bloomfield, Railton, Bishop, Buckingham, Harper, Meek, Wheeler, Clarke.

Ques I Any objection against any of the bretheren? Ans Bro. Birmingham neglected Hampton Poyle.

II Any to be recieved on full plan? No.

III Any [to be received on][3] trial? Bro. Fowler.

IV Any removals. 1. Bro. Bloomfield from Tackley to Kirtlington. 2. Bro. Preston has entered the ministry.[4]

V Any alteration in times or places?

Ans During the winter months the usual change in the times of Evening Services in the country.

P.B. Wamsley

18 December 1861

Local Preacher's Meeting held Dec 18th 1861

Present Revs W.R. Rogers & P.B. Wamsley Bros Smith Meek Foster Barratt Holloway Grimmett Adams Railton Buckingham Faulkner Skidmore Hitchman Nix Bishop Jones Hunt Roberts Howard Ecclestone Harper Birmingham Kent Wheeler Palmer

I Objections 1 ans Bro. Foster was objected to by Mr[s] Smith &c. As result of enquiry & conversation Bro Nix moved Bro Jones seconded a resolution of confidence, considering Bro. Foster, as a father, had a perfect right to advise his son in certain matters of family dispute & trouble.[5]

II Any recieved on full plan? Ans no.

III Any [received] on trial? [Ans][6] No.

IV Any removals? Bro. Skidmore from Kirtlington to Witney.

V Any alterations in time or Place? None.

Philip B. Wamsley.

---

1   William R. Rogers (1810–68), Superintendent of the Oxford Circuit, 1861–64: *Minutes of Conference* 1868: 259.

2   Philip Broster Wamsley (1832–86), junior minister in the Oxford Circuit, 1861–64: *Minutes of Conference* 1887, 14–15.

3   Indicated in original by a line.

4   Charles Preston was accepted for the ministry at the Conference of 1861 and sent immediately to an appointment in the Bridgewater Circuit: *Minutes of Conference* 1861, 6, 29.

5   Although precise details are not given, Joseph Foster's son Edwin was married to Esther, née Smith. Ann Smith, Esther's widowed mother, was a baker in Woodstock. It may be suggested that the 'family dispute & trouble' involved Edwin Foster's relationship with his wife's family. By 1871 the younger Fosters had left Woodstock for Abergavenny.

6   Indicated in original by a line.

31 March 1862

Local Preacher's Meeting held in Oxford March 31st
Present Revs W.R. Rogers & P.B. Wamsley Bros Adams Smith Nix Hitchman Skidmore Colegrove Railton Bishop Danbury Foster Harper Buckingham
I Any objections? None.
II Any recieved on full plan? None.
III Any recieved on trial? Bro. Fowler to be put on trial. Moved by Bro. Danbury seconded by Bro. Railton, that Bro. Sumner[1] be recieved on trial.
IV Any removals? Bro. T. Barratt is removed to the Brackley Circuit.[2] Bro. Reynolds recieved on recommendation from Birmingham Circuit as on trial.
V Any alteration in time or place? No.

        Philip B. Wamsley.

25 June 1862

Quarterly Local Preachers Meeting held in Oxford June 25th 1862
Present Rev. W.R. Rogers P.B. Wamsley Bros Adams Howard Nix Kent Hitchman Railton Meek Danbury Colegrove Fowler Reynolds Grimmett Buckingham Fathers Clarke Foster Sumner Ecclestone Hunt Harper
I Ques Any objections? Bro. Hunt neglected New Osney & New Hinksey. Bro. Roberts neglected Islip. The explanation given was considered satisfactory.
II Any to be recieved on full plan? No.
That Bro. Reynolds be retained on trial six months longer his examination being unsatisfactory.
III Any to be recieved on trial? No.
IV Any Removals to, or from the Circuit? No.
V Any alteration in time or place? Moved by Bro. Ecclestone seconded by Bro. Grimmett that the service at Headington Quarry be altered from afternoon to morning, and that Mr Rogers be requested to inquire & arrange accordingly.

        Philip B. Wamsley.

24 September 1862

Local Preachers Meeting held in Oxford September 24th 1862
Present Revs W.R. Rogers & P.B. Wamsley Bros Adams Railton Fowler Meek Hitchman Smith Grimmett Sumner Bishop Nix Hunt Harper
I Ques. Any objection to any of the bretheren? Ans. No.
II Any to be recieved on full plan? Ans. No.
III Any to be recieved on Trial? Ans. Bro. Taylor by a unanimous vote.
IV Any Removals to or from the Circuit? Ans. No.

---

1 Elijah Henry Sumner (1842–1916), engine cleaner, of Oxford (though from a Bladon family). He entered the Wesleyan ministry in 1866: *Minutes of Conference* 1916, 158.
2 Thomas Barrett was recorded in the 1871 Census living at Hethe, and was buried there in 1878.

V Any alteration in Times or Place of service?

Ans: From 7 to 6 ½ in all the country places on week-night as usual during the winter months.

Local Preachers Meeting held in Oxford Dec 24th 1862

Present Rev W.R. Rogers & P.B. Wamsley Bros Foster Clarke Fathers Birmingham Hunt Jones Fowler Sumner Nix Taylor Faulkner Howard

I Ques. Any objection to any bretheren? No.

II Any bretheren to be recieved on Full plan?

Moved by Bro. Adams & seconded by Bro. Jones that Bro. Fowler be recieved.

III Any to be recieved on Trial? No.

IV Any Removals to or from the Circuit? Bro. Bishop removed to Watlington as a Hired Local Preacher.[1]

V Any alteration in Time or Places?

1. Moved by Bro. Hunt & seconded by Bro. Nix that the service at Headington Quarry be changed from Morning to Afternoon 2 ¾ and that Headington New be discontinued or altered to once a month according to the superintendent's discretion.

2. That Hampton Poyle be altered to Evening only instead of Afternoon & Evening.

Philip B. Wamsley.

25 March 1863

Local Preachers Meeting held in Oxford March 25th 1863

Present Revs W.R. Rogers Philip B. Wamsley Bros Smith Jones Hitchman Colegrove Ecclestone Foster Fowler Buckingham Adams Nix Railton Hunt

I Ques: Any objection to any of the bretheren? No.

II Any bretheren to be recieved on the full plan? No. Bro. Sumner who is very busy wishes to remain on trial another Quarter.

III Any to be recieved on trial?

Ans. No.

IV Any Removals to, or from the Circuit? Bro. Reynolds has removed to London. Bro. Taylor declines to continue on the Plan. Bro. Henman[2] of Bedford having brought his credentials is cordially recieved on the Plan.

V Any alterations in Times or Place

1. Hampton Poyle Afternoon and Evening ½ past two and six.

2. New Headington is to be discontinued unless the friends on the spot more heartily cooperate.

---

1   By the time he offered for the Wesleyan ministry in 1864 Albert Bishop had been a Hired Local Preacher in the Watlington Circuit for two years. Paying a salary to secure the full-time services of a Local Preacher was an option for circuits which could not afford the costs of stipend, housing and allowances associated with increasing the number of ministers.

2   William Albert Henman (1840–1911), farmer, of Islip.

1 July 1863

Local preachers Meeting held at Oxford July 1 1863

Present Rev W.R. Rogers in the Chair with the Brethren Adams Jones Danbury Grimmett Henman Nix Fathers Roberts Hunt Howard & Sumner

1. Any objection to any of the Brethren? No.

2. Any to be received on full plan?

Proposed by Bro Adams seconded by Bro Nix that Bro Sumner be received. Carr[d].

3. Any to be received on trial?

Bro Irons of St Clements.[1]

4. Any removals to or from the Circuit. No.

5. Any alteration in time or place.

Bladon if agreeable to the Friends to have Service at 11 a.m. 6 p.m.

Local Preachers Meeting held in Oxford September 24th 1863

Present Revs W.R. Rogers Philip B. Wamsley Skidmore Colegrove Ecclestone Roberts Roberts[2] Kent Clarke Nix Palmer Howard Jones Adams.

I Question Any objection to any bretheren. No.

II Question Any to be recieved on Full Plan? No.

III Question Are there any to be recieved on Trial? No.

IV Ques. Any Removals to or from the Circuit? Bro Fowler has removed to the Abingdon Circuit.

V Ques. Any alterations in time or places? None, except the usual alteration on week nights during the winter months.

23 December 1863

Local Preachers Meeting held in Oxford on Wednesday Dec 23rd 1863

Present Revs W.R. Rogers Philip B. Wamsley Bros Fathers Jones Clarke Nix Henman Meek Foster Howard

I Question Any objection to any of the Bretheren. Bro Danbury neglected Islip on Sunday Dec 20 & Trafford neglected Charlton neglected Nov 29th.

II Ques Any to be recieved on full plan. No.

III Ques Any to be recieved on trial? No.

IV Ques Any removed to or from the Circuit? No.

V Ques Any alteration in time or place?

N.B. As several cases of neglected [appointments] were reported, there was a serious conversation held upon the evils arising therefrom & it was moved by Mr Fathers & seconded by Mr Henman 'that henceforth every Bro neglecting an appointment without giving satisfactory reason shall be dropped two numbers on the plan.'

23 March 1864

Local Preachers Meeting held in Oxford on Wednesday March 23rd /64.

1   Thomas Irons (c. 1804–?), fruiterer, of St Clement's. Irons was in Reading at the time of the 1861 Census: see below, minute for March 1865.
2   Roberts is listed twice.

Present Revs W.R. Rogers Philip B. Wamsley Bros Foster Hitchman Nix Roberts Jones Howard Railton Adams

I Ques Any objection to any of the bretheren? None.

II Ques Any to be recieved on full plan? No.

III Ques Any to be recieved on Trial?

IV Ques Any Removals to or from the Circuit? Bro Embury[1] who cam[e] duly accredited from the Banbury Circuit.

V Ques Any alteration in time or place? Service in the country places at 7 o'clock week day instead of 6 ½.

Philip B. Wamsley.

22 June 1864

Local Preachers Meeting held in Oxford June 22nd 1864

I Ques. Any objection? No.

II Ques. Any to be recieved on Full Plan? Ans. Yes. Bro. Irons unanimously received.

III Ques. Any to be recieved on Trial? No.

IV Ques. Any Removals to or from the Circuit? Bro. Sumner has removed to London.

V Ques. Any alteration in time or place?

Present Revs W.R. Rogers P.B. Wamsley Bros Ecclestone Palmer Henman Kent Bloomfield Irons Clarke Colegrove Hunt Roberts Howard Nix Foster Holloway.

20 September 1864

Local Preachers' Meeting held September 20th 1864

Question I Are there any objections against any of the brethren?

A. None.

　II Are there any to be received on the full plan?

A. None.

　III Are there any to be received on trial?

A. None.

　IV Are there any alterations in the time or place of services?

A. Kirtlington is to be dropped from the plan.

Present: - Revd T. Derry[2] and J. Scott[3] Brothers Jones Danbury Adams Smith Hunt Foster Harper Nix Grimmett Roberts Clarke Hitchman Ecclestone Holloway Henman and Irons.

Signed

Thomas Derry

1　William Shepherd Embury (1825–68), printer.

2　Thomas Derry, Superintendent of the Oxford Circuit, 1864–66: *Minutes of Conference* 1897, 22–3.

3　John Scott, junior minister in the Oxford Circuit, 1864–65: *Minutes of Conference* 1895, 34–5. Scott spent most of his ministry in Ceylon and had been there for nine years before his one-year appointment in Oxford.

21 December 1864

Local Preachers' Meeting held in Oxford December 21st 1864
Present Rev T. Derry & J. Scott Bros Jones, Adams, Smith, Nix, Grimmett, Colegrove, Roberts, Hitchman, Ecclestone & Skidmore.
Q 1 Are there any objections against any of the Brethren?
A None.
Brother Howard, having written to request that his name might be removed from the plan on account of his preaching appointments interfering with his duty as assistant Class Leader - the Brethren expressed their regret that the congregations should be deprived of Bro. Howard's services & resolved that he be requested to continue a Local Preacher though he should preach more rarely than before.
Q 2 Are there any to be received on the full plan?
A. None.
Q 3 Are there any to be received on trial?
A. None.
Q 4 Are there any alterations to be made in the time or place of services?
A. A unanimous opinion was expressed in favour of the first Sunday service at Headington Quarry being held in the morning so as to benefit the afternoon service at New Headington but no resolution was come to on the subject.
Q 5 Are there any new places to be taken on the plan?
A. The superintendent was requested to make inquiries as to the adviseableness of commencing preaching at Marston.
Signed
Thomas Derry.

22 March 1865

Local Preachers' Meeting held in Oxford March 22 1865
Present Revs T. Derry & J. Scott. Brothers Jones, Danbury, Adams, Fathers, Kent, Howard, Hunt, Foster, Nix, Grimmett, Roberts, Clarke, Hitchman, Ecclestone, Railton, Henman & Irons.
Question I Are there any objections against any of the Brethren?
A. Certain facts relative to Brother T.G. Smith having been considered it was unanimously resolved That his name be dropped from the plan.
Some inquiries were made as to the circumstances under which Brother Irons left Reading which were answered satisfactorily to the Meeting.
Q II Are there any to be received on the full plan?
A. None.
Q III Are there any to be received on trial? A. None.
Q IV Are there any to be received from other circuits?
A. Brother Keene[1] from Witney Brother Scarfe from Ipswich and Brother Phipps[2] from Swansea.

---

1   George Keene (1843–1931), grocer.
2   Austin Phipps (1838–1920), tailor.

Q V Are there any alterations in the time or place of services?
A. The week night services to begin at 7. Bladon to have morning instead of afternoon service. Kidlington to have afternoon service only & Hampton Poyle Evening service only.

Signed Thomas Derry.

22 June 1865

Local Preachers' Meeting held in Oxford June 22, 1865
Present Rev. T. Derry & J. Scott – Br[s] Danbury, Adams, Howard, Hunt, Foster, Harper, Nix, Hitchman, Ecclestone, Trafford, Holloway, Henman & Irons.
Question 1 Are there any objections against any of the Brethren?
A. Brother Grimmett has resigned his plan to the superintendent. It was stated Br. Keene had neglected his appointment to Bladon on May 7 & it was determined that he be spoken to by the superintendent.
Q. 2 Are there any to be received on the full plan?
A. No.
Q. 3 Are there any to be received on trial?
A. No. Resolved: That in future before any person be received as a Local Preacher on trial he be examined in Wesley's first twelve sermons[1] & the Conference catechisms[2] & be heard preach by a Committee of three Local Preachers to be appointed by the Superintendent.
Q. 4 Are there any Brethren received from or gone to other circuits?
A. Brother William Symons is received from the Brackley Circuit. Brother Scarfe has removed from Oxford.
Q. 5 Are there any alterations in the time or place of service?
A. New Headington to be given up. Forest Hill to have an additional service on the Sunday afternoon.

27 September 1865

Local Preachers' Meeting held in Oxford, September 27: 1865.
<u>Present</u>: Revs T. Derry & S.R. Williams[3] – Messrs Birmingham, Adams, Fathers, Hunt, Foster, Nix, Hitchman, Railton, Trafford, Henman & Symons.
In reference to the last meeting, the Superintendent stated that Bro. Keene, being usefully engaged in Sabbath-School work, would wish for all his appointments to be for the evening services.

---

1   The first twelve sermons in John Wesley's *Sermons on Several Occasions*, part of the doctrinal standards of Wesleyan Methodism.
2   The Wesleyan Conference published a series of graded catechisms, for children, young people and adults, and mandated their use in Sunday Schools from 1827: William Peirce, *The Ecclesiastical Principles and Polity of the Wesleyan Methodists* (revised edition, London: Wesleyan Conference Office, 1873), 147.
3   Samuel R. Williams (1842–1924), junior minister in the Oxford Circuit, 1865–67: *Minutes of Conference* 1925, 104–5.

Since it is not acceptable to the parties concerned, Forest Hill is not to have another service.

Quest. I Are there any objections against any of the Brethren?

Ans. 1 Objection was raised to Bro. Birmingham's non-attendance upon public service. Bro. B said that he <u>was</u> improved, and promised further improvement.

2. Objection was also taken to the conduct of Bro. Symons in engaging in a game unbefitting the position and character of a Local Preacher. He admitted his fault and promised that such conduct should not be repeated.

Quest. II Are any to be received on full plan?

Ans. None.

Quest III Are there any to be received on trial?

Ans. None.

Quest IV Are there any Removals to or from the Circuit?

Ans. Brethren Jones and Ecclestone are removing to London. <u>Resolved</u> That a letter to addressed to each of them, expressive of our Christian sympathy and deep regret at their removal.

Quest V Any alterations in times of preaching?

Ans. <u>Headington Quarry</u> to be 3 o'clock.

<u>Charlton</u> to be half past 5 o/c.

Quest VI Any new places to be taken on the plan?

Ans. Enquiries to be made concerning Eynsham, and, if possible, arrangements to be entered into for commencing a cause there.

Samuel R. Williams.

27 December 1865

Local Preachers' Meeting held in Oxford December 27/65

Present Revs T. Derry & S.R. Williams & J. Hobkirk.[1] Messrs Adams, Fathers, Hunt, Railton, Nix, Colegrove, Bloomfield, Henman, Palmer.

The Superintendent read a letter from Bro. Embury laying the fact of his illness before the Meeting , and requesting the supply of his appointments. <u>Resolved</u>: That the Christian sympathies of this Meeting be conveyed to Bro. Embury in his present affliction, with the hope that it may please Almighty God soon to restore him to health and that he may soon be able again to take his work among us.

Quest. I Are there any objections against any of the Brethren?

Ans. Bro. Palmer has several times neglected his appointments: but this was explained on the ground of Mrs Palmer's ill-health. Bro. Palmer promised that he would try to attend his Class a little oftener.

Quest. II Are any received on full plan?

Ans. None.

Quest III Are there any received on Trial?

Ans. None.

---

1   John Hobkirk (1813–71), supernumerary minister in the Oxford Circuit, 1865–68; *Minutes of Conference* 1871, 255–6.

Quest IV Any Removals to or from the Circuit?

Ans. Bro. Symons has removed to Chipping Norton.

Quest V Any alterations in times of preaching?

Ans. None.

Quest VI Any new places to be taken on the plan?

Ans. 1 The Ministers of the Circuit to go over to Eynsham to see if a preaching place can be procured.

2 Marston to be placed under the supervision of Messrs Railton, Hunt and Nix during the ensuing quarter.

Samuel R. Williams.

21 March 1866

Local Preachers' Meeting, held in Oxford, March 21:1866

Present: Revs T. Derry, S.R. Williams, & J. Hobkirk – Messrs Birmingham, Adams, Kent, Hunt, Foster, Harper, Nix, Roberts, Hitchman, Railton, Henman, Irons, Trafford.

I Are there any objections against any of the Brethren?

Ans – None.

II Are there any to be received on full plan?

Ans – None.

III Are there any to be received on Trial?

Ans – None.

IV Any alterations in times of preaching?

Ans – Woodstock to have extra service in afternoon.

The weeknight services to begin at 7 o/c.

With reference to Eynsham and Marston it was agreed that the former name be taken off the plan, as no opening appears, at present, to present itself; and that Marston be put upon the plan, and have services appointed, ~~afternoon and~~ in the evening.

Samuel R. Williams.

27 June 1866

Local preachers' Meeting, held in Oxford, June 27:1866.

Present: The Revs T. Derry & S.R. Williams. Messrs Adams, Kent, Howard, Foster, Nix, Danbury, Railton, Henman, Irons.

I Are there any objections against any of the Brethren?

Ans 1 Brother Harris has yielded to sudden temptation, and, under circumstances of great provocation, quarrelled with his wife, which quarrel, at last, came to blows. This Meeting, taking into consideration the peculiar nature of the case, ~~recommends~~ determines that his name be left off the plan for a quarter but that his number be retained.[1]

---

1   The plans for May–August and September–November 1866 are extant and confirm that Harris was omitted from the later plan. His number in the list of preachers (18) was left blank so that there was no loss of seniority.

2 The Meeting wishes Brother Skidmore to be written to, requesting him to pay more attention to pulpit preparation and reading.
II Are there any to be received on full plan?
<u>Ans</u> None.
III Are there any to be received on trial
<u>Ans</u> None.
IV Are there any alterations in times of preaching?
<u>Ans</u> The afternoon service at Woodstock to be given up.
Marston to have service on Wednesday evening occasionally as may be convenient.
Samuel R. Williams
Secretary.

26 September 1866

Local Preachers' Meeting held in Oxford Sept: 26:1866
<u>Present</u>: The Revs H. Young[1] & S.R. Williams. Messrs Birmingham, Hunt, Adams, Foster, Nix, Colegrove, Roberts, Clarke, Hitchman, Railton, Skidmore, Henman, Danbury, Irons.
I Are there any objections against any of the Brethren?
<u>Ans</u> 1 <u>Bro. Palmer</u> has neglected some of his appointments during the quarter.
   2 <u>Bro. Harper</u> neglected Marston, July 22nd
<u>Resolved</u> That they be written to by the Secretary upon the subject.
   3 That Bro. Harris' name be dropped.
   4 The Chairman to see Brother Keene about his continuance on the plan.
   5 That Brother Phipps acquaint the Chairman when the dates when he will be able to take appointments.
II Are any to be received on full plan?
<u>Ans</u>: None.
III Are any to be received on Trial?
<u>Ans</u>: The Superintendent to see Bro. Turtle of Woodstock,[2] and, if he thinks proper, to give him a note, authorizing him to accompany one or more local preachers.
IV Are there any alterations in times of preaching?
<u>Ans</u>: None.
Samuel R. Williams
Secretary.

26 December 1866

Local Preachers' Meeting held Dec: 26: 1866.
<u>Present</u>: Revs H. Young & S.R. Williams. Messrs Wheeler, Adams, Nix, Roberts, Hitchman, Railton, Trafford, Skidmore, Holloway, Henman, Faulkner.

---

1   Henry Young (1813–86), Superintendent of the Oxford Circuit, 1867–69: *Minutes of Conference* 1886, 36–7.
2   Probably Edward Turtle (1834/5–1910), shoemaker, of Woodstock.

In reference to minutes of last Meeting – the Chairman announced that he had seen Bro. Keene, & as he wished to devote his time to the Bible class, the Super: thought it best to omit his name. Bro. Phipps gave in a list of Sundays when he can take appointments, and he has been planned in accordance with that. The Chairman considered that, under the circumstances, it would be better that Bro: Turtle remain at home.[1]

I Are there any objections against any of the Brethren?

Ans 1 <u>Bro Harper</u> to be written to in reference to the omission of Charlton – to acquaint the next Meeting with the particulars.

    2 <u>Bro: Colegrove</u> to be seen by the Super: & if he cannot engage to take his appointments, the Meeting regrets to feel that his name must be omitted.

II Are there any to be received on full plan?

Ans: None.

III Are there any to be received on Trial?

Ans: None.

IV Are there any Removals to or from the Circuit?

<u>Ans</u>: Bro: Choules[2] has come duly accredited from Wantage.

V Are there any alterations in times of preaching?

Ans: None.

Samuel R. Williams
Secretary.

[Inside the back cover of the book is a list of names and amounts – perhaps subscriptions]

	2/6
	2/6
T.R.	1/-
Smith	1/-
	2/6
Danbury	1/-
Trafford	1/-
Hunt	
Nix	
Cripps	1/-
Brown	1/-

---

1   Turtle resumed local preaching in 1885.

2   William Young Choules (1836–1904), railway ticket collector.

Minute Book

of

LOCAL PREACHERS'

Meetings

Oxford.

Mar. 27, 1867

to

Dec. 22, 1902

27 March 1867

Minutes of a Meeting held in Oxford March 27:1867

<u>Present</u>: Revd H. Young & S.R. Williams. Messrs Birmingham, Danbury, Adams, Howard, Hunt, Foster, Nix, Colegrove, Roberts, Hitchman, Railton, Trafford & Henman.

I. Are there any objections against any of the Brethren?

Ans: None.

II. Are there any to be received on full plan?

Ans: None.

III. Are there any to be received on Trial?

Ans: None.

IV. Are there any Removals to or from the Circuit?

Ans: Bro: Harris has recently come to Oxford from Walton on Thames, duly accredited as a Local Preacher. The Brethren, however, not feeling assured that he has received his last Quarterly Ticket,[1] the Super is requested to see him on the subject, before making the next plan.

V. Are there any alterations in times or places of preaching?

Ans: It was suggested, with respect to Kidlington, that Mr Thurland[2] should be asked to give notice of leaving the Chapel at present rented by him, & that, in the meantime, another more suitable place of worship be sought for.

It was resolved also that Kidlington & Hampton Poyle have two services each on Sunday, afternoon & evening.

Bro: Grimmett, of Bladon, having written a letter which was read to the Meeting, asking his re-appointment on the plan, the Meeting, though thankful to hear of his improved state of mind, felt that sufficient time had not elapsed, to allow of his reinstatement.

Samuel R. Williams,

<u>Secretary</u>.

3 July 1867

Minutes of a Meeting held in Oxford July 3: 1867.

<u>Present</u>: Revs H. Young & S.R. Williams: the Brethren Adams, Howard, Hunt, Foster, Nix, Roberts, Clarke, Hitchman, Railton & Henman.

I. Are there any objections against any of the Brethren?

Ans: 1. A conversation arose on the subject of Bro: Kent's meeting in Class: and the Secretary was instructed to express to him the opinion of the Brethren that he ought now to meet at Woodstock.[3] The Superintendent also to see him on the matter.

---

1   i.e., confirming his status as a member in good standing in a local Wesleyan class.

2   Edward Thurland (1794–1879), chemist and druggist, a prominent Oxford Wesleyan.

3   Although it is unclear when Edwin Kent moved from Oxford to Woodstock, he was a trustee of the Woodstock chapel by 1863.

2. The Meeting learnt with regret that Bro: Colegrove had resigned his plan.[1]
II. Are there any to be received on full plan?
Ans: None.
III. Are there any to be received on Trial?
Ans: None.
IV. Are there any Removals to or from the Circuit?
Ans: None.
V. Are there any alterations in times or places of preaching?
Ans: The services at Marston have been given up, in consequence of there not being a suitable place for preaching.
Samuel R. Williams
Secretary.

25 September 1867

Minutes of a Meeting held Sep 25 1867 at Oxford
Present: Revds H. Young & Joshua Hawkins.[2] Brethren Adams, Foster, Nix, Hitchman, Henman & Railton.
I. Are there any objections against any of the Brethren?
Ans: No.
II. Are there any to be rec'd on full Plan?
Ans: No.
III. Are there any to be rec'd on Trial?
Ans: Yes. 1. Bro: E.W. Miles, from Swindon.
    2. Bro: W. Danbury[3] to be seen by the Superintendent and receive a note.
IV. Are there any Removals to or from the Circuit?
Ans: Bro: Miles from Swindon.
V. Are there any alterations in times or places of Preaching?
Ans: Marston again to be brought on the Plan.
After the general business had been gone through a committee was appointed to consist of the Rev. H. Young, Messrs Nix, Railton, Hunt & Roberts for examination of Treasurers Book in connexion with Horse-hire Fund & further to set right business connected therewith.[4] To meet on Tuesday Oct 1 at 2 o'clock.

25 December 1867

Minutes of a Meeting held Xmas 1867 at Oxford
Present: Revs H. Young & Jos. Hawkins. Messrs Hunt, Nix, Henman, Howard, Railton, Birmingham.

1   i.e., resigned as a Local Preacher.
2   Joshua Hawkins (1845–92), junior minister in the Oxford Circuit, 1867–68. Hawkins left the Wesleyan ministry in 1877, having 'changed [his] doctrinal views': *Minutes of Conference* 1877, 55.
3   John Wesley Danbury (1849–77), mason, of Bladon.
4   Previous minutes had referred to subscriptions to pay for a conveyance for the preachers; this is the first use of the term 'Horse Hire Fund'.

I. Are there any objections against any of the Brethren?
Bro: Harris to be written to concerning neglect of Forest Hill.
II. Are there any to be rec'd on Full Plan?
Ans. Bro: Miles is to preach a Trial Sermon & be examined at the next meeting.
III. Are there any to be rec'd on Trial?
Ans. J.W. Danbury.
IV. Are there any removals to or from the Circuit?
Ans: None.
V. Are there any alterations in times or places of Preaching?
Ans: None.
Resolved:- That the Horse-Hire Fund Committee shall meet on the 1st [*conj.*]
Wednesday in February.
Jos. Hawkins, Sec.

25 March 1868

Minutes of a Meeting held at Oxford Lady Day 1868.
Present: Revds H. Young & J. Hawkins. Messrs Meek, Foster, Adams, Nix, Henman,
Hitchman, Harper, Railton, Hunt, Harris, Irons.
I. Are there any objections against any of the Brethren?
It was stated that Bro: Roberts had not met in Class for some time & Mr Young was
requested to see him.
II. Are there any to be rec'd on Full Plan?
Bro: Miles not having preached a Trial Sermon to be apptd to do so & to be examined
at the next meeting.
III. Are there any to be rec'd on Trial?
None.
IV. Are there any removals?
None.
V. Are there any alterations in times or places of Preaching?
None.

24 June 1868

Minutes of a Meeting held at Oxford June 24 1868.
Revs H. Young & J. Hawkins, Messrs Foster, Henman, Jas Nix, Hunt, Railton, Miles,
Harris, Howard.
I. Are there any objections to any of the Brethren?
Mr Young reported that he had seen Mr Roberts & his explanation was satisfactory.
II. Are there any to be rec'd on Full Plan?
Bro: Miles had been heard preach & passing his exam was unanimously rec'd.
III. Are there any to be rec'd on Trial?
Bro: Jas King[1] to be seen by Mr Young & if he thinks fit receive a note.
IV. Are there any removals?

---

1   James King (1846–74), shopman, of Oxford.

None.

V. Are there any alterations etc?

None.

Bro: Palmer has been removed by death during the Quarter.[1]

30 September 1868

Minutes of a Local Preachers Meeting held at Oxford Sep. 30 1868

Present: Revds H. Young & J. Hawkins – Messrs Foster, Henman, Railton, J. Nix, Harris.

I. Are there any objections to any of the Brethren?

None.

II. Are there any to be rec'd on Full Plan?

Bro: J.W. Danbury to be heard preach a Trial Sermon & to be examined at the next meeting.

III. Are there any to be rec'd on Trial?

Bro: Barfield[2] to be seen by Mr Young & to receive a note.

IV. Are there any removals to or from the Circuit?

None.

V. Are there any alterations in times or places of Preaching?

None.

J. Hawkins.

2 December 1868

Minutes of a Local Preachers Meeting held at Oxford Dec 2d 1868

Present: Revds H. Young & J. Hawkins – Messrs Adams, Nix, Henman, Hunt, Harris.

I. Are there any objections to any of the Brethren?

Ans: Bro: Trafford having neglected an appt to be written to concerning it.

II. Are there any to be rec'd on Full Plan?

Bro: J.W. Danbury having preached & passed a creditable exam was unanimously received.

Bro: Colegrove again to have his name on the Plan.

III. Are there any to be rec'd on Trial?

Bro: Barfield & Bro: Austin.[3]

Bro: King to be seen by Mr Young & if he sees fit to receive a note.

Bro: J. Belcher[4] to be seen by Mr Young etc.

---

1   John Palmer (1801–68), farmer, of Murcot, died in April 1868.

2   Possibly Thomas Barfield (1848–1920), who married in Banbury in 1871. His son Harold (1872–1953) was a Local Preacher in Banbury from 1889: *Methodist Local Preachers' Who's Who 1934* (London: Shaw Publishing Co., 1934), 58.

3   Possibly Alfred George Austin (1847–1911), compositor, of Oxford. Austin emigrated to the USA in 1873, and later became a Methodist minister.

4   Joseph Belcher (1838–1912), carrier.

IV. Are there any removals to or from the Circuit?
None.
V. Are there any alterations in times or places of Preaching?
None.
Jos. Hawkins <u>Sec</u>.

24 March 1869

Minutes of a Local Preachers Meeting held at Oxford Mar 24 '69
Present: Revds H. Young & Jos Hawkins, Messrs Foster, Irons, Harper, Railton,
Hunt, Colegrove, Nix, Adams, Henman, Howard.
I. Are there any objections to any of the Brethren?
Ans: That Bro: Roberts be written to concerning neglect of appts at Forest Hill on
Jan 3 & at Marston on Mar 21
Bro: Trafford for neglecting Forest Hill Jan 24
Bro: Harris for neglecting Forest Hill Jan 17 & Charlton Feb 14.
II. Are there any to be rec'd on Full Plan?
None.
III. Are there any to be rec'd on Trial?
Ans: Bro: Jas King.
Bro: Belcher not having been heard to receive a note for another Quarter.
IV. Are there any removals to or from the Circuit?
Ans: Bro: Barfield has removed to Banbury.
V. Are there any alterations in times or places of Preaching?
Ans: None.

23 June 1869

Minutes of a Local Preachers Meeting held at Oxford June 23 '69
<u>Present</u>: Revds H. Young & Jos Hawkins, Messrs Adams, Henman, Birmingham,
King, Foster, Harris, Railton, Hunt, Harper, Meek, Irons.
I. Are there any objections to any of the Brethren?
Ans: None.
II. Are there any to be rec'd on Full Plan?
Ans: None.
III. Are there any to be rec'd on Trial?
Ans: Bro: Belcher to retain the same position.
IV. Are there any removals to or from the Circuit?
Ans: None.
V. Are there any alterations in times or places of Preaching?
Ans: None.
Bro: Colegrove to be placed in the position on the Plan that he formally occupied.

29 September 1869

Minutes of Local Preachers Meeting held at Oxford Sep. 29th 1869
Present: The Revds Richard Bell[1] & R.W.G. Hunter,[2] Bros Nix, Adams, Colegrove, Railton, Hunt, Irons and J.W. Danbury.
Q1 Are there any objections to any of the brethren?
Ans. They were examined, one by one.
Q2 Any of the brethren leaving?
Bro: Choules, going to the Brackley circuit.[3]
Q3 Any to be examined next quarter?
Bro: Austin.
Q4 Any to come on trial?
From his report it was thought advisable to postpone Bro: Belcher's name to another quarter.
Q5 Any changes in the places?
Marston to be left off.
Q6 Any place to come onto the plan?
The report in reference to Botley to be received at the next meeting.
R.W.G. Hunter Secretary.

29 December 1869

Minutes of Local Preachers' Meeting held at Oxford Decr 29th 1869
Present: The Revds Richard Bell & R.W.G. Hunter, Messrs ~~Smith~~, Adams, Nix, Railton, Fathers, Birmingham, Hunt, [*indeciph.*],[4] Harper, Harris, Howard & Irons.
Q1 Are there any objections to any of the brethren?
Ans. They were examined, one by one.
Q2 Are there any to be received on full plan?
Brother King to preach a trial sermon during the Quarter. Brother Austin to be spoken to by Mr Bell.
Q3 Are there any removals to and from the Circuit?
Brother Smith from the Malton Circuit.
Q4 Are there any to come upon trial?
Mr Styles[5] to be heard by the brethren, Mr Dingle[6] to be spoken to by Mr Bell.

---

1   Richard Bell (1820–74), who served in the Oxford Circuit, 1849–50, and returned as Superintendent, 1869–72: *Minutes of Conference* 1875, 562.
2   Ralph G.W. Hunter (1843–1917), junior minister in the Oxford Circuit, 1869–70: *Minutes of Conference* 1917, 169–70. Hunter retired to Oxford, after two periods of service in the Circuit.
3   Choules continued to appear in the minutes, so evidently did not leave the Circuit, or not for long.
4   Name indecipherable and crossed out.
5   George Stiles (1845–1930), baker, of Headington Quarry.
6   William Dingle (1814–79), whitesmith, of Oxford.

30 March 1870

Minutes of Local Preachers' Meeting held at Oxford March 30 1870
Present: The Revds Richard Bell & R.W.G. Hunter, Messrs Nix, King, Trafford, Foster, Henman, Colegrove, Railton, Adams, Harper, Howard, Skidmore & Harris.
1 Any objections to any of the brethren?
They were examined, one by one.
2. Any removals to or from the Circuit?
Brother Smith to the Driffield Circuit.
Brother Austin has sent in his resignation.
3. Any to come upon full plan?
Brother King. Heard by the Rev. R. Bell, & Messrs Howard & Colegrove. Sermon and examination considered fair. Passed unanimously.
Ralph W.G. Hunter
Secy.

29 June 1870

Minutes of the Local Preachers' Meeting held at ~~Oxford~~ Bladon June 29th
Present the Revds R. Bell & R.W.G. Hunter, Messrs Adams, Holloway, Birmingham, Danbury, J. Danbury Jnr, Hunt, Nix, Railton, Meek, ~~Smith~~, Clark, Choules, Skidmore, Harper, Miles, Colegrove, Trafford, Kent, Henman & Fathers.
1. Any objections to any of the brethren?
They were examined, one by one.
2. Any to be received on full plan?
William Dingle, who has recently left the Primitive Methodist Connexion.[1]
3. Any to come upon trial?
1. Brother B.A. Gregory,[2] Brasenose College. Heard by the Revd R.W.G. Hunter & Bro. Railton.
2. Brother Styles[3] of Headington.
Ralph W.G. Hunter
Secy.

28 September 1870

Minutes of Local Preachers' meeting held Sept 28th 1870 in Oxford at 2 o'c.

---

1   Dingle was a Primitive Methodist Local Preacher of long standing, fully accredited by 1847: see the 1847 Primitive Methodist plan in Kate Tiller, '"The desert begins to blossom": Oxfordshire and Primitive Methodism, 1824–1860', *Oxoniensia*, 71 (2006), (Oxford: OAHS, 2007), between pages 102 and 103.
2   Benjamin Alfred Gregory (1850–76). Son of Benjamin Gregory, Superintendent of the Oxford Circuit, 1857–60, he entered the Wesleyan ministry in 1874. See *Minutes of Conference* 1877, 21–2, and Benjamin Gregory, *Consecrated Culture: Memorials of Benjamin Alfred Gregory* (London: T. Woolmer, 1885).
3   Corrected in pencil to 'Stiles'.

Present Rev. R. Bell chairman Rev John Norton Vine[1] Bros Clarke, Hitchman, Railton, Henman, Harris, King, J. Nix, Roberts, Stiles, Birmingham, Hunt, Adams, Harper.

I Any objections to any of the brethren?

They were examined, one by one.

II Any to be received on full plan?

None!

III Any to be received on trial?

None!

IV Any removals to or from the Circuit?

None!

V Any alteration in time or places?

It was understood that Woodstock would [have] henceforth a week evening service every week and Bladon, Wooten, Coombe & Tackley once a fortnight.[2]

Prop by Mr Nix, secd by Mr Henman that Mr Railton be Secy of the Local Preachers meeting for the ensuing year. Car'd unanimously.[3] ~~Hugh Railton. Secy.~~

It was suggested by the chairman that at the Christmas meeting two papers be read bearing on the work of preaching. Subject to be left to the brethern reading them. Hugh Railton Secy.

21 December 1870

Minutes of Meeting held in Oxford Dec 21st 1870.

Present Revd R. Bell chairman Rev. J.N. Vine. Bros Dingle, Nix, Henman, Holloway, J. Danbury, J.W. Danbury, Harper, King, Hunt, Harris, Birmingham, Kent, Howard, Stiles & Railton.

Propd by Mr Vine Secd by Mr Nix that the minutes of last meeting be confirmed.

Qy I Any objection to any of the brethern?

They were examined one by one!

II Any to be received on full plan?

None!

III Any to be received on Trial?

None!

IV Any removals to or from the Circuit?

None!

---

1   John Norton Vine (1842–81), junior minister in the Oxford Circuit, 1870–71: *Minutes of Conference* 1881, 45–7.

2   The provision of additional services in Woodstock and its surrounding villages reflected the decision of the Circuit Quarterly Meeting to locate the junior minister in Woodstock rather than Oxford. First discussed in 1867, the proposal was agreed in June 1870, and J.N. Vine was the first minister to be based in Woodstock: OHC, OMCA, NM5/A/A3/1, Circuit Quarterly Meeting Minute Book, 1861–88, minutes for 27 March 1867 and 29 June 1870; *Minutes of Conference* 1870, 34.

3   Railton was the first formally appointed lay secretary of the Local Preachers' Meeting.

V Any alteration in time etc?

None!

Propd by Mr Henman and secd by Mr Nix that a letter be written to the trustees of Wooten and Charlton Chapels suggesting that a stove be provided during the cold season of the year.

A conversation arose out of several complaints relative to the change of appointments by brethren when it was urged that every brother attend to his own appointments as far as he is able.

Two papers were read in the afternoon on subjects relating to the work of preaching by Bro. J. King on 'Our Work' and by Bro. Stiles on the 'Conditions of a Sinner's Acceptance with God'. After a conversation a vote of thanks was presented to each of the brethren for their excellent papers.

Hugh Railton Secy.

29 March 1871

Minutes of Meeting held March 29 1871 in Oxford

Present: Rev. R. Bell Chair Rv. J.N. Vine Bros Adams, Dingle, Harper, Birmingham, Harris, Henman, Nix, Hunt, Choules, Hitchman, Skidmore, Stiles & Railton.

Propd by Mr Vine Secd by Bro Harper that the minutes of last meeting be adopted. Unan.

I Any objection to any of the brethern?

Ans: None!

II Any to be received on full plan?

Bro Trotman[1] who has left the Free Methodists asks to be admitted in connexion with us.

Propd by Bro Nix Secd Bro Adams & supd by Rev. J.N. Vine & Bro Dingle that Bro Trotman be received on full plan. Unan!

III Any to be received on TriaL?

None!

IV Any removals to or from the Circuit?

Bro Ford[2] is received from the Chichester Circuit!

V Any alterations in time etc

Jericho to come on the Plan![3]

1   Alfred Davis Trotman (1845–90), hairdresser, of Oxford.

2   George Ford (1832–84), who came to work for the Oxford Circuit as a Home Missionary, based in Jericho: *OC*, 25 November 1871, 5.

3   The development of Wesleyan work in the growing suburb of Jericho was part of Richard Bell's plan for the extension of Methodism in Oxford. In addition to the employment of George Ford as a Home Missionary, in December 1871 a Mission School was opened in Cranham Street, intended as the precursor of a new chapel: 'Wesleyanism', *OC*, 25 November 1871, 5.

As Bro Stiles will have completed his probation at the June Qy Meeting it was intimated he should preach a Trial Sermon & prepare for Examination at that time. Hugh Railton Secy.

28 June 1871

Minutes of Meeting held June 28th 1871
Present Revs R. Bell J.N. Vine Bros Henman, Adams, Harper, Hitchman, Trotman, Nix, Ford, Harris, Dingle, Hunt, Stiles, Gregory & Railton.
Minutes of last meeting were read & confirmed.
Question I Any objection to any of the brethren? None!
II Any to be received on full plan?
Bros Stiles & Gregory having completed their probation were examined and received.
IV Any removals to or from the circuit?
Bro J.W. Danbury has removed to the Reading Circuit.
III Any to be received on trial?
None!
V Any alteration in time or places?
Ans: Bro Trotman to make enquiry respecting the operations of the Evangelical Union & to express the desire of this meeting to take Botley as a permanent preaching place.
Hugh Railton
Secy.

27 September 1871

Minutes of meeting held Sep27/71
Present Revs R. Bell J.N. Vine Bros Ford, Hitchman, Henman, Trotman, Railton, Hunt, Stiles, Harris, Howard.
Minutes of last meeting read & confirmed.
I Bro Irons to be seen by Mr Bell respecting Class meeting & shorter sermons – a general conversation resulted in recommending short prayer & Sermon.
II None!
III None!
IV Bro Danbury Jnr returns to the Circuit.
V Horspath to come on the Plan & have Quarterly Visitation.[1] Bro. Railton to take charge of Horspath.
Reapt of Secy of meeting.
Hugh Railton
Secy.

---

1   Suggesting the existence or expectation of a society class: the ministers visited each class once a quarter to issue tickets of membership.

27 December 1871

Minutes of meeting held Decr 27th 1871.

Present Rev. R. Bell & J.N. Vine. Bros Ford, Danbury, Henman, Nix, Birmingham, Hunt, Stiles & Railton.

I Any objection to any of the Brethren? None!

II Any to be received on full plan? None!

III Any to be received on trial?

Bro Thornton who has been on trial [ ]¹ months in the Banbury Circuit.

IV Any removals to or from the Circuit?

Bro William King from Southampton!

V Any alteration in time or place? None!

Hugh Railton

Secy.

27 March 1872

Minutes of meeting March 27th 1872

Present Rev R. Bell J.N. Vine Bro Adams, Foster, Clarke, Ford, Choules, Harris, Nix, Trotman, Henman, Roberts, Howard, Stiles, Harper, Railton.

I Any objection to any of the brethren?

Bro Colegrove to be seen by Mr Bell & Mr Nix respecting his position on the Plan, objection was also taken to the preaching of Bros Harris & Faulkner.

Bro Harris resigned. The meeting resolved that Bro Faulkner's name be kept on the Plan but that he have no appointment the next quarter.

II Any to be received on full plan?

None!

III Any to be received on Trial? None!

IV Any removal to or from the Circuit? None!

V Any alteration in time or place?

Coombe is understood to be at ½ past 2 It was suggested that the appointments for Hampton Poyle, Charlton, and Islip be so arranged that the conveyance should go occasionally in that direction.

2. In future, Local Preachers coming to reside in the Oxford Circuit have no appointments until they have been heard and pass a² satisfactory Examination.³

Hugh Railton Secy.

---

1   Gap left for a number.

2   Word 'some' inserted in the text.

3   Methodism had no nationwide system of testing and accreditation for its Local Preachers until the 1930s and before that, training was left to each circuit. Although it was generally assumed that any fully accredited Local Preacher moving to a new circuit should be accepted onto the preaching plan, some circuits introduced their own tests. This practice was prohibited when the 1894 Conference codified the regulations governing Local Preachers: Wellings and Wood, 'Facets of formation: theology through training', 75–6; *Minutes of Conference* 1894, 458–9.

26 June 1872

Minutes of meeting held June 26/72

Present Rev R. Bell J.N. Vine Bro Danbury, Dingle, Trotman, Clarke, Ford, Henman, Hunt, Nix, Irons, Stiles, Railton.

Minutes of last meeting confirmed.

Mr Vine explained that he had seen Bro Kent respg several rumours afloat in the Circuit & he promised to abstain in future from the appearance of evil and also to attend more regularly the means of grace.[1]

A conversation arose respecting the readmission of Bro Harris, but as he had made no application to the Superintendent the subject dropped.

I Any objection to any of the Brethren? On Bro Kent's name being called over it was moved by Bro Railton sec'd by Bro Danbury that he have no appointment on the next Plan and that he be summoned to the Sept meeting and be urged to meet in class and that the Secretary write a letter to him embodying the above. Car^d

Bro Holloway was requested to attend his own appointments or provide a substitute whose name is on the plan and a note to that effect be sent.

Bro Thornton having left Horspath unsupplied it was resolved that a letter of admonition be sent him and that his Examination be postponed till Xmas [conj.] 1872.[2]

II Any to be received on full plan?

Bro Keene being now able to render a little assistance it was resolved unanimously that his name appear again on the Plan in his former position.

III Any to be received on Trial? None!

IV Any alteration in time or place? None!

V Any removals to or from the Circuit? None!

Hugh Railton, Secy.

Correct Records. Richard Bell, June 28th 1872.

25 September 1872

Minutes of meeting Sepr 25th 1872

Present Rev. F. Greeves[3] W. Brookes[4] Bro Nix, Adams, Clarke, Skidmore, Ford, Holloway, Harper, Danbury Jr, Howard, Henman, Railton.

1　No explanation is extant concerning the 'rumours', but reputation was important for Local Preachers. 'Abstain … from the appearance of evil' quotes 1 Thessalonians 5:22; 'means of grace' is Wesleyan shorthand for the class meeting, prayer meeting, public worship and Holy Communion, set out in John Wesley's sermon 'The Means of Grace', in his *Sermons on Several Occasions.*
2　There is no record of an examination taking place and Thornton does not appear on the 1876 plan.
3　Frederic Greeves (1833–95), Superintendent of the Oxford Circuit, 1872–75: *Minutes of Conference* 1895, 25–7.
4　William Brookes (1844–1928), junior minister in the Oxford Circuit, 1872–73: *Minutes of Conference* 1928, 109–10.

I Bro Holloway was objected to by Bro Henman on account of his taking so prominent a part in the labour agitation … the meeting declined to entertain the question.[1]
II None.
IV III Bro Nix & Railton to hear
III Bro Belcher from Faringdon at Jericho chapel and report.
III Bro W. King to[2]
V None.
Bros Kent & Henman resigned.
Cowley Road to be put on the plan if arrangements can be made.

18 December 1872

Minutes of meeting Decr 18/72.
Present Rev F. Greeves. Brooks. Bro Ford, Harper, Nix, Hunt & Railton.
I Any objection none.
II Any to be received none.
III Any on trial. Bro J. Smith & Gilder[3] to have a star on the new plan[4] & to have a few appointments.
IV Any removals to or from the Circuit? Bro Blazé from Ceylon.[5]
V Any alteration in time or place? None.
The Horse Hire Fund being in difficulties a committee to be formed & consist of all the Oxford Local Preachers.
Hugh Railton Secy.

26 March 1873

Minutes of meeting March 26th 1873
Present Rev F. Greeves W Brooks Bro Keen Adams Choules Ford Dingle Harper Nix Blaze Birmingham Stiles & Railton.

---

1   Christopher Holloway was a local leader of the National Agricultural Labourers' Union and was involved in the strikes in the area around Wootton in the summer of 1872: see Pamela L.R. Horn, 'Christopher Holloway: an Oxfordshire Trade Union Leader', *Oxoniensia* 33 (1968), 125–36. Attention was drawn to Holloway's position as a Wesleyan Local Preacher in a letter from 'A Subscriber' to *JOJ*, 14 September 1872, 5, and Holloway rebutted any incompatibility between his work for the NALU and his status as a Local Preacher a week later (*JOJ*, 21 September 1872, 7). W.A. Henman was a substantial farmer, holding the tenancy of Manor Farm, Islip and farming 320 acres in 1871, with fourteen employees. His wider connections are explored in Richard Smart (ed.), *The Bousfield Diaries* (Woodbridge: Boydell, for the Bedfordshire Historical Record Society, 2007), 58–9.
2   Railton probably intended to record that King had moved away from Oxford during the previous quarter.
3   Walter Gilder (1852–1936), tailor, of Oxford.
4   Either instead of name or initials or an asterisk to mark them as trainees.
5   John Thomas Blazé (1853–1921), who matriculated at Merton College in October 1872.

I Any objection to any of the brethren? None.

II Any to be received on the plan? None!

III Any to be received on Trial?

Prop. Bro Dingle Sec Bro Keene that Bro Gilder be put on Trial if residing in the Circuit when the new Plan is made.

Prop Bro Choules sec Bro Dingle that Bro Smith be put on Trial.

Prop Mr Dingle sec Mr Choules that Mr Shirley[1] be put on Trial.

Prop by Mr Keene sec by Mr Dingle that Bro Richings[2] be put on as Supply. Bro Lyford[3] to be put on as do [ditto].

IV Bro Gregory removed to Manchester. Bro J. King to Bury St Edmunds.

V Any alteration in time & place? None.

H. Railton Secy.

~~Horse Hire Fund Committee to meet~~

25 June 1873

Minutes of Meeting held June 25th 1873

Present the Revs F. Greeves & W. Brookes & Messrs Nix, Blazè, Railton, Hunt, Stiles, Irons, Harper, & Ford.

1. Any objection to any brother? Bro Fathers having ceased to meet in class & gone from the Circuit to be dropped from the plan.

2. Any one to be received on full plan? No.

3. Any one to be received on trial? Bro. Richings who appeared on the last plan as supply to have his name put on the next.

4. Any one removed to another Circuit? Bro. Railton to the Ross circuit & Bro. J.W. Danbury to the Bedford.

5. Any alteration to the times & places of service? Cowley Road to have a morning service at 11 o'clock.

Bro. Nix proposed & Bro. Hunt seconded a motion that Bro. Roberts be requested to act as secretary in Bro. Railton's place. Passed nem. con.

Wm Brookes Sec. pro tem.

24 September 1873

Minutes of Meeting held Sept 24th 1873

Present Revds F. Greeves & R.W. Moss;[4] & Messrs Trotman, Harper, Adams, Nix, Ford, Keene & Stiles.

The Minutes of last meeting were read & confirmed.

1. Any objection to any brother? No.

---

1   Joseph Shirley (1854–1944), plumber, of Oxford.
2   William Richings (1841–1910), plumber, of Oxford.
3   John Lyford (1839–85), grocer's porter, of Oxford.
4   Richard Waddy Moss (1850–1935), junior minister in the Oxford Circuit, 1873–75: *Minutes of Conference* 1936, 188.

2. Any one to be received on the full plan? No.
3. Any one to be received on trial? Bro. Plater.[1]
4. Any one removed to anther circuit? No.
5. Any alterations in time or place of service?
Week-night service at Jericho to be at 7 instead of 7.30.
[week-night service at] Charlton 6.30 [instead of] 7.
Sunday evening [service at] Coombe [to be at] 5.30 [instead of] 6.[2]
Proposed by Bro. Adams & Seconded by Bro. Nix: that the thanks of this meeting
be presented to Bro. Railton for the diligent and regular discharge of his duties as
Secretary to the quarterly Local Preachers Meeting. Carried unanimously.
R. Waddy Moss.
(Secy pro tem).

7 January 1874

Minutes of Meeting held Jany 7/74
Present Revs F. Greeves & R.M Moss: Messrs Adams, Ford, J. Nix, Danbury, Stiles,
Hunt & Roberts.
Minutes of last Meeting were read & confirmed.
1. Any objection to any brother? No.
2. Any one to be received on the full plan? No.
3. Any one to be received on trial? Yes. Brother Joseph Danbury.[3]
4. Any one removed to another Circuit? Yes. Brother Choules.
5. It was unanimously proposed by the Meeting that Bro. Harris be restored to the
full plan.[4]
6. Any Alterations in time or place of service? Yes.
Charlton to have Evening Service at 5.30.
Wm Roberts
Secretary.

25 March 1874

Minutes of Meeting held March 25/74
Present Rev F. Greeves R.W. Moss Messrs Howard, Adams, Ford, J. Nix, Clarke,
Keene, Hunt, Danbury, Trotman, Stiles, Irons, & Harper & Roberts.
1. Any objection to any brother? Bro. Colegrove's case deferred till next meeting.
2. Any one to be received on full plan? No. Bro. Harris's Case left over.
3. Any one to be received on trial? No.

---

1   Identified on the 1876 plan as W.E. Plater, Blackhall Road. Possibly William Edward
Plater (1854–1933), student in Oxford from 1872, and later ordained in the Church of England.
2   Repetition indicated in the text by ditto marks.
3   Joseph Danbury (1845–1929), harness maker, of Bladon.
4   Probably John Harris, dropped from the plan in September 1866.

4. Any removals to or from the Circuit? Bro. Foster to Cheltenham. Bro. J. King from Bury St Edmunds.
5. Any alterations in time or place?
The morning service at Cowley Road to be discontinued for present.
Wm Roberts
Secretary.

24 June 1874

Minutes of Meeting held June 24th 1874
Present Revs F. Greeves & R.W. Moss Messrs J. Nix, Adams, Trotman, Ford, Richings, Shirley, Roberts.
1. Any objection to any of the brethren? Mr Greeves promised to see Bro. Colegrove as to his name [*indeciph.*] on the plan.
2. Any one to be received on full plan? Brothers Richings & Shirley were examined. Bro Shirley passed satisfactorily and was requested to preach a trial Sermon before some of the brethren during the ensuing quarter. Bro. Richings examination was not so satisfactory & he was desired to present himself at some future time for another examination.
3. Any one to be received on trial? Yes. Brother A. Green.
It was suggested that Bro. Lyford present himself for examination next quarter.
4. Any removals to or from the Circuit? Yes. Bro. Gilder to Rye, Sussex.
5. Any alterations in time or place? Yes. The weeknight service at Jericho to held at ½ past 7 oc instead of 7.
Wm Roberts
Secretary.

23 September 1874

Minutes of Meeting held Sept 23rd 1874
Present Revs F. Greeves R.W. Moss & R. Green.[1] Messrs J. Nix, Skidmore, Ford, Danbury, Adams, Trotman, Birmingham, Hunt, Blazé and Roberts.
1. Any objection to any of the brethren? None.
2. Any one to be received on full plan? Bro. Shirley. It was proposed that Brothers Lyford, Richings & Plater be requested to prepare for examination next quarter, notice of which was conveyed to them accordingly.
Bro. Smith having sent in his resignation, it was accepted.
3. Any one to be received on trial? No.
4. Any removals to or from the Circuit? None.
5. Any alterations in time or place of services? Yes. Weeknight service at Jericho at 7 o'clock instead of ½ p 7 oc and Wootton, Bladon, Coombe and Tackley at ½ p. 6 oc.

---

1   Ralph Green (1845–1920), minister in the Oxford Circuit, 1874–76: *Minutes of Conference* 1920, 122. The Conference of 1874 assigned additional 'home missionary' ministers to seventy-two circuits, and Green was stationed in the Oxford Circuit, to be based at Woodstock: *Minutes of Conference* 1874, 355–6.

Wm Roberts
Secretary.

30 December 1874

Minutes of Meeting held December 30th 1874
Present Revs F. Greeves, R.W. Moss & R. Green. Messrs J. Danbury, J. Danbury Jnr,
Adams, Shirley, Stiles, Nix & Roberts.
1. Any objection to any of the brethren? It was stated that charges had been made
against Brother Irons, but that he had left the Circuit, and there had been no opportunity for investigation that his name be removed from the plan and it was agreed
that on the event of his return to the circuit his name should not be placed upon
the plan till he had cleared himself to the satisfaction of this Meeting.
2. Any one to be received on full plan? It was proposed that Bro. Richings name be
put on the plan on condition that he passed an examination before a Committee
consisting of the Oxford Local Preachers before the plan as made or during the
ensuing quarter.
3. Any one to receive on Trial? No.
4. Any removals to or from the Circuit? Brother J.W. Danbury from Bedford and
Brother Ford to King St. Circuit, Bristol.
5. Any alterations in time or place of Services? No.
Wm Roberts
Secretary.

31 March 1875

Minutes of Meeting held held[1] March 31st 1875
Present Revs F. Greeves, R.W. Moss & R. Green. Messrs Clarke, Plater, J. Danbury,
J. Danbury Jnr, Shirley, Gilder, Hunt, Stiles, Keene, Harper, Nix, Roberts.
1. Any objection to any brother? No.
2. Any one to be received on full plan? Yes. Bro. Plater passed his examination, but
Bro. Danbury was recommended to come again for assessment.
3. Any one to be received on trial? Yes. Bro. Green.
4. Any removals to or from the Circuit? Yes. Bro. Gilder from the Rye Circuit &
Bro. J.W. Danbury to the Aylesbury.
5. Any alterations in time or place? It was decided that Botley should have a Sunday
evening for a quarter to be supplied by private arrangement.
Wm Roberts.

30 June 1875

Minutes of Meeting held June 30th 1875
Minutes of previous meeting read and confirmed.

---

1   Repetition in text.

Present Revds F. Greeves, R.W. Moss & R. Green. Messrs J. Danbury Jr, Gilder, Adams, Shirley & Roberts.

1. Any objections to any of the brethren? No.

2. Any one to be received on full plan? No. Bro A. Green to come up for examination next quarter.

3. Any one to be received on trial? Yes. Bro Gabriel Woodward[1] & Joseph Hunt[2] to have a few appointments. Bro Butler[3] to come on trial for 1 quarter, then to be received if approved, providing his credentials from the Primitive Methodist Society are satisfactory.

4. Any removals to or from the Circuit? Bro Belcher[4] from the Swindon Circuit and Brother J. Kerby from Witney provided his credentials are satisfactory.[5]

5. Any alterations in time or place of Service?

Botley to be placed on the plan for Sunday Evening Service.

Wm Roberts.

29 September 1875

Minutes of Meeting held Sept 29th 1875

Minutes of previous meeting read and confirmed.

Present Rev J. Mason,[6] J. Leal[7] & R. Green. Messrs J. Adams, J. Danbury, Clarke, Shirley, Plater, Roberts, Nix, Hunt, Harper & Keene.

1. Any objection to any of the brethren? Bro Nix overlooked his appointment at Horspath, being away at the time.

Rev. J. Mason to have a conversation with Mr Savory[8] in reference to taking appointments. The Meeting regrets that Brother Gilder had not informed Mr Mason of his intended removal from Circuit.

Mr Kerry's case was reported. The Meeting was informed that he was not in the Circuit.[9]

---

1   Gabriel Woodward (1856–1937), gardener, of Bladon.

2   Joseph Hunt (1851–1927), glove cutter, of Bladon.

3   Alfred Butler (1845–1919), builder, of Oxford.

4   See above, December 1868. It seems to have taken some years for Belcher to move from Faringdon to Woodstock and transfer fully to the Oxford Circuit.

5   Kerby is not listed on the 1876 plan, so perhaps his credentials were not satisfactory.

6   Joshua Mason (1825–1907), Superintendent of the Oxford Circuit, 1875–76: *Minutes of Conference* 1907, 137–8.

7   John Leal (born 1843), junior minister in the Oxford Circuit, 1875–76. Leal left the Wesleyan ministry in 1877 and later served as a Congregationalist minister: *Minutes of Conference* 1877, 55. I am grateful to John Lenton for this information.

8   Perhaps George Mearns Savery (1850–1905), who matriculated at Oxford in 1872 and graduated in 1876. Savery's father, George (1815–85), was a Wesleyan minister who retired to Oxford in 1881.

9   No further explanation of this matter is extant. Henry and Anna Kerry were active Oxford Wesleyans, as were several of their children, so it is possible that 'Mr Kerry' was one

The Case of Bro A. Green to stand over another quarter.

2. Any one to be received on trial? Brothers Gabriel Woodward and Joseph Hunt. Mr Mason to see Brother Butler with reference to his name appearing on the plan.

3. Any one to be received on full plan? No.

4. Any removals to or from the Circuit? Bro Gilder to Bristol.[1]

5. Any alteration in time or place of Service? Yes. Woodstock side of Circuit Bladon Coombe Tackley & Wootton to have weeknight service at ½ past 6 oc instead of 7 oc. Mr Wheeler of Hampton Poyle to be seen either by Mr Mason or Mr Leal with reference to a service at 5 o.c. Sunday afternoon.[2]

Wm Roberts
Secretary.

29 December 1875

Minutes of Meeting held December 29th 1875

Present Revs J. Mason J. Leal & R. Green.

Messrs J. Nix, Trotman, Shirley, Adams, Roberts, Howard, Hunt, Keene & Styles.

1. Any objection of the Brethren? None. Brothers Savory & Plater tendered their resignation which were accepted.

2. Any one to be received on trial? No. Brother A. Green's case to stand over for the present.

3. Any one to be received on full plan? Yes. Bro. Butler.

4. Any removals to or from the Circuit? None.

5. Any alteration in time or place? No.

The Meeting regrets to hear that Horspath has been disappointed so often.

Wm R.

29 March 1876

Minutes of Meeting held March 29th 1876

Present Revs J. Mason J. Leal & R. Green.

Messrs Nix, Hunt, Richings, Styles, Shirley, Belcher, Butler, Harper, Danbury, Adams, Keene, J. Hunt, Trotman & Roberts.

1. Any objection to any of the brethren? Brother Colegrove's resignation was accepted. Bro Coppock[3] did not go to Botley to his appointment. The Secretary to write to him. Brother A. Green's resignation accepted.

2. Any one to be received on trial? No.

---

of their sons. It is also possible that this is a misspelling of 'Kerby' from the previous meeting.

1   If Gilder moved, he was back in Oxford twelve months later: see minutes for September 1876.

2   William Wheeler (1806–88) was the most senior Local Preacher in the Circuit, and a farm labourer in Hampton Poyle.

3   Identified on the 1876 plan as W. Coppock, Headington Quarry, and probably William Coppock (1851–1924), bricklayer, of Headington Quarry.

3. Any one to be received on full plan? Brother J.J. Moore.[1]
4. Any removals to or from the Circuit? Bro. J. Brough from Taunton.
5. Any alteration in place or time of Services?
Jericho Thursday Evening Service to be ½ p 7 oc instead of 7 oc.
Bladon, Coombe, Wootton & Tackley to have weeknight service at 7 oc in place of ½ p 6.
Wm Roberts
Secretary.

28 June 1876

Minutes of Meeting held June 28th 1876
Present Revs J. Mason J Leal and R. Green. Messrs Clarke, Moore, Trafford, Roberts & Nix.
1. Any objection to any of the brethren? Mr Dingle's case referred to. The Rev. J. Mason was requested to see him & report result of the interview to the next Local Preachers' Meeting.
2. Any one to be received on full plan? Bro J.W. Danbury owing to ill-health and removing from place to place his name has not for some time appeared upon any circuit plan, but as the brethren are well acquainted with him, and have perfect confidence in him, they agree to restore him to his place on the Local Preachers' plan.
3. Any one to be received on trial? Bro. J.M. King[2] and Bro Skinner.[3] Bro J. Bloomfield to come on plan as Exhorter.[4]
4. Any removals to or from the Circuit? Bro Wm Gibson[5] from the Thame Circt, as soon as his credentials are received, the Superint to place his name on full plan. Bro. J. Hunt removed to the South Petherton circuit.
5. Any alterations in time or place of Service?
A Room in the Crescent was mentioned to the Meeting which has been occupied by the Free Church of England,[6] but the proposal did not seem ripe to be undertaken at present.[7]
Wm Roberts
Secretary.

1   James John Moore (1835–88), printer, of Oxford.
2   John Matthias King (1843–1913), tailor's clerk, of Oxford.
3   Tom Skinner (1855–1934), draper, of Oxford.
4   Although listed on the 1876 and 1878 plans as 'J. Bloomfield, Bladon', cross-referencing to his death in September 1884 suggests that this was Thomas Bloomfield (1807–84), shepherd, of Bladon.
5   Probably William D. Gibson (1852–1930), agricultural labourer, of Brill. As a Local Preacher in the Thame Circuit, Gibson became part of the enlarged Oxford Circuit in 1905.
6   Secession provoked by the controversy between Bishop Henry Phillpotts and the Revd James Shore in the 1840s: Grayson Carter, *Anglican Evangelicals. Protestant Secessions from the Via Media, c.1800–1850* (Oxford: OUP, 2001), 356–90. The Free Church of England advertised afternoon and evening services in The Crescent, Park Town, in the Oxford newspapers in the early months of 1874: for instance, *OC*, 10 January 1874, 8.
7   See below, September 1880, for the 'Room'.

27 September 1876

Minutes of Meeting held September 27th 1876

Present Rev. G. Maunder[1] J. Chapman[2] J.T. Harrison[3] & R.W.G. Hunter

Messrs Howard, Nix, Adams, J. Danbury, Gilder, J. Danbury Jr, Trotman, Moore, Keene, Stiles, Hunt & Roberts.

1. Any objections to any of the brethren? No. A Letter from Bro Dingle tendering his resignation which resignation was accepted by the Meeting.

2. Any one to be received on full plan? Bro. Plater. Bro. G. Woodward to present himself for examination next quarter.

3. Any one to be received on trial? No.

4. Any removals to or from Circuit? Bro Gibson to Thame Circuit.

5. Any alteration in time or place? Headington Quarry to have service on Wednesday Evenings at 7 oc instead of Thursday.

Bladon, Coombe, Woodstock, Wootton & Tackley to have weeknight service at ½ p 6 oc in lieu of 7 oc.

The Service at Botley to be discontinued.

The Meeting thought it advisable to ask for two collections for the Horse Hire Fund.

Wm Roberts Secretary

Geo Maunder Chairman.

27 December 1876

Minutes of Meeting held Decr 27/76

Present Rev G. Maunder & J. Chapman

Messrs Shirley, Trotman, J. King, J. Danbury, Moore, Kent, Gibson, J. Nix & Roberts.

1. Any objections to any of the brethren? No.

2. Any one to be received on full plan? Bro. G. Woodward.

3. Any one to be received on trial? No.

4. Any removals to or from the Circuit? Bro. J.W. Danbury to [ ].[4]

5. Any alteration in time or place of service? To have a morning service at William St Chapel, Cowley, as well as Evening.[5]

Wm Roberts Secretary.

1   George Maunder (1815–78), Superintendent of the Oxford Circuit, 1876–78: *Minutes of Conference* 1878, 48–9. See also Thomas F. Maunder, 'Memorials of the Rev. George and Mrs Maunder', *WMM* 1881 (series 6, volume 5), 322–9 (May) and 401–9 (June).

2   James Chapman (1849–1913), third minister in the Oxford Circuit, 1876–78: *Minutes of Conference* 1914, 138–40. Chapman returned as Superintendent in 1890.

3   John T. Harrison (1851–1918), stationed as home missionary minister at Woodstock, 1876–77: *Minutes of Conference* 1876, 91 and 1918, 110.

4   Space left for a place to be added, but left blank.

5   The Wesleyans took over the former Primitive Methodist premises in Alma Place, off William Street, in 1875, replacing this with a new chapel in 1882–83: John and Boylan, *Cowley Road Methodist Church Centre Oxford. Centenary 1904–2004* (Oxford: Cowley Road Methodist Church, 2004), 2–8.

21 March 1877

Minutes of Local Preachers' Meeting held March 21st 1877
Present Revds G. Maunder, J. Chapman, J.T. Harrison & R.W. Hunter.
Messrs Belcher, Trotman, Adams, Keene, Nix, Moore & Roberts.
1st Any objection to any of the brethren? No.
2nd Any one to be received on the full plan? Brother Plater's name to remain on the plan. Bro Findlay passed the ordinary examination at Trowbridge.[1]
3rd Any one to be received on trial? No.
4th Any removals to or from the Circuit? Bro Harper removed to Abingdon.
5th Any alteration in place or times of service? The week night service to be altered from ½ p 6 oc to 7 oc on the Woodstock side of the Circuit.
Wm Roberts Secretary.

20 June 1877

Minutes of Local Preachers' Meeting held June 20th 1877
Present Rev G. Maunder, J. Chapman, J.T. Harrison, & R.W. Hunter.
Messrs Adams, Trotman, Moore, Styles, King, Nix & Roberts.
1. Any objection to any Brother? No.
2. Any one to be received on full plan? Brother King was examined & received on full plan.
3. Any one to be received on trial? No.
4. Any removals to or from the Circuit? No.
5. Any alteration in time or place of service? No.
Wm Roberts Secy.

26 September 1877

Minutes of Local Preachers' Meeting held Septr 26th 1877.
Minutes of previous Meeting read and confirmed.
Present Rev. G. Maunder, J. Chapman, J.T. Harrison, R.W. Hunter.
Messrs Moore, Nix, Keene, J. Danbury, Gilder & Roberts.
1. Any objection to any brother? Brother Blazé being absent from the Circuit, it was agreed that his name should be retained on the plan.
Brother Butler, having failed to fulfil two appointments, a letter to be sent to him asking for explanation.
2. Any one to be received on trial? No.
3. Any one to be received on full plan? No.
4. Any removals to or from the Circuit? No.

---

1   William Hare Findlay (1857–1919), undergraduate at Merton College from 1875. Findlay's father James (1815–77) was Superintendent of the Bradford-on-Avon Circuit and died at Trowbridge in March 1877: *Minutes of Conference* 1877, 33–4. William entered the Wesleyan ministry in 1879: *Minutes of Conference* 1920, 118–19.

5. Any alterations in time or place? Woodstock side of Circuit to have service on week night at ½ p 6 oc Woodstock excepted.
George Maunder Chairman
Wm Roberts Secretary.

26 December 1877
Minutes of Local Preachers' Meeting held Decr 26th 1878[1]
Present Rev G. Maunder, J. Chapman & J.T. Harrison.
Messrs Moore, Keene, Adams, Richings. King, Nix & Roberts.
1st Any objection? No. Bro Coppock tendered his resignation. Accepted.
2. Any one to be received on trial? No.
3. Any one to be received on full plan? No.
4. Any removals? No.
5. Any alteration in time or place? Charlton Sunday Evening Service at ½ p 5 oc in lieu of 6 oc.
Note the Superintendent has handed the plans to the Meeting in order that they may be farmed [*conj.*] the profit to go to the Horse Hire Fund.[2] Further it was resolved that a Secretary be appointed for this work and that Mr Trotman be requested to act.
Wm Roberts
Secretary.

27 March 1878
Minutes of Local Preachers' Meeting held Mar 27th 1878
Present Rev G. Maunder, J. Chapman, R.W. Hunter & J.T. Harrison.
Messrs Clarke, Adams, Moore, Hunt, Skidmore, J. Danbury, Styles & Roberts.
1. Any objections? No.
2. Any one to be received on trial? No.
3. Any one to be received in full? No.
4. Any removals to or from the Circuit? Bro Wakerley[3] from Leicester.
5. Any alteration in time or place of service? No.
Resolved that the Conveyance be discontinued to Charlton for the future, and that this ~~Brethren~~ to supply be optional with those brethren appointed.
Wm Roberts.

3 July 1878
Minutes of Local Preachers' Meeting held July 3rd 1878
Present Rev R.W. Hunter, J. Chapman & J.T. Harrison.

---

1   Mistake in the text: should be 1877.
2   Quarterly preaching plans were sold to subscribers and congregation members. Presumably Maunder had decided to devote the quarter's proceeds to the Horse Hire Fund.
3   John E. Wakerley (1858–1923). Wakerley entered the Wesleyan ministry in 1879: *Minutes of Conference* 1924, 119–20.

Messrs J. Nix, Moore, King, Styles & Roberts. Trotman. Keene.[1]

1. Any objections? No.

2. Any one to be received on trial? No. Bro. Barlow.[2]

3. Any one to be received on full plan? No.

4. Any alteration in time or place of service? No.

5. Any removals to or from the Circuit? No.

6. Has any Local Preacher died during quarter? Yes. Bro Falkner of Tackley died on the 23rd May 1878. Proposed that a letter of sympathy be sent to his Widow.[3]

Resolved that a special appeal be made to the brethren for the supply of Charlton. The following resolution was proposed and carried unanimously.

The Local Preachers of the Oxford Circuit in their Quarterly Meeting mournfully record the great loss which has befallen them in the death of the Rev. George Maunder.[4] His preaching will ever remain in their memories, as a model of faithfulness and earnestness. His administration of their affairs was most patient & thorough.

His personal relations with them were eminently affectionate & gracious. They would also record their deep sympathy with the bereaved family in this great sorrow and their earnest prayer that all the consolations of the Comforter may be afforded them.

A letter embodying the above was sent to Mrs Maunder.

Wm Roberts Secretary.

25 September 1878

Minutes of Local Preachers' Meeting held Septr 25th 1878

Minutes of previous Meeting read and confirmed.

Present Rev C.H. Floyd,[5] J. Chapman & J.B. Nicholls.[6]

Messrs Keene, Gilder, Richings, Belcher, Skidmore, Trotman, King, Styles, Nix, Wakerley & Roberts.

1. Any objection to any of the brethren? No.

2. Any one to be received on full plan? Bro. Skinner.

---

1   The last two names seem to have been added later.

2   Barlow's name was added later, after the answer 'No' to the question.

3   The July–September 1878 Plan records the death of 'Mr W. Faulkner', at Tackley on 23 May 1878. Other evidence, including the probate record, indicates that this was Samuel Faulkner.

4   'The Late Rev. G. Maunder', OC, 13 July 1878, 5.

5   Charles Hulme Floyd (1836–1919), who served as junior minister in the Oxford Circuit, 1860–61 and returned as Superintendent, 1878–81: Minutes of Conference 1920, 113.

6   John Broadhurst Nichols (1855–1927), stationed at Woodstock in 1878–79 as a home missionary minister: Minutes of Conference 1878, 112. Nichols left the Wesleyan ministry in 1882 and later served as a Congregationalist minister in Leicester and London.

3. Any one to be received on trial? Mr Wells of Tackley.[1]
4. Any removals to or from the Circuit? Brother Woodward to Box Hill, Surrey.
5. Any alterations in time or place of Service? Woodstock side of Circuit to have weeknight service at ½ p 6 instead of 7 oc.
Wm Roberts
Secretary

23 December 1878

Minutes of Local Preachers' Meeting held December 23rd 1878
Present Rev C.H. Floyd, Mr Trotman, Skinner, King, Nix & Roberts.
1. Any objection to any brother? No.
2. Any one to be received on trial? Bro Prescott to be regarded as having been on trial 3 months.
Bro Wells of Tackley.
3. Any removals to or from Circuit? No.
4. Any alteration in time or place of Services? No.
5. Any one to be received on full plan? Bro Skinner passed his examination and was accepted as a fully accredited local preacher.
Wm Roberts
Secretary.

26 March 1879

Minutes of Local Preachers' Meeting held March 26th 1879
Present Rev C.H. Floyd, J. Chapman, J.B. Nicholls, Messrs King, Brough, Clarke, Trafford, Trotman, Gilder, Wakerley, Styles, Nix, Hunt & Roberts.
1st Any objection to any of the brethren? No.
2. Any one to be received on trial? Bro Geden.[2]
3. Any one to be received on full plan? Bro Barlow to present himself for examination next quarter, to preach a Sermon in the interim, & Messrs Nix, Howard & Trotman to hear him.
4. Any removals to or from the Circuit? No.
5. Any alteration in time or place of Service? No. Horspath to have open air Services during the month of June.
Resolved that a Committee be formed consisting of the Rev C.H. Floyd & Messrs Nix & Trotman who shall make inquiries at Wheatley as to the desirability of holding services there.
Wm Roberts
Secretary.

1   Richard Wells (1823–98), agricultural labourer, of Tackley.
2   Alfred Shenington Geden (1857–1936), undergraduate at Magdalen College. Geden entered the Wesleyan ministry in 1881: *Minutes of Conference* 1937, 184.

25 June 1879

Minutes of Local Preachers' Meeting held June 25/79

Present Rev C.H. Floyd, J. Chapman, Messrs Trotman, Butler, Styles, Hunt, Nix, King, Gilder & Roberts.

Minutes of previous Meeting read and confirmed.

1. Any objection to any of the brethren? No.
2. Any brother to be received on trial? Bro Lilly of Woodstock.
3. Any alteration in time or place of service? No.
4. Any brother to be received on full plan? Bro Barlow to remain on trial.
5. Resolved that the Committee appointed for to enquire as to desirability of holding services at Wheatley be re-appointed.

Wm Roberts
Secretary.

24 September 1879

Minutes of Local Preachers' Meeting held Sept 24th 1879

Present Rev C.H. Floyd, E. Morgan,[1] Messrs Skidmore, Trotman, King, Clarke, Nix, Adams, Trafford, Gilder, Keene, Styles & Roberts Luffman[2]

1st Any objections? No.

2. Any one to be received on trial? Bro Findlay,[3] Ashdown[4] & Dingle[5] to be Exhorters.
3. Any one to be received on full plan? Bro Barlow to present himself for examination. Bro Prescott to be examined.
4. Any removals to or from the Circuit? Bro Wakerley removed to the Eastbourne Circuit. Bro Findlay to Richmond.[6]
5. Any alteration in time or place of Service? Service on Woodstock side of Circuit to be ½ pt 6 oc on week night.

---

1   Ebenezer Morgan (1851–1916), second minister in the Oxford Circuit, 1879–81: *Minutes of Conference* 1916, 161.

2   Samuel Luffman (1854–1930), stationed to the Oxford Circuit as home missionary minister at Woodstock, 1879–80: *Minutes of Conference* 1879, 117. In the summer of 1880 Luffman married Maria Adams, daughter of Joseph Adams, Local Preacher, of Bladon, but by this time he was describing himself as 'gentleman' and he was in Anglican orders by the census of the following year.

3   Possibly Joseph John Findlay (1860–1940), who matriculated at Wadham College in May 1879. A younger brother of W.H. Findlay, who had just left Oxford to train for the Wesleyan ministry.

4   Horace Ashdown (1860–1929), grocer, of Oxford.

5   Unlikely to be William Dingle (1814–79), who resigned as a Local Preacher in 1876. His younger brother Daniel (1825–85), dealer, brought two children for baptism with the Wesleyans in the early 1880s and two of his executors were Walter Slaughter and William Richings, Wesleyan Local Preachers.

6   Richmond College, the London branch of the Wesleyan Theological Institution, where ministers were trained.

Resolved that the Committee on Wheatley subject be re-appointed.
Wm Roberts.

17 December 1879

Minutes of Local Preachers' Meeting held Decr 17th 1879
Minutes of previous meeting read and confirmed.
Present Rev C.H. Floyd
Messrs King, Trotman, Styles, Nix & Roberts.
1st Any objections? No.
2. Any one to be received on full plan? Bro Prescott to be examined next quarter.
3. Any one to be received on trial? No.
Brother Morris name to be dropped from plan having ceased to be a member of Society.[1]
4. Any removal to or from the Circuit? Bro Barlow removed to Lincoln Circuit.
5. Any alteration in time or place of Service? No.
Wm Roberts
Secretary.

17 March 1880

Minutes of Local Preachers' Meeting held Mar 17th 1880
Present Rev. C.H. Floyd, E. Morgan, Jas Moorhouse[2]
Messrs Nix, Hunt, Styles, Skidmore, Wells, Butler & Keene.
1. Any objection? No.
2. Any one to be received on trial? No. Mr Floyd stated that he had seen Mr Josiah Nix[3] & Mr Lawrence & would give them a note to preach once or twice in the course of the quarter.
3. Any one to be received on full plan? Bros Prescott & Geden were examined and a report of their Sermons was given. By a unanimous vote they were received as fully accredited Local Preachers.
4. Any removals to or from the Circuit? Mr Brough had removed to Newcastle under Lyne.
5. Any alteration? It was agreed that the service at New Hincksey should be put on the plan.[4]
Wm Roberts.

---

1   i.e., a member of the Wesleyan Society.
2   The listing after Floyd and Morgan suggests that Moorhouse was a minister, but the only Moorhouse in the Wesleyan ministry in 1880 was Joseph (1808–91), a supernumerary in the Stourbridge Circuit: *Minutes of Conference* 1879, 87 and 1891, 51–2.
3   Josiah Nix (1847–1924), provision merchant, of Oxford. Younger brother of James Nix. For his subsequent career as an evangelist, see 'Nix, Josiah', in *DMBI*.
4   The wording suggests that preaching had been taking place at New Hinksey for some time and that the Methodist presence was now sufficiently well established to warrant listing on the plan.

22 September 1880

Minutes of Local Preachers' Meeting held Sept 22nd 1880[1]
Present Rev C.H. Floyd, E. Morgan & A. Martin.[2] Messrs Adams, King, Butler, Baker,[3] Trotman, Styles & Roberts.
1. Any objection to any brother? No.
2. Any one to be received on trial? Bro Griffin[4] of Bladon.
3. Any one to be received on full plan? No.
4. Any removals to or from the Circuit? Bro Skuse[5] from Brackley. Bro Dunn from Thetford. Bro Prescott removed to Rochdale.
Bro Ashdown to be examined next Quarter.
5. Any alteration in time or place of service? Woodstock side of Circuit to have weeknight services at ½ p 6 instead of 7 oc.
Resolved that Mr Gardner's offer of Room in the Crescent for Sunday Service be accepted.[6]
Wm Roberts
Secretary.

16 June 1880

Local Preachers' Meeting June 16 1880
Present Rev. C.H. Floyd Messrs King Moorhouse Shirley Skinner Rev. E. Morgan Nix Keene Holloway.
Any objection? No.
Any one to be received on trial? Mr Baker.
Mr Sinfield and Mr Griffin to be received as exhorters. Mr Wells[7] also to be received as exhorter.
Any one to be received on full plan? No.
Any one removed to or from the Circuit? Mr Lilly removed from Woodstock to [ ][8]
Charles H. Floyd

23 December 1880

Minutes of Local Preachers' Meeting held Decr 23rd 1880
Present Revs C.H. Floyd, E. Morgan & A. Martin. Messrs Nix, Skidmore, King, Baker & Skinner.

1   The June and September minutes appear out of sequence in the minute book.
2   Arthur Martin (1854–1908), stationed as home missionary minister at Woodstock, 1880–82: *Minutes of Conference* 1880, 111 and 1908, 141–2. Martin returned to the Oxford Circuit in 1889 and stayed for three years.
3   George Aron Baker (1851–1945), watchmaker and jeweller, of Oxford.
4   James Reuben Griffin (1857–1932), tailor, of Bladon.
5   John Skuce (1844–1914), traveller in coal.
6   First suggested in 1876. Probably The Studio at North Mews, Park Town, owned by James and Mary Gardiner. I am very grateful to Liz Woolley, Stephanie Jenkins and Malcolm Graham for their help in identifying this reference.
7   Richard Wells: see above, September 1878.
8   Space left for the place-name, but not filled in.

1st Any objection? Several appointments unsupplied.
Mr Roberts Tackley & Headington Quarry
Mr Shirley Tackley, Horspath, Wootton
Mr J. Danbury Horspath
Mr Ashdown
Moved by Rev. E. Morgan seconded by Mr Nix that letters be written to these brethren & the answers read at the next LP Meeting.
2. Any one to be received on trial? Mr Saunders from Romford Circuit.
3. Any one to be received on full plan? Ans No.
4. Any removals to or from the Circuit?
Mr Fryer[1] from Bedale. Mr Forrest from [*indeciph.*]. Mr Sharr from Leeds (Oxford Place).
5. Any alteration in time or place of Service? Moved sec'd and carried that service be held at Forest Hill on Sunday afternoon at 3 o/c.
It was moved that Mr Findlay be examined next Quarter. Moved that Messrs Trotman & Skinner be requested to go to Hincksey to make arrangements for continuing the Services.
Moved by Mr Nix, secd by Mr Skinner that Mr Morgan be requested to see Mr Gardiner respecting an evening service at the Crescent.
~~Moved by Mr Skinner secd by Mr Morgan that a service be held at Forest Hill on Sunday afternoon at 3 o/c.~~
Upon Mr Trotman's resigning the office of Secy to the Horse Hire Fund the meeting proposed that a hearty vote of thanks be given to him & also to Mr Jakeman for the help he has rendered. Proposed and seconded that Mr G.A. Baker be appointed Secy of the Horse Hire Fund. Moved by Mr Nix and seconded by Mr Baker that Mr Skinner be appointed Secy to the Local Preachers' Meeting.
T. Skinner
Secy.

23 March 1881

Minutes of Local Preachers' Meeting Mch 23rd 81.
Present Revs C.H. Floyd, E. Morgan and A. Martin, Messrs Howard, Adams, Gilder, Hunt, Butler, Baker, Trafford, Styles, Danbury & Skinner.
Minutes of last meeting read & confirmed.
1st Any objection? Mr Shirley did not answer the letter sent him respecting his appointments that were unsupplied (as requested by the last meeting). He also failed to supply Headington Quarry and Forest Hill on the last Plan.
It was therefore resolved upon the proposal of Rev. E. Morgan that he be requested to see Mr Floyd this evening 23rd inst.
Mr J. Danbury sent satisfactory explanation to similar letter.
Messrs Roberts & Ashdown sent in their resignations which were accepted.

---

1   John Fryer (1844–1918), farmer, of Bladon.

2nd Any one to be received on Trial? Mr Wm Elme's[1] name was mentioned. Mr Nix to hear him preach & to report.

3rd Any one to be recd on full plan? Bro Findlay should have been examd, but wished for a postponement for a few quarters.

Bros Baker & Saunders to be examined next qtr & to preach trial sermons. Messrs Howard, Nix & Butler to hear Mr Baker and Bros King, Hunt & Skinner Mr Saunders.

4. Any removals? Bro Dunn to Alton. Bro Griffin to Ross. Bro Wm Hawkin recd from Guernsey. Bro Railton from Ross, his name to be restored to its original place on the plan.

5. Any alterations in times or places? The afternoon Service at Forest Hill was dropped from the plan. Bro Butler enqd whether anything more be done for Hincksey. Mr King volunteered a site if a chapel could be built. It was agreed that Rev C.H. Floyd & Mr Nix see him on the subject.

It was thought desirable that the Local Preachers spend an evening together during the next qtr & that one or two papers be read bearing upon the work.

The rev. E. Morgan & Messrs Nix, King & Skinner were appointed a committee to arrange for the meeting.

T. Skinner
Secretary.

22 June 1881

Local Preachers' Meeting June 22 1881
Present Revs C.H. Floyd, E. Morgan & A. Martin. Messrs King, Trafford, Danbury, Butler, Adams, Hunt, Baker & Skinner.
Minutes of last meeting confirmed.
1. Any objection to any of the brethren? None.
2. Any one to be received on Trial? No.
3. Any one to be received on full plan? Bro. Baker. Examined & passed unanimously.
4. Any removals to or from the Circuit? Yes. Bro. Saunders to Croydon.
5. Any change in time or place of Service? No.

Mr Baker upon resigning the office of Secretary to the Horse Hire Fund was thanked for his services & upon the proposal of Rev. E. Morgan secd by Mr Adams it was resolved that a request be sent to Mr Railton asking him to succeed Mr Baker in the office.

H.P. Hughes.
T. Skinner
Secretary.

---

1   Walter Elmes (1858–1936), stone mason, of Headington Quarry. The minute book records his first name with a capital W and a small superscript, which might be 'm' or possibly 'r'. Elms was mentioned again in December 1882.

28 September 1881

Minutes of Local Preachers' Meeting held Septr 28/81

Present Revs H.P. Hughes,[1] M. Munro,[2] and A. Martin.

Messrs Adams, Danbury, Hunt, Keene, J. Danbury, Clarke, Gilder & Skinner & J. Nix.

Minutes of last meeting confirmed.

1st question Any objection to any of the brethren? None.

2nd Any to be received on full plan? Ans. No.

3rd Any to be received on Trial? Bro. J. Cross[3] & Bro. W.E. Colegrove.[4]

4th Any removals to or from the Circuit? Mr Baker to Gloucester.

5th Any change in time or place of Service? Hincksey Sunday Evening Service from 7 o/clock to 6.30. The week evening services at Bladon, Coombe, Wootton, Tackley, Islip, Forest Hill & Horspath from 7 to 6.30.

The desirability of recommencing the Services at Charlton was referred to.

The Horse Hire Fund, Mr Railton being unable to take Secretaryship of this Fund, Bro Skinner was appointed, the fund for the future to be called the Circuit Mission Fund.

T. Skinner

Secy.

21 December 1881

Minutes of Local Preachers' Meeting held Decr 21st 1881

Present Rev. H.P. Hughes, G. Savory,[5] M. Munro & A. Martin. Messrs Jas Nix, Danbury, Howard, Skidmore, Railton & Hunt.

I Any objection to any of the brethren? None.

II Any to be rec'd on full plan? Mr O.K. Hobbs[6] rec'd from the Bible Christians.

III Any to be received on trial? None.

IV Any removals to or from the Circuit? None.

V Any change in time or place of service? None.

1   Hugh Price Hughes (1847–1902), Superintendent of the Oxford Circuit, 1881–84: *Minutes of Conference* 1903, 131–4. For his ministry in Oxford, see also Dorothea Price Hughes, *The Life of Hugh Price Hughes* (London: Hodder and Stoughton, 1904), 130–64.

2   Macdonald Munro (1850–1907), second minister in the Oxford Circuit, 1881–84. Munro married Emily Boffin, daughter of the confectioner James Boffin, a prominent Oxford Wesleyan. He resigned from the Wesleyan ministry in 1893 and was ordained into the Church of England: *Minutes of Conference* 1893, 55; *MR*, 6 June 1907, 8.

3   Probably James Cross (1855–1924), cordwainer, of Oxford, whose address in Little Clarendon Street in local directories for the 1880s corresponds with the 1886–88 plans.

4   William Edward Colegrove (1859–1940), undergraduate.

5   George Savery (1815–85), Wesleyan minister, who retired to Oxford in 1881: *Minutes of Conference* 1885, 28–9.

6   Possibly Owen Knights Hobbs (1861–1932), non-collegiate student, who graduated through Exeter College in 1882.

A conversation arose about the possession of a stable at Tackley[1] and upon the prop of Rev A. Martin sec'd by Mr Howard the matter was left in the hands of Rev. H.P. Hughes & Messrs Nix & Skidmore to make further enquiries.

H.P. Hughes

T. Skinner

Secy.

29 March 1882

Minutes of Local Preachers' Meeting held Mch 29th '82

Present Revs H.P. Hughes, M. Munro & A. Martin. Messrs Railton, Nix, Wheeler, J. Danbury, Findlay, Hobbs, Colegrove, Belcher, Solloway,[2] Clarke & Skinner.

I Any objection to any of the brethren? None.

II Any to be received on full plan? Yes, Mr R. Buckell,[3] from the Methodist Free Church, Mr John Solloway, from another[4] Circuit, and Mr Findlay, who successfully passed his examination were fully received.

III Any to be rec'd on Trial? Yes, Mr Josiah Nix, Mr Wickham,[5] Mr John Curtis & Mr John H. Harwood.[6]

IV Any removals to or from the Circuit? Bro Hawkin to Hertford & Bro Curtis from Derby.

V Any change in time or place of Service? An afternoon service was appointed for Islip in lieu of the morning one & an evening service at the Crescent in addition to the one held in the afternoon. The services at Charlton to be resumed.

It was decided that the conveyance for Islip & Charlton should start at 1 o'clock unless the Local Preachers appointed are advised to the contrary.

Mr Hughes proposed & Mr Jas Nix seconded that a Theological Society be formed to assist the Local Preachers & those preparing for examination, meeting to be held from 3 to 4 o'clock on Sunday afternoons. Carried unan'y.

Hugh Price Hughes

T. Skinner

Secy.

10 May 1882

Minutes of Special Local Preachers' Meeting of Oxford Local Preachers held May 10/82

1   Tackley was the furthest point on the journey of the preachers' conveyance from Oxford to the villages. Acquisition of a stable was perhaps an attempt to improve care for the horse. See below, December 1885, for a minute explicitly addressing this issue.

2   Possibly John Solloway (1860–1946), non-collegiate student.

3   Robert Buckell (1841–1925), coal merchant, of Oxford. The key figure in Oxford's Liberal organisation for half a century, Buckell was Mayor six times between 1885 and 1919: 'Buckell, Sir Robert', DMBI.

4   Space left for the name of the circuit to be inserted, but 'another' added in lighter ink.

5   Walter Wickham (1857–1913), astronomer assistant.

6   John Henry Harwood (1858–1921), printer, of Oxford.

Present Rev H.P. Hughes, Messrs Railton, Jas Nix, Wickham, Josiah Nix, Shirley, Gilder, Solloway, Hedges, Richardson[1] & Skinner.

It was resolved that open air services be held (morning, afternoon & evening) at the following places in the following order

Horspath	May 28th
Tackley	June 11 Messrs Richings, Nix, Solloway & Harwood
Headington Quarry	June 18 Messrs Nix, Wickham, Buckell, Keene
Wootton	June 25 Buckell, Keene, Holloway, Crosse & T. Harris[2]
Bladon	July 2 J Nix, Harris, Railton, Danbury, [*indeciph.*] & French.[3]
Charlton	July 9 Railton, Gilder, Lyford & Keene
Woodstock	July 16 Keene, Shirley, Buckell, T. Harris & Fryer
Coombe	July 23 J. Nix, Gilder, Cross & Colegrove.

Upon the proposal of Mr Jas Nix, secd by Mr Railton it was resolved that a preaching place be procured at Eynsham to be opened as quickly as possible.

The claims of the following villages were mentioned, Wolvercote, Wheatley, Eynsham, Littlemore, Nuneham, Cowley & Marston, & it was agreed that open air work should be commenced in each place in August next.

T. Skinner

Secy.

21 June 1882

Local Preachers' Meeting held June 21 1882

Present Revs H.P. Hughes, M. Munro, Messrs Holloway, Colegrove, Buckell, Jas & Josiah Nix, King, Cross, Keene, Hunt & Styles.

Minutes of last Meeting read and confirmed.

I. Any objection to any of the Brethren?

Ans. None.

II. Are there any to be received on full plan? Ans. No.

III. Are there any to be rec'd on trial? Yes. Mr John Savery.[4]

Mr Ward[5] of Exeter College to be placed on the plan if he has passed the usual examination.

---

1   Possibly Joseph William Champness Richardson, for whom see below, December 1882.

2   Thomas James Harris (1863–1940), carpenter, of Oxford.

3   Possibly Daniel French (1848–1913), platelayer, of Wolvercote.

4   John Manly Savery (1858–1939), non-collegiate undergraduate.

5   William John Ward (1861–1952), undergraduate, Exeter College. Ward was a founder-member of the Oxford University Wesley Guild and later an Anglican clergyman.

Mr Chitty's[1] name being mentioned Mr Hughes undertook to see if he has been on trial and give him some work this quarter.

Mr Keene was asked to take Mr Grimmet with him to some appointments and report at next quarterly meeting.

Also Mr Josiah Nix to take Messrs Embury,[2] Foster[3] & Saunders out to some afternoon service & report.

IV. Any removals to or from the Circuit? Mr A. Taylor (Local Preacher on trial) from Rickmansworth. Mr J. Curtis removed to Derby. Mr J.H. Harwood removed.

V. Any change in time or place of Service.

The service at the new chapel at Hinksey to be held at 11 oc in the morning and half past six in the evening.

Resolved, that the Cranham St Local Preachers take the service alternately with the Ministers on Thursday evening.

That, it is desirable that the House and Premises belonging to Mr Boreman at Eynsham be taken for 3 years at a rental of £12 per annum with the option of purchasing the whole property at any time during that period for the sum of £450. And provided also that the tenancy might be terminated by giving 6 months notice at the expiration of one year.

That Mr Josiah Nix arrange for conveyance to Islip & Charlton.

H.P. Hughes.

26 June 1882

Special Meeting of the Oxford Local Preachers held June 26th 1882

Present Rev H.P. Hughes & M. Munro Messrs Jas and Josiah Nix, Solloway, Buckell, Wickham, & Skinner.

Resolved that open air services be held in the following order

Forest Hill	August 6th
Eynsham	[August] 6th (if ready to be opened)[4]
New Inn Hall St	[August] 13th to commence with prayer meeting at 9.45 open air Service from 2.30 to 4 and in the evening from 5.30 to 7.
Islip	Aug 20th
Tackley	[August][5] 27th
Hinksey	Sep 3rd

---

1   Perhaps Arthur John Chitty (1859–1908), student, Balliol College.

2   Thomas Francis Embury (1864–1932), carpenter, of Oxford.

3   James Barnett Foster (1865–1940), milkman, of Oxford. Later a Wesleyan minister: *Minutes of Conference* 1941, 161.

4   See 21 June minutes, making arrangements to rent a house in Eynsham for Wesleyan preaching.

5   All indicated by ditto marks in original.

11 August 1882

Special Meeting of the Oxford Local Preachers held Aug 11/82
Present Rev H.P. Hughes Messrs Gilder, Cross, Buckell, Richings, Harwood, Findlay, Solloway, Colegrove, Josiah Nix & Skinner.
Resolved, that open air services be held at the following places
Tackley Aug 27 Rev Dixon[1] Messrs Skuce, Lyford, Colegrove, French, J. Savery
Islip Aug 20 Rev M. Munro Messrs Richings, Gilder, Wickham, Solloway
Hincksey Sep 3 Rev M. Munro, Messrs Jas Nix, Josh Nix, Railton, Buckell, Wickham.
T. Skinner Secy.

20 September 1882

Minutes of Meeting held Sep 20/82
Present Revs H.P. Hughes, M. Munro & A. Martin, Messrs Findlay, Gilder, King, Jas Nix, Cross, Wheeler, Railton & Skinner.
Minutes of previous meeting read & confirmed.
1st question Any objection to any of the Bretheren? None.
II Any to be received on trial?
Bro. Chitty.
The names of Messrs Embury, Foster, Sumner & G. Adams[2] were brought before the meeting and it was decided to give them a few appointments on the next plan, also Bro Saunders, Mr Railton being asked to hear him preach & report.
III Any to be received on full plan? Bro Colegrove & Bro Cross should have been examined but wished for postponement till next quarter.
IV Any removals to or from the Circuit? Bro Hedges has removed to Coventry. Bro Hobbs & Bro Taylor have also left the Circuit.
V Any change in time or place of Service?
Charlton afternoon service from 2.30 o'clock to 3.[3] Evening 6 o/c instead of 5.30.
Eynsham to have a morning service at 11 instead of afternoon at 3.
Week night services
Hincksey from 7 to 7.30
Bladon, Coombe, Tackley & Wootton 7 to 6.30
Forest Hill & Horspath 7 to 6 o/c.
To prevent mistake in future, the bretheren were asked to understand distinctly that the Conveyance for Woodstock to start from Mr Stroud's[4] punctually at 9 o/c & the one for Charlton from the Martyrs Memorial at 1.15.
T. Skinner Secy.

---

1   There were eleven Dixons in the Wesleyan ministry in 1882. Seth Dixon was stationed in the neighbouring Swindon Circuit, so he might have supported Hughes' evangelistic plans, although he moved to Redruth after the Conference of 1882, making the timing difficult for a late August open-air service at Tackey: *Minutes of Conference* 1882, 67 and 1896, 35
2   George Adams (1856–1941), grocer's assistant, of Bladon.
3   Original text '3 o'clock to [*indeciph*.]', obliterated by the correction.
4   Possibly John Stroud, farmer, 35 New Inn Hall Street.

27 December 1882

Minutes of Local Preachers Meeting held Dec 27th 1882
Present Revs H.P. Hughes & M. Munro Messrs Jos[h] Nix, Keene, Cross, Fryer, Trafford, Findlay, King, Hunt, Skidmore, Danbury, Railton, Jas Nix, & Skinner.
Minutes of previous meeting read & confirmed.
I. Any objection to any of the Brethren? None.
II. Any to be recd on Trial? Bro Embury & Bro Foster were proposed & accepted.
Messrs G. Adams, Harry Danbury,[1] Jackson[2] & Saunders to have a few more appointments. The name of Walter Elms was mentioned Mr Hughes promising to see him.[3]
III. Any to be rec'd on full plan? Bro. Colegrove sh'd have presented himself for examination but wished for a further postponement. Bro Cross was examined: the result being satisfactory he was unanimously accepted subject to ~~the~~ a favourable report of his trial sermon from Mr Munro.
IV. Any removals? Bro Allen[4] from the Camborne Ct.
V. Any change in time or place of service?
Week evening services at Horspath & Forest Hill from 6 to 6/30. Upon the proposal of Mr Jas Nix secd by Mr Trafford it was decided that Beckley be placed on the plan; subject to the approval of the Quarterly Meeting.
H.P. Hughes.

11 March 1883

Minutes of meeting held Mch 11/83
Present Revs H.P. Hughes, M. Munro & A. Martin Messrs Jas Nix, Cross, Clarke, Allen, Colegrove, Wickham, Solloway, Jos[h] Nix, Railton, Hunt & Skinner.
I question Any objection to any of the Bretheren?
It being stated that Mr Shirley failed to supply his Beckley app[t] the secretary was asked to obtain an explanation.
II Any to be rec[d] on Trial?
Mr G. Adams was proposed & accepted.
Messrs Saunders & H. Danbury wished that that they sh[d] have no more appointments for the present.
III Any to be received on full plan?
Mr Simpson was received as a Local Preacher from Yorkshire. Messrs Colegrove, Jos[h] Nix & Wickham having completed the usual time on trial were examined & having satisfied the Meeting were unanimously received.
IV Any removals?
Mr Keene has left the Circuit. Mr Simpson received.

---

1   Possibly Harry Danbury (1859–85), builder, of Bladon.
2   Possibly Samuel Jackson (1861–1925), undergraduate at Merton College and a founder-member of the Oxford University Wesley Guild.
3   See above, March 1881.
4   Hugh Allen (1814–86), tailor.

V Any change in time or place of Service?

The week evening Services at Bladon, Coombe, Tackley & Wootton from 6.30 to 7 o/c.

Charlton week evening service to Wednesday.

The communication from Eynsham expressing a wish that the service sh^d be held in the afternoon instead of the morning, not ~~meeting with the entire approval of~~ being unanimously approved – it was left with Mr Munro to consult with the people at the Home Missionary Meeting that a final decision might be come to.

Mr Jas Nix to make enquiries & secure a suitable trap for Charlton at a sum not exceeding £13 per annum.

9 April 1883

Minutes of Special LPs Meeting held Apr 9/83
Present Rev. M. Munro Messrs Jos^h Nix, Gilder, Chitty, Solloway & Wickham.
The following dates were suggested for open air services

May	6	Tackley
	13	Horspath (Messrs Jos^h Nix & Railton)
	20	Eynsham
	27	Bladon
June	3	Headington Quarry
	10	Islip
	17	Wootton
	24	St Clements
July	1	Beckley
	8.	New Hinckesy
	15	Woodstock
	22	Forest Hill
July	29	Coombe
Aug	5	Charlton
	12	Oxford Combined Chapels
	19	Cranham St

Resolved that a collection be made once during the day.

That the Rev H.P. Hughes be requested to choose the Hymns and Mr Jos^h Nix to arrange for the printing of 10,000 copies.

That the Preacher appointed for the day on the Circuit Plan shall control the meetings.

20 June 1883

Minutes of Local Preachers Meeting held at Woodstock June 20/83
Present Rev H.P. Hughes & A. Martin Messrs Fryer, Cannon, Clarke & Skidmore.
I Question Any objection to any of the Bretheren? None.
II Any to be received on trial? Ans No.
III Any to be received on full plan? Answer No.
IV Any removals to or from the Circuit? Mr C. Cannon received from another circuit.
V Any change in time or place of service? No.
H.P. Hughes.

19 September 1883

Minutes of Meeting held Sep 19th/83
Present Revs H.P. Hughes, M. Munro, G. Marris[1] & L. Walton.[2]
Messrs Findlay, Wickham, Gilder, Shirley, Cross, Wheeler, Jos[h] Nix, Jas Nix, Railton, Colegrove, Hunt, & Skinner.
Minutes of previous meeting read & confirmed.
Ist question. Any objection to any of the bretheren? Complaint was made that Mr Howard did not send an accredited supply to Cranham St; the secretary was requested to write him & produce the reply at the next meeting.
Mr Trotman's name was mentioned Mr Hughes promising to see him.
II Any to be received on Trial?
Mr W. Slaughter[3] was proposed & received ~~also Mr Cooper of Horspath as an Exhorter.~~
~~Also Mr Pearson;~~ Mr Jos[h] Nix Mr Jas Nix & Mr Railton to hear Mr Pearson[4] preach during the qr and report with a view to his coming on the plan.
The names of Messrs Vanes,[5] Brown & Kellett[6] were also mentioned.

---

1   George Marris (1854–1952), second minister in the Oxford Circuit, 1883–86: *Minutes of Conference* 1952, 147–8.
2   Thomas Lionel Walton (1852–94), home missionary minister in the Oxford Circuit, 1883–86: *Minutes of Conference* 1894, 23–4.
3   Walter Slaughter (1853–1909), grocer, of Oxford. For a brief biography, see 'Death of Mr Walter Slaughter', *OC*, 5 February 1909, 12.
4   Arthur Pearson (1860–1926), ironmonger and businessman, of Oxford. A brief biography of Pearson was published in the *MR*, 23 July 1891, 557, and an obituary in the *Local Preachers' Magazine*, June 1926, 185. Pearson also received an entry in the *Methodist Who's Who* (1914), 218.
5   Sidney Albert Vanes (1864–1901), undergraduate, Jesus College and a founder-member of the Oxford University Wesley Guild.
6   Ernest Edward Kellett (1864–1950), undergraduate, Wadham College and a founder-member of the Oxford University Wesley Guild. Kellett's memoir, *As I Remember* (London: Victor Gollancz, 1936), includes a chapter of 'Some Oxford Memories' (316–39), but says little about Methodism; more may be gleaned from a letter of reminiscence about Hugh Price

Mr Cooper[1] of Horspath was proposed & received as an Exhorter.

III Any to be received on Full Plan? Mr Chitty sh^d have presented himself for examination but asked for a postponement till next qr.

IV Any removals? Mr Stiles who has emigrated to Canada.

V Any change in time or place of Service? Yes.

Week evening services at Forest Hill & Horspath from 7 to 6 o/c. Bladon, Coombe, Tackley, & Wotton from 7 to 6/30.

Mr Cross was appointed Secretary to the Horse Hire Fund in the place of Mr Skinner who resigned.

H.P. Hughes.

13 October 1883

Minutes of Special Meeting held Oct 13/83

Present Revs H.P. Hughes & M. Munro, Messrs Jos^h Nix, Colegrove, Findlay, Foster, Embury, Wickham, Jas Nix, Gilder & Skinner.

How the Mission Chapel in Cranham St could be best utilized was the question before the Meeting, and after considerable discussion it was resolved that Mission Services be held each Sunday Evening at 7 o/c with a view to reach those persons who go to no place of worship.[2]

It was also decided to appoint Mission Bands to visit the houses in the neighbourhood, to sing in the streets &c, and also to assist in the Services.

The question of the Catherine[3] St St Mary's Rd Service also came before the meeting.

H.P. Hughes.

19 December 1883

Minutes of meeting held Dec 19 1883

Present Revs H.P. Hughes, M. Munro, G. Marris & L. Walton. Messrs Wickham, Cross, Foster, Embury, Chitty, Railton & Skinner.

I Question Any objection to any of the Bretheren? Complaint was made that Mr Jas Nix did not send duly accredited supply to Charlton (last quarter) the secy to write him.

Hughes, reproduced in Dorothea Price Hughes, *Life of Hugh Price Hughes* , 137–42. See also 'Kellett, Ernest Edward', in *ODNB*.

1   Michael Cooper (1837–1914), market gardener, of Horspath.

2   On 16 September the Wesleyans opened a new chapel in Walton Street, finally fulfilling Richard Bell's ambition of a purpose-built sanctuary in Jericho. This raised the question of how best to use the Cranham Street premises. See 'New Wesleyan Chapel, Walton Street, Oxford', *OC*, 15 September 1883, 5.

3   Inserted. The Catherine Street Mission opened in January 1883 and was staffed by student volunteers. See M. Wellings, '"In perfect harmony with the spirit of the age": the Oxford University Wesley Guild, 1883–1914', *SCH* 55 (2019), 479 and 485.

II Any to be received on Trial? Yes. Mr C. Richardson,[1] Mr J. Osborn[2] & Mr Pearson. Mr Ison[3] to be heard; the names of Messrs Kellett, Moulton,[4] Hoare,[5] and Horwell[6] were also mentioned.

III Any to be received on Full Plan? Yes. Mr Barrett from another circuit, also Messrs Foster, Embury & Chitty, who having passed their examination were unanimously received.

IV Any removals? Mr Barrett received from another Circuit.

V Any change in time or place of Service? St Clements to 7.30.

The Secretary to the Horse Hire Fund (Mr Cross) intimated his intention of resigning that office. Mr ~~Allen's~~ Pearson's name was mentioned as likely if asked to succeed him.

H.P. Hughes.

19 March 1884

Minutes of Local Preachers Meeting Mch 19/84

Present Revs H.P. Hughes, M. Munro, G. Marris & L. Walton.

Messrs Jas Nix, Railton, Wickham, Gilder, Slaughter, Jos[h] Nix, Embury, Richardson, Foster, Hunt & Colegrove.

Ist Question Any objection to any of the Bretheren? Mr Hughes to see Mr Trotman before leaving his name off the plan. Also Mr Butler.

II Any to be rec[d] on Trial? Mr White[7] (St Clements) and Mr Ashdown[8] to have one or two appointments. Mr Ison to be heard

III Any to be rec[d] on Full Plan? Mr Champness Richardson having passed his Examination successfully was fully received.

IV Any removals to or from the Circuit? Mr Cannon to another Circuit.

V Any change in time or place of Service? Week night services in the country places from 6/30 to 7.

A resolution of congratulation to Mr Pearson on the occasion of his marriage was passed.[9]

H.P. Hughes.

---

1   Joseph William Champness Richardson (1865–1946), grocer's apprentice, of Oxford.
2   James Osborne (1849–1911), monumental mason, of Kidlington.
3   Henry Halford Ison (1860–1941), ironmonger, of Oxford.
4   Thomas William Moulton (1861–1937), non-collegiate undergraduate and a founder-member of the Oxford University Wesley Guild.
5   Wilfred Ernest Hoare (1864–1929), undergraduate, Merton College and a founder-member of the Oxford University Wesley Guild.
6   Herbert William Horwill (1864–1952), undergraduate, Wadham College and a founder-member of the Oxford University Wesley Guild. Later a Bible Christian and United Methodist minister: *Minutes of Conference* 1952, 143.
7   William Samuel White (1840–1919), shoemaker, of Oxford.
8   Reinstatement following resignation in 1881.
9   Arthur Pearson married Eunice Mary Hearne in the January–March quarter of 1884.

16 April 1884

Minutes of Special Meeting of the Oxford L. Preachers Apr 16/84

Present Rev H.P. Hughes Messrs Railton, Jas Nix, Jos^h Nix, Chitty, Colegrove, Cross & Wickham.

Resolved that Rev H.P. Hughes arrange on next plan for the usual open air Services at various places in the Circuit.

That two collections be made each day.

That three Oxford preachers be appointed at each place.

That necessary hymns be selected by Rev H.P. Hughes & a sufficient number be printed.

In addition to the ordinary open air work, it was decided that 4 preachers should visit the following villages taking them as grouped, and that Mr Railton should render service with a cornet.

Cuddesdon }
Baldon }
Garsington }
Dorchester}
Nuneham}
Sandford}
Wytham }
Wolvercote }
Woodeaton }
Noke }
Elsfield }
G. Stringer Rowe.[1]

25 June 1884

Local Preachers Meeting June 25th 1884

Present Revs H.P. Hughes, M. Munro, L. Walton, G. Marris.

Messrs Embury, Skuce, Foster, Ashdown, Holloway, Osborn, Josh Nix, G. Adams, Slaughter, Danbury, King, Trafford, Gilder, Belcher, Skidmore, Fryer, Railton, Adams Snr, Clarke, Wickham, Jas Nix, Cross, Colegrove & Hunt.

Report of last meeting read & adopted.

Ist Question Any objection to any of the bretheren? Messrs Trotman & Butler having ceased to meet in class are disqualified as Local Preachers; their names to be dropped. Also the names of Messrs Findlay[2] & Forest. Mr Chitty to be charged with neglecting his appt at Wootton May 4 and at Cranham St May 11. Mr Douglas with failing to send an accredited substitute to Beckley.

1   George Stringer Rowe (1830–1913), Superintendent of the Oxford Circuit, 1884–87: *Minutes of Conference* 1914, 125–6.
2   J.J. Findlay was teaching at Bath College in 1884–85, so may have left the Oxford Circuit by the summer: see Findlay, Joseph John, *Who was Who*.

II Any to be received on Trial? Yes. Messrs White, Ashdown & A.F. Solloway[1] having been heard and a favourable report given were recd on trial. Mr Eden's[2] name was mentioned, but was left for consideration till next meeting. Messrs Smith, McLean, J. Colegrove,[3] G. Ward, G. Handy[4] & T. Harris to have a few appointments & report made to next meeting.

III Any to be recd on Full Plan? Messrs G. Adams & J. Osborn were examined & recd on full plan.

IV Any removals? Mr Watson[5] from the Banbury Circuit.

V Any change in time or place of Service? None.

On the proposition of Mr Adams secd by Mr Railton and supported by Mr Jas Nix a hearty vote of thanks was rendered to the Revs H.P. Hughes & M. Munro in acknowledgment of their valuable services rendered to the Circuit great regret was felt that they must so soon leave.

At the close of the meeting the bretheren adjourned to the front of the old chapel where they were photographed in a group by Mr Sumner.[6]

G. Stringer Rowe.

24 September 1884

Minutes of Meeting held Sep 24/84

Present Rev G.S. Rowe, G. Marris & T.L. Walton, Messrs Embury, Foster, Cross, Wickham, Fryer, Barrett, G. Adams, Jas Nix, Watson, Jos[h] Nix, Hunt, Allen, Railton, White, Slaughter, Holloway & Skinner.

~~Minutes of previous meeting~~

Ist Question Any objection to any of the Bretheren? Mr Gilder's name being mentioned it was resolved that the consideration of his case be postponed till next quarter meanwhile his name not to appear on the plan.[7]

II Any to be received on Trial?

---

1   Arthur Frederick Solloway (1864–1949), grocer's assistant, of Oxford. See also A.F. Solloway, *Life More Abundant* (London: Pickering and Inglis, 1924).

2   Possibly Frederick Edens: see below, December 1887.

3   Joseph Colegrove (1865–1951), stationer, of Oxford. See Edward Colegrove, *Joseph Colegrove … A Short Appreciation* (privately printed, n.d.).

4   Probably George William Handy (1863–1904), commercial traveller, of Oxford.

5   Samuel Watson (1848–1920), carpenter and joiner.

6   Jabez Sumner (1843–1908) was a photographic printer by 1871 and a photographer ten years later. Born in Bladon, he was connected to the Danburys and Grimmetts, and his wife Elizabeth (1842–1929) was the sister of James and Josiah Nix; Joseph Colegrove was a nephew by marriage.

7   There is no indication in the minutes of what Gilder's 'case' involved, but the Oxford press reported his conviction for indecent exposure: 'Indecent conduct in the University Parks', *OC*, 16 August 1884, 5 and 'Latest News', *Oxford Times*, 16 August 1884, 8.

Mr J. Colegrove was proposed by Rev G. Marris seconded by Mr Railton & rec^d on Trial also Mr T. Harris proposed by Mr Jas Nix seconded by Mr Cross & Mr J. Smith proposed by Mr Jos^h Nix seconded by Mr Marris.

Messrs Ward & Handy to be left till next quarter.

III Any to be received on Full plan? No.

IV Any removals to or from the Circuit? Mr A. Solloway has left the Circuit & Mr G.V. Rowe was fully received from the Finsbury Park Circuit.[1]

Brother Bloomfield having died during the qr the meeting desired to place on record its high appreciation of his Christian character & the valuable service he has rendered to the circuit. A copy of the resolution to be sent to his widow.[2]

V Any change in time or place of Service? Yes. Bladon, Coombe, Tackley & Wootton week Evening service from 7 to 6/30.

Morning Service to be held at Eynsham in place of the afternoon.

It was also resolved that a preaching place be opened at Wheatley as soon as arrangements can be made.

Dec 17 1884 G. Stringer Rowe.

T. Skinner

Secretary.

17 December 1884

Minutes of Meeting held Dec 17/84

Present Revs G.S. Rowe, G. Marris & T.L. Walton.

Messrs Embury, Wickham, Foster, Pearson, Watson, Skuce, Skidmore, White, G.V. Rowe, Cross, Nix, King, Fryer, Ashdown, G. Adams, Shirley & Skinner.

Business arising out of former minutes.

It was resolved upon the proposal of Mr Nix sec^d by Mr Walton that the consideration of Mr Gilder's case be adjourned sine die.[3]

Preaching has been commenced at Wheatley under very promising auspices.

Ist Question Any objection to any of the bretheren? ~~Mr Allen failed to keep his appt at St Clements Nov 30.~~ The supply sent by Mr Chitty ~~a supply~~ to Cranham St not being an accredited one the secretary was directed to write him upon the matter & report to the next meeting also to Mr Colegrove his supply to Islip being also unaccredited.

II Any to be rec^d on trial? Mr Kellett was proposed by Mr G. Adams sec by Mr Skinner to be rec^d on trial if he so wished.

Messrs McAleese, Handy, Ward, Hoare, ~~John Howard & Peattie~~ to have a few appointments.

---

1   George Vanner Rowe (1862–1936), who moved from Finsbury Park with his father, the new Superintendent.

2   Thomas Bloomfield was interred at Bladon in September 1884 by T. Lionel Walton.

3   In September there was a prospect of an appeal, but by December Gilder had served a prison sentence. The family moved to Hinckley later in the decade.

III Any to be rec[d] on Full plan? Mr Pearson presented himself for examination, but the meeting feeling it would be to his advantage postponed his examination till next qr requesting ~~that~~ him in the meantime to read Wesley's Notes on the New Testament.

IV Any removals. Mr Jos[h] Nix has removed to another circuit, this being the first meeting since his removal the meeting desired to place on record the loss the Circuit had sustained thereby & the hearty good wishes of the bretheren for his future prosperity. Mr Perkins has been rec[d] from the Banbury circuit.[1] Mr Hastings from Thame,[2] both fully accredited. Also Mr Dunbar a ~~from~~ Free Methodist Local Preacher who has come to reside in the Circuit.

V Any change in time or place of service? None.

G. Stringer Rowe

T. Skinner Secy.

25 March 1885

Minutes of Meeting held March 25th 1885

Present Revs G.S. Rowe, G. Marris, T.L. Walton

Messrs Embury, G.V. Rowe, Foster, Osborne, Adams, Pearson, Perkins, King, Hastings, Watson, Fryer, Cross, Douglas, Trafford, Barrett, Clarke Slaughter, Allen, Nix, Railton, Ashdown, White, Hunt & Wickham.

Minutes of last Meeting were read and confirmed.

Business arising from former minutes:-

Bro Gilder's case has settled itself by his removal from the Circuit.

Bro Kellett has been received on trial.

Bro Pearson requests his examination to be deferred till next Quarter.

It was announced that Bro Holloway had formally retired from the Plan.

Question I Any objection to any of the brethren? Bros J. Colegrove, Douglas & Cooper had failed to keep their appointments at Beckley, and further neglect of the work at that place was mentioned, to remedy this several preachers volunteered for appointments. Bro Belcher's case was reported and, after careful consideration it was decided 'that his name be removed from the plan for next Quarter, and that a letter be sent to the effect that his restoration to the Plan depends upon his sobriety and good conduct in the interval.'[3]

Question II Any to be received on Trial? Bro George Arthur Banks from the Lincoln Circuit as already accredited 'on trial' in that Circuit.

Bro Horwill, and Bro Handy.

The following to have a few appointments: Bros Hoare, Walter Elmes, Ernest Turtle,[4] Thomas Dawson.[5]

---

1   John William Perkins (1860–1938), carpenter and joiner.
2   John Hastings (1830–1924), shoemaker.
3   Marginal note: 'This letter was sent'. Initialled, but illegible.
4   Ernest Turtle (1863–1942), assurance agent, of Oxford.
5   Thomas (or Tom) Dawson (1863–1946), joiner, of Oxford.

Question III Any to be received on Full Plan.
Bros Pearson, Slaughter, Ashdown, & White to be examined next Quarter.
Bro D.P. Clifford[1] fully received from Primitive Methodist Plan.
Question IV Any removals?
Bro Banks from Lincoln circuit.
Question V Any change of time or place of Service?
Wheatley, Evening service from 6 to ½ past 6.
Question VI Any place to come on the Plan?
New Headington – A service has been held for some time in Bro Vallis' house,[2] and it
was decided to place New Headington on the Plan for a Sunday evening appointmt.
The claims of Kidlington and Cumnor were mentioned.
A conversation ensued on the question of Trap Hire.
G. Stringer Rowe.

10 April 1885

Minutes of Special Meeting of the Oxford Local Preachers, April 10th 1885
Present Rev. Geo. Marris, Messrs Nix, Chitty, G. Rowe, Harris, Perkins, Hastings,
Railton, Pearson, Wickham, Watson.
Subject for discussion – the open air Services during the Ensuing season.
Resolved that open air Services be held on a similar plan to those of last year.
That Mr Wickham act as Secretary and Treasurer for this work.
That suitable Hymns be selected by a sub-committee consisting of Rev. G. Stringer
Rowe, Messrs Nix, Watson & Railton (sec).
That May 24 be fixed to commence the series.
It was recommended that the Oxford 'open air' Service consist of a Prayer Meeting
in the Field at 10 a.m., Services in the 3 Chapels at 11 a.m., Service in the Field at
2.30 or 3 p.m. and again at 6 p.m. After the close of the Evening Field Service that a
procession be formed & march to New Inn Hall St Chapel for a 'testimony meeting.'
That necessary Bills be printed announcing the Services at each place.

30 June 1885

Meeting held at Bladon, June 30th, 1885 at 11 a.m.
Present Revs G.S. Rowe, G. Marris, T.L. Walton. Messrs Danbury, Nix, Skidmore,
Railton, Allen, Fryer, Clifford, Hunt, Watson, Skuce, Adams, Ashdown, Howard,
King, G. Adams, G.V. Rowe, Hastings, Slaughter, White, Pearson & Wickham.
The Minutes of Meeting held March 25th were read and confirmed.

---

1   David Price Clifford (1838–1902), tailor, of Oxford. See J.N. [James Nix], 'David Price
Clifford: in Memoriam', *ODFCM*, September 1902, 37–8. Clifford's brothers-in-law included
Tom Skinner and John and James Salter.
2   In the 1891 Census Thomas Vallis, grocer, was living at 52 High Street, New Headington;
see also Michael S. Edwards, *The Lime Walk Story* (Witney: The Witney Press, 1972), 5.

Question I Any objection to any of the brethren? The secretary was requested to write to Bro Richings asking him to be at the starting place punctually.[1] Resolved: 'That Bro Belcher's name be restored to its former place on the Plan and that the Sec. write him to that effect.'

Question II Any to come on trial? Bros Hoare, Elmes, Turtle, Dawson, Fletcher, Choldcroft,[2] T.C. Piggott.[3]

The following to be heard Bros Baker,[4] Turtle Sen[r],[5] Bydawell,[6] East; E. Maycock of Wootton, Berks to have one or two appointments.[7]

Question III Any to come on Full Plan? Bros Pearson, Slaughter, Ashdown, & White passed a satisfactory examination and were unanimously received on Full Plan.

Question IV Any removals?

Bro Davis fully accredited from the Swindon Circuit.

Bro Banks acting under medical advice has resigned his position as preacher.

Question V Any change in time or place of Service? None.

Question VI Any place to come on the Plan? Garsington; and if a suitable place for worship can be obtained, Dorchester.[8] The following places were mentioned: Cuddesdon & Old Woodstock, but action deferred for the present.

Bro Slaughter kindly offered the use of his trap for 3 months if service be commenced at Dorchester.

G. Marris.

---

1   For the shared transport, taking preachers to their appointments in the rural chapels.

2   Christopher James Choldcroft (1859–1943), hairdresser, of Oxford.

3   Theodore Caro Piggott (1867–1944), undergraduate, Christ Church, and son and biographer of Henry J. Piggott, junior minister in Oxford, 1854–55. In T.C. Piggott and T. Durley, *Life and Letters of Henry James Piggott, BA, of Rome* (London: Epworth Press, 1921), 284 and 286, Piggott refers to a crisis in his own religious experience which he was able to discuss frankly with his father.

4   Thomas Henry Baker (1854–1936), draper's assistant, of Oxford.

5   Edward Turtle (1834/5–1910), assurance agent, of Oxford. It is probable that Turtle had started exploring preaching in 1866.

6   John Bydawell (1861–1929), of Oxford. By 1891 Bydawell was a postal telegraphs linesman.

7   Edward Maycock (1833–96), furniture dealer, of Wootton. Maycock's wife Martha was sister of David Price Clifford.

8   The minutes for June 1887, indicating that open-air services were continuing in Dorchester, suggest that a suitable place had not been obtained. A further discussion on 'the needs of Dorchester' was held in September 1902. From 1856 until 1920 the living of Dorchester Abbey was held by two High Churchmen, W.C. Macfarlane and Nathaniel Poyntz, who devoted considerable energy and resources to restoring the parish church, strengthening parochial organisation, and excluding Nonconformists: Kate Tiller, 'Religion and Community: Dorchester to 1920', in Kate Tiller (ed.), *Dorchester Abbey: Church and People 635–2005* (Stonesfield: The Stonesfield Press, 2005), 61–83, esp. 72 and 82. The Wesleyans obtained a foothold in the village, but decided to withdraw in 1908, maintaining the possibility of occasional open-air services: *OWMCM*, July 1908, 69.

30 September 1885

Minutes of Meeting held Sep 30/85
Present Revs G. Marris, T.L. Walton & W. Wood.[1] Messrs Ashdown, Perkins, Harris, Railton, Watson, Davis, Fryer, Clifford, Fletcher, Skuce, Cross, Nix, Hunt, G.V. Rowe, Elms, Douglas, Hastings, Embury, King, Trafford, Wickham, Skinner.
1st Question Any objection to any of the brethren? Brother Trafford failed to keep his app[t] at Hincksey.
2nd Question Any to be rec[d] on Trial? Bros Bydeawell & Baker.
The following to be heard during the qr H. Danbury Albert Titcomb[2] & J. Salter.[3] Jos[h] Colegrove's name was mentioned & it was proposed that Mr Rowe be asked to see him before making the plan. The names of Messrs Handy & Hedges were also mentioned.
Bro Turtle Sen[r] was proposed and received as an Exhorter.
3rd Question Any to be rec[d] on Full Plan? Bro Harris, who having passed his examination was unanimously received.
4th Question Any removals?
Bro Chitty has left the Circuit.
Bro Foster for Richmond College.[4]
Bro Barrett removed to Buckingham Circuit.
Bro Belcher has resigned his membership & position on the plan.
Bro Solloway[5] & Bro Colegrove[6] have also resigned.
5th Question Any change in time or place of service?
Wheatley from 6/30 to 6.
Woodstock, Bladon, Wootton, Coombe & Tackley week evening service from 7 to 6/30.
6th Quest. Any place to come on the plan?
Old Woodstock, if it can be secured.
G. Stringer Rowe.

30 December 1885

Meeting held Dec 30/85
Present Revs G.S. Rowe, G. Marris, T.L. Walton, W. Wood. Messrs Nix, Watson, Pearson, G.V. Rowe, Railton, Howard, Elmes, Douglas, Harris, Clifford, Wickham, Hunt, Ashdown, Embury, Skinner.

---

1   William Wood (1855–1917), minister in the Oxford Circuit, 1885–86: *Minutes of Conference* 1918, 103.
2   Albert Titcomb (1864–1924), of Oxford. One of four brothers, all of whom became Local Preachers.
3   John Henry Salter (1854–1930), boatbuilder, of Oxford. Brother-in-law of Tom Skinner and David Price Clifford. For the Salter family, see Simon Wenham, *Pleasure Boating on the Thames. A History of Salter Bros* (Stroud: The History Press, 2014), 186–201.
4   To train for the Wesleyan ministry.
5   John Solloway.
6   William E. Colegrove. According to *The Clergy List 1897*, 193, Colegrove was ordained deacon by the bishop of Worcester in 1886, serving as curate of Immanuel, Birmingham.

1st Question Any objection to any of the bretheren? Mr Fryer failed to keep his appt at Charlton.

Mr Buckell's name being reached it was agreed that the following resolution be sent him – 'That this meeting joins in a brotherly congratulation to Mr Buckell upon the dignity conferred upon him by being made Mayor of Oxford.'[1]

2nd Question Any to be recd on Trial? Yes. Bro Armstrong[2] (from another Circuit accredited as Local Preacher on Trial) & Brother Titcomb.

Bro Gibbons[3] to be heard. Bro John Salter to have a few appointments.

The case of Bro H. Stanley[4] being discussed it was agreed that if Mr Walton's further enquiries be satisfactory to receive him in the same status that he had held before. Bro Archer's (Wootton) name also came before the meeting.[5]

3rd Question Are any to be recd on Full Plan? None.

4th Question Any removals to or from the Circuit? Yes. Bro Geo Williams from the Witney Circuit, fully accredited.[6]

5 Question Any change in time or place of service?

Old Woodstock from 3 to 2/30.

6th Question Any place to come on the Plan? No.

Mr Walton was requested to convey to the friends at Tackley & Wootton the sense of the meeting, to the effect that they might reasonably be expected to bear the Expense of stabling the Horse for the appointed preacher.

31 March 1886

Minutes of meeting held Mch 31/86

Present Revs G.S. Rowe, G. Marris, T.L. Walton & W. Woods.

Messrs King, Hastings, Pearson, Watson, Railton, Clifford, Ashdown, Harris, Perkins, G.V. Rowe, Wickham, Fryer, Nix, Richings & Skinner.

Minutes of former meeting read & confirmed.

Ist Question Any objection to any of the bretheren?

Messrs Elmes, Douglas, Skuce & Skinner failed to keep their appt at Charlton, The Crescent & Woodstock respectively.[7]

IInd Question Any to be recd on Trial?

---

1   This was the first of Buckell's six terms as Mayor of Oxford: see https://www.oxford-history.org.uk/mayors/1836_1962/buckell_robert_1885_1918.html, accessed 30 November 2021.

2   Percy Armstrong (1866–1946), undergraduate, Jesus College. Armstrong matriculated in October 1886, from Kingswood School, so the other circuit was probably Bath.

3   Probably Thomas James Gibbins (1866–1945), draper's assistant, of Oxford.

4   Probably Harry Stanley (1852–?), grocer's assistant, of Woodstock.

5   The 1886–87 plan lists J.T. Archer, of Wootton, among the preachers on trial, and A.J. Archer, of Oxford, as a fully-accredited Local Preacher. In 1888 the latter is listed as A.G. Archer.

6   George Williams (1848–1922), hurdle maker and carpenter, of Combe.

7   Four preachers listed, but only three places.

The names of A. Titcomb & G. S. Salter[1] to be put on the plan. Messrs J.T. Archer, P. Nix[2] & Gibbons to have a few appointments with initials.

III Question Any to be rec^d on Full Plan? ~~Bro~~ [*indeciph.*] ~~& Bro Wetherill from other Circuits. Stanley~~. No.

IV Any removals? Brother Maycock has removed to Abingdon. Brother Wetherill[3] rec^d from another circuit & Bro Stanley from the Methodist Free Church both fully accredited.

Brother Allen has died during the qr.[4]

It was resolved that a letter of condolence be sent to his widow.

V Question Any change in time or place of service?

Cranham St to have a morning service at 11, the Evening service to be altered from 7 o/c to 6/30.

Garsington an afternoon service at 3 as well as the Evening at 6.

Tackley Evening service to begin at 5/45 instead of 5/30.

Week evening services at Wootton, Coombe, Bladon & Tackley from 6/30 to 7 o/c.

VI Any places to come on the plan?

Cuddesdon & Wheatley to appear as open air Stations the service at Cuddesdon commencing at 3 & Wheatley at 5 o/c.

Bro Bydawell resigned his position on the plan.

G. Stringer Rowe.

5 July 1886

Minutes of meeting held in Oxford July 5/86

Present Revs G.S. Rowe, G. Marris, T.L. Walton, Messrs Clifford, Railton, Watson, Ashdown, Douglas, Howard, King, Archer, G.V. Rowe, Wetherill, Wickham, Cross, Turtle, Harris, Perkins & Skinner.

Minutes of previous meeting read & confirmed.

I Question Any objection to any of the bretheren?

The following failed to keep their app^t

Mr Railton at Charlton

[Mr][5] Richings at Cuddesdon

[Mr] Buckell at Woodstock

[Mr] Embury at Charlton

[Mr] Ashdown at New Head^n

II Question Any to be rec^d on Trial?

---

1   George Stephen Salter (1859–1950), boat builder, of Oxford.
2   Philip Wamsley Nix (1866–1924), watchmaker, of Oxford; son of James Nix.
3   Joseph Robert Weatherill (1856–1940). Weatherill was a paid temperance advocate for the United Kingdom Alliance.
4   Hugh Allen died on 26 January 1886, according to the probate records.
5   All indicated by ditto marks in original.

Messrs Byles,[1] P.W. Nix & Archer. Messrs Vallis,[2] Gibbons & Hay to have a few appointments with initials.

III Question Any to be rec[d] on full plan? None.

IV Any removals? Bro Elmes and Brother Richardson removed from the Circuit. Messrs Archer,[3] A. Solloway[4] & Jas Hastings[5] have removed into the Circuit.

V Any change in time or place of Service?

Cranham St to have a week evening service at 7.30.

Services at Charlton & Wheatley to be discontinued. /over

Cuddesdon to have a service at 6 o/c as well as 3/30.

A conversation took place respecting Kidlington but no decision was arrived at.

G. Stringer Rowe.

29 September 1886

Minutes of meeting held Sep 29. 86

Present Revs G.S. Rowe, C.R. Burroughs[6] & W.M. Butters,[7] Messrs Wickham, Cross, Nix, Railton, Turtle, Hunt, Watson, King, Archer, Fryer, Dawson, Hastings (B),[8] Perkins, Embury, Pearson, Harris & Skinner.

Ist Question Any objection to any of the bretheren? The following failed to keep their appt

Bro Cross at Bladon

Messrs Trafford, Vallis & Shirley at Cuddesdon.

2nd Question any to be received on trial? Yes.

Bro Vallis, proposed by Mr Hunt, sec[d] Mr Nix

[Bro][9] Gibbins, [proposed by] Mr Railton [seconded] Mr Pearson

[Bro] Hay, [proposed by Mr Railton, seconded Mr Pearson].

[Bro] Douglas[10] Mr Nix sec[d] Mr King.

3rd question Any to be rec[d] on Full Plan?

Yes, Bro Dawson, who having passed his examination was unanimously rec[d].

---

1   Probably Robert MacBrair Biles (1864–89), undergraduate, Balliol College.

2   Thomas Vallis (1861–1922), grocer and baker, of Headington.

3   Alfred George Archer (1848–1913), Inland Revenue officer, of Oxford.

4   Arthur Solloway had left the Oxford Circuit in 1884.

5   James Hastings (1857–1928), auctioneer, of Oxford.

6   Charles Robert Burroughs (1854–1932), minister in the Oxford Circuit, 1886–89, based at Woodstock: *Minutes of Conference* 1933, 240–1.

7   William Middleton Butters (1858–?), minister in the Oxford Circuit, 1886–89. Butters retired from the Wesleyan ministry in 1897: *Minutes of Conference* 1897, 58.

8   The minutes follow the convention adopted by the Wesleyan Conference of using letters to differentiate between preachers with the same surname and initials. In the minutes and on the preaching plan, therefore, John Hastings appeared as J. Hastings (A) and James Hastings as J. Hastings (B).

9   Indicated by ditto marks in original.

10   Edward Douglas (1844–1908), labourer, of Headington Quarry.

IVth question, Any removals? Bros G.V. Rowe & Fletcher removed from the circuit.
V quest. Any change in time or place of Service? None.
The following were appointed a Committee to confer with Mr Inskip in allotting the
members of the Mission Band among the Local Preachers, Messrs Nix, Wickham,
Clifford and Pearson.
G. Stringer Rowe
T. Skinner
Secy.

29 December 1886

Minutes of Quarterly Meeting held Dec 29th 1886
Present Rev G.S. Rowe
    Revs J. Thompson,[1] W.M. Butters
    Messrs Nix, Railton, Solloway, Clifford, Embury, Watson, Pearson, Hunt,
Weatherill, E. Turtle, Wickham.
Minutes of last meeting read & confirmed.
I Any objection? None.
II Any to be received on trial?
Bro H. Flory from Woodville and Swadlingcote comes accredited as a preacher
on trial.[2]
Bros Larkin & Ritson[3] to come on with initials.
III Any to be received on Full Plan?
Bros E. Turtle, Baker & Titcomb to be examined next Quarter.
IV Any removals?
Bro Hay has left the Circuit.
Bro Horwill [has left the Circuit][4]
Bro G. Salter withdraws his name.
Bro J.T. Archer of Wootton resigns.
Bro Torr[5] from Bible Xtian Church, Australia is accepted on 'Full Plan'.
V Any change in time or place of Service?
Islip from 2.30 to 3 (?)[6]
Tackley 5 ¾ to 5 ½

---

1   John Thompson (1847–1938), minister in the Oxford Circuit, 1886–87: *Minutes of
Conference* 1938, 191.
2   Henry William Flory (1868–1956), tailor. Although received from a Derbyshire circuit,
Flory was born in Oxford.
3   John Holland Ritson (1868–1953), undergraduate, Balliol College. Later a Wesleyan
minister: *Minutes of Conference* 1954, 118–19. For Ritson's years in Oxford and his call to
preach, see John H. Ritson, *The World is Our Parish* (London: Hodder and Stoughton, 1939),
17–33.
4   Indicated by ditto marks in original.
5   William George Torr (1853–1939), undergraduate, non-collegiate.
6   Question mark in the original minute.

Method of Service at Cranham St was discussed, but it was eventually decided to make no radical change at present.
G. Stringer Rowe
Mar 30 1887

30 March 1887

Minutes of Meeting held Mch 30/87
Present Revs G.S. Rowe, C.R. Burroughs & W.M. Butters
Messrs Harris, Dawson, Trafford, Douglas, King, Taylor, Perkins, Johnson, Watson, Cross, Embury, Turtle, Titcomb, Railton, Nix, Hunt, Howard, Hastings B, Shirley, Wickham, Ashdown, Skinner.
1st question Any objection? The case of Bro Hastings A was discussed & it was left from Mr Rowe to see him.
2nd Any to be recd on Trial?
Bro Ritson, and Bro P.W. Nix, subject to his consent. Bro J.H. Salter with initials & Bro Duck[1] with an asterisk.
3rd questn Any to be recd on full plan?
Bros E. Turtle, Baker, Titcomb & Douglas passed their Examination successfully & were unanimously received.
4th question Any removals?
Bro Larkin represented on the plan by initials has left the Circuit.
Bro Skuce has retired from the plan.
Bro Taylor[2] has been recd from the Rugby Circuit as a fully accredited local preacher as also Brother Johnson[3] from Stockton.
5th question Any change in time or place of Service? None.
G. Stringer Rowe.

29 June 1887

Minutes of Meeting held June 29/87
Present Revs G.S. Rowe & W.M. Butters. Messrs Archer, Ashdown, Johnson, King, Clifford, Dawson, Turtle, Nix, Richings, Taylor, Wickham, Pearson, Howard, Harris, Embury, Railton, Hunt, Skinner.
The Chairman reported that Bro Clarke had died during the quarter & the secretary was directed to send a letter of condolence to his widow.[4]
A letter of sympathyising with Bro Jonathan Skidmore in the bereavement he has been called to endure owing to the death of his wife was also directed to be sent.[5]
Ist question Any objection to any of the bretheren?

1   William Duck (1868–1948), tailor, of Oxford.
2   Not listed on the July–October 1888 plan, and not mentioned again in the minutes.
3   Edwin Johnson was employed as Circuit Missionary or Evangelist, 1886–88.
4   Jonas Clarke, of Woodstock, died in June 1887.
5   Sarah Skidmore died in April 1887.

It was named that Bro Shirley failed to keep his appointment at Horspath but an explanation was given.

2nd Question Any to be rec[d] on trial?

Bro Buckingham[1] having been heard by Messrs Fryer & Adams & report being favourable it was decided that he come on with initials.

3rd question Any to be received on full plan? None.

4th question Any removals?

Bro Reed has removed into the Circuit from Bath.[2]

5th question Any change in time or place of service? None.

It was decided to continue open air services at Dorchester on the next plan.

J. Martin.

28 September 1887

Minutes of Meeting held Sep 28/87

Present Rev J. Martin[3] (Chairman), Revs H. Jefford,[4] C.R. Burroughs & W.M. Butters, Messrs Solloway, Reed, Archer, Hastings, Hunt, Baker, Osborne, Fryer, Turtle, Railton, Johnson, Harris, Watson, Howard, Adams, G. Adams, Wickham, Nix, Embury & Skinner.

Minutes of June Meeting read & passed.

1st question Any objection to any of the bretheren? Bro Vallis failed to keep his appointment at Forest Hill but the omission was satisfactorily explained.

2nd question Any to be received on Full plan? None this qr, but Messrs Turtle, Vallis, Flory & Gibbins having been the accostomed time on trial shall be asked to present themselves for Examination next quarter & trial sermon arranged for.

3rd Question Any to be received on Trial? Bro J.H. Salter to continue with initials & Bro W. Whitfield[5] to have a few appointments also with initials. Messrs T. Buckingham, J.H. Ritson & F. Murfitt. Bro W. Duck proposed by Bro Hastings B & sec[d] Bro Nix ~~was also~~ not being well known was received by a small majority. Bro Timotheus Brown[6] was received as an Exhorter.

4th Question Any removals?

Bro W. Whitfield has removed into the Circuit & Bro Simpson has left it.

5th Question Any change in time or place of service?

1   Perhaps Thomas Buckingham (1847–99), mason's labourer, of Eynsham, but probably Stephen Thomas Buckingham (1868–1954), carpenter, of Eynsham.

2   Edward Reed (1811–91), retired Inland Revenue officer, and father-in-law of Alfred Archer.

3   John Martin (1817–1908), Superintendent of the Oxford Circuit, 1887–90: *Minutes of Conference* 1909, 130–1.

4   Henry Jefford (1840–1907), minister in the Oxford Circuit, 1887–90: *Minutes of Conference* 1907, 134–5.

5   W. Whitfield, Magdalen Street, is listed on the 1888 plan as a Local Preacher on trial, but does not appear on the 1890 plan.

6   Timotheus Brown (1859–1937), carter, of Garsington.

It was proposed to alter the time of the Islip week evening service but before doing so Mr Jefford was asked to get the mind of the Islip people on the subject.

Bladon, Coombe, Wootton & Tackley week evening services from 7 to 6/30.

Tackley Sunday Evening service from 5/45 to 5/30.

It was proposed & agreed to plan 2 bretheren at Horspath on the Sunday.

An alteration in the conveyances was suggested & it was finally arranged that 2 pony traps sh^d be hired for the Woodstock side of the Circuit to reduce the expenditure & to facilitate the app^t of the Coombe preacher. Both traps to leave the Martyrs Memorial at 9 a.m. one carrying the preachers for Woodstock, Wootton & Tackley & the other supplying Eynsham, Coombe & Bladon.

J. Martin

T. Skinner (Secy).

28 December 1887

Minutes of Meeting held Dec 28/87

Present Revs J. Martin, H. Jefford, W.M. Butters. Messrs Hunt, Reed, Nix, Embury, Railton, Turtle, Douglas, Trafford, Dawson, Pearson, Howard & Skinner.

Minutes of previous meeting read & passed.

1st Question Any objection?

It was reported that Bro Armstrong had preached un-methodistic doctrine at Headington Quarry & the Chairman was desired to interview him upon the matter.[1]

Bro Flory failed to keep his app^t at Cranham St, it was explained that illness was the cause.

Bro Duck failed similarly at F. Hill & Horspath, the Secy to write to him for an explanation.

2 Question Any to be rec^d on Full Plan? It was expected that Messrs Turtle, Vallis, Flory & Gibbons would present themselves for Examination but they wished it postponed for a qr.

3rd Question Any to be received on Trial? Messrs J.H. Salter, Whitfield, Davis,[2] Edens[3] & Holland.[4]

Bro Haltey as an Exhorter.

Messrs Pheysey[5] and Ray[6] with initials.

4th Question Any removals?

Messrs E.R. Turtle & Biles have removed from the Circuit.

---

1   Sadly, no further details are provided. Armstrong's father was a Wesleyan minister and he was educated at Kingswood School, so he should have been well-acquainted with Methodist doctrine.

2   William Davis (1853–1937), farmer, of Oxford.

3   Frederick Edens (1851–1930), coal merchant, of Oxford. Brother-in-law of James Nix.

4   Frederick Holland (1858–1926), grocer's assistant, of Oxford. F. Holland, Bullingdon [Road], is listed on the 1888 plan, but not the 1890 plan, and is joint Superintendent of the St Clement's Sunday School with Walter Slaughter.

5   Percy Wootton Pheysey (1868–1954), undergraduate, Wadham College.

6   Herbert Edward Ray (1866–1950), saddle and harness maker, of Forest Hill.

Bro Styles[1] has removed into the Circuit from Bishop Stortford as a L.P. on Trial.
5th Question Any alt[n] in time or place of Service? Beckley Services at 3/15 and 6 o/clock. Cuddesdon at 3 & 6.
It was agreed to start a Sunday School at Horspath as soon as possible & the Local Preacher for the day to assist. In order that he may reach the Chapel by 2/30 it was decided that the Garsington conveyance sh[d] go through Horspath.
The Secretary was requested to send letters to Messrs Harris & Baker congratulating them upon their recent marriage.[2]
The Chairman stated that if the routine business of the Meeting could be got through more expeditiously a discussion upon some Theological or other subject might profitably be taken up at the close. This seemed to be the unanimous opinion of the meeting.
J. Martin
T. Skinner Sec'y.

28 March 1888

Minutes of Meeting held Mch 28/88
Present Revs J. Martin, H. Jefford, C.R. Burroughs & W.M. Butters. Messrs Wickham, Fryer, G. Adams, Dawson, Whitfield, Richings, Archer, Turtle, Railton, Reed, Davis, Pearson, Watson & Skinner.
Minutes of former meeting read & signed.
1st Question Any objection? It was objected that Bro Flory failed to keep his appointment at Tackley on 11th Mch; which was satisfactorily explained.
2nd Quest[n] Any to be rec[d] on Full Plan? The bretheren who sh[d] have been examined with that view wished for further postponement.
Bro Nix proposed, sec[d] by Bro Hunt ~~and supported by Bro Wickham~~ that Bro Belcher be rec[d] on Full Plan. The resolution was carried without opposition, a few abstained from voting.
3rd Question Any to be rec[d] on Trial? Bro Pheysey was proposed as also Bro Rogers from another Circuit. Messrs Shayler[3] & Albert Vallis[4] to receive notes to preach from the Sup[t].
Brother Douglas undertook to form a Society Class at Beckley.
Bro Skinner & Bro Clifford were asked to do what they could to revive the languishing cause at Horspath; Bro Turtle promising to visit Cuddesden as frequently as possible to assist in the work there.

1   Alfred George Ernest Styles (1863–1944), draper's assistant. A.G.E. Styles, 72 Walton Street, is listed on the 1888 plan, but not the 1890 plan.
2   Thomas Harris married Mary Anne Rees and Thomas Henry Baker married Rosa Jane Winter in December 1887.
3   John Shayler (1860–1944), baker, of Eynsham.
4   Albert George Vallis (1868–1940), baker, of Headington Quarry. Brother of Thomas Vallis.

4th Question Any removals? Bro Rogers has removed into the Circuit. Bro Murfitt has left it.

5th Question Any change in time or place of service?

Week evening services on the Woodstock side of the Circuit from 6/30 to 7 o/c.

The following were asked to form the Library Committee to frame rules for & take charge of the Volumes presented for the use of Local Preachers (Rev W.M. Butters, Messrs Nix, Railton, Pearson & Wickham (convener). The books to be trust property.[1]

T. Skinner Sec'y.

6 April 1888

A special meeting was held Apl 6/88 to make arrangements for open air work during next plan.

Present Rev J. Martin Messrs Clifford, Railton, Watson, Baker, Edens, Johnson, Pearson & Skinner.

Mr Wickham (Sec'y of this work) was unable to be present but sent his book showing a balance in hand of £4-2-8 ¾.

The dates & places proposed to be visited during the quarter were decided upon & the following committee appointed to group the workers & prepare Hymn Sheets. Messrs Nix, Railton, Watson, Embury & Wickham (Sec'y).

It was decided to print a separate plan for the open air Services.

J. Martin

T. Skinner.

27 June 1888

Minutes of Meeting held June 27/88

Present Revs J. Martin, H. Jefford & W.M. Butters, Messrs King, Reed, Nix, Davis, Turtle, Solloway, Wickham, Johnson, Watson, Douglas, Adams Sen[r], Hastings B, Railton, Buckingham, Archer, Fryer, Hunt, Pearson & Skinner.

Ist Question Any objections? None.

2nd Any to be rec[d] on Trial? J. Shayler, Arthur Vallis,[2] & Albert G. Vallis to come with initials.

3rd Any to come on full plan? Bro Turtle and Bro Vallis[3] were examined & rec[d] , the former proposed by Bro Adams, sec[d] Bro Nix, the latter proposed Bro Nix, and sec[d] by Bro Hunt.

4th Question Any removals?

Bro Williams into the Witney Circuit. Bro Rogers has also left the Circuit.

---

1   See below, September 1888, for further discussion on the best way of holding the library in trust.

2   Arthur Edward Vallis (1866–1944), bricklayer, of Headington Quarry. Brother of Thomas and Albert Vallis.

3   Thomas Vallis.

5th Question Any change in time or place of Service? None.

It was agreed to incorporate the open air appointments in the regular plan for the future.

Mr Wickham (convener of the Library Committee) stated that he had not been able to call the members together as yet but hoped to do so soon.

J. Martin

T. Skinner

Secy.

27 September 1888

Minutes of Meeting Sep 27/88

Present Revs J. Martin, H. Jefford, C.R. Burroughs & W.M. Butters. Messrs Davis, Railton, Watson, Pearson, Hunt, Perkins, Wickham, Hastings B, Dawson, Embury, Fryer, Skidmore, King, Ashdown, Harris & Skinner.

Minutes of previous Meeting read & passed.

1st question Any objections? Several bretheren failed to keep their appointments, but the failures were satisfactorily accounted for.

2nd Question Any to be rec^d on full plan? Bro Ritson who has passed his Examination in the Bolton Circuit was rec^d as a fully accredited Local Preacher.

3rd Question Any to be rec^d on trial? Messrs Reeves[1] & Gourlay[2] to have notes from the superintendent & accompany some of the bretheren.

4th Question Any removals?

Messrs Baker & Whitfield have removed from the Circuit.

5 Question Any change in time or place of Service? Bladon, Coombe, Wootton & Tackley week Evening services from 7 to 6/30.

Mr Wickham reported that the L.P. Library Committee had met & desired information as to the advisability or otherwise of making a subscription for members also enquiring whether the books sh^d be vested in the New Inn Hall St Trustees or a separate Trust be formed by a selection from the L. Preachers.

The Meeting deemed it unnecessary to make a subscription & thought the property sh^d be held by the New Inn Hall St Trustees in trust for the Local Preachers.

Bro Weatherill was heartily congratulated by the meeting upon his recent marriage & received its best wishes for his future happiness, he thanked the bretheren for their hearty congratulations & kind wishes.[3]

J. Martin

T. Skinner

  Secretary.

---

1   Possibly Henry Joseph Reeves (1858–1928), coach builder, of Oxford.

2   Probably Samuel Gourlay (1860–1902), tailor's cutter.

3   Weatherill married Elizabeth Branton in the autumn of 1888.

27 December 1888

Minutes of Meeting Dec 27/88

Present Revs J. Martin, H. Jefford & W.M. Butters.

Messrs Hastings B, Railton, Embury, Dawson, Douglas, Wickham, Edens, Skidmore, Clifford, Watson, Reed, Nix, Archer, Shirley & Skinner.

Minutes of previous Meeting read & passed.

First Question, Are there any objections against any of the Bretheren? Yes, Bro Duck neglected his app^t at Horspath.

Sec^d Question, Are there any to be rec^d on Full Plan? No.

Third Question, Are there any to be rec^d on Trial? Yes. Messrs Gourlay, Reeves & Martin[1] to have a note from the Superintendent. Messrs Flory, Duck, Salter, Styles, Davis & Edens, having been on trial the usual time the Secretary was directed to write them, asking that they present themselves for Examination next qr. Enquiries to be made respecting Bro Archer of Wootton.[2]

Fourth Question, Any removals? Bro Johnson has removed from the Circuit. Bro Baker was understood to be returning to the Circuit & his name was to occupy its former place on the plan. Bro Buckell wrote the Superintendent resigning his position as a Local Preacher. Mr Martin saw him & advised him to reconsider his decision afterwards getting another letter from him saying that he felt he ought to adhere to his former decision purpose, the Bretheren regretted to hear it & deemed it desirable that the Secretary shd write him expressing their feeling & hoping that upon further reconsideration he wd consent to remain with them.

5th Question, Any change in time or place of Service.

A morning service at 11 at New Headn [conj.] as well as an evening service.[3]

It was agreed that at the Expiration of the present contract the University Press authorities shd be asked for an estimate for printing the plan.[4]

J. Martin

T. Skinner Secy.

27 March 1889

Minutes of Meeting held Mch 27/89

Present Revs J. Martin, H. Jefford & W.M. Butters, Messrs Solloway, Reed, Davis, Embury, Harris, Fryer, G. Adams, Clifford, Turtle, Railton, Douglas, Nix, Hastings B, Watson, Perkins, Richings, Skidmore, Shirley, Dawson, Styles, Slaughter, Vallis, Weatherill & Skinner.

---

1   Henry Martin (1870–?), non-collegiate undergraduate, and son of John Martin: H. Martin, Blackhall Road, is listed on the summer 1890 plan as a fully accredited Local Preacher.

2   Last sentence added at the top of the page.

3   On the July–October 1888 plan New Headington was listed, but without specific service times; by summer 1890 services were appointed at 11 and 6 each Sunday.

4   Both the 1888 and 1890 plans were printed by Alden and Co., of Oxford, so the University Press did not take over the contract.

Minutes of former Meeting read & passed.

Ist Question Any objection to any of the bretheren? Complaint was made that Bro Ashdown failed to keep his Eynsham morning appointment & the Secretary was instructed to write him.

II Any to be received on Trial? Yes. Messrs H.E. Ray, A.G. Vallis, A. Vallis, Gibbins, H. Martin & Holland. Bro J. Colegrove to be seen by Mr Martin & if he wishes it, he also to be recd on Trial.[1]

III Any to be received on Full Plan? Messrs Styles, Davis & Edens having passed their Examination were unanimously received on Full Plan.

IV Any removals? Bro Chas Burroughs[2] recd from the Abingdon Circuit – as a fully accredited Local Preacher. Bro Styles has left the Circuit. Bro Buckell's resignation was accepted. Messrs Flory & Duck were dropped from the plan agreeably with their wishes.

V Any change in time or place of Service?

The week evening Services at Bladon, Coombe, Wootton & Tackley to be at 7 instead of 6/30.

Mr Butters who had examined the candidates for full membership was asked to read a paper on 'Inspiration' at the next meeting. He said he would do so if possible. The rule of the Connexion requiring every Local Preacher to meet in Class was brought prominently before the meeting & it was unanimously agreed that a circular letter (drawn up by the Superintendent & the Secretary) be sent to every Local Preacher giving the Rule in full and desiring that he inform the next meeting in whose class he met.

A letter recd from Bro Wickham (who was absent through illness) stated that he had summoned the members of the L.P. Library Committee but they failed to attend at the time appointed.

J. Martin

T. Skinner

 (Secretary).

26 June 1889

Minutes of Meeting held June 26/89

Present Revs J. Martin & H. Jefford. Messrs Howard, Davis, Turtle, Edens, Clifford, Hunt, Pearson, Hastings B, Douglas, Watson, King, Fryer, Osborne, Dawson, Railton, G. Adams, Burroughs, Nix & Skinner.

The minutes of former Meeting read & passed.

Bro Shirley did not reply to the circular letter sent him in common with the rest of the bretheren asking him to inform the Meeting in what class he was a member & the Secretary was instructed to write him again. Bro J. Hastings B told the Meeting

---

1   Joseph Colegrove, who was on trial in 1884–85.

2   C. Burroughs, James Street, is listed on the summer 1890 plan.

that he was not a member of any class after carefully considering the matter it was defferred for a quarter.

Messrs Howard, Watson & King were added to the Library Committee.

Ist Question Any objection to any of the bretheren?

Bro Shirley failed to keep his Eynsham app^t.

[Bro]^1 Cross failed at Coombe & Eynsham.

[Bro] Archer at Bladon but he gave a satisfactory explanation.

II Question Any to be rec^d on full plan? None.

III [Question] Any to be rec^d on Trial? Yes. Bro Robinson.^{2}

IV Any change in time or place of service? Beckley to have an Evening service only.

J. Martin

T. Skinner

(Secy)

29 September 1889

Minutes of Meeting held Sep 29/89

Present Revd J. Martin who presided

Rev A. Martin.^{3} Messrs Edens, Skidmore, Dawson, Turtle, Fryer, Railton, Adams, Osborne, Douglas, Pearson, Hunt, Clifford, Watson, King, Reed, Solloway, Howard & Skinner.

Minutes of previous Meeting read & passed.

1st question Any objection?

Bro Vallis failed to keep his Hincksey app^t but a satisfactory explanation was given. Bro Ashdown's name to be left on the plan for another qr.^{4}

2nd question Any to be rec^d on Trial? Bro Strothard^5 was proposed sec^d & rec^d . Messrs Freeman,^{6} W. Titcomb^7 & Roff^8 to receive a note from the Superintendent. The Rev A. Martin to see Bro Clark recently arrived in Woodstock.^{9}

3rd question Any to be rec^d on Full Plan? None.

4th [question]^{10} Any removals. Messrs Torr, Baker, Armstrong, Pheysey & Buckingham have left the Circuit. Bro Harris sent a letter to the Meeting asking

---

1   Indicated by ditto marks in original.

2   Apparently not followed up.

3   Arthur Martin (1854–1908), who served in the Oxford Circuit 1880–82, and returned for a second appointment, 1889–92.

4   Behind this cryptic reference lay a failure in business: see below, December 1889 and March 1890.

5   William Henry Strothard (1861–1920), printer, of Oxford.

6   John Freeman (1870–1952), banker's clerk, of Oxford. Freeman entered the Wesleyan ministry in 1896: *Minutes of Conference* 1953, 135.

7   William Edward Titcomb (1858–91), insurance agent, of Oxford.

8   John Henry Roff (1870–1932), confectioner's clerk, of Headington.

9   Henry George Clark (1866–?), carpenter.

10   Indicated by ditto marks in original.

that his name be left off the plan, ill health preventing his work. The Meeting were sorry for him in his illness but w^d not think of dropping his name & the Sec was directed to send him a letter of sympathy.

5th Any change in time or place of Service. Woodstock week Evg service to 745. Coombe, Bladon, Wootton & Tackley to 730.

Bro Shirley was to be seen by the Sup^t for an explanation of his position with regard to his non-attendance at Class.

Bro Pearson prop^d sec^d by Bro Watson that a letter be sent to Bro Hastings B from this meeting deprecating his action at St Giles Fair.[1]

J. Martin.

30 December 1889

Minutes of Meeting held Dec 30/89

Rev. J. Martin in the Chair. Present Revs H. Jefford & A. Martin. Messrs Nix, Railton, Hastings B, Watson, Skidmore, Perkins, Reed, Harris, Dawson, Shirley, Archer, Solloway, Embury & Skinner.

Minutes of former Meeting read & passed.

1st question Any objection? Bro Cross failed to keep his St Clements app , the secy to write him for an explanation.

Bro Nix proposed, sec^d Bro Pearson that Bro Ashdown's name be kept on the Minute Book but dropped from the plan & that he be asked to attend the next meeting & give explanation needed.[2]

[line at foot of page – *indeciph.*]

2nd question Any to rec^d on full plan? None.

3rd question Any to be rec^d on Trial?

Bro John Roff & Bro Thomas.[3]

Bro E. Titcomb[4] to come on with initials.

Messrs Gibson[5] & Taylor[6] to receive notes from the Superintendent.

Messrs Strothard & W. Titcomb could not undertake work at present.

Bro Freeman wished to keep to Sunday School work.

---

1   An article on St Giles's Fair appears in *JOJ*, 14 September 1889, 8, reporting good weather and 'the most orderly and well-conducted' attendance for some years. No reference to Hastings appears in the newspaper account of the Fair or of subsequent sittings of the City Police Court. Hastings might perhaps have taken part in the Salvation Army Prayer Meeting at the Fair.

2   See below, March 1890.

3   Apparently not taken further. Thomas may be Alfred Eaton Thomas (1869–1959), undergraduate, Jesus College, a member of the OU Wesley Guild: OHC, OMCA, NM5/F/A1/1, John Wesley Society minute book, 1882–89, list of members, November 1889.

4   Ernest Titcomb (1871–1941), upholsterer, of Oxford. Entered the Wesleyan ministry in 1896, serving in South Africa.

5   William Ralph Boyce Gibson (1869–1935), undergraduate, The Queen's College.

6   Alfred Edward Taylor (1869–1945), undergraduate, New College.

4th question Any removals? None.

5th [question][1] Any change in time or place of Service? Beckley to have an Evening service only.

Mr Wickham was asked to see Mrs Gardner & get her sanction for the work at the Crescent to be put on Methodist lines.[2]

Bro Shirley expressed his strong sympathy with Class Meetings & said he intended joining a class during the qr.

Mr Wickham presented the report of the Summer Open Air Services.

Income 17-8-3 17-10-9

Expenses 9-8-1 6-12-1 ½

Surplus 8-0-2 10-18-7 ½

which was divided as follows [ ] £ to the Local Preachers Library Fund [ ] to the C. Mission Fund & the balance carried forward.[3]

The Library Committee were said to have 11/5 in hand.

Mr Hastings was asked to audit the open air a/c.

J. Martin.

26 March 1890

Minutes of Meeting held Mch 26/90

Present Revs J. Martin, H. Jefford & A. Martin. Messrs Hastings, Nix, Reed, Edens, G. Adams, Fryer, Adams Sen[r], Railton, Shirley, Ashdown, Trafford, Hunt, Perkins, Watson, Embury, Archer, King, Davis, Howard.

Minutes of former meeting read & passed.

1st question, Any objection? None.

2nd Any to come on full plan? No.

3rd Any to come on Trial? Yes. E. Titcomb, W. Titcomb, Taylor, Clark, G. Horn, J. Stanton.[4] Messrs Salter, A.G. Vallis, A. Vallis, Ray and H. Martin to be asked to come up for Examination next qr.

4th question, Any removals? Bro Cross sent in his resignation & pressed for its acceptance to which the meeting agreed. Bro King also tendered his resignation, as his health prevented his giving more than fragmentary service, but several of the bretheren testified to the value of his work & the loss it w[d] be to allow his resignation & feeling that he had the full confidence of the meeting he withdrew his resignation.

5th question Any change in time or place of service

Week evening service at Bladon, Coombe, Wootton & Tackley from 6/30 to 7. Walton St week evg to 7.30. Eynsham to substitute aft[n] service for morning if Mr Jefford finds the members generally desire the change.

---

1   Indicated by ditto marks in original.
2   No elucidation is offered about the 'Methodist lines' in question. Apart from ensuring that services were led by accredited preachers, possible causes of concern might have been neglect of classes or reluctance to contribute to circuit funds.
3   Figures not filled in.
4   John Stanton (1869–?), labourer, of Bladon.

Owing to ill-health Mr Wickham resigned the secretaryship of the open air work & received the hearty thanks of the meeting for his services. He handed 4£ to his successor Mr Edens to be retained together with 4-18-7 to be devoted to the payment of bills sent to the Qtly Meeting for extra travelling expenses of the ministers, the remaining surplus to go to the Circuit Mission Fund.

Mr Watson proposed sec[d] by Mr Davis that a monthly meeting of the Local Preachers be held the 1st Friday in each month at 8 o/c for the improvement & intercourse of its members.

Messrs Embury, Clifford & Watson (secy) to organise the meetings.

Mr Ashdown explained to the satisfaction of the meeting his position with regard to his failure in business & received the sincere & practical sympathy of its members with him in his personal, family & business trials.[1]

J. Martin

T. Skinner
    Secy.

25 June 1890

Minutes of Meeting June 25/90

Present Rev[d] J. Martin (chairman) Revs H. Jefford & A. Martin

Messrs Embury, Dawson, Watson, Edens, Shirley, Perkins, Clifford, Douglas, Railton, Nix, King, Wickham, Davis & Skinner.

Minutes of former meeting read & passed.

Mr Nix proposed Mr Watson sec[d] that Mr Cross having resigned his name be left off for this qr and be reinstated next plan shd he write asking for it to be so. Carried by 8 votes to 4.

1st Question Any objection? None.

2nd [Question][2] Any to be received on full plan? Yes. Mr H. Martin who passed a very successful examination was upon the proposal of Mr Wickham sec[d] by Mr Hastings rec[d] upon the full plan. Bro Butler to be rec[d] sh[d] he so desire.[3]

3rd Question Any to be rec[d] on trial? None.

4th Question Any removals? Bro Horn has left the Circuit.

5th Question Any change in time or place of service.

~~Bladon, Coombe, Wootton & Tackley week evening service from~~ Eynsham, morning service to be substituted for aftn.

Requests were made for open air services from New Head[n] & Cuddesden Methodist services being asked for at Sunnymede[4] Mr Jas Nix was asked to pay a visit & report.

---

1   In addition to the hints in the minutes of September and December 1889, see 'Notice of dividend', *JOJ*, 11 January 1890, 5, reporting on Ashdown's arrangement with his creditors.

2   Indicated by ditto mark in original.

3   Butler had been dropped from the plan in June 1884.

4   At the northern end of Summertown.

It was resolved to send a letter of sympathy jointly with the one from the Qtly Meeting to Mr Brockless & family in their loss by death of Mrs Brockless.[1]
James Chapman
T. Skinner
  (Secy)

24 September 1890

Minutes of Quarterly Meeting held Sept 24th 1890
Present Revs J. Chapman,[2] A. Martin, G. Rose.[3] Messrs Howard, Embury, Solloway, King, Weatherill, Skidmore, Perkins, Clifford, Adams, Ballard,[4] A. Vallis, Archer, Dawson, Watson, Hunt, Shirley, Fryer, Ballard,[5] Pearson & Wickham.
The Minutes of last Meeting were read & confirmed.
The Meeting passed a Vote of deep Sympathy with Bro Hastings (B) in his recent bereavement.[6]
I question Any objection?
Bro Vallis on Aug 17 failed to send a supply to Cranham St but a note arrived on Sunday morning that he would be unable to attend. The Superintendent promised to point out to him the inconvenience of such a course.
Question 2 Any to be received on Full Plan? None.
Question 3 Any to be received on Trial?
Bro Arthur Smart, of 13 Queen St,[7] strongly recommended by Rev. A. Martin & Mr Solloway.
The Superintendent was also requested to see Bro Smith of Hayfield Road,[8] formerly on trial in Buckingham Circuit, and lately in Society at Headington Quarry: also T.E. Gibbins, 13 Queen Street, formerly on trial on our plan.[9]
Question 4 Any Removals?
Bro Burroughs to Hackney.
[Bro][10] H. Martin to Stockport (Trinity).[11]

---

1   Ann Brockless (1827–90) was buried at Islip on 29 May 1890. Edmund and Ann Brockless ran a baker's business in Islip. See also 24 September 1890 and 22 June 1891.
2   James Chapman (1849–1913), who served in the Oxford Circuit 1876–79 and returned as Superintendent, 1890–93.
3   George F. Rose (1861–1932), minister in the Oxford Circuit, 1890–93: *Minutes of Conference* 1932, 73–4.
4   Adolphus Ballard (1867–1915), solicitor, of Woodstock.
5   Listed twice.
6   Florence Hastings died in September 1890.
7   Smart's address, like that of T.E. Gibbins (see note below) indicates employment in the drapery business of Charles Badcock and Co., whose premises at 13–15 Queen Street included accommodation for single employees.
8   Moses Smith (1857–1946), coachman, of Oxford.
9   Gibbins was on trial in 1886–87.
10   Indicated by ditto mark in original.
11   Moving with his father, who retired to Stockport.

[Bro] Stanton moves out of Oxford Circuit tomorrow.
Question 5 Any change in time or place?
Week night services on Woodstock side (except Woodstock itself) to ½ past 6.
Question 6 Any to come up for examination?
Superintendent to see the brethren whose time of probation has been more than one year.
It was decided to have a Local Preachers' Convention ~~Wednesday October 29 being suggested as the date. Mr King kindly promised to give a paper~~ consisting of the brethren of this Circuit and if possible of the neighbouring Circuits all arrangements to be made by the following Committee ~~appointed to arrange~~ The ministers and Messrs Pearson, Nix, Edens, Weatherill, Watson, Clifford, Hastings (B), Skinner, Wickham (convener of 1st meeting).
The following gentlemen volunteered to go in twos on alternate Sundays to Eynsham to try to revive the work there Messrs Edens } W. Harris}

J. Nix} Shirley}

The Local Preachers decided to erect a small memorial brass in Islip Chapel to perpetuate the memory of Mrs Brockliss.[1] Mr Wickham to receive the subscriptions.
There was no report on the opening of Cottage Services at Sunnymede.
Some conversation took place on the state of the Temperance work in the Circuit and brethren were requested to prosecute it with revived energy. Rev. A. Martin announced that Mr Alison, M.P. for Carlisle,[2] would attend a Temperance Meeting in the Oxford Chapel on Nov. 22.
The Monthly Meetings of the Local Preachers for mutual help and encouragement to be continued; the next meeting to be on Wednesday, October 29, Mr King kindly consenting to give a paper.
James Chapman.

29 December 1890

Minutes of Meeting held Dec 29th 90
Present Revs J. Chapman, A. Martin, G. Rose. Messrs G. Adams, Railton, Fryer, Howard, King, Archer, Skidmore, Watson, Somerton,[3] Weatherill, Solloway, Vallis, Trafford, W. Titcomb, J. Titcomb,[4] Adams Senr, Osborn, Harris, Hunt, Embury, Turtle, Hastings (B), Ray, Reed, W. Slaughter, Douglas, White, Clifford & Skinner.
1st question, Any objection? None.

---

1   See 25 June 1890 above. The inscription read: 'Ann Brockless. Died May 25 1890, aged 63 years. Erected by the Local Preachers of the Oxford Circuit.' I am indebted to Shirley Martin for supplying these details and for a photograph taken before Islip Chapel closed in 1988. This recognition by the Local Preachers was unprecedented and it is not explained, but it may be inferred that Mrs Brockless offered support and hospitality to visiting preachers.
2   Robert Andrew Allison (1838–96), Liberal MP for Eskdale.
3   Listed on the 1890 plan as 'Somerton, Cowley Road'.
4   Possibly Walter John Titcomb, listed as 'J' to distinguish him from his brother William.

2nd question, Any to be rec[d] on full Plan? Yes. Bro Butler, a fully accredited Local Preacher.[1] The bretheren on trial whose probation has expired to come for Examination next quarter.

3rd question Any to be rec[d] on Trial? Yes! Bro Lofthouse[2] from another circuit.

4th question, Any removals? Yes.

Bro A. Smart to Manchester.

Bro G. Vallis[3] sent in his resignation which was accepted.

5 question Any change in time or place of Service? None.

The thanks of the Meeting were given to Bro Skinner for his services as Secretary during the past 10 years.

It was resolved upon the proposal of Bro Skinner, sec[d] Bro Adams Sen[r] that Bro Hastings (B) be the future Secretary.

The Chairman reported that two monthly meetings of the Local Preachers had been held during the quarter. Bro King & Bro Taylor had given papers, followed by profitable discussion.

Bro Clifford promised to introduce a subject at the next meeting 'The relation of Repentance to Faith'.

The Chairman expressed a wish that similar meetings might be held occasionally on the Woodstock side of the Circuit.

The Local Preachers Convention was deferred for the present.

James Chapman.

1 April 1891

Minutes of Quarterly Meeting held April 1st 1891

Present Revs J. Chapman, A. Martin. G.F. Rose. Messrs J. Adams, Hunt, Howard, Railton, Nix, Trafford, Skidmore, Shirley, King, Skinner, Fryer, Wickham, Embury, G. Adams, Watson, Clifford, Slaughter, Pearson, Harris, Archer, Solloway, Davis, Turtle, Edens, Salter, Vallis, Roff, E. Titcombe & Hastings.

The minutes of last meeting were read & confirmed after which the following questions were put to the meeting –

Question 1 Any objections? None.

Question 2 Any to be received on full plan?

The meeting unanimously approved of the names of the following brethren being received on full plan after passing the usual Exam. [*indeciph.*] Messrs Salter, Vallis, Roff & E. Titcombe.

Question 3 Any to be received on trial?

Rev. J. Chapman & Mr Watson strongly recommended Bro Freeman which met with the unanimous approval of the brethren.

---

1   Alfred Butler (1845–1919), restored after six years' absence from the plan.

2   William Frederick Lofthouse (1871–1965), undergraduate, Trinity College. He entered the Wesleyan ministry in 1896: *Minutes of Conference* 1966, 185–6.

3   Albert George Vallis.

Question 4 Any removals?

Bro F.W. Lewis[1] fully accredited from Birmingham.

Question 5 Any change in time or place?

Bladon 7 on week nights.

The meeting decided that the committee for making the necessary arrangements for the Open air Services should be composed of the Local Preachers Resident in Oxford & the society stewards of the ~~country places~~ city societies. It was pro by Rev A. Martin & sec[d] by Mr Watson that Mr F. Embury act as sec.

It was pro by Mr Watson & sec[d] by Rev. A. Martin that the matters pertaining Horspath, Eynsham & Islip be transferred to the ~~Special Local Preachers~~ committee referred to above, a meeting of which is to be held shortly.

James Chapman

James Hastings

Secy.

22 June 1891

Minutes of meeting held at Bladon June 22/91

Present Revs J. Chapman, A. Martin, G.F. Rose. Messrs Danbury, Wells, Slaughter, Davis, Solloway, Adams, Watson, Roff, Douglas, G. Adams, Fryer, Hunt, Edens, Railton, Nix, Skidmore & Skinner.

The minutes of former meeting were read & confirmed.

The secretary was requested to send a letter of sympathy to Bro Archer, assuring him of the sympathy of the Brethren under the long continued illness of Mrs Archer & praying that she may be speedily restored to health.

Also a letter be sent to the parents of Bro W. Titcombe (who has died during the qtr) acknowledging the services he has rendered the circuit and sympathizing with them in their bereavement.[2]

Question 1 Any objection? None.

Question 2 Any to be received on Full plan? None.

Question 3 Any to be received on trial?

Bro Drory[3] to receive a note from the Superintendent if he desires it.

Question 4 Any removals?

Bro Perkins to Portsmouth.

A resolution was passed asking Bro Pearson to secure if possible a stronger horse & larger trap for Garsington, Cuddesdon & Horspath.

A resolution was unanimously passed sanctioning the extra outlay requested in erecting the memorial brass in Islip Chapel to the memory of the late Mrs Brockliss.[4]

---

1   Frank Warburton Lewis (1871–1952), non-collegiate student. Lewis entered the Wesleyan ministry in 1893: *Minutes of Conference* 1952, 149–50.
2   William Titcomb died on 20 April 1891, aged 32.
3   John Drory (1867–1935), draper's assistant, of Oxford.
4   See 25 June and 24 September 1890 above.

The Chairman suggested that the Local Preachers with their friends should have a picnic during the summer & the following committee were appointed to learn the opinion of the Brethren & if desired by a majority of the Brethren to make arrangements.

J. Nix. S. Watson. Clifford. Edens. Railton.

James Chapman
James Hastings
Secy.

16 September 1891

Minutes of Quarterly Meeting held Sept 16/91

Present Revs J. Chapman, G.H. Rose & E.H. Summers.[1] Messrs Davis, King, Howard, Edens, Archer, Watson, Skinner, Hunt, Harris, Embury, Smith, Douglas, Roff, Clifford, Dawson, Wickham, Titcombe, Pearson, Solloway, Vallis, Skidmore, Turtle, Shirley & Hastings.

The minutes of last meeting were read & confirmed.

Question 1 Any objection? Mr Osborne to be written to asking him why he did not take his appointment at Islip Sept 13.

Question 2 Any to come on full Plan?

Bro J. Richards fully accredited from the Bolton [conj.] Circuit.

3 Any to come on trial?

Bro Dorry refused to receive a note.

The Superintendent to see Bro Smith[2] of Bladon & give a note if fitting.

Question 4 Any removals from the circuit?

Bro H.G. Clark.

5 Have any died? Bro Reed.[3]

This meeting desires to place on record its great appreciation of the character & work of the late Bro Reed & its sympathy with his family. For a great number of years Bro Reed has been a Local Preacher & Inland Revenue Officer he resided in various places in all of which he did vigorous & valuable work for our church in one or two cases becoming the chief support of a village cause. His work was nearly done when he came to Oxford & to most of the brethren he was only known in his days of weakness & comparative retirement. He was among us long enough to impress us with his sterling character & deep interest in Methodism. His last days were full of weakness & was a result [indeciph.] of depression but his life had given

---

1   Elijah Henry Sumner (1842–1916). A Local Preacher in Oxford 1862–64, Sumner entered the Wesleyan ministry in 1866, serving in the Bahamas. The *Minutes of Conference* 1891, 179, note that Sumner 'is visiting England' and he conducted the Harvest Festival services in his native village of Bladon in September: *MR*, 22 October 1891, 827.

2   Probably Edward James Smith (1873–1948), stone mason, of Bladon.

3   Edward Reed died on 17 August 1891, aged 80: *MR*, 3 September 1891, 713.

clear testimony of his living faith & hope. He rests from his labours & Methodism is the better in many places for his loving service.

16 December 1891
Minutes of Quarterly Meeting held [ ][1]
Present Revs J. Chapman, A. Martin, G.F. Rose. Messrs Hunt, Nix, Shirley, King, Skinner, Fryer, Wickham, Embury, Archer, Pearson, Hastings, Turtle, Davis, Ballard, Vallis, Roff & Titcombe.
The minutes of last meeting were read & confirmed.
Question 1 Any objection?
The following brethren were requested by the meeting to wait on Bro Railton & report at the next Local Preachers Meeting – J. Nix, Clifford & the Superintendent.[2]
The brethren requested that letters be written to Bro Edens & Bro Osborn calling their attention to certain appointments which they had missed.
Bro T. Vallis sent a letter in which he tendered his resignation. The brethren thought it advisable for the Super to see him before the resignation was accepted.
Question 2 Any to come on full Plan? It was proposed and seconded that the following brethren come up for examination next quarter – Bros Ray, Lofthouse & Freeman.
Question 3 Any to come on trial? Messrs Drory & Harris[3] were nominated.
Question 4 Any removals? None.
Question 5 Any change in time or place? None.
The meeting requested that a letter be written to Bro Pearson calling his attention to the inconvenience the brethren had been put to owing to his not having provided a trap for Garsington on Nov 1 & 8 & Dec 20.
Bro Chapman informed the meeting of his intention to arrange for a Local Preachers Convention to be held at New Inn Hall St Church during the ensuing Quarter.
James Hastings
Secy.

30 March 1892
Minutes of Quarterly Meeting held March 30/92
Present Revs J. Chapman, A. Martin, G.F. Rose. Messrs Watson, Adams, Fryer, G. Adams, Lofthouse, Nix, Roff, Freeman, Ballard, Archer, Hunt, Slaughter, Harris, Howard, Embury, Pearson, Richings, Solloway, Eden, Clifford, White, Dawson, King, Titcombe.

1   The preaching plan for October 1891 to January 1892 gives the date for the Local Preachers' Meeting as Wednesday 16 December.
2   See below, March 1892.
3   Alfred Herschell Harris (1863–1953), undergraduate, Trinity College. Harris appears in the list of Local Preachers on the plan for January to April 1892: OHC, OMCA, NM5/A/A1/1, Circuit plans and directories.

The minutes of last meeting were read & confirmed.

Question 1 Any objection?

Bro Ray is to be put among the Exhorters with the understanding that he may come up for exam. next quarter if he chooses.

Question 2 Any to come on Full Plan?

Bro Nix pro. & Bro G. Adams sec. that Bro Ashdown's name be restored to the plan. Bros Freeman & Lofthouse were both received on full plan after passing a successful Examination.

Bro Railton sent the following letter of resignation-

'Dear Sir,

I beg to resign my position as a Local Preacher on the Plan. I deeply regret what has taken place, & throw myself on the kindness of my brethren.

I am resply

Hugh Railton.'

The committee appointed by the last Local Preachers' Meeting recommended that Bro Railton's resignation be not accepted, but that he receive no appointments for the present, which was adopted.[1]

(three members of the meeting did not vote).

Question 3 Any to come on trial? Yes. Messrs H.A. Liddell,[2] T.S. Goudge[3] & J.B. Eames.[4]

Question 4 Any removals? Yes. Bro Richards to Abingdon.

Question 5 Any change in time or place?

New Headington 6 instead of half past.

It was proposed & carried that the following brethren Brother Wickham act as joint secretary in arranging for open air services Bros Wickham Bros Freeman & Titcombe to assist him.

James Chapman

James Hastings Sec.

29 June 1892

Minutes Quarterly Meeting held June 29/92

Present Revs J. Chapman, A. Martin, G.F. Rose. Messrs Watson, Freeman, Skinner, Wickham, Solloway, Hunt, Dawson, Titcombe, Davis, Pearson & Hastings.

Question 1 Any objection?

A letter was received from Brother Taylor containing his resignation which was accepted. Bro Ashdown wrote asking that his name might be restored to its original place on the plan. Bro Wickham pro & Bro Solloway sec that this should be done, the meeting supporting.

---

1   No indication is given as to what had happened.
2   Henry Andrew Liddell (1864–1933), schoolteacher, of Oxford.
3   Thomas Sidney Goudge (1870–1954), undergraduate, Merton College.
4   James Bromley Eames (1872–1916), undergraduate, Worcester College.

Bro Roff to be relieved of work on the Plan for a time so that he may devote himself to the work in the Sunday School.[1]

Question 2 Any removals?

Bro Embury to Africa.

Bro White to Brighton.

Bro Martin pro & Bro Wickham sec that a letter be sent to Bro Embury expressing the loss the Brethren feel in his removal.

Question 3 Any to come on trial?

Bro Pearson pro & Bro Solloway sec that Bro [*indeciph.*][2] be appointed once or twice with one or two of the brethren agreed to.

Bro Rose pro & Bro Wickham sec that a note be sent to Bro F. Buckingham[3] by the Superintendent.

Mr P.J. Horton[4] sent a letter to the Rev J. Chapman asking him to convey to the Brethren the thanks of the Christian Workers Association for the help & assistance which they had rendered them.

Bros Skinner & Watson to arrange for the Oxford Open Air meeting.

It was thought desirable by the meeting that Special Services should be held in all the villages & the names of the following Brethren were mentioned to form a committee. Messrs Nix, Skinner, Shirley, Calloway,[5] Pearson, Wickham, Watson, Clifford, Freeman & Titcombe.

James Chapman

James Hastings

Secy.

28 September 1892

Minutes of Quarterly Meeting held Sept 28/92

Present Revs J. Chapman, R.M. Rees,[6] G.F. Rose. Messrs Watson, Clifford, King, Edens, Solloway, Archer, Wickham, Salter, Roff, Dawson, Richings, T. Vallis, Freeman, Skidmore & Hastings.

Question (1) Any objection? None.

[Question][7] (2) Any removals?

---

1   Roff was the first Superintendent of the Sunday School at New Headington: Edwards, *Lime Walk Story*, 7.

2   Added in pencil.

3   Frederick Buckingham (1871–?), apprentice to smith, of Oxford. The initial in the minutes could be a 'B', but the plan for October 1892 to January 1893 lists 'F.B.' and the next quarter 'F. Buckingham', at 15 Albert Street, Oxford: OHC, OMCA, NM5/A/A1/1, Circuit plans and directories.

4   Percy James Horton (1872–1954), member at Wesley Memorial Church.

5   Perhaps a slip of the pen for 'Solloway'.

6   Robert Montgomery Rees (1853–1925), minister in the Oxford Circuit, 1892–93: *Minutes of Conference* 1925, 107–8.

7   Indicated by ditto mark in original.

Mr H.A. Lester[1] from Maidstone & Mr D. Mead[2] from Rochester.

Bro T.S. Goudge resigned.

[Question] 3 Any to come on Full Plan?

Bro Smith to receive a note asking him to come up for exam. at next meeting.

Question (4) Any to come on Trial?

Bro Wickham pro & Bro Clifford sec^d that Bro Buckingham come on trial & that he should be examined in the Sec^d catechism & the elements of English grammar.

[Question] (5) Any change in time or place? None.

Conversation on the work at Beckley. The following Bros to see Mr Hutt with respect to their closing the chapel when the Band was out[3] - Bros Slaughter, Solloway & Titcombe.

After a conversation on the work at Horspath Bro Richings volunteered to go every Sunday & Bro Clifford to go every other Sunday to try & revive the work.

The Report of the open air work was read. The financial statement showed a bal in hand of £3-14-1 ½ 30/- of which the meeting decided should be retained & the bal of £2-4-1 ½ be handed to the treasurer of the Circuit Mission Fund. The meeting passed a vote of thanks to Bro Wickham for his services in conducting the work of the open air mission.

James Chapman

Sec James Hastings.

25 December 1892

Minutes of Quarterly Meeting held Dec 25/932

Present Revs J. Chapman, R.M. Rees, G.F. Rose. Messrs Watson, Solloway, Mead, Skinner, Wickham, Richings, Roff, Ashdown, Hunt, Osborne, Howard & Hastings.

The usual questions were then asked –

Question (1) Any objection? None.

[Question][4] (2) Any to come on Full Plan? Bro D. Mead Evangelist was admitted on full plan after passing the usual Exam.

[Question] (3) Any to come on Trial?

Bro Collins to receive a note from the superintendent asking him to go with two or three of the brethren if the Superintendent think desirable.

Question 4 Any change in time or place? None.

A conversation to[ok] place respecting The Crescent & several of the brethren thought it would be better to let it drop off the plan, but it was decided by the

---

1   Probably Henry Arthur Lester (1869–1922), non-collegiate undergraduate.

2   David Mead (1870–1943), who came to Oxford as a lay evangelist, under the auspices of Thomas Champness's Joyful News Mission. For the Mission, see 'Joyful News', in DMBI. The Mission trained workers particularly for village evangelism and Mead, the son of a farm labourer, was based at Eynsham.

3   Perhaps a reference to open-air services led by a Mission Band.

4   Indicated by ditto mark in original.

meeting that it would be better for the Superintendent & Mr Watson to see Mrs Gardener before any alterations were made.

Bro T. Vallis to be written to asking the cause of his missing his appointment at Garsington on the 13th Nov.

The secretary received the thanks of the Brethren & was reelected.

The Superintendent informed the meeting that he had been successful in obtaining the services of the District Evangelist Mr Sandeford for the purpose of working up the villages during ~~the winter months~~ January. The following Brethren to form a committee for arranging the mission work. Rev. J. Chapman, Messrs Nix, Watson, Wickham, Eden & Hastings.

James Chapman

James Hastings Sec.

29 March 1893

Minutes of meeting held March 29/93

Present Revs J. Chapman & G.F. Rose. Messrs King, Howard, Turtle, Hunt, Butter, Ashdown, Skidmore, Archer, Clifford, Skinner, Mead, Roff, Richings, Trafford, Freeman, Titcomb, Smith, Watson & Railton.

Question (1) Any objection? None.

[Question]¹ (2) Any to come on full plan? None.

[Question] (3) Any to come on Trial? Bro Collins to have a note.

[Question] (4) Any Removals? Bro Drory to West Bromwich.

[Question] (5) Any change in time or place? Proposed that service be in afternoon instead of morning at Eynsham if the Eynsham people are agreeable.

The secretary to [ ] Messrs Wickham & Solloway expressing sympathy of meeting & hope for their recovery.

Bro Smith who should have come up for exam this Quarter requested that his exam should be postponed for a Quarter the meeting consented.

Proposed that the following Brethren Messrs Wickham, Edens & Mead form a committee to arrange for the summer open air services.

sec James Hastings

27 June 1893

Minutes of Quarterly Meeting held at Bladon June 27/93

Present Revs J. Chapman R.M. Rees. Messrs Watson, Weatherhill, J. Adams, G. Adams, Eden, Solloway, Clifford, Harris, Fryer, Railton, Pearson, Hunt, Nix, Archer, Richings, Skinner, Belcher, Wells, Turtle, J. Salter, Vallis & Hastings.

Question (1) Any objection? None.

[Question]² (2) Any to come on from other circuits?

---

1   Indicated by ditto mark in original.
2   Indicated by ditto mark in original.

E. Turtle from Cheltenham.[1]
[Question] (3) Any to come for exam.
Bro Smith's exam to be postponed for a Quarter.
[Question] 4 Any to come on Trial?
Bro Collings to wait another Quarter.
Question (5) Any change in time or place?
It was thought best for Eynsham to remain as before.
Bro Richings gave a good report of the good work done at Horsepath & the meeting closed.
Enoch Salt
sec James Hastings

28 September 1893
Minutes of Quarterly Meeting held Sept 28/93
Present Revs E. Salt[2] T.F. Nicholson[3] Isaac Newton[4] Messrs Wickham, Salter, Dawson, Lester, Solloway, Hunt, Clifford, Osborne, Richings, Harris, Turtle, Eden, Skidmore, Railton, Watson, Davis, Skinner, Archer, Pearson, Nix & Hastings.
Question (1) Any objections? None.
　(2) Any to come on Full Plan? None.
　(3) Any to come on trial?
　Bros E. Collins & R. Pullen.[5]
　The Super to sees Bros[6]
　(4) Any to come for exam?
　Bros Liddle & Buckingham. The Super to see Bro Smith.
　(5) Any change in time or place?
The Crescent to be continued as before.
Question (6) Any Removals?
Bros Titcombe, Lewis & Freeman to Theological Institute.[7]
The Super suggested that it would be a good thing if some Bro would read a paper at a future meeting on the best method of conducting the ordinary preaching service.

1　Probably Ernest Turtle (1863–1942), a Local Preacher in the Oxford Circuit from 1885, who left Oxford in 1887.
2　Enoch Salt (1845–1919), Superintendent of the Oxford Circuit, 1893–96: *Minutes of Conference* 1919, 114–15.
3　Thomas Frederick Nicholson (1846–1925), minister in the Oxford Circuit, 1893–96: *Minutes of Conference* 1925, 111–12.
4　Isaac Newton (1862–1918), minister in the Oxford Circuit, 1893–96: *Minutes of Conference* 1918, 115–16.
5　Reginald Pullen (1874–1942), printer's compositor, of Oxford.
6　Space left for names to be added, with some faint pencillings.
7　Ernest Titcomb and John Freeman to Headingley College; F. Warburton Lewis was allocated to the President's List, to fill vacancies occurring during the year.

Bro Wickham kindly promised to do so in 6 months time. Bro Edens read a report of the open air work showing a Bal in hand of £2-4-4.

Enoch Salt

James Hastings
    Sec.

27 December 1893

Minutes of Quarterly meeting held Dec 27/93

Present Revs E. Salt T.F. Nicholson I Newton

Messrs Wickham, Dawson, Watson, Skinner, Weatherill, Daunt, Turtle, Skidmore, Roff, Archer, Pearson, E. Turtle, Ashdown, Liddle & Hastings.

Question (1) Any objection? None.

[Question]¹ (2) Any Removals? Mr E. Collins.

[Question] (3) Any to come on Full Plan?

Bro Liddle after passing a Successful Examination was unanimously received by the Brethren as a fully accredited Local Preacher.

Bro Smith to be written to informing him that his name must be moved down among the Exhorters owing to his failing to come up for Exam.

Question (4) Any to come up for Exam?

The Super to write to Bro Buckingham & ask him to come up for Exam in 3 or 6 months from this date.

[Question](5) Any to come on Trial?

The Super to see Mr Ison² & Mr Brown of Woodstock to ask them if they would take any work on the Plan.

[Question] Any change in time or place? None.

A conversation to[ok] place on on³ the desirability of making a Special effort to work the cause at Eynsham more successfully & the following four Brethren promised to give special attention during the coming quarter – Bros Wickham, Skinner, Archer & Watson.

Enoch Salt

Jas Hastings Sec.

28 March 1894

Minutes of Quarterly Meeting held March 28ᵗʰ 1894

Present Revs Enoch Salt, T.F. Nicholson, I Newton.

Bros Hunt, Railton, Nix, Skidmore, Shirley, Richings, King, Wickham, Osborne, Watson, Clifford, Ashdown, Harris, Archer, Solloway, Hastings (B), Dawson, Turtle, Davis, Edens, Butler, Roff, Liddell.

---

1   Indicated by ditto mark in original.
2   Henry Halford Ison (1860–1941), ironmonger, of Oxford.
3   Repetition in original.

1. Any objections? Bro Wickham reported that Bro Ashdown on Jan 21 had sent to Cranham Street an unsuitable and unaccredited supply. The superintendent exhorted the brethren to strict attention to prescribed duties and strongly urged them in cases of necessity to supply only comprehensively accredited substitutes.
Bro Buckingham requested to have his name removed from those on trial.
Bro Smith preferred to be removed from the plan rather than to be transferred to the exhorters. This was agreed to by the meeting.
Bro Douglas sent in his resignation. Proposed by Bro Clifford and seconded by Bro Davis 'That his resignation be accepted.' The motion was carried a few not voting.
2. Any removals to or from circuit? None.
3. Any to come on full plan? No.
4. Any to come on trial? The superintendent proposed and Bro Clifford seconded 'That Mr Ison be received on trial' Carried unanimously.
It was agreed that Mr Hodgkinson be requested to come on trial.
5. Any change to come up for exam? No.
Any change in time or place? No.
Bros Edens, Nix, Turtle, Wm Harris, with Bro Solloway as secretary were unanimously appointed a committee for arranging and carrying out open air services.
It was agreed by the meeting that one of the ministers together with Bros Nix, Clifford and Wickham visit Islip to confer with the brethren there on the best method of improving the state of the Society and of conducting the Sunday school.
Bro Wickham gave an address on the best way of conducting effective preaching services in the country chapels. A vote of thanks to Bro Wickham was unanimously passed. Bro Clifford promised a sermon outline on Luke viii 28[1] at the next meeting.
Enoch Salt
H.A. Liddell
Sec.

25 June 1894

Minutes of Local Preachers' Meeting held June 25 1894
Present Revs Enoch Salt, I. Newton. Bro[s] Hunt, Railton, Skidmore, Richings, Wickham, Watson, Clifford, Pearson, Weatherill, Archer, T. Vallis, Davis, A. Vallis, Liddell.
Any Objections? Brother Skidmore reported the Cuddesdon services to have been neglected on June 17 by Mr Ison. An enquiry was directed to be made.
Bro Pearson reported that Woodstock had been neglected on May 20 by Bro Nix.
The Superintendent called attention to correspondence with Bro Lester.[2]
Any Removals to or from Circuit? No.
Any to come on full plan? No.

1 'When he saw Jesus, he cried out, and fell down before him, and with a loud voice said, What have I to do with thee, Jesus, thou Son of God most high? I beseech thee, torment me not.'
2 Sadly, not extant, but in 1896 Lester was ordained deacon by the bishop of Rochester.

Any to come on trial? Bro Watson proposed, Bro Clifford seconded that Mr Morris be heard and reported on three months hence. Carried unanimously.[1]
Any to come up for Exam.? No.
Any change in time or place? No.
Bro Pearson moved, Bro Archer seconded a vote of condolence to Bro Solloway in his recent bereavement.[2] Carried unanimously.
Bro Pearson moved, Bro Wickham seconded a vote of hearty congratulation to Bro Ballard on his marriage.[3] Carried unanimously.
Bro Pearson moved a vote of sympathy with Mr Hodgkinson on his recent accident on his way to Eynsham. This was agreed to.
A conversation then followed on the best means of supporting the Open Air work for the remainder of the summer.
Bro Clifford proposed and Bro Skinner seconded that the committee for arranging a special Open Air Day for the Oxford churches consist of the Oxford Local Preachers and the officers of the societies, and that the following constitute the executive committee Bros Clifford, Pearson, Davis, Richings, Solloway (convener), Liddell (secretary) and Mr Kerry.[4] Carried unanimously.
Bro Clifford proposed, Bro Skinner seconded that Dr Fairbairn[5] be approached with the idea of obtaining to use Mansfield Coll grounds for the Oxford open air services. Car. unam.
The Islip Committee was supplemented by Bros Skinner, Watson, Richings. Bro Wickham was appointed convener.
Bro Clifford's address on Luke vii 28[6] was postponed till next meeting.
Enoch Salt
H.A. Liddell
Sec.

24 September 1894

Minutes of Local Preachers' Quarterly Meeting held September 24th 1894
Present Revs Enoch Salt Isaac Newton.

1   This resolution was not followed through and was rescinded at the next meeting: see below, September 1894. Alfred Morris (1860–1929), gardener's labourer, was a class leader at New Headington; his son Alfred William (1883–1961) became a Local Preacher in the early 1900s.
2   Arthur Solloway's son, Arthur Clarence, died in June 1894, aged 5.
3   Adolphus Ballard married Mary Elizabeth Henman (1867–1965), daughter of William Albert Henman, at Islip parish church, on 7 June 1894.
4   Probably Arthur Frank Kerry (1862–?), schoolteacher and musician; organist at Wesley Memorial Church in the early 1900s.
5   Andrew Martin Fairbairn (1838–1912), Principal of Mansfield College. The college opened in Oxford in 1886.
6   'For I say unto you, Among those that are born of women there is not a greater prophet than John the Baptist: but he that is least in the kingdom of God is greater than he.'

Bros Wickham, Railton, King, Ashdown, Edens, Skidmore, Archer, Watson, Weatherill, Pearson, Davis, Turtle, Embury, Salter, Nix, Skinner, Whiteman, Liddell. The minutes of the previous meeting were read and confirmed. The meeting having heard Bro Nix in respect to the matter reported at the last meeting expressed its entire satisfaction in his explanation. The Superintendent reported that Mr Ison had made proper provision for the Cuddesdon service reported in the preceding meeting.

The Superintendent adopted the Revised Course of Procedure recommended by the Conference and gave the necessary information as to the scope and application of each article as it occurred.[1]

I Any objection? The meeting was informed that Cuddesdon had been neglected by Bro T. Vallis on July 8, Bro Hunt on July 15 and Bro A. Vallis on July 22. It was unanimously agreed 'That this meeting hears with serious concern of the failure of the services at Cuddesdon and desires the brethren concerned to send an explanation to the next meeting.'

II Any one died? No.

III Has any one resigned? No.

IV Has any one removed to another circuit? Bro Lofthouse to Croydon circuit. The secretary was instructed to convey to Bro Lofthouse the hearty appreciation of the brethren for the invaluable assistance which he had rendered in the Oxford Circuit.

V Has any duly accredited brother entered the circuit? Bro C.H. Underwood from Madeley[2] and Bro Edw. Whiteman from Fareham & Bro T.F. Embury from the Orange River Free State.[3] It was unan. agreed that Bros Embury and E. Turtle should be reinstated in the positions occupied previous to their absence from Oxford. Rev Isaac Newton was requested to see Mr Leworthy of Bullingdon Road.[4]

VI Any one on trial to be fully received? No.

VII Who continue on trial? Bro Eames – 10 quarters. Bro Pullen – 4 quarters. Bro Ison – 2 quarters.

VIII Who are received on trial? None.

It was unanimously agreed 'That since the resolution respecting Mr Morris had not been carried out, no further notice should be taken of the matter.'

1   The Conference of 1894 adopted a revised 'Order and Form of Business' for Local Preachers' Meetings. The traditional question-and-answer format was retained, as were the familiar themes of discipline, transfer and training, but some questions were amplified and others, particularly referring to the spiritual health of the circuit and the encouragement of theological study by the Local Preachers, were added. See *Minutes of Conference* 1894, 456–62.

2   In the plan for October 1894 to January 1895 Underwood's address is given as 13 Queen Street, the accommodation for employees of Charles Badcock and Co., drapers: OHC, OMCA, NM5/A/A1/1, Circuit plans and directories.

3   Frank Embury left Oxford for South Africa in June 1892.

4   Although listed on the plans as 'J. Leworthy', probably Isaac Leworthy (1838–1918).

IX Any to receive a note? The superintendent undertook to see Mr Richings Jn^{r1} and Mr Wm Hoare.

X Any change of service? No.

XI Any new place to be opened? No.

XII Any place to be given up? No.

Bro Solloway presented a report on the open air services during the summer and a financial statement recording total balance in hand from 1893 and 1894 of £3-8-1 (He further suggested that £1 of the balance should be given to the Headington Band[2]). It was unanimously agreed on the proposition of the Superintendent – 'That this meeting expresses its very high appreciation of the services rendered by Bro Edens to the Open Air Mission.'

Bro Wickham placed before the meeting the advisability of forming a Home Reading Union in connection with the Allan Library.[3] It was proposed by Bro Nix, seconded by Bro Archer, 'That the balance of £3-8-1 on the Open Air Mission Fund be devoted to assist the formation of a Home Reading Union in connection with the Allan Library.'

Amendment No. 1: Bro Pearson proposed and Bro Skinner seconded 'That the whole of the balance of £3-8-1 be devoted to the use of the Eynsham committee.' The amendment was lost.

Amendment No. 2: Bro Pearson proposed and Bro Railton seconded 'That the balance of £3-8-1 be given in three equal portions to a Home Reading Union Fund, the Eynsham Committee and the New Headington Brass Band.' The amendment was lost.

The original motion was then put to the meeting and carried.

Bro Pearson proposed and Bro Salter seconded 'That Bros Nix, Davis, Ison, Salter with Bros Wickham and Liddell as secretaries be appointed, with power to add to their number as a committee to arrange for the formation and conducting of the Home Reading Union.' Carried unan.

Bro Nix gave notice that at the Local Preachers' meeting in March he would bring forward a resolution in respect to the suggestions made by Conference concerning the position of Local preachers in the Quarterly Meeting.[4]

1   Albert George Richings (1876–1944), tailor's assistant, of Oxford. Son of William Richings.

2   Edwards, *Lime Walk Story*, 6, notes the formation of the New Headington Wesleyan Temperance Brass Band, but dates this to 1897.

3   The Allan Library was donated to the Wesleyan Connexion in 1884 by Thomas Robinson Allan, and was intended for the use of Wesleyan ministers. A new building was provided for the Library in 1889–90, as part of the redevelopment of a site close to Wesley's Chapel in City Road: 'Allan Library', in *DMBI*, and Clive Field, 'The Allan Library: A Victorian Methodist Odyssey', *Bulletin of the John Rylands Library* 89.2 (2013), 69–105.

4   As part of the consideration of the training, organisation and status of Local Preachers, the Conference of 1894 resolved that every accredited Local Preacher should be a member of the Circuit Quarterly Meeting. As 'new legislation', this proposal had to be submitted to

A discussion followed in respect to the work at Eynsham. Bro Archer proposed and Bro Skinner seconded that the Circuit Mission committee be requested to provide a conveyance for Eynsham. Carried unanimously.

H.A. Liddell

Sec.

17 December 1894

Minutes Local Preachers' Meeting December 17 1894

I Any Objection? The meeting heard with much pleasure that Bro Hunt's reported omission was a mistake and that the appointment was duly kept.

The secretary was instructed to request Bros T. and A. Vallis to communicate with the next meeting in respect to the failure in appointments at Cuddesdon on July 8 & 22.

II Any one died? No.

III Any one resigned? No.

IV Any one removed? No.

V Any one entered? No.

VI Any one on trial to be fully received? No.

Who continue on trial? Bros Eames, Pullen, Ison.

Who are received on trial? Messrs Hoare, Richings, E. Smith nominated by the superintendent & unanimously received.

X Any change of service? No.

XI Any new place to be opened? No.

XII Any place to be given up? No.

Present Rev Enoch Salt

Bros Howard, Hunt, Railton, Nix, Skidmore, Shirley, King, Skinner, Wickham, Osborne, Watson, Clifford, Pearson, Ashdown, Weatherill, Archer, Davis, Butler, Liddell, Whiteman.

T.B. Nicholson

H.A. Liddell

Sec.

18 March 1895

Minutes of Local Preachers' Meeting Monday March 18th 1895

Present Revs T.F. Nicholson and Isaac Newton. Bro[s] Hunt, Wickham, Watson, Ashdown, Archer, Solloway, Liddell.

I Any objection? No.

2 Any one died? No.

3 Any one resigned? Bro Osborn sent in his resignation. It was accepted.

---

the District Synods for consultation, before ratification by the Conference of 1895: *Minutes of Conference* 1894, 310 and 'Local Preachers' Meetings and the District Synods', *MR*, 6 September 1894, 653.

4 Anyone removed? Brothers Embury & Whiteman.

5 Anyone entered? Bro Swift from Weston-s-Mare.[1]

6. Anyone on trial to be fully received? No.

7. Who continue on trial? Bros Eames, Pullen, Ison, Richings, Hoare, Smith.

8. Who are received on trial? The Superintendent proposed Mr C Rydal Mason Trinity Coll.[2] Proposal accepted.

9. Who receive a note? Bro Solloway proposed P. Hunt[3] & H. Sumner[4]. It was agreed that they should be seen by one of the ministers.

10. Any change of service? No.

11. Any new place to be opened? No.

12. Any place to be given up? No.

Enoch Salt

H.A. Liddell
    Sec.

17 June 1895

Minutes Local Preachers' Meeting June 17 1895

Present Revs Enoch Salt, T.F. Nicholson, I. Newton. Bros Railton, Nix, Skidmore, Shirley, Richings, Skinner, Wickham, G. Adams, S. Watson, Clifford, Archer, Dawson, Turtle, E. Turtle, Davis, Edens, Salter, Liddell, Underwood, Leyland.[5]

1. Any Objection. Bro Stanley failed to supply Bladon on June 16 - A note to be sent. The committee accepted Bro A. Vallis' excuse for omission of appointment on July 8 last.

2. Anyone died? No.

3. Anyone resigned? No.

4. Any one removed? No.

5. Any one entered? Mr Nicholson to enquire about Mr Harper.[6]

6. To be fully received: Mr R. Pullen was examined and was accepted.

7. Who continue on trial? Messrs Eames, Ison (6), Richings (3), Hoare (3), E. Smith, Rydal Mason.

8. Received on trial? Messrs H. Sumner, P. Hunt, E.J. Brown.[7]

1   Frank Cook Swift (1872–1953), commercial traveller.

2   Charles Rydal Mason (1876–?), undergraduate, Trinity College. Mason, a son of the Wesleyan missionary Frederick Mason (1834–1911), matriculated in 1893.

3   Arthur Percy Hunt (1878–1942), assistant librarian, of Oxford.

4   Henry Elijah Sumner (1877–1963), photographer, of Oxford. Sumner entered the Congregational ministry in 1905: *Congregational Year Book 1963–64* (London: CUEW, 1963–64), 441–2.

5   Arthur William Leyland (1872–1952), schoolmaster, of Oxford.

6   Charles Harper (1813–97), who moved to Abingdon in March 1877 but returned to Oxford eighteen years later.

7   Ernest John Brown (1873–1943), draper's traveller, of Woodstock.

9. Who receives a note? Mr Hubert Field[1] to be heard and reported on.

10. Change of service. None.

11. Any new place? No.

12. Any place to be given up? No.

Enoch Salt

H.A. Liddell

Sec.

16 September 1895

Minutes Local Preachers' Meeting September 16th 1895

Present Rev Enoch Salt. Bros Hunt, Railton, Nix, Skidmore, Shirley, Fryer, Wickham, G. Adams, Watson, Clifford, Pearson, Ashdown, Weatherill, Solloway, Dawson, E. Turtle, Turtle, Edens, Liddell, Underwood, Leyland, Swift.

1. Any objection? No.

2. Any one died? No.

3. Any one resigned? No.

4. Any one removed? Bro W. Hoare to Winchester.

5. Any one entered? No.

6. Anyone to be fully received? The brethren consented to Mr Ison's exam being postponed for six months. Bros A. Richings and E. Smith come up for exam next quarter. Bro Wickham gave notice that at the next meeting he would bring forward a resolution proposing a written exam in addition to an oral one.

7. Who continue on trial? Bros Ison, Richings, Smith, Rydal Mason, Sumner, P. Hunt.

8. Who are received on trial? A discussion on Mr Hubert Field ended in an arrangement for Bros Solloway and Clifford to hear him and report.

9. Who receive a note? None.

10. Any change of service? No.

11. Any new place? No.

12. Any place to be given up? No.

A discussion followed on the state of the work in the circuit.

The secretary was re-elected.

Enoch Salt

H.A. Liddell

   Sec.

16 December 1895

Minutes of Quarterly Local Preachers' Meeting held December 16 1895

Present Revs Enoch Salt, Isaac Newton. Bros J. Nix, Skidmore, Shirley, Skinner, Fryer, Wickham, G. Adams, S. Watson, Clifford, Pearson, Ashdown, Archer, Solloway, Hastings B, Turtle, Davis, Edens, Liddell, Underwood, Swift.

1. Any objection. In respect to brother A.W. Leyland it was proposed by Bro G. Adams, seconded by Bro Fryer

---

1   Hubert Field (1868–1962), cabinet maker, of Oxford.

That the meeting records with sorrow and deep sympathy the trouble which has befallen Bro Leyland. It fully believes that the bicycle fatality in which he was concerned was purely accidental, and that he did what he could to avoid it: and while condemning his subsequent action in giving a wrong name and address, believes that he did it under the influence of strong temptation and that it did not represent his true character. Having regard to what Bro Leyland has already suffered and his own great sorrow on account of this wrong step, the Meeting thinks that the justice of the case will be met by his having no appointments on the forthcoming plan.[1]

2. Any one died? No.

3. Any one resigned? Bro Roff sent in his resignation. The meeting agreed, provided that an interview which the superintendent offered to arrange permitted of no other course.

4. Any one removed? Bro A.G. Richings to Watford.

5. Anyone entered? No.

6. Anyone to be fully received? Bro E.J. Smith was examined. Proposed by Bro Clifford, seconded by Bro Pearson that he be accepted. Carried unanimously.

7. Who continue on trial? Bros Ison, Rydal Mason, Brown, Sumner, P. Hunt.

8. Who are received on trial? Bro Rickard[2] was proposed by Bro Pearson, seconded by Bro Solloway. The meeting agreed. The meeting further agreed that Bro Hubert Field should be heard and reported on at the next meeting.

9. Who receive a note? None.

10. Who are rec[d] as exhorters? None.

11. Any change of service? No.

12. Any new place? No.

13. Any place to be given up? No.

The meeting discussed a circular issued by the District Local Preachers' Committee.[3] Bro Archer introduced a discussion on the best means of increasing the Local Preachers' efficiency in the villages.[4]

Enoch Salt

H.A. Liddell

    Sec.

---

1   For an account of the case, see 'An Oxford Schoolmaster charged with Manslaughter', *JOJ*, 14 December 1895, 8.

2   Possibly Edward Martin Rickard (1876–1945), commercial traveller. E.M. Rickard preached 'an appropriate sermon' at the Woodstock Harvest Festival on 29 September 1895: 'District News', *JOJ*, 5 October 1895, 7.

3   The changes proposed by the 1894 Conference, ratified in 1895, included the establishment of a Local Preachers' Committee in each District of the Wesleyan Connexion: *Minutes of Conference* 1894, 315.

4   In 1894–95 the Joyful News Book Depot, Rochdale, published *Homely Counsels for Village Preachers*, by Joseph Bush, a Past President of the Wesleyan Conference, and C.O. Eldridge's *Local Preachers and Village Methodism*. These books were part of a wider conversation about the position of Methodism in rural areas.

16 March 1896

Minutes of Quarterly Local Preachers' Meeting March 16th 1896

Present Revs Enoch Salt, T.F. Nicholson, Isaac Newton. Bros Nix, Howard, Pearson, Weatherill, Railton, G. Adams, Fryer, Swift, Clifford, Archer, Skidmore, Dawson, Turtle, E. Turtle, Watson, Solloway, Hunt, Liddell.

1. Any objection? The superintendent read a letter from Forest Hill, stating that Bro T. Vallis had missed his appointment on Sunday Mar 15. The secretary instructed to write to him.

2. Anyone died? Bro J. Hitchman.[1] The secretary was instructed to convey to the deceased brother's relatives the brethren's ~~appreciation~~ sympathy in their bereavement and their appreciation of his character and work.

3. Any one resigned? No.

4. Any one removed? No.

5. Any one entered? Bro J. Jeynes transferred from Charlbury by Rev. T. Hackett.[2]

6. Any one to be fully received? The brethren agreed that Bro Ison's probation should be extended for six months.

7. Who continue on trial? Bros Ison, Rydal Mason, Brown, Sumner, Hunt, Rickard.

8. Who are received on trial? Mr Hubert Field, proposed by Bro Watson, sec[d] by Bro Solloway and received nem con.

Mr Duck,[3] proposed Bro Archer, sec[d] Bro E. Turtle. Received.

9. Who receive a note? The brethren agreed that Mr Harry Danbury[4] receive a note.

10. Any exhorters? No.

11. Any change time or place? No.

12. Any new place? No.

13. Any place to be surrendered? No.

A Discussion followed on the efficiency of the class meetings[5] and arrangements were made for open air services.

Bro Solloway brought forward Bro Douglas' name with a view to his being reinstated on the plan, but circumstances prevented any further discussion at the time.

Enoch Salt

H.A. Liddell

 Sec.

---

1   James Hitchman (1812–96), buried at Holy Trinity, Oxford, on 18 February 1896.

2   Probably James Jeynes (1872–1964), grocer. Born in Newent, in the Forest of Dean, Jeynes transferred a year later to the Ledbury Circuit: see minutes for June 1897. James Jeynes married Ellen Clary, of Enstone, in summer 1897, so was perhaps in Charlbury in the mid-1890s. Thomas Hackett was the Superintendent of the Witney Circuit, responsible for the Wesleyan chapel in Charlbury.

3   William Duck, who was on trial in 1887–89.

4   Harry William Danbury (1879–1958), of Bladon.

5   Debate on the place and effectiveness of the class meeting ran on through the 1880s, leading to a major report to the Conference in 1889: Henry D. Rack, 'Wesleyan Methodism 1849–1902', HMCGB, 3, 158–62.

15 June 1896

Minutes of Local Preachers' Meeting June 15th 1896

Present Rev Enoch Salt. Bros Solloway, Archer, Skidmore, Turtle, Fryer, Richings, Butler, Field, Clifford, Railton, Ashdown, Pullen, P. Hunt, Jeynes, Sumner, Duck, Vallis T, Swift, C. Hunt, E. Turtle, Pearson, E.J. Smith, Nix, Rickard, Wickham, Liddell.

Any Objection? None this quarter. Bro Vallis explained to the ~~meeting~~ satisfaction of the Meeting that his failure to supply Forest Hill on March 15 was due to a sudden emergency.

Any one died? No.

Any one resigned? No.

Any one removed out? No.

Any one entered? No.

Any one to be fully received?

Bros Percy Hunt and Henry Elijah Sumner were examined and unanimously passed for 'Full Plan' on their promising to complete the Reading of Wesley's 53 Sermons by Christmas.

Bros Ison and Rydal Mason were not present. It was therefore decided to ~~hold over~~ adjourn the Meeting till Friday June 19th at 7 p.m. to complete the examinations.

It was also considered desirable that Bro Brown of Woodstock should be requested to come up at the same time although he had not yet preached a trial sermon.

Who continue on trial? Bros Ison, Rydal Mason, Brown, Rickard, Field, Duck.

Who are received on trial? Mr Harry Danbury, prop Bro Solloway, seconded Bro Fryer.

Who receive a note? None.

Any one to be placed among Exhorters? No.

Any change in time or place? No.

Any place to be given up? No.

The Meeting gave permission for Miss Richings[1] to travel on Sunday by the preachers' conveyance to Horspath to assist in services and directed that trap should proceed via Horspath.

The classes at New Hincksey, Islip and Cuddesdon were being met by Messrs Clifford Solloway Field respectively. These brethren were thanked by the Meeting.

The minutes of the last meeting were read and confirmed.

William J. Hutton[2]

H.A. Liddell

    Sec.[3]

---

1   Ada, Gertrude or Ethel, daughters of William Richings.

2   Superintendent from September 1896; see below.

3   Note added in pencil: '14 Sep 1896'.

19 June 1896

Minutes of Adjourned Meeting held Friday June 19th at 7 p.m.

Present Revs Enoch Salt, T.F. Nicholson, Isaac Newton. Bros Turtle, Skidmore, Butler, Wickham, Field, Hunt, Sumner, E. Turtle, Railton, Ison, Swift, Nix, Clifford.

The Secretary read letters from Messrs Rydal Mason and Brown explaining their inability to attend.

It was resolved that Mr Brown should be appointed to preach a trial sermon and requested to attend for examination at the September meeting.

Mr Mason's absence was due to unavoidable causes but the brethren considered that his trial sermon had been to the satisfaction of the meeting.

The examination of Bro Ison was then conducted by the Superintendent. He was afterwards unanimously received by the brethren.

William J. Hutton

H.A. Liddell

14 Sep 1896 Sec.

14 September 1896

Minutes of Local Preachers' Meeting held Sept 14th 1896

Present Rev. W.J. Hutton[1] Bros H. Railton, J. Skidmore, T. Skinner, Fryer, Wickham, G. Adams, Watson, Pearson, Weatherill, Archer, Solloway, Dawson, Turtle, Davis, Butler, Liddell, Leyland, Swift, Smith, Sumner, Hunt, Rickard, Duck.

1. Any objection? No.

2. Any one died? No.

3. Any one resigned? A letter was read from brother King, requesting to be permitted to resign. The meeting desired that his name should be retained in hope of future services and expressed its high appreciation of his past work. The secretary was instructed to write him to this effect.

4. Any one removed? No.

5. Any one entered? No.

6. To be fully received? The Superintendent explained that Bro Rydal Mason had asked for a postponement of his exam. The matter was left in his hands.

The superintendent also undertook to see Bro Brown who is already due for examination and Bro Rickard who is due at the next meeting.

7. Who continue on trial? Bros Rydal Mason (7), Bro Brown (6), Bro Rickard (4), Bro Field (3), Bro Duck (3).

8. Who are received on trial? Bro H. Danbury who had been nominated by the late Superintendent and approved at the last meeting was received.

---

1   William James Hutton (1838–1916), Superintendent of the Oxford Circuit, 1896–99: *Minutes of Conference* 1917, 146–7.

9. Any one to receive a note? Mr Arthur Watson[1] of 24 Juxon St was accepted by the meeting. The Superintendent undertook to see Mr Duncankin.[2]

10. Any one to be received as exhorter? No.

11. Any change time? No.

12. Any new place? No.

13. Any place to be given up? No.

A discussion followed on the State of the Work. The Meeting gladly recognised Bro Rickard's offer to make special efforts to revive the work at Beckley.

The secretary was re-appointed with a vote of thanks for past services.

The secretary was instructed to request the secretary of the Circuit Mission Fund to provide a conveyance for Islip.

Bro Solloway presented the balance sheet for Open Air services held during the past summer.

William J. Hutton

H.A. Liddell Sec.

14 December 1896

Dec. 14th 1896.

Minutes of Local Preachers' Meeting held December 14th 1896

Present Revds W.J. Hutton, Campbell Jefferies,[3] E.J. Oldmeadow.[4] Bros Howard, Railton, Nix, Skidmore, Richings, Skinner, Fryer, Wickham, Pearson, Ashdown, Archer, E. Turtle, Davis, Salter, Liddell, Swift, E.J. Smith, Ison, Rickard, Danbury. The minutes of the preceding meeting were read and confirmed.

1. Any Objection? No.

2. Any one died? No.

3. Any one resigned? Bro T. Vallis sent in his resignation. The meeting duly noted the fact, but expressed a wish that his name should stand until the Superintendent had had an opportunity of seeing him.

4. Any one left circuit? Bro Solloway to Glasgow, Cathcart Road.[5] A motion proposed by Bro Wickham, seconded by Bro Pearson, expressing appreciation of his past services was unanimously carried. Secretary instructed to write him.

---

1   Arthur Ernest Watson (1878–1957), clerk, of Oxford.

2   Frederick Silas Dunkin (1864–1948), dentist, of Oxford.

3   Campbell Jefferies (1850–1919), minister in the Oxford Circuit, 1896–98: *Minutes of Conference* 1920, 114.

4   Ernest James Oldmeadow (1867–1949), minister in the Oxford Circuit, 1896–97. Oldmeadow was admitted into full connexion with the Conference in 1894, was without pastoral charge in 1897 and 1898, and 'voluntarily retired' from the Wesleyan ministry in 1899: *Minutes of Conference* 1899, 64. He subsequently became a Roman Catholic, and served as editor of *The Tablet*. Frank Nix recorded that Oldmeadow's conversion did not surprise Oxford Methodists: *OMM*, March 1934, 26.

5   Solloway, *Life More Abundant*, 36–44, describes his appointment as superintendent of the Tolbooth Hall, Glasgow.

5. Any one entered? Mr Josiah Nix.
Proposed by Bro Wickham and seconded by Bro Pearson 'that his name be restored to its original position.' Carried unan.
6. To be fully received? The Superintendent reported that he had advised Bro Rydal-Mason to defer his examination. Bro Brown had not been seen and Bro Rickard requested permission to defer his exam till March. It was agreed that these brethren should be requested to present themselves to the next meeting.
7. Who continue on Trial? Bros Rydal-Mason 8, Brown 7, Rickard 5, Field 4, Duck 4, Richings A.G. 4, Danbury 2.
8. Who are received on trial? Mr Arthur Watson was reported on by Bro Pearson, nominated by superintendent, and unan received.
Mr Dunkin was reported on by Bro Howard, nominated by Superintendent and unan received.
Mr E.E. Genner[1] was nominated by Superintendent and unan received.
9. Anyone to receive a note? No.
10. Anyone to be exhorter? No.
11. Any change in time? No.
12. Any new place? No.
13. Any place to be given up? No.
Under General Question I
The condition of several of the weaker places in the circuit having been referred to it was held to be desirable that some effort should be made to strengthen the congregations and services. In order to this it was thought desirable to attempt a revival of the Mission Band on lines similar to those by which it was regulated in 1882, according to a printed plan of that date which was laid before the meeting. As a method of procedure it was deemed convenient that the names of persons so employed should be suggested by the Quarterly Local Preachers' Mtg and that from quarter to quarter the same meeting should revise the list as circumstances might require.
It was further agreed that the operation of the band should for the present be limited to Beckley, Forest Hill, Garsington, Horspath and Eynsham and that in each case appointments should be made fortnightly, monthly or otherwise at the discretion of the Superintendent.
A discussion then followed on a circular issued by the Oxford District Local Preachers' Committee. It was proposed by Bro Wickham and seconded by Bro Salter 'That although some of the brethren considered an examination inexpedient, the Local Preachers of the Oxford Circuit desired to express their appreciation of the consideration of the committee and undertook to read the book prescribed.' Carried unan.
A further discussion followed in respect to the subscription to the Allan Library.

1 Ernest Ely Genner (1877–1930), undergraduate, Balliol College. See 'Genner, Ernest Ely', *DMBI*.

Mar. 15: 1897 William J. Hutton
H.A. Liddell
   Sec.

15 March 1897

Minutes of Local Preachers' Meeting held March 15th 1897
Present Revds W.J. Hutton, E.J. Oldmeadow. Bros C. Hunt, Railton, J. Nix, Skidmore, Shirley, Richings, Skinner, Wickham, G. Adams, Watson, Pearson, Ashdown, Weatherill, Archer, Dawson, Turtle, Edens, Liddell, Leyland, Swift, Smith, Jeynes, Sumner, P. Hunt, Rickard, Field, Duck.
1. Any objection? Bro Stanley was reported to have omitted an engagement at Woodstock & Bro Hastings at New Headington. The Superintendent was asked to see them.
Bro Rickard's explanation as to an omission at New Headington was accepted and Bro T. Vallis had communicated to the Superintendent his desire to continue on the plan.
2. Anyone died? No.
3. Anyone resigned? No.
4. Anyone left circuit? Bro Ernest Turtle to Ross.
5. Anyone entered? No.
6. To be fully received? The Superintendent informed the meeting that Bro Rydal-Mason had withdrawn from the plan. Bro Brown sent in his withdrawal but the meeting determined to continue his name during the next quarter to give the Superintendent an opportunity of seeing him. Bro Richings wished to defer his examination for further preparation.
7. Who continue on trial? Bros E.J. Brown, A.G. Richings, H. Danbury, Dunkin, Watson, Genner.
8. Who are rec[d] on trial? None.
9. Any one to receive a note? No.
10. Any one to be exhorter? No.
11. Any change in time? No.
12. Any ~~change in~~ new place? No.
13. Any place to be given up? No.
Bros Field, Duck and Rickard were examined, nominated by the Superintendent and accepted by the Meeting.
June 14:1897 William J. Hutton
                    H.A. Liddell
                      Sec.

14 June 1897

Minutes of Local Preachers' Meeting held June 14 1897
Present Rev W.J. Hutton. Bros Dawson, Skidmore, Skinner, Railton, Smith, Pearson, Swift, Turtle, Richings, Weatherill, Liddell.

1. Any Objection? The Superintendent reported that he had written to Bro Stanley but had received no reply. The Meeting requested the Super to repeat his enquiries.
2. Any one died? No.
3. Any one resigned? Bro J. Hastings B sent in his resignation. The Meeting decided to hold the matter over until the Super who had already called on Bro Hastings once might be able to obtain an interview.
4. Any one left the Circuit? Bro Jeynes to Ledbury circuit. The Superintendent undertook to convey the kind wishes of the meeting to him.
5. Anyone entered? No.
6. Any to be fully received? No.
7. Who continue on trial? Bros Brown, A.G. Richings, Danbury, A.E. Watson, Dunkin, Genner.
8. Who are received on trial? None.
9. Anyone to receive a note? No.
10. Anyone to be an exhorter? No.
11. Any change in time or place? No.
12. Any new place to be opened? No.
13. Any place to be given up? No.
Sep 20:1897. William J. Hutton

H.A. Liddell.

20 September 1897

Minutes of Local Preachers' Meeting held Sept 20th 1897
Present:- Rev. W.J. Hutton. Bros Hunt, Railton, W. Richings, Fryer, G. Adams, Watson, Pearson, Ashdown, Weatherill, Archer, Dawson, Liddell, Swift, Smith, Sumner, P. Hunt.
1. Any Objection? Bro Edens was reported as having omitted New Headington on Sept 12.
Bro Sumner explained to the meeting his omission of Tackley on Aug 22.
2. Any one died? No.
3. Any one resigned? Bro J. Hastings (B)'s resignation was again considered. It was proposed by Bro Fryer and seconded by Bro G. Adams that 'In further considering the desire of Mr James Hastings that his name should be withdrawn from the plan the Meeting regretfully acceded to his request; recording at the same time its appreciation of valued services which he had rendered for many years past and especially expressing its grateful satisfaction that in other forms, and as opportunity may offer, the work of the Wesleyan Methodist Church will continue to have his sympathy and active support.'
4. Any one left? Bro A.G. Richings to Banbury.
5. Any one entered? No.
6. Any one to be fully Received? No.
7. Who continue on trial? Bros Brown, Danbury, A.E. Watson, Dunkin, Genner.
8. Who are received on trial? None.

9. Any one to receive a note? No.
10. Any one to be an exhorter? No.
11. Any change in time or place? No.
12. Any new place to be opened? No.
13. Any place to be given up? No.
The Secretary was thanked for past services and unan re-elected.
Dec 13th 1897 William J. Hutton
H.A. Liddell

13 December 1897

Minutes of Local Preachers' Meeting held Dec 13th 1897
Present Revs W.J. Hutton, A.E. Butler,[1] Campbell Jefferies. Bros Nix, Salter, Sumner, Railton, Richings, Dawson, G. Adams, H. Danbury, Smith, Archer, Genner, Liddell, Swift, Pearson, Shirley, Duck.
Any objection? It was stated that Brother Edens had during the quarter made an arrangement with his creditors. This Meeting is of opinion that the circumstances are such as to justify his continuance on the plan but considers it expedient that he should be left without appointments on the next plan. Prop Bro Salter, sec Bro G. Adams. Carried nem. con.
2. Any one died? Bro C. Harper.
3. Any one resigned? No.
4. Any one left the Circuit?
    Bro Underwood to Gloucester.
    Bro Rickard to Weston-super-Mare.
5. Any one entered? No.
6. Any to be fully received? No.
7. Who continue on trial? Bros H.W. Danbury, A.E. Watson, Dunkin, Genner, Brown.
8. Who are received on trial? None.
9. Any one to receive a note? The Superintendent nominated Mr John K. Wilkins.[2]
10. Any one to be an exhorter? Mr T. Bennett.[3]
11. Any change in time or place? No.
12. Any new place to be opened? No.
13. Any place to be given up? No.
Mar 14: 1898 William J. Hutton

                    H.A. Liddell

---

1   Albert Edwyn Butler (1868–1931), minister in the Oxford Circuit, 1897–1900: *Minutes of Conference* 1931, 108.
2   John Knowles Wilkins (1877–1960), non-collegiate undergraduate, elected a member of the Wesley Guild in October 1897: OHC, OMCA, NM5/F/A1/2, John Wesley Society Minute Book, 1889–1900, minutes of 22 October 1897.
3   From the January to April 1898 plan Bennett is listed as a member of the No. 1 Mission Band: OHC, OMCA, NM5/A/A1/1, Circuit plans and directories.

14 March 1898

Minutes of Local Preachers' Mtg held Mar 14th 1898

Present:- Revs W.J. Hutton, A.E. Butler. Bros J. Nix, J. Skidmore, Skinner, S. Watson, Pearson, Archer, Dawson, Liddell, Leyland, Pullen, Genner.

The brethren passed a vote of sympathy with Bro Clifford in his painful illness.

1. Any objection? No.

2. Any one died? No.

3. Any one resigned? No.

4. Any one left circuit? Bro Swift to Reading.

5. Any one entered? Mr W.H. Franks from S. Leonards.[1]

6. Any one to be fully received? The Brethren discussed Bro Douglas' request to come on the plan but the general opinion expressed was in direction of the matter being indefinitely deferred.

7. Who continue on trial? The foll[g] arrangements were made for exams next meeting.

Bro Danbury heard by Bros Liddell, Slaughter, Pullen.

Bro A.E. Watson by S. Watson, Archer, Dawson.

Bro Dunkin by J. Nix, Clifford, Leyland.

Bro Genner by Pearson, Wickham, Skinner.

8. Who are received on trial? None.

9. Any one to receive a note? The Super nominated Mr Corley.[2]

10. Any one to be an exhorter? No.

11. Any change in time or place? No.

12. Any new place to be opened? No.

13. Any place to be given up? No.

A discussion on the work of the Mission bands followed. The brethren recognised with much pleasure the offer of the University contingent to work Cuddesdon. Messrs Burnett,[3] Adair[4] and Miller[5] were added to No. 2 band.

Bros Shirley, Watson A.E. & H. Danbury were appointed secs for open air services on the proposal of Bro Pearson & seconding of Bro Skinner.

13 June, 1898 William J. Hutton

H.A. Liddell

Sec.

13 June 1898

Minutes of Local Preachers' Meeting held June 13 1898

Present – Rev W.J. Hutton

---

1   Walter Harman Franks (1873–1958), clothier.

2   Ferrand Edward Corley (1877–1937), undergraduate, St John's College. See 'Corley Family', *DMBI*.

3   W.C. Burnet, Worcester College.

4   Herbert Norman Adair (1879–1956), Jesus College.

5   J.H. Millett, non-collegiate student.

Bros Skidmore, Wickham, G. Adams, Watson, Archer, Dawson, Liddell, E.J. Smith, Genner, Richings, Pearson, Fryer, Skinner, A.E. Watson. Danbury H, Duck, Pullen, Leyland, Sumner, Clifford.

Any objection? No.

Any one died? Brother Wells of Tackley.[1] The brethren wished to place on record their high appreciation of the fidelity and conscientious labours of Bro Wells in the cause of Christ during his prolonged connection with this church. Pro Bro Skidmore, sec[d] by Bro Richings and carried unan.

3. Any one resigned? No.

4. Any one left the circuit? No.

5. Any one entered? No.

6. Any one to be fully received?

Bros Genner, A.E. Watson and H. Danbury were examined, nominated by the Super and unanimously received.

Mr Dunkin wrote expressing his wish to retire.

7. Who continue on trial? None.

8. Who are received on trial? Mr F.E. Corley S. John's and Mr J.K. Wilkins of 2 Kingston Road were nominated by the Superintendent and unanimously received.

9. Any one to receive a note? The Super nominated Mr H. Smith[2] of Bladon who was unanimously received.

10. Any one to be an exhorter? Ppd by Secy seconded by Bro Wickham that Bro E.J. Brown should be placed on the exhorters' list. Carried nem con.

The super nominated Bros J. Nappin[3] and W. Hobbs[4] who were unan rec[d].

11. Any change in time or place? No.

12. Any new place to be opened? No.

13. Any place to be given up? No.

A discussion on open air work followed and a Special Local Preachers' Mtg was arranged for Thursday June 16th at 6.30 p.m.

William J. Hutton

16 June 1898

Special Local Preachers' Meeting held June 16 1898

Present Rev W.J. Hutton. Bros Salter, Watson, Richings, Dawson, Turtle, Wickham, Watson A.E., Danbury H., Field, Clifford, Shirley, Liddell.

The business consisted in making arrangements for Open Air services throughout the circuit.

Sep. 12: 1898 William J. Hutton

H.A. Liddell

Sec.

1   Richard Wells.
2   Henry Albert Smith (1878–1971), labourer, of Bladon.
3   Joseph William Nappin (1863–1935), carrier, of Bladon.
4   William Hobbs (1862–1919), baker, of Oxford.

12 September 1898

Minutes of Quarterly Local Preachers' Meeting held Sept 12 1898
Pres. Rev W.J. Hutton
Bros Skidmore, Richings, Archer, Dawson, Clifford, Sumner, A.P. Hunt, Liddell.
1. Any objection?
Omissions of appointments were reported as follows
Wootton Mr Sumner on Aug 28
Tackley Mr P. Hunt on Aug 28
Eynsham Mr Duck on Aug 21
Cuddesdon Mr T. Vallis on Sept 11.
Mr Duck had already explained to the Superintendent and Messrs Sumner and Hunt were present at the Meeting. Their explanation was accepted by the brethren. The Superintendent undertook to see Mr T. Vallis.
2. Any one died? No.
3. Any one resigned? No.
4. Any one left the circuit? No.
5. Any one entered? No.
6. Any one to be fully received? No.
7. Who continue on trial? Brs Brown, Corley & Wilkins. The Superintendent explained why Mr Brown's name was continued 'On Trial' and it was agreed by the Meeting that it should continue so.
8. Who are received on trial? Mr Simmonds who has been received from Tunbridge Wells was nominated by the Superintendent and unanimously received.
9. Any one to receive a note? No.
10. Any one to be an exhorter? No.
11. Any change in time or place? No.
12. Any new place to be opened? No.
13. Any place to be given up? No.
Dec. 12th 1898 William J. Hutton

H.A. Liddell

12 December 1898

Minutes of Quarterly Local Preachers' Meeting held Dec 12 1898
Present Rev. W.J. Hutton
Bros Nix, Watson, ~~Genner~~, Richings, H. Danbury, A.E. Watson, Archer, Pearson, Weatherill, Wickham, E.J. Smith, Genner, Corley, Dawson, Clifford, Skinner, Shirley, Ison, Nappin, Liddell.
1. Any objection? The Superintendent read a letter of explanation from Mr T. Vallis which was accepted by the meeting.
2. Any one died? No.
3. Any one resigned? No.
4. Any one left the circuit? No.

5. Any one entered? No.

6. Any one to be fully received? No.

7. Who continue on trial? Bros Brown, Corley, Wilkins, Simmonds.

8. Who are received on trial? None.

9. Who receive a note? None.

10. Any one to be an exhorter? No.

11. Any change in time or place?

The brethren agreed to two services at Forest Hill, at 3 and 6 p.m. *

12. Any new place to be opened? No.

13. Any place to be given up? No.

* The brethren agreed that the Sunday preaching services at Eynsham should be held afternoon & evening and that the morning should be devoted to Sunday school work.

William J. Hutton

H.A. Liddell.

13 March 1899

Minutes of Quarterly Local Preachers' Meeting held March 13 1899

Present:- Rev W.J. Hutton

Bros Skinner, Clifford, Watson, Corley, Dawson, Smith, G. Adams, H. Danbury, Richings, Pearson, Liddell, Genner, Weatherill, Ison, Nappin.

1. Any Objection? No.

The brethren agreed that a letter of sympathy and kind wishes should be sent to brother Wickham in his ill-health.

2. Any one died? No.

3. Any one resigned? No.

4. Any one left the Circuit? Bro C.J. Simmonds to Thame Circuit.

5. Any one entered? No.

6. Any one to be fully received? No.

7. Who continue on trial? Bros Brown, Corley, Wilkins.

8. Who are received on trial? The super nominated Bro H. Smith. Arrangements were made by the Superintendent for hearing trial sermons by Bros Corley & Wilkins.

9. Who receive a note? None.

10. Any one to be an exhorter? The superintendent nominated Bro Felix Minn[1] of Tackley. Bro Bricknell of Cuddesdon was also suggested. Both were unanimously accepted. Bro Bricknell subject to an interview arranged by super.

11. Any change in time or place? No.

12. Any new place to be opened? No.

13. Any place to be given up? No.

1   Felix Minn (1862–1929), farm labourer, of Tackley.

A conversation followed on the state of the work in the circuit. It was agreed to continue the arrangements for Eynsham.

15 May 1899

Minutes of Special Local Preachers' Meeting held May 15 1899
Present: Rev W.J. Hutton. Bros Archer, Clifford, G. Adams, E.J. Smith, Genner, Corley, Pullen, Shirley, Turtle, Skinner, A.E. Watson, H. Danbury, Liddell.
The business consisted in making arrangements for speakers for the open air services at the following places Tackley, Hinckley, Horspath, Beckley, Garsington, Cuddesdon, Coombe, Headington Quarry, Woodstock, Bladon, Eynsham, Wootton.
June 12th 1899 William J. Hutton

H.A. Liddell.

12 June 1899

Minutes of Quarterly Local Preachers' Meeting held June 12 1899
Present: Rev W.J. Hutton.
Bros Skidmore, Dawson, Clifford, Railton, Corley, Genner, Pearson, Archer, A.E. Watson, Skinner, Liddell.
1. Any objection:-
Bro Edens was reported to have omitted Cuddesdon on ~~July~~ April 9. Bro Sumner on April 2. Bro Ison on May 14. The secretary was instructed to ask for an explanation in each case.
Bro Danbury was to be written to in respect to his substitute at Eynsham on June 11.
2. Any one died? No.
3. Any one resigned? No.
4. Any one left the circuit? Bro Leworthy has removed to Barnstaple.
5. Any one entered? Bro Archer proposed and Bro Pearson seconded the reinstatement of Bro J.H. Roff's name to its original place. Carried unan.
The superintendent nominated Mr Perry S. Dobson,[1] who was unanimously received.
6. Any one to be fully received?
Bro Corley presented himself for examination and was unanimously accepted by the Meeting.
7. Who continue on trial? Bros Brown and Wilkins and H. Smith.
8. Who are received on trial? None.
9. Who receive a note? None.
10. Any one to be an exhorter? No.
11. Any change in time or place? No.
12. Any new place to be opened? No.
13. Any place to be given up? No.

---

1   Perry Silas Dobson (1876–1962), non-collegiate undergraduate.

The name of Mr Watkins was suggested by Mr Clifford for Mission Band work. The Superintendent promised to enquire.

In reference to Beckley the Superintendent reported the formation of three mission bands from among the friends at New Headington and Headington Quarry for the purpose of regular visitation and help.

Open air arrangements for the summer were then completed by appointments for New Headington, Islip and Forest Hill.

Wm Bradfield[1] 11/9/99

H.A. Liddell Hon. Sec.

11 September 1899

Minutes of Quarterly Meeting of Local Preachers held Sept 11 1899

Present: Rev W. Bradfield[2]

Bros Shirley, Archer, P. Hunt, Sumner, Wickham, Dobson, Ashdown, Skinner, E.J. Smith, Skidmore, Richings, Weatherill, Pearson, Roff, Butler, Dawson, Fryer, Leyland, G. Adams, Edens, Duck, Ison, Field, Watson, Davis, A.E. Watson, H. Danbury, Turtle, Clifford.

1. Any objection? Mr Sumner explained to the satisfaction of the meeting his omission of Cuddesdon on April 2. Mr Edens explained that his absence was caused by an appointment in Abingdon Circuit. Mr Ison also explained that for his appointment arrangements had been made.

* see end.

2. Any one died? Bro J. Danbury of Bladon.[3] It was proposed by Bro Wickham and seconded by Bro G. Adams 'That the local preachers place on record their grateful appreciation of the devout Christian life and loyal service both to the cause of Christ and the Methodist Church which their departed brother maintained both throughout his prolonged service as a Methodist Local Preacher.' Carried unanimously.

3. Any one resigned? No.

4. Any one left the Circuit? Bro J.K. Wilkins to Manchester Mission circuit, Manchester. The sec was desired to express to him their appreciation of his past services.

5. Any one entered? No.

6. Any one to be fully received? No.

7. Who continue on trial? Bro E.J. Brown and H. Smith.

8. Who are received on trial? None.

1   Superintendent of the Circuit from September 1899.

2   William Bradfield (1859–1923), Superintendent of the Oxford Circuit, 1899–1902: *Minutes of Conference* 1923, 108.

3   John Danbury's death is reported in *JOJ*, 12 August 1899, 10.

9. Who receive a note? Bros E. Bowers and G. Gomm[1] were nominated and received.

10. Any one to be an exhorter? No.

11. Any change in time or place? No.

12. Any new place to be opened? No.

13. Any place to be given up? No.

Mr A.E. Watson presented a balance sheet dealing with the finances of the open air services. It showed – Income £4-18-9 ½ Exs £4-0-6 ½ Balance in hand 18/3. A discussion then followed on the spiritual aspect of the work.

* The following omission were noted

Bro Hobbs Horspath Aug 13

Cuddesdon Sept 3

Bro Ray Horspath Aug 27

Bro T. Vallis Cuddesdon Aug 27.

The Sec was instructed to ask for an explanation.

Wm Bradfield 11/12/99

H.A. Liddell

11 December 1899

Minutes of Quarterly Local Preachers' Meeting held Dec 11 1899

Present: Revs W. Bradfield A.E. Butler.

Bros J. Nix, S. Watson, Salter, Davis, Skidmore, Wickham, Archer, Dobson, Weatherill, Hunt, Turtle, Hastings, Roff, A. Vallis, G. Adams, Richings, Fryer, Clifford, Edens, Genner, Corley, A.E. Watson, Danbury, Railton, Sumner, Weatherill, Shirley, Skinner, Pearson, Ison.

Any objection? No.

Any one died? No.

Any resigned? Bro A.P. Hunt. The resignation was agreed to nem. con. The Superintendent read a letter of resignation from Bro Cooper but it was decided to retain his name during the ensuing quarter.[2]

Anyone left the Circuit? No.

Anyone entered? No.

Anyone received? Bro Cross's name was proposed for reinstatement. Carried unan.

Who continue on trial? Bros E.J. Brown and H. Smith. Arrangements were made for Bro Smith's trial sermon.

Who are received on trial? Mr Albert Antliffe[3] was proposed by the Superintendent and seconded by Mr Nix. Carried unan. Mr E. Bowers, ppd by Mr Richings and sec[d] by Bro Hunt and accepted.

1   Gilbert Gomm (1878–1968), of Oxford. Gomm emigrated to Canada in 1902 and later became a Presbyterian minister.

2   Michael Cooper, of Horspath, stayed on the plan as an exhorter well into the next century.

3   Albert Antliff (1879–1964). Antliff came to Oxford to improve his education, was working as a paid lay agent for the Wesleyan Circuit in 1901, and then entered the Wesleyan

Who receive a note? None.
Any one to be an exhorter? No.
Any change in time or place? A suggested change at Eynsham was referred to the Eynsham committee.
Any new place to be opened? No.
Any place to be given up? No.
A conversation followed on the state of the Spiritual work in the circuit.
The following Mission Band arrangements were made – No 2 Messrs Hooper, Courtney Brown, Baker, Kumarakulasinghe, Walker, Hopwood.[1]
Wm Bradfield 12/3/00
H.A. Liddell

12 March 1900

Minutes of Quarterly Local Preachers' Meeting held March 12 1900
Present Rev W. Bradfield
Bros Skinner, Davis, Roff, Railton, Ashdown, E.J. Smith, G. Adams, Clifford, Skidmore, Richings, Danbury, Antliff, Corley, Ison, Genner, Dobson, Turtle, Freeman, Watson, Liddell.
Any objection. Bro A. Vallis was reported to have missed Cuddesdon Feb [ ].[2]
On the motion of Bro Clifford it was unanimously agreed that the secretary should write.
Any one died: no.
Any one resigned: no.
Any one left the circuit: no.
Any fully accredited local preacher entered: Bro W.A. Freeman.[3]
Any one to be fully received? Mr Albert Antliffe was examined. He was nominated by the Superintendent and accepted by the meeting.
Who continue on trial? Bros E.J. Brown and H. Smith. The meeting consented to Bro Smith's examination being deferred for a quarter.
Who are received on trial? None.
Who receive a note? Mr G. Banting,[4] Bayswater Mill, and Mr W. Allen,[5] Forest Hill were received by the meeting.

---

ministry: *Minutes of Conference* 1965, 189.
1   All members of the Oxford University Wesley Guild: Ronald Morley Hooper (Worcester), Courtney Brown (St John's), B.W. Baker (University College), C.B. Kumarakulasinghe (Merton), W.J. Walker (Balliol) and H.R. Hopwood (Brasenose), listed on the Guild's term card for October 1899: OHC, OMCA, NM5/F/A1/2, John Wesley Society Minute Book, 1889–1900. Hooper's younger brother, John S.M. Hooper, was a Local Preacher in the Oxford Circuit from September 1901.
2   Space left for date to be inserted.
3   William Alfred Freeman (1869–1950).
4   George Preston Banting (1881–1960), farmer, of Forest Hill.
5   William Allen (1865–1943), gardener, of Forest Hill.

Any one to be an exhorter? No.

Any change in time or place? A discussion concerning the morning service at Eynsham led to no definite conclusion.

Any place to be opened? No.

To be given up? No.

The names of Mr Woodsworth,[1] accepted probationer of the Canadian Methodist Church,[2] and Mr W.J. Walker,[3] Balliol, were added to those of the helpers from other circuits.

The name of Mr C. Smith[4] was added to the Bladon mission band.

A Special Meeting was arranged for March 28 at 6 p.m. to consider arrangements for the summer Open Air services.

Wm Bradfield 11/6/00

H.A. Liddell

11 June 1900

Minutes of Local Preachers' Meeting held June 11 1900

Present: Rev. W. Bradfield.

Bros: Railton, Skidmore, Skinner, Watson, Clifford, Weatherill, Dawson, Turtle, Liddell, Sumner, Corley, Dobson, H. Clifford, Genner.

Any objection? Bro T. Vallis was reported as missing Bladon June 3. The secretary was instructed to write.

Any one died? No.

Any one resigned? No.

Any one left the circuit? No.

---

1   James Shaver Woodsworth (1874–1942), of Toronto, an honorary member of the OU Wesley Guild in Michaelmas Term 1899: OHC, OMCA, NM5/F/A1/2, John Wesley Society Minute Book, 1889–1900, minutes of 21 November 1899. Woodsworth was a Methodist minister in Canada from 1900–18: Neil Semple, *The Lord's Dominion. The History of Canadian Methodism* (Montreal and Kingston: McGill-Queen's University Press, 1996), 350, and Kenneth McNaught, *A Prophet in Politics. A Biography of J.S. Woodsworth* (Toronto: University of Toronto Press, 1959), 10–19. According to McNaught, Woodsworth was not impressed by the Wesley Guild and Methodist sermons, preferring to attend the Church of England while in Oxford.

2   Slightly unusual terminology: a probationer was a person accepted and trained for the ministry who was serving a period of probation in a circuit appointment prior to reception into full connexion and ordination. In the Wesleyan Connexion, probation typically lasted for two years.

3   Wilfrid James Walker (1880–1952), undergraduate, Balliol College, and member of the Mission Band noted in the December 1899 minutes. For Walker's subsequent career, see *The Methodist Local Preachers' Who's Who 1934*, 537, and F.C. Pritchard, *The Story of Woodhouse Grove School* (Bradford: Woodhouse Grove School, 1978), 287–97.

4   Probably Charles William Smith (1880–1954), grocer, of Bladon, who became a Local Preacher in 1909.

Any fully accredited local preacher entered? Bro Howard Clifford[1] from Witney and Bro Arthur E. Clifford[2] of Mr Cook's Mission.[3]

Any one to be fully received? No.

Who continue on trial? Bros E.J. Brown and H. Smith.

Who are received on trial? Bros G. Banting and W. Allen were nominated by the superintendent and received by the meeting.

Who receive a note? The name of Mr Walter Titcomb[4] was mentioned. Mr Clifford[5] was asked to see him.

Any one to be an exhorter? No.

Any change in time or place? No.

Any new place to be opened? No.

Any place to be given up? No.

It was suggested that at the next meeting the time after business should be devoted to devotional discussion and the Secretary was instructed to ask Mr J. Vanner Early[6] to read a paper.

A resolution supporting Mr Souttar's 'Sale of Intoxicating Liquors to Children Bill' was passed and the secretary was instructed to forward it to the proper quarters.[7]

Wm Bradfield 24/9/00

H.A. Liddell

24 September 1900

Minutes of Local Preachers' Meeting held Sept 24 1900

1   Howard James Clifford (1875–1935), carpenter and joiner. Nephew of David Price Clifford.

2   Probably Arthur Ernest Clifford (1873–1948), also a nephew of David Price Clifford and cousin of Howard Clifford.

3   Thomas Cook (1859–1912), Wesleyan Connexional Evangelist, led a mission for the Oxford and District Free Church Council in February 1899: *ODFCM*, February 1899, 7 and March 1899, 15–16. The implication is that Clifford was a member of Cook's itinerant mission team.

4   Walter John Titcomb (1868–1924), tailor, of Cowley.

5   David Price Clifford.

6   James Vanner Early (1853–1920), of the Witney blanket-making firm: Alfred Plummer and Richard E. Early, *The Blanket Makers* (London: Routledge and Kegan Paul, 1969), 111–20. The Earlys were strong supporters of the Wesleyan cause in Witney, and J.V. Early was a Local Preacher.

7   The 'Sale of Intoxicating Liquors to Children (No. 2)' bill was a private member's bill sponsored by Robinson Souttar (1848–1912), Liberal MP for Dumfriesshire. Souttar was well known in Oxford: a non-collegiate student at the university from 1884–88, he was a member of New Road Baptist Church while resident, served as President of the Oxford YMCA, and stood unsuccessfully for the city's single parliamentary seat in the 1892 General Election: D.W. Bebbington, 'Baptist MPs in the Nineteenth Century', *Baptist Quarterly*, 29.1 (1981), 3–24, at 22.

Present: Revs W. Bradfield, J. Pellow[1] J.S.W. Shrewsbury.[2] Bros S. Watson, Railton, Dawson, G. Adams, E.J. Smith, H. Sumner, Antliff, Skinner, Richings, Ison, Danbury, A.E. Watson, Genner, Archer, Liddell, ~~H. Smith~~, Pearson.

Any objection? The following omissions were noted and the secretary was instructed to write.

Bro Field Eynsham Aug 26

Bro Butler New Hinksey Sep 23

Bro Edens Forest Hill Aug 26

In the case of Bro Banting's omissions at Cuddesdon, Beckley, Horspath Bro Antliff was requested to call on him for an explanation.

Any one died? No.

Any one resigned? No.

Any one left the circuit? No.

Any fully accredited local preacher entered the circuit? No.

Any one to be fully received? No.

Who continue on trial? Bros E.J. Brown and Bro H. Smith with arrangements for examination next quarter, Bro W. Allen and Bro G. Banting subject to the Superintendent's discretion.

Who are received on trial? None.

Who receive a note? None.

Any one to be an exhorter? No.

Any change in time or place? No.

Any new place to be opened? No.

Any place to be given up? No.

Mr Sumner read a very encouraging report on the work of the Cycle Mission during the past summer.[3]

The meeting unanimously expressed its heartfelt gratitude for the interest and sympathy shown.

A collection ~~to~~ on the spot to liquidate a debt of 9/- realised 15/3.

The work of the past summer's open air work was then discussed by the brethren and a financial statement was presented by Mr Danbury shewing a balance of £1-8-9 in favour of the account.

Wm Bradfield 10/12/00

H.A. Liddell

---

1   John Pellow (1849–1920), minister in the Oxford Circuit, 1898–1901: *Minutes of Conference* 1920, 127.

2   John Sutcliffe Wesley Shrewsbury (1866–1931), minister in the Oxford Circuit, 1900–03: *Minutes of Conference* 1932, 61.

3   Nine years later the attempt to form a Cycle Corps of preachers and other workers to reach villages without Nonconformist places of worship failed to attract recruits: OHC, OMCA, NM5/A/A4/3: Local Preachers' Meeting Minute Book, 1903–30, minutes for 17 June and 16 September 1909.

10 December 1900

Minutes of Local Preachers' Meeting held Dec 10 1900
Present Revs W. Bradfield J.W.S. Shrewsbury. Bros Skinner, Fryer, Wickham, G. Adams, J.R. Weatherill, Liddell, E.J. Smith, Sumner, Danbury, A.E. Watson, Genner, Corley, Dobson, H. Smith, Allen, Nappin, Hobbs.
Any objection? The following omissions were noted and the secretary instructed to write to the brethren concerned.
Bro Shirley, Bladon Nov 18, A. Vallis Cuddesdon Oct 21, Ashdown Eynsham Oct 28 (morning). In the case of Bro H. Clifford who neglected his appointment at Tackley on Nov 11 the reply was to be sent to the Superintendent as early as possible.[1]
Any one died? No.
Any one resigned? Bro T. Vallis. The resignation was accepted by the meeting.
Any one left the circuit? No.
Any one to be fully received? Bro H. Smith was examined, nominated and unanimously received by the meeting.
Who continue on trial? Bros E.J. Brown, Allen and Kernick.[2] On the proposition of the superintendent it was agreed that Bro Banting should not continue.
Who are received on trial? The superintendent nominated Messrs A.J. Costaign,[3] W. Woodward,[4] J. Nappin, W. Hobbs who were received by the meeting.
Who receive a note? None.
Any to be an exhorter? No.
Any change in time or place? No.
Any new place to be opened? No.
Any place to be given up? No.
Mr Adams proposed and Mr Skinner seconded 'That the next Local Preachers Meeting be held on the same day as the Quarterly Meeting.'[5] This was carried.
The Meeting recommended Mr H. Danbury to the Circuit Mission Committee as Secretary in place of Mr A.E. Watson.
Wm Bradfield 27/3/01
H.A. Liddell
Sec.

1   See below, July 1901. The unusual urgency in following up Clifford's missed appointment was perhaps connected to a sense of his waning loyalty to Methodism.
2   Frederick Walwyn Kernick (1882–1933), undergraduate, Christ Church. Kernick entered the Wesleyan ministry in 1905 and was Master of Queen's College, Melbourne, 1929–33: *Wesley College Chronicle*, December 1933, 12.
3   Alfred James Costain (1881–1963), undergraduate, Lincoln College. Costain entered the Wesleyan ministry in 1904 and was Headmaster of Rydal School, 1915–46: *Minutes of Conference* 1963, 206.
4   William Woodward (1875–1962), carter, of Bladon.
5   Since the 1894 reforms, all fully accredited Local Preachers were *ex officio* members of the Circuit Quarterly Meeting. Holding both meetings on the same day might encourage attendance.

27 March 1901

Minutes of Local Preachers' Meeting held March 27 19~~0001~~

Present Revs W. Bradfield, J.S.W. Shrewsbury. Bros J. Nix, S. Watson, H. Railton, C. Hunt, J.R. Weatherill, D.P. Clifford, T. Skinner, A. Pearson, Fryer, Field, H. Sumner, Ison, Wickham, Genner, G. Adams, E.J. Smith, Dawson, Edens, H. Danbury.

Any objection. It was noted that Bro Shirley had omitted Cuddesdon on March 17. It was moved by Bro Wickham and seconded by Bro Clifford that he be asked to explain this omission and the previous omission at Bladon. This was carried.

Any one died? No.

Any one resigned? Bro J.M. King sent a letter of resignation to the Superintendent who undertook to see him and explain that his name might be retained.

Any one left the Circuit: Bro A.E. Watson to the Kentish Town Circuit.

Any one to be fully received? No.

Who continue on trial? Messrs E.J. Brown, W. Allen, Kernick, A.J. Costaign, W. Woodward, J. Nappin, W. Hobbs, G. Gomm.

Who are received on trial: Mr A.E. Dawe[1] was accepted by the Meeting.

Who receive a note: Mr Clifford suggested Bro Mortimer of Forest Hill.[2] Accepted by Meeting. Mr Buckingham was to be accepted on trial subject to a satisfactory interview with Superintendent. Mr Baker was received by the meeting.[3]

Any one to be an exhorter? No.

Any change in time or place? No.

Any new place to be opened? No.

Any place to be given up? No.

The Meeting agreed to Mr Baker taking Beckley eleven Sundays out of 13. Service to be indicated by initials.[4]

Arrangements for Open Air Services were deferred to a meeting to be held on Tuesday April 2 at 6 p.m.

Wm Bradfield 2/7/01

H.A. Liddell

2 July 1901

Minutes of Local Preachers' Meeting held at Bladon, July 2nd 1901.

Present Revs W. Bradfield, J. Pellow & J.S.W. Shrewsbury.

---

1   Probably Alfred Robert Daw (1877–1955), shop assistant. of Oxford.

2   Owen Mortimer (1875–1935), postman, of Forest Hill.

3   Robert Wreford Baker (1883–?). In the 1901 Census Baker is listed as a brewer's clerk, which by 1902 might have been an uncomfortable occupation for a Wesleyan Local Preacher. The arrangement for Baker, still on trial as a preacher, to conduct almost every service at Beckley, suggests employment as a lay agent by the Oxford Circuit.

4   From October 1900 Beckley's appointments on the plan are marked 'to be arranged'; on the April–July 1901 plan they are marked by asterisks; by the autumn of 1901 Baker is no longer leading all of the Beckley services: OHC, OMCA, NM5/A/A1/1, Circuit plans and directories.

Bros Richings, Skinner, Fryer, G. Adams, D.P. Clifford, Weatherill, Belcher, E.J. Smith, Sumner, Genner, Antliff, H. Smith, Nappin, Hobbs, Woodward, H.W. Danbury.

1. Any objection? No.

2. Any one died? No.

3. Anyone resigned? A letter was read from Bro J.M. King, asking that his name might be removed from the Plan, as its retention would only cause 'extra work' to the Meeting. It was unanimously resolved on the proposition of Bro Adams seconded by Bro Clifford 'That the Meeting most sympathetically refuse to remove Bro King's name.'

Mr Howard Clifford, having ceased to be a member of Society and having joined another church was disqualified from being a Local Preacher, & it was resolved to take his name off the Plan.[1]

4. Anyone left the Circuit? Brother Duck, removed to Cambridge.

5. Any fully accredited local Preacher entered the Circuit. Bro T.P. Starke from Norwich.[2]

* See next page.

6. Anyone to be fully received? No.

7. Who continue on trial? Bros E.J. Brown, W. Allen, F.W. Kernick, A.J. Costain, J. Nappin, W. Hobbs, W. Woodward, G. Gomm & A.R. Daw, also Bro Metcalf, a Local Preacher on Trial from Birmingham.

8. Who are received on Trial? Messrs O. Mortimer & R.W. Baker were accepted by the Meeting.

Mr Alder of Woodstock was suggested,[3] & it was left to the Superintendent to see him & give him a few appointments if he thought desirable.

The Superintendent reported that Mr Buckingham declined to have his name put on the plan as a local preacher on trial.

9. Who receive a note? None.

10. Anyone to be an Exhorter? No.

11. Any change in time or place? No.

12. Any new place to be opened? No.

13. Any place to be given up? No.

The names of Messrs H.G.F. Micklewright (of Merton Coll) and C.L. Hare (Corpus) were added to No. 2 Mission Band.[4]

1   Clifford emigrated to the United States in autumn 1901. By the time of his naturalization in 1912 he was a Salvation Army officer.

2   Theodore Philip Starke (1864–1939), NSPCC Inspector.

3   Possibly John Joseph Alder (1872–1949), boot repairer.

4   H.G.F. Micklewright and C.L. Hare were elected members of the OU Wesley Guild in Michaelmas Term 1900: OHC, OMCA, NM5/F/A1/3, John Wesley Society Minute Book, 1900–11, minute of 20 October 1900. Harry Micklewright (1882–1972) became a Local Preacher in the Oxford Circuit in March 1903.

* It was unanimously resolved on the proposition of Bro Sumner, seconded by Rev. J. Pellow That Bro A.P. Hunt's name be re-instated on the Plan.
A letter of sympathy was ordered to be sent to Bro Skidmore, who was lying seriously ill, & also to Bro C. Hunt whose wife was also very ill.
Wm Bradfield 25/9/01
H.A. Liddell

25 September 1901

Minutes of Local Preachers' Meeting held Sept 25 1901
Pres: Rev W. Bradfield BA, J.S.W. Shrewsbury BA, F.C. Wright.
Bros Jas Nix, Watson, Railton, Sumner, Roff, Richings, Ashdown, Dawson, G. Adams, E.J. Smith, Clifford, Weatherill, Wickham, Genner, Corley, Danbury, Archer, Liddell, Skinner, Shirley, Fryer.
Any objection:- No.
Any one died:- Brother Johnathan Skidmore. The Secretary was instructed to place on record the Meetings' appreciation of the devoted life and service of Bro Skidmore.
Any one resigned? No.
Any one left the circuit? Bro Stanley to [ ],[1] Bro Freeman to Newport, Mon, Bro Antliff to Raunds and Bro Metcalf to Birmingham Mission.
Any one entered? Bro Golby of Stroud.[2]
The question of Messrs Hooper & Spooner from Kingswood School was left to the Superintendent's discretion.[3]
Any one to be fully received. No.
Who continue on trial? Messrs E.J. Brown, W. Allen, F.W. Kernick, A.J. Costain, J. Nappin, W. Hobbs, W. Woodward, G. Gomm, A.R. Daw, O. Mortimer, R.W. Baker.
Who are received on trial. None.
Who receive a note: none.
Any one to be an exhorter. No.
The Late Mr Jonathan Skidmore[4]
On Monday, July 15th, 1901, a large number of Oxford Methodists followed with the family mourners to the grave the remains of Brother Jonathan Skidmore, who was interred in the growingly beautiful Cemetery at Rose Hill, near Oxford. The deceased was born in the village of Tackley, Oxon, in the year 1829. His father was accustomed to worship in the Wesleyan Chapel, which was one of the first established in what is now the Oxford Circuit. The services were carried on by a few earnest and simple believers, who were noted for their enthusiasm in singing, praying, and preaching, and soon became a model and type of the glow and unction

1   Gap left for place to be inserted.
2   Harry Golby (1869–1949), workhouse porter.
3   See notes of 2 December meeting. Kingswood School, Bath, was founded by John Wesley as a school for the sons of his Travelling Preachers.
4   Transcription of cutting from *ODFCM*, Vol V, No. 57, Sept 1901, 45–6.

attending Methodist worship in rural England. The services mostly depended on the local preachers, with a visit from the Circuit Minister at long intervals; but the impassioned appeals of the preachers, the instruments of brass and wood in the choir, the old tunes to the old and favourite hymns, which made the place ring, filled the worshippers with love for their chapel and service. A majority of the inhabitants of the village, with at least two of the prominent farmers, were worshippers and members. Into this society young Skidmore was introduced, and there was soon kindled in his heart a love for the sanctuary, and at the age of sixteen he was converted to God and became a member of the Methodist Society. He was converted in his own home after a prayer meeting. So intense was his desire for the conversion of his mother, that he began to pray for her and with her, and he was not satisfied till she gave evidence of her change of heart.

During revival services in the village, he displayed great fervour and aptitude in appealing to men of his own class, and in directing any who were penitent to the Saviour. The minister at once urged the work of preaching upon him, and the appeal resulted in his being admitted as an Exhorter on the 23rd March 1859, and on the 21st September, 1859, he was appointed as a Local Preacher on trial, and on 26th Dec., 1860, he was examined, and as a fully accredited Local Preacher commenced the labours faithfully and punctually discharged in the preaching of the simple Gospel in the villages in the Oxford and adjoining circuits.

Brother Skidmore had few educational advantages; there was but the dame school, and in his early years he had to go to work to help the family eke out a hard living. The Scriptures were to him the Book of books, and taught by the Holy Spirit, with an experience which responded to the light and grace which shone through the Word, made him a living expositor of the "truth as it is in Jesus." His pulpit addresses inspired the hearers with the simplicity and genuineness of his character. Notwithstanding the fact that his sentences were many of them ungrammatical, yet one seldom failed in obtaining clear light on the subject of his address.

This sketch of our brother would be incomplete if it did not specially allude to his visitation of the sick; in this his aptitude was tactful and sympathetic; he ministered consolation and comfort to many souls, and was successful in dealing with men and women who had put off the search for salvation till a dying hour. His joy seemed greatest when on a Sunday afternoon he took a round of visitation at Tackley with the preacher for the day. He was a labourer on the Great Western Railway for many years, living at Tackley; his house was always open, and he gladly dispensed such things as he had. His wife died at Tackley a few years ago, and he married a second time, gave up his employment, and came to live in Oxford. Soon after, his health became uncertain, and gradually began to fail; a grave sickness two years ago brought him within sight of eternity; but he was spared and laboured on, till on the 16th of June he was appointed to take part in an Open Air Service at Tackley. This was his last service. He was a member of the Local Preachers' Mutual Aid

Association,[1] and took great interest in its work. He died at Sunset Cottage, St Clement's, Oxford, on the 11th of June 1901, in a home provided by Mr Walter Slaughter for poor aged Christians who while not entirely destitute may without any payment occupy till the Master should come. His body was in Oxford but his heart was still at Tackley.

Servant of God, well done! Well hast thou fought

The better fight!

J.N.

Any change in time or place. No.

Any new place to be opened. No.

Any place to be given up. No.

A discussion followed on the condition of the society at Beckley. The Superintendent and Messrs Watson, Genner, Richings & J. Nix were appointed a committee to investigate.

Wm Bradfield 30/12/01

H.A. Liddell

2 December 1901

Minutes of Special Local Preachers' Meeting held at New Inn Hall Street Dec 2 1901 Present Rev W. Bradfield BA, F.C. Wright,[2] J.S.W. Shrewsbury BA and J. Wright. Messrs Genner, Corley, Clifford, Nix, G. Adams, Wickham, Skinner, Railton, Turtle, Gomm, Allen, Kernick, Costain, Nappin, Hobbs, Woodward, G. Spooner[3] & J.M.S. Hooper.[4]

The Chairman stated that the meeting was called in accordance with the resolution passed at the September Meeting for the purpose of examining for full plan Bros Allen, Kernick, Costain, Nappin, Hobbs and Woodward.

The Chairman also stated that since the September Meeting Bros G. Spooner & J.S.M. Hooper had come to reside in the circuit having removed from the Bath Circuit.[5] Their examination for full plan was due and would have taken place

---

1   Inaugurated in October 1849 and independent of the denominational structures, the Local Preachers' Mutual Aid Association was set up to provide relief to sick and elderly Local Preachers. See Alan Parker, *Confidence in Mutual Aid* (Peterborough: Methodist Publishing House for LPMA, 1998), Part 2.

2   Frederick Charles Wright (1861–1933), minister in the Oxford Circuit, 1901–04: *Minutes of Conference* 1933, 256.

3   George Spooner (1882–1963), undergraduate, Brasenose College. Spooner entered the Wesleyan ministry in 1906 and served in India for many years: *Minutes of Conference* 1963, 207.

4   John Stirling Morley Hooper (1882–1974), undergraduate, Corpus Christi College. Hooper was the younger brother of R.M. Hooper, and he entered the Wesleyan ministry in 1905, serving in India until retirement: *Minutes of Conference* 1974, 141–2.

5   As pupils at Kingswood School, Spooner and Hooper began their training as Local Preachers in the Bath Circuit.

last ~~September~~ June at Bath had it been possible for them to have been present at the Local Preachers' Meeting. He therefore asked the meeting to allow these two brethren to be examined with the other six. This was unanimously agreed to.

The examination of the eight brethren was then conducted by the Chairman at the close of which reports of their preaching were given by several of the brethren present. After each name had been separately voted upon the eight brethren were unanimously recommended to be received on full plan.

30 December 1901

Minutes of Local Preachers' Meeting held at New Inn Hall St Dec 30 1901
Present:- Revs W. Bradfield BA & J.S.W. Shrewsbury. Bros J. Nix, Watson, Railton, Fryer, Roff, Vallis, Smith, Wickham, Richings, Weatherill, Starke, Turtle, Skinner, Archer, Pearson, Liddell, H. Smith, Nappin, Dawson, Woodward.

1. Any objection: Mr Sumner was mentioned as having omitted Beckley on Dec 1. The secretary was instructed to ask for an explanation.
2. Has any one died? No.
3. Any one resigned? On the proposition of Bros Wickham & Vallis it was agreed that Bro Edens' resignation be accepted.[1]
4. Any one left the circuit? No.
5. Any one entered the circuit? No.
6. Who continue on trial?

On the proposition of Messrs Nix and Wickham it was agreed 'That this meeting having heard the report of the special meeting held Dec 2 confirms its action in receiving the brethren there named on full plan.'

The following continue on trial E.J. Brown, Gomm, Daw, Mortimer, Baker.

The meeting resolved that the Superintendent be asked to make arrangements for Bro Gomm's trial sermon and examination.

Any one to be fully received? No.

Who are received on trial? Mr Wm George[2] was unanimously accepted by the meeting.

Any one to receive a note? The Superintendent was requested to see brother Ray.[3]

Any one to be an exhorter? No.

Any change in time or place? No.

Any new place to be opened? No.

Any place to be given up? No.

Wm Bradfield 24/3/02

H.A. Liddell

---

1   No reason given, but in March 1903 Edens applied for reinstatement and it was asked 'if Bro Edens had obtained his discharge', suggesting that he had been declared bankrupt.
2   William Blissett George (1877–1925), chemist's manager, of Oxford.
3   Probably Herbert Edward Ray, who continued on the plan as an exhorter.

3 February 1902

Minutes of Special Local Preachers' Meeting held Monday Feb 3 1902

Present – Revs W. Bradfield, F.C. Wright, J. Wright.[1] Bros Genner, Ashdown, Archer, Field, Clifford, Nix, Wetherill, Davis, Shirley, Turtle, Gomm, Richings, Railton, Corley, Ison, Spooner, Hooper, Watson, Danbury, Smith, Woodward, Hobbs, Nappin, Allen, Wickham, Skinner, Starke, George, Golby.

Tea was kindly provided by Mr James Nix at six o'clock to which about twenty-four members sat down.

After tea Mr Genner delivered an address on 'Bible Study for Local Preachers'.

The question was dealt with under the following heads.

1. What are our objects in studying it.
2. Bible study is a necessity.
3. It is a matter of personal appropriation.
4. How to use it.
5. Practical suggestions.

The address was heartily and thankfully received and an animated discussion followed maintained by Messrs Watson, Nix, Clifford, Wickham, Liddell and the chairman.

On the proposition of Mr Watson supported by the Rev Jas Wright and Mr Archer a hearty vote of thanks was accorded to Mr Genner for his address and Mr Nix for his hospitality.

24 March 1902

Minutes of Local Preachers' Meeting held March 24 1902 at New Inn Hall Street

Present: Revs W. Bradfield, F.C. Wright, J.S.W. Shrewsbury BA. Bros Jas Nix, Watson, Danbury, Skinner, Archer, Turtle, Wickham, Starke, Dawson, Pearson, Railton, Corley, Genner, Richings, E.J. Smith, Liddell, Shirley, Ison.

1. Any objection?

Mr H. Sumner wrote to the meeting and explained that the charge of missing Beckley was erroneous. The meeting accepted his statement and regretted that the charge had been made.

Any objection?

Bro Shirley was reported as having missed Wootton on Feb 23 and Cuddesdon Mar 2. The meeting agreed that he should be asked for an explanation.

Bro A. Vallis was reported for Hinksey Mar 9 and was to be asked for an explanation. Any one died? The Rev J. Wilson of Islip.[2] The meeting expressed its appreciation of his services and requested Mr Archer to convey to the relatives their sincere sympathy.

---

1   James Wright (1832–1920), resident in the Oxford Circuit as a supernumerary minister from 1901: *Minutes of Conference* 1920, 124.

2   James Wilson (1814–1902), a minister of the Methodist New Connexion, who retired to Oxfordshire in 1875 and was in Islip by the end of 1886: *MNC Minutes of Conference* 1902, 8–10.

Any one resigned? Mr A. Ballard sends his resignation. On the proposition of Messrs Nix and Wickham it was regretfully received.

Any one left the Circuit?

Bro A.E. Clifford to the Manchester Mission and Bro A.R. Daw to Newcastle, Brunswick.

Any fully accredited local preacher entered the Circuit. Bro T.A. Baker of Bedford St Iffley Rd from the Stonehouse Circuit.[1]

Bro T. Vallis sent a letter to the Superintendent asking for reinstatement. The Meeting unanimously agreed that he should be received.

Any one to be fully received?

Mr Gomm wrote stating that he was ill and asking that his exam. might be deferred till the March quarter. The meeting agreed.

Who continue on trial? Bros Brown, Gomm, Mortimer, Baker, George.

Who receive a note? It was agreed that Mr H. Pullen[2] receive a note.

Any one to be an exhorter? No.

Any change in time or place?

Horspath week evening agreed to at 7.

Eynsham week evening at 6.30.

Any new place to be opened? No.

The meeting expressed its sympathy with Mr Howard on the death of his wife and requested Mr Archer to convey their expressions in writing on behalf of the Quarterly Meeting.[3]

The Secretary was instructed to convey to Bro Clifford their sincere sympathy in his illness and their best wishes for his speedy restoration.

Bro Shirley who arrived during the process of the meeting explained his absences and the explanations were duly accepted by the meeting.

There were 54 local preachers to be reported to the Connexional Committee.[4]

The meeting unanimously invited Mr Corley to read a paper to the brethren during the coming quarter.

Wm Bradfield 30/6/02

H.A. Liddell

30 June 1902

Minutes of Meeting held June 30th at New Inn Hall St

Present: Revs W. Bradfield, F.C. Wright and J.S.W. Shrewsbury.

1   Thomas Arnold Baker (1856–1940), steel boat builder.
2   Harry Howard Pullen (1880–1934), grocer's assistant, of Oxford.
3   Mary Anne Howard died in the spring of 1902.
4   The 1894 scheme required the Local Preachers' Secretary in each circuit to report annually to the District LP Committee on 'the various statistical facts relating to the Local Preachers in that Circuit'. District statistics were reported to the Connexional LP Committee and then published in the *Minutes of Conference*.

Bros Nix, Watson, Corley, Shirley, Weatherill, Skinner, Richings, Genner, Liddell, Archer, Dawson, Ashdown, Danbury, Hancock.

Any objection:- the meeting agreed that bros Butler, Dawson and A. Vallis should be asked to explain absences from Cuddesdon on April 20, 27 and May 4 respectively.

Any one died? No.

Any one resigned? A letter of resignation was received from bro W.B. George. The meeting agreed that the matter should stand over for a quarter, the Rev F.C. Wright to see Mr George meanwhile.

Any one left the circuit? Mr T.A. Baker to the Oxford (UMFC) circuit. Mr Dobson to Stanstead Quebec. The secretary was instructed to convey to Mr Dobson the meeting's appreciation of ~~the meeting~~ his past services and its best wishes for his future success.

Any fully accredited preacher entered the circuit? Bro H.M. Hancock from Bristol ~~Queen~~ King St.

Any one to be fully received? No.

Who continue on trial? Bros E.J. Brown, G. Gomm, O. Mortimer, R.W. Baker, W.E. George.

Who receive a note? Mr H. Pullen's name was again suggested to the meeting.

Any one to be an exhorter? No.

Any change in time or place? No.

Any new place to be opened? No.

Any place to be given up? No.

Mr Dawson explained that his absence from Cuddesdon was due to illness an explanation which was received by the meeting with sympathy.

Sep 29 '02 Arthur Hoyle[1]

H.A. Liddell

29 September 1902

Minutes of Meeting held Sept 29 at New Inn Hall St

Present:- Revs Arthur Hoyle,[2] J.S.W. Shrewsbury. Bros Dawson, E.J. Smith, Genner, Richings, Ashdown, T. Vallis, H. Danbury, Archer, Railton, Wickham, Liddell, Skinner, Nappin, Woodward, Hobbs.

Any objection:- the following omissions were noted Bro Pearson Beckley, Bro Roff Beckley Aug 3, Bro Mortimer Beckley July 20. Mr Roff explained that his omission was due to an oversight. The secretary was instructed to write to the other brethren. Any one died: Bro D.P. Clifford. The secretary was instructed to convey to Mrs Clifford and family the sincere sympathy of the Meeting in their loss and

---

1   Superintendent from September 1902.

2   Arthur Hoyle (1857–1928), Superintendent of the Oxford Circuit, 1902–05: *Minutes of Conference* 1928, 111.

bereavement and to express its unanimous appreciation of his loyal service to the cause of Christ.[1]

Any one resigned. The superintendent undertook to see Bro George about his letter of resignation.

Any one left the Circuit. Bro Hill Hancock to Barnsley.

Any fully accredited local preacher entered the circuit: Bro A.T. Smith from Gainsborough.[2]

Any one to be fully received: No.

Who continue on trial: Bros E.J. Brown, G. Gomm, O. Mortimer, R.W. Baker, W.B. George.

Who are received on trial? Mr Barron[3] already on trial in the Bath Circuit[4] was accepted on the nomination of the superintendent and Mr Archer. Mr H. Pullen on the nomination of the superintendent and Mr Railton.

Who receive a note? None.

Any one to be an exhorter? No.

Any change in time or place? No.

Any new place to be opened? No, but a discussion was held on the needs of Dorchester.[5]

Any place to be given up? No.

The meeting agreed on the ~~nomination~~ proposition of Bros Ashdown and Richings to restore Bro T. Vallis' name to its original position on the plan.

Dec. 22 '02 Arthur Hoyle

H.A. Liddell

1   Clifford died on 11 July 1902. A tribute by 'J.N'. (James Nix) was published in the *ODFCM* in September 1902.

2   Probably Albert Thomas Smith (1873–?), draper's assistant. Smith's address is listed on the July–October 1902 plan as 15 Pembroke Street, and this was an accommodation block for draper's assistants and apprentices: OHC, OMCA, NM5/A/A1/1, Circuit plans and directories and census returns for 1901 and 1911.

3   William Arthur Barron (1883–1958), undergraduate, New College.

4   Barron came to Oxford from Kingswood School and was therefore attached to the Bath Circuit.

5   See note for June 1885. According to *Kelly's Directory of Berkshire, Bucks and Oxon* for 1907, 96, there was a Wesleyan chapel in Dorchester in that year, but the Local Preachers' meeting in March 1908 resolved 'to discontinue the services there for the present'. and the Quarterly Meeting resolved to dispose of the property, retaining the possibility of occasional open-air services. Dorchester remained on the Wesleyan plan at least until 1913, but with no preachers appointed.

Select Bibliography

Banbury, G.G., 'Oxford Circuit', *UMFC Magazine*, May 1863

Batty, Margaret, 'The contribution of local preachers to the life of the Wesleyan Methodist Church until 1932, and to the Methodist Church after 1932, in England', MA thesis, University of Leeds, 1969

Bebbington, David W., 'The Mid-Victorian Revolution in Wesleyan Methodist Home Mission', *Journal of Ecclesiastical History* 70.1 (January 2019)

Binfield, Clyde, *So Down to Prayers. Studies in English Nonconformity 1780–1920* (London: J.M. Dent and Sons, 1977)

Bowmer, John, *Pastor and People. A Study of Church and Ministry in Methodism from the death of John Wesley (1791) to the death of Jabez Bunting (1858)* (London: Epworth Press, 1975)

Boylan, John, *Cowley Road Methodist Church Centre Oxford. Centenary 1904–2004* (Oxford: Cowley Road Methodist Church Centre, 2004)

Cashdollar, Charles D., *A Spiritual Home. Life in British and American Reformed Congregations, 1830–1915* (University Park, PA: Penn State UP, 2000)

[Cooke, M.A.], *The Upright Man; A Memorial Volume of the Rev. Corbett Cooke, Wesleyan Minister* (London: Conference Office and Guernsey: E. Le Lievre, 1868)

Crossley, Alan, (ed.), *The City of Oxford* (VCH Oxfordshire, 4) (Oxford: OUP, 1979)

Curthoys, Mark, 'Oxfordshire's Tolpuddle? The Case of the Ascott Martyrs', *Oxoniensia* 86 (2021)

Davies, Rupert, and Rupp, Gordon (eds), *A History of the Methodist Church in Great Britain*, 1 (London: Epworth Press, 1965)

Davies, Rupert, George, A. Raymond and Rupp, Gordon (eds), *A History of the Methodist Church in Great Britain*, 2 (London: Epworth Press, 1978)

Davies, Rupert, George, A. Raymond and Rupp, Gordon (eds), *A History of the Methodist Church in Great Britain*, 3 (London: Epworth Press, 1983)

Edwards, Michael S., The *Lime Walk Story. A Fortieth Anniversary Souvenir History, 1885–1972* (Witney: The Witney Press, 1972)

Eldridge, C.O., *Local Preachers and Village Methodism* (Rochdale: Joyful News Book Depot, 1895)

Francis, Keith A., and Gibson, William (eds), *The Oxford Handbook of the British Sermon 1689–1901* (Oxford: OUP, 2012)

Graham, Malcolm, 'The suburbs of Victorian Oxford: growth in a pre-industrial city', PhD thesis, University of Leicester, 1985

Gregory, Benjamin, *Consecrated Culture: Memorials of Benjamin Alfred Gregory* (London: T. Woolmer, 1885).

Gregory, Benjamin, *Side Lights on the Conflicts of Methodism during the Second Quarter of the Nineteenth Century* (London: Cassell and Co., 1898)

[Gregory, J.R.], *Benjamin Gregory, DD. Autobiographical Reflections, edited, with Memorials of his Later Life, by his Eldest Son* (London: Hodder and Stoughton, 1903)

Hatton, William, *A Brief Account of the Rise and Progress of the Local Preachers, and of Local Preaching, among the Methodists* (Leeds: E. Baines, n.d. [1817])

Heitzenrater, Richard P., *Wesley and the People Called Methodists* (Nashville: Abingdon Press, 2013 [second edition])

Hempton, David, *Methodism: Empire of the Spirit* (New Haven and London: Yale UP, 2005)

Horn, Pamela L.R., 'Christopher Holloway: an Oxfordshire Trade Union Leader', *Oxoniensia* 33 (1968)

Hughes, Dorothea Price, *The Life of Hugh Price Hughes* (London: Hodder and Stoughton, 1904)

Knight, Frances, *The Nineteenth Century Church and English Society* (Cambridge: CUP, 1995)

Law, Brian, *Building Oxford's Heritage* (Stadhampton: Prelude Promotion, 1998)

Lobel, Mary D., (ed.), *Ploughley Hundred* (VCH Oxfordshire, 6) (London: OUP, 1959)

McNaught, Kenneth, *A Prophet in Politics. A Biography of J.S. Woodsworth* (Toronto: University of Toronto Press, 1959)

Milburn, Geoffrey, and Batty, Margaret (eds), *Workaday Preachers. The Story of Methodist Local Preaching* (London: Methodist Publishing House, 1995)

Mills, W. Haslam, *Grey Pastures* (London: Chatto and Windus, 1924)

Nightingale, Joseph, *A Portraiture of Methodism* (London: Longman, Hurst, Rees, and Orme, 1807)

Oxley, J.E., *A History of Wesley Memorial Church, Oxford 1818–1968* (Oxford: The Oxonian Press, 1968)

Peirce, William, *The Ecclesiastical Principles and Polity of the Wesleyan Methodists* (London: Hamilton, Adams and Co., 1854, revised 1868; Wesleyan Conference Office, 1873)

Piggott, T.C., and Durley, T., *Life and Letters of Henry James Piggott, BA, of Rome* (London: Epworth Press, 1921)

Pocock, Christine Margaret, 'The origins, development and significance of the circuit in Wesleyan and Primitive Methodism in England, 1740–1914', PhD thesis, University of Nottingham, 2015

Rack, Henry D., *Reasonable Enthusiast. John Wesley and the Rise of Methodism* (London: Epworth Press, 1989)

Ritson, John H., *The World is Our Parish* (London: Hodder and Stoughton, 1939)

Rix, Mary Bright, *Life of Emma Mathews* (Oxford: Hall, 1960)

Robinson, William, *An Essay on Lay Ministry; particularly on that of Wesleyan Local Preachers* (London: Mason, 1832)

Royle, Edward, 'When did the Methodists stop attending their parish churches?', *Proceedings of the Wesley Historical Society* 56.6 (2008)

Smart, Richard (ed.), *The Bousfield Diaries* (Woodbridge: Boydell, for the Bedfordshire Historical Record Society, 2007)

Solloway, A.F., *Life More Abundant* (London: Pickering and Inglis, 1924)

Tiller, Kate, *Church and Chapel in Oxfordshire 1851*, (Oxford: Oxfordshire Record Society, 1987)

Tiller, Kate, 'Religion and Community: Dorchester to 1920', in Kate Tiller (ed.), *Dorchester Abbey: Church and People 635–2005* (Stonesfield: The Stonesfield Press, 2005)

Tiller, Kate, '"The desert begins to blossom": Oxfordshire and Primitive Methodism, 1824–1860', *Oxoniensia* 71 (2006)

Tiller, Kate (ed.), *Berkshire Religious Census 1851* (Reading: Berkshire Record Society, 2010)

Vickers, John A. (ed.), *A Dictionary of Methodism in Britain and Ireland* (Peterborough: Epworth Press, 2000) (and accessible in an expanded and updated version online at https://dmbi.online/)

Wellings, Martin, and Wood, Andrew, 'Facets of Formation: Theology through Training', in Clive Marsh, Brian Beck, Angela Shier-Jones and Helen Wareing (eds), *Unmasking Methodist Theology* (London: Continuum, 2004)

Wellings, Martin, 'The building of Wesley Memorial Church, Oxford', in *Building the Church* (*The Chapels Society Journal*, volume 2) (2016)

Wellings, Martin, '"In perfect harmony with the spirit of the age": The Oxford University Wesley Guild, 1883–1914', in Morwenna Ludlow, Charlotte Methuen and Andrew Spicer (eds), *Churches and Education* (*Studies in Church History* 55) (Cambridge: CUP, 2019)

Wellings, Martin, 'Hugh Price Hughes and "The Revival of Oxford Methodism"', *Methodist History* 58.3 (April 2020)

Wellings, Martin, 'Wesleyan Methodism and Nonconformity', in David Bebbington and David Ceri Jones (eds), *Evangelicalism and Dissent in Modern England and Wales* (Abingdon and New York: Routledge, 2021)

Wenham, Simon, *Pleasure Boating on the Thames. A History of Salter Bros 1858–Present Day* (Stroud: The History Press, 2014)

Wilson, F. Rought, *Life of George Sargeant. Wesleyan Missionary and First President of the West Indian Conference* (London: Charles H. Kelly, 1901)

Index

1870 meetings   169
authorized as exhorter   112
to be heard preaching   117
committee to investigate charge of
    drunkenness against George
    Osborn   141
received a note on trial   95
received on the plan   119, 120
to supply Charlton's
    appointments   131
taken off the plan   176
Faulkner, Samuel
    1855 meetings   135
    1856 meetings   136
    1857 meetings   139
    1861 meetings   149
    1862 meetings   151
    1866 meetings   158
    to be heard preaching for
        assessment   133
    to be placed on exhorters' list   139
    death of   186
    kept on the plan without
        appointments   173
    note authorizing preaching   131, 132
    received as exhorter   134
    received on trial   136
    trial sermons and to be
        examined   138
Field, Hubert
    1896 meetings   247, 248
    1897 meetings   251
    1898 meetings   255
    1901 meetings   266
    1902 meetings   272
    to be heard preaching   244, 245
    class meeting at Cuddesdon   58, 247
    may receive a note   244
    neglected Eynsham   264
    received on the plan   251
    received on trial   246, 247, 248, 250
financial difficulties *see* debt
Findlay, Joseph John
    1882 meetings   194, 197, 198
    1883 meetings   200, 201
    to be examined for
        accreditation   191
    received as exhorter   188

received on the plan   194
requested postponement of
    examination   192
taken off the plan   203
Findlay, William Hare   184, 188
Finsbury Park Wesleyan Circuit   205
Fisher, Thomas R.   53, 108, 109, 110,
    111, 112, 113
Fletcher, Mr (unidentified)   208, 209,
    213
Fletcher, John   32, 35
Flory, Henry William   213, 215, 216,
    217, 220, 221
Floyd, Charles Hulme
    1860 meetings   147
    1861 meetings   148
    1878 meetings   186, 187
    1879 meetings   187, 188, 189
    1880 meetings   189, 190
    1881 meetings   191, 192
    committee to enquire about Wheatley
        as preaching place   187, 188, 189
    to enquire about possible chapel at
        Hincksey   192
Fly Sheets from the Private
    Correspondent   11, 14, 18
Ford, George
    1871 meetings   172, 173
    1872 meetings   173, 174, 175
    1873 meetings   175, 176
    1874 meetings   177, 178
    removed to King St. Circuit,
        Bristol   179
    school chapel,(mission
        school)   57n271, 171n3
    transfer from Chichester
        Circuit   171
Forest, Mr   191, 203
Forest Hill
    to be put with Littleworth   96
    to be regularly supplied   133
    class meetings   58n275
    deputation for building a chapel   117
    Mission Bands   250
    neglected by Frederick Edens   264
    neglected by Henry Jackson   77
    neglected by Joseph Shirley   191
    neglected by Mr Harris   165, 167

Hugh Price Hughes' initiatives   22, 23, 57
by Wesley brothers   2
in Wesleyan evangelism   56
Osborn, George
  1854 meetings   132, 133
  1855 meetings   133, 135
  1856 meetings   138
  1857 meetings   141
  credentials from other Circuit not provided   53, 129
  'injurious' rumours   134
  'injurious' rumours deemed unfounded   135
  reprimanded for drunkenness   49, 134n2, 141
  taken off the plan for immorality   142
Osborne, James (farmer c.1841)   88, 89, 90, 96, 99, 101
Osborne, James (1849–1911)
  1884 meetings   203
  1885 meetings   206
  1887 meetings   215
  1889 meetings   221, 222
  1890 meetings   227
  1892 meetings   234
  1893 meetings   236
  1894 meetings   237, 242
  to be heard preaching   202
  neglected appointments   231
  neglected Islip   230
  received on the plan   204
  resignation accepted   242
Ostler, Joseph
  1830 meetings   69, 71, 72, 73
  1831 meetings   74, 75, 76
  1832 meetings   77, 78
  1833 meetings   79, 80, 81, 82
  1834 meetings   82, 83, 84
  1835 meetings   85, 86, 87, 88
  1836 meetings   88, 89, 90
  1837 meetings   91, 92
  1838 meetings   93, 94, 95, 96
  1839 meetings   96
  1840 meetings   98, 99, 100
  1841 meetings   100
  1842 meetings   102, 103
  1843 meetings   104, 105, 106
  1844 meetings   107, 108, 109

1845 meetings   110, 111, 112
1846 meetings   113, 114, 115
1847 meetings   115, 117
1848 meetings   118, 119
1849 meetings   120
age of when preacher   46
candidates' preaching abilities and training   52, 87, 88, 95, 99, 104, 107
chapel family   47
committee on preachers' transport   93
committee on subscriptions for purchase of books   93
covering fifty miles a day for preaching   59
death of   121
head of list on preaching plan   38n200
to inquire into Meek case   96
Oxford
  neglected by George Scarsbrook and Daniel Young   48, 94
  neglected by Joseph Adams   128
  open-air preaching   199, 207, 233, 239
  times of worship   119, 147
Oxford and District Free Church Council   58
Oxford and District Free Church Magazine   55
Oxford Chronicle   18, 19, 121n1
Oxford Local Preachers' Book
  description of book
    minute-takers   39
    missing entries   39
    oldest records (1830–66; 1867–1902)   39
    one previous volume lost   38–9
  description of entries
    dates, days and times   39–40
    question-and-answer format   47, 240n1
    record of attendance and titles   40
    venues   40
  lists of attendees
    all men   41–2
    preachers 'on trial' and exhorters   41, 69n2